WILLIAM BLAKE
and the MODERNS

WILLIAM BLAKE *and the* MODERNS

ROBERT J. BERTHOLF *and*
ANNETTE S. LEVITT, *Editors*

State University of New York Press

ALBANY

Published by
State University of New York Press, Albany

Printed in the United States of America

For information, address State University of New York Press, State University Plaza, Albany, N.Y., 12246

Library of Congress Cataloging in Publication Data
Main entry under title:

William Blake and the moderns.

1. Blake, William, 1757-1827—Influence—Addresses, essays, lectures. 2. Literature, Modern—20th century—History and criticism—Addresses, essays, lectures. 3. Philosophy, Modern—20th century—Addresses, essays, lectures. I. Bertholf, Robert J. II. Levitt, Annette S., 1938-
PR4148.I52W5 821′.7 82-656
ISBN 0-87395-615-X AACR2
ISBN 0-87395-616-9 (pbk.)

10 9 8 7 6 5 4 3 2 1

In memory of my parents,
SAMUEL *and* SARA SHANDLER,
and for MORT,
with love and gratitude

For ANNE,
her mindful patience

Contents

Introduction: The Tradition of Enacted Forms

Discussions of literary traditions and the ways they operate in the origins of new works have been intense in this century. In fact, the terms "literary history" and "literary influence" have been given over to a variety of definitions, as well as methodologies of speculation about the value of a text, its context, and its relational linguistic structures. Even without a survey of contemporary criticism—which would not be to the point here—the fundamental principle persists that a poet names the preceding artists who will comprise his essential literary history, the authors and the texts which extend into his own work, either consciously or unconsciously. Harold Bloom, following in part the discussions of the modes of recurring forms in Northrop Frye's *The Anatomy of Criticism* in his own *The Anxiety of Influence* and *A Map of Misreading*, has argued strenuously about the need of the poet to expunge antecedent influences; and his notions about the "anxiety" of being influenced have forced reconsideration of the notions of literary history. The roles of literary history and influences have been peculiar preoccupations of modern poets.

After Yeats, whose antithetical thinking about history and the poet's place in that recurring force was directed more toward a mode of poetry than toward a theory of influence, the two poets who have altered the thinking about the traditions most radically have also been critics who have stabilized their positions with influential critical essays. T. S. Eliot attempted to devalue the nineteenth century, especially in his essays "Dante" and "Swinburne as Poet," and to display a basis for modern poetry in the metaphysical styles of poets and the Jacobean styles of playwrights; behind those writers was the figure of Dante as the final spiritual source for the modern poet. Eliot attempted to exclude the Romantic in poetry from the active tradition and to replace it with a tradition built on the formality of poetic procedures, instead of the intensity of personal feelings realized in unique literary form. And Ezra Pound, while he praised the efforts of the Pre-Raphaelites to revive "The Spirit of Romance," pushed the traditions in a different direction, to the base of music and poetry in the Provençal poets, and then to the great spiritual energy of Dante. As the collected *Literary Essays* show, Pound's interest was antiquarian and not projective.

Behind Eliot stands Irving Babbitt, whose *Rousseau and Romanticism* justified the rejection of the Romantic in literature; after Eliot come Brooks and Warren's *Understanding Poetry*, the New Criticism, and the devaluation of the relationship of an individual poem to its historical context and to the larger literary traditions in which it belonged. It is ironic perhaps that the Kantian principle of the contained apprehension of a poem constituting its essential life was transformed into the rules of the regularity of stanzas and meters and operations of wit and irony, as a basis of literary merit. In a poetic sense, behind Pound stand Blake and Whitman, the generative advocates of poetry as a projective fiction of the imagination's life; after him come William Carlos Williams, Robert Duncan, and a group of poets seeking out their own relationships to the past, and announcing them in poems which enact their own forms. As Blake and Whitman generated poetic forms for the habitation of the poet's vision, so Pound and the poets after him maintain the effort of deriving passional forms from historical materials.

A literary tradition is not merely the compilation of explicated verbal echoes, or the outline of the persistent recurrence of themes, images, and structures. A tradition of enacted forms postulates a literary tradition that is inclusive and not exclusive. The poet seeks out, both consciously and unconsciously, influences, attunements, and disruptions that provoke his awareness of his engagement in a literary history of recurring forms. His occupations are not driven by a creative anxiety into intricate procedures of misreading in an effort to do away with his predecessors. The forms of expressions dominate. The generation of particular forms to present a vision specifies a line of writing that grew out of the period of the Romantic in literature. The forms develop within the vision, present and enact it; they are not imposed as external agents of structure. But while the freedom of the imagination acts as a bulwark against the passivity of conventional structures, the active principle of insistent reference to preceding literature picks out what is most vital in the line. If Blake had not taken up Milton's *Paradise Lost*, for example, as a projection of what he called "The One Central Form," that omission would have been an indication that Milton's poem had so mismanaged itself that it was not part of the common form of the imagination's life. The tradition of enacted forms by necessity refers to itself because it seeks out examples that most vigorously present the vision of the imagination engaged in an area of meaning greater than itself. If there is one central form of the imagination, then the possibilities of imaginative literature are manifestations, as approximations, of that central form. The literature which contains reference to preceding literatures becomes an indication that the central imagination is alive and provocative, and not an indication of a metaphysical scheme of influence dominated by the anxiety of that influence and the obligation to remove that antecedent force. Harold Bloom's system in the end only explains the psychology of itself, and not the literature it raids for illustrations. Instead of declaring a necessary independence from antecedent masters, writers in this tradition seek out (often consciously) examples of this central imagination in order to penetrate further into the life of the sustaining vision. In that sense, one artist comes into the possibilities of his own imagination in the works of another, as Whitman was stirred by reading Emerson, and as Melville rewrote *Moby-Dick* into its present form after reading Shakespeare. Pound's call to "make it new" was not a rejection of the past, but a call for re-vision, a recasting of the antique and generative vision into the active forms of the present. His procedure was inclusive, as was Blake's in seeking out the line backward from Milton to Shakespeare to Dante, and his poetry was derivative in the most impeccable sense: it reenacted the past in the self-made forms of prophecy as a fictive assertion of wholeness. Eliot's procedures, on the other hand, were exclusive. His was a plan of depersonalized procedures, of structures which could be imposed, and not the revelation of the imagination creating form.

Blake is the most extreme and the most modern of the Romantics; none of his contemporaries or immediate followers went as far as he in pursuit of political, philosophical, or artistic revolutions. Aside from his early *Poetical Sketches*, which reflect the modes and some of the ideas of his time, Blake's work continuously challenges accepted standards, from the encyclopedic style and religious attack of *The Marriage of Heaven and Hell* to the reflexivity and simultaneity of *Milton* and *Jerusalem*, with their own critiques of psychological and religious stasis. The prevailing urgency in Blake's work is to repudiate entrenched ideas and forms, and to create new ones. But the rejection of established ideas and literary forms initiates fractures and discontinuity. All of Blake's protagonists endure the crisis of alienation, from their soul mates and their societies, and even within their own psyches. From the simplistic and solipsistic Thel to the rebellious Orc and the tyrannical Urizen, and even Blake's Milton, "in Eden without his Emanation," and Albion, who stands for all men, but stands without Jerusalem, his "feminine portion," they discover their need for union, which comes through the imagination, synonymous with love. Blake moves forward apocalyptically, out of the Orc cycles of freedom and repression

—artistic, political, and psychological. The new Jerusalem is not a mere replica of an old religious city, but the projection of a spiritual wholeness which can be re-visioned. It is this plunging into chaos and emerging into order, as a process, which makes Blake so appealing to creative artists. And whether they go to him for imaginative vision, or ideas, or form—or do not go to him, but have recognizable spiritual affinities with him—he stands as a central voice molding modern literature and thought. The action of the imagination is first destructive, and the deconstructive necessity is the allowance for the emergence of the imagination itself in comprehensive forms of communication. The deconstructive modalities of Nietzsche and Heidegger were operative in Blake's vision, and in a sense Nietzsche and Heidegger reenacted them in their own terms.

The thirteen essays in this collection map out the lines of direct literary influences and indirect intellectual affinities that make up the tradition of enacted forms. In using aspects of Blake's forms and ideas, they reassert the idea of continuity, the drive for wholeness (not built on the conclusions of disillusionment), and the arrival of new poetic forms. In Part I, which deals with modern poetry, Hazard Adams, in "The Seven Eyes of Yeats," asserts that there was no significant direct absorption of Blake's poetry in Yeats, and discusses seven areas of continuity which Yeats altered for his own purposes. In contrast, Donald Pease, in "Blake, Whitman, Crane: The Hand of Fire," traces an affinity between Blake and Whitman, and claims that in searching into Whitman, Hart Crane activated and added to the vision of Blake in ways that reformulate the terms of the epic in the twentieth century.

The tradition is clarified further by Leroy Searle in "Blake, Eliot, and Williams: The Continuity of Imaginative Labor." While the school of poets and critics who follow after Eliot's lack of sympathy for Blake's prophecies—which leads from Allen Tate and John Crowe Ransom, and then to Robert Lowell, John Berryman and the poets of the confessional mode—shows only slight connections with Blake, the poets who follow after Williams (who did not know Blake as a poet)—leading to Allen Ginsberg and Robert Duncan—show an intimate knowledge of the poems and a huge sympathy with Blake's visionary process. A similar theme is taken up by Jay Parini. In "Blake and Roethke: When Everything Comes to One," he shows how Roethke, who took Blake directly as a master, follows the same procedures of resolving the process from chaos to order, and finally, in the later poems, discloses a kinship with Blake in the land of visionary wholeness. Robert Duncan, as Robert Bertholf shows in his essay "Robert Duncan: Blake's Comtemporary Voice," came to Blake first through the Songs. Later he found in the intricacies of the great prophecies a revelation of his own vision, which he proclaims as a basis for the continuance of the mythopoetic process. Part I closes with an essay by Alicia Ostriker. In "*Blake, Ginsberg, Madness, and the Prophet as Shaman,*" she discusses the manifestations of Blake's voice and presence in Ginsberg's poetry, in a thorough discussion of the similarities of their treatment of madness and the stance of the poet as a shaman.

In Part II the topic is Blake and the modern novel. Robert Gleckner reexamines Joyce's use of Blake and finds that E. J. Ellis's *The Real Blake* is the essential source of Joyce's knowledge of Blake, and not primarily the poems; and that while there are sustained references to Blake throughout Joyce's work, the outright determining influence that was previously thought to operate is not present. Lawrence and Blake, as discussed by Myra Glazer in "Sex and the Psyche: William Blake and D. H. Lawrence," have a common ideal, that of the freedom of the imagination, but also a common contention, that of the struggle between the male and female aspects of the generative imagination. Both claim that equality is necessary for creation, but both fear the appearance of the female principle as it manifests itself as the anima, or the Great Mother. For Joyce Cary, as for Blake, the supremacy of the imagination overcomes the strictures of society, as Annette Levitt demonstrates in " 'The Mental Traveller' in *The Horse's Mouth*: New Light on the Old Cycle." Reviewing Cary's working manuscripts, she shows just how conscious and pervasive a force Blake's poem was on Cary's novel, and how their interaction achieves added dimensions of meaning for both works. But Cary is not the only novelist who went to Blake for primary ideas. In "A Fourfold Vision: William Blake and Doris Lessing," Susan Levin illustrates how Lessing adapted Blake's ideas on the necessity to cleanse the sight of predeterminations and attain the full view of the fourfold vision in the process of revelation. This aspect of Blake's thought enters the characterization in Lessing's novels, while the idea of four as a structural principle occurs in *The Four-Gated City* as the definition of a completed city.

The three essays in Part III demonstrate how the force of Blake as a thinker has reached into modern thought in an indirect but active line of affinity. Minna Doskow, in "The Humanized Universe of Blake and Marx," explains how Blake and Marx dealt with the eighteenth century's mechanical notion of the split between the perceiving subject and the unfeeling object. Blake created in the realm of the imagination, while Marx declared the economic rights of man, but both were concerned to integrate, and thus humanize, man with his immediate environments. That mankind has a future, in evolutionary and spiritual events, is the assumption of the Jesuit Teilhard de Chardin. In "Blake, Teilhard, and the Idea of the Future of Man," Eileen Sanzo relates how Blake's prophecies in *Milton* and *Jerusalem* set out a clear idea of the future growth of spiritual understanding available to mankind, and shows how Chardin, although he was not a reader of Blake, proposed a similar definition of man's future spiritual growth as the central point of his theology. The concluding essay, by William Dennis Horn, "William Blake and the Problematic of the Self," specifies Blake as the forerunner who announced what the "self" in the imaginative vision can be, and traces the emergence of Blake's procedures in the writing of Harold Bloom, Hegel, Jacques Lacan, and Paul de Man. At the end, the collection returns to the particular self, as Blake proposed, alive in the process of enacting forms, and fully capable of continued revelation.

Abbreviations

All quotations from Blake's work, unless otherwise indicated, are from *The Poetry and Prose of William Blake*, ed. David V. Erdman, commentary by Harold Bloom (Garden City, N.Y.: Doubleday, 1965). References to this edition have been indicated within the text of the essays by E, plus a page number. In addition, the following abbreviations have been used:

MHH	The Marriage of Heaven and Hell
VDA	Visions of the Daughters of Albion
U	The Book of Urizen
M	Milton
J	Jerusalem
FZ	The Four Zoas
VLJ	A Vision of The Last Judgment
BA	The Book of Ahania

Abbreviations appear following quotations. Roman numerals refer to chapters, scenes, or nights; Arabic numbers to indicate plate or page, and line number. Thus, (M I: 27, 8–10) refers to *Milton*, the first book, plate 27, lines 8–10. Other abbreviations are designated in the notes of the individual essays.

PART I

Hazard Adams

The Seven Eyes of Yeats

Yeats's devotion to Blake had, as far as I can tell, little effect on his poetic style, that is to say, what is roughly called the form of his poems.[1] There are, of course, echoes of Blake here and there, though perhaps not so many as one might expect from a man who apparently knew much of Blake by heart. One may be tempted to discover the genesis of "Byzantium" in the following lines from *The Four Zoas*, particularly since we know that Yeats was the work's first editor and one of its first readers:

> The flames rolling intense through the wide Universe
> Began to Enter the Holy City Entring the dismal clouds
> In furrowd lightnings break their way the wild flames whirring up
> The Bloody Deluge living flames winged with intellect
> And Reason round the Earth They march in order flame by flame . . . .
> (FZ IX: 119, 16–20)

Still, it is quite a distance from the intent of this passage to "Byzantium."

A more obvious echo is the following from "The Double Vision of Michael Robartes":

> For what but eye and ear silence the mind
> With the minute particulars of mankind? [2]

These, incidentally, are not among Yeats's best lines. The word "mankind" is not quite right and seems to have been chosen for the rhyme. For that matter, the word "mind" is not quite right. I take it that Yeats means something more materialistic, like "brain." [3] If he were really trying to write in Blake's spirit that would be a better word. But the whole idea seems to depart from Blake, in spite of the Blakean term "minute particulars." Yeats sharply distinguishes thought and emotion, and mixes the Blakean idea of minute particulars with the Keatsian notion of being teased out of thought. If one is interested in the sources of Yeats's poetic techniques one is better advised to look in Spenser, Shakespeare, Wordsworth, Shelley, Keats, and even Dante Rossetti.

The situation is different when one looks into Yeats's prose—especially the early prose, where Blake is frequently echoed, alluded to, or directly quoted. But here again Yeats's tone is more like Pater's—hardly Blakean—and frequently smothers or subtly changes the Blakean thought. The reason for this—if it requires a reason in a poet of great and unmistakable voice—is that Blake's influence was mixed and filtered through John Butler Yeats, Pre-Raphaelitism, and occultist thought.

John Butler Yeats, himself heavily influenced by the Pre-Raphaelites in his son's formative years, appreciated the wild free side of Blake—the happy thoughtlessness that he attributed to Blake and to artists generally[4]—and was prone to reducing Blake's complex ideas to overly simple distinctions. One of these was that between thought and emotion. The emphasis on emotion W. B. Yeats took into his own work and then, as Harold Bloom has pointed out, foisted it on Blake, who never used the term "emotion" and was suspicious of the divisions it implies.[5] Blake's term "intellect" means an exercise of the whole mind, not pure abstract thought or wild free irrational feeling.

The Pre-Raphaelite connection with Blake is a curious one and a means by which Blake came to Yeats in somewhat distorted form. There can hardly be a greater contrast between Blake, once out of his *Poetical Sketches* stage, and Rossetti, particularly with respect to poetic tone. The principal Pre-Raphaelite distortion of Blake, it seems to me, lies in their interpretation of the "minute particular" to mean an imitative minuteness of accurate detail. Blake would certainly not have accepted W. M. Rossetti's remark that the painter must base his personal vision on a "direct study of Nature." Yeats did not accept Rossetti's distortion of Blake's thought, but his taste was formed in part on the Pre-Raphaelite nostalgia for things medieval and the languid emotion of D. G. Rossetti's and Burne-Jone's paintings—a quality Blake rarely exhibits.

Occultist thought, which Yeats assimilated in many ways and in part from his collaborator in the edition of Blake, Edwin J. Ellis, was a prism through which he distorted Blake.[6] One is hard pressed to imagine a more inaccurate treatment of a poet in the history of modern criticism. Nothing approaches it since the Gnostic allegorical interpreters of Scripture. Harold Bloom, mystified by his own brand of occultist interpretation—the theory of the anxiety of influence—imagines that Yeats's misinterpretation of Blake is a deliberate *clinamen* or creative swerve.[7] This seems to me quite wrong. It can, of course, never be proved or disproved. I prefer a simpler, more mundane explanation: an inexperienced or fanatical interpreter will interpret through what is either familiar or an *idée fixe*. Yeats's collaborator, Ellis, was a fanatic, and Yeats was still an inexperienced critic absorbed by his occult studies and without a lot of formal learning. He had been educated principally by his father. The reasons for Yeats's misinterpretation of Blake were principally his lack of critical sophistication and the occultist thoughts that dominated him at the time. There have been other books badly misinterpreting Blake. One, a strict Jungian reading, makes a similar mess of things, but its author was hardly suffering an anxiety of influence.[8] He was suffering a fixed idea and a naïve conception of hermeneutic enterprise.

In spite of continued efforts to prove otherwise by a number of more recent critics, Blake was temperamentally about as far from being an occultist as apparently he was from being Irish. Yeats's efforts to read him through Swedenborg, Boehme, and such other occultists as he knew was disastrous. The effort throws a veil over Blake that robs him, among other things, of his humor and his ability to evade all systems. The essay that Yeats wrote for the Blake volumes, "The Necessity of Symbolism," is a very interesting, indirect statement about poets of the late nineteenth century and their desperate search for order or sense of its lack, but it has almost nothing to do with Blake.

What then *is* the influence of Blake on Yeats, since clearly there is a profound one? It lies in certain fundamental notions that Yeats picked up at least in part from Blake, often changed, and assimilated to his own way of looking at things. A little artificially, I shall try to isolate and discuss several of these separately. I choose seven of them. I shall discuss each as briefly as I can.

1. Contraries and Negations. In *A Vision*, Yeats states that his idea of conflict came, at least in part, from Blake's notion of contraries: "I had never read Hegel, but my mind had been full of Blake from boyhood up and I saw the world as a conflict—Spectre and Emanation—and could distinguish between a contrary and a negation." [9] Both Blake and Yeats seek a way out of the subject-object problem. In that opposition the object inevitably negates the subject, as in the body-soul opposition the soul negates the body. In both cases one side of the opposition claims a superior reality for itself: the objective world over the subjective, the soul over the body. A true contrary would be one in which these oppositions are themselves opposed by a principle of radical unification. Yeats's opposition of "primary" and "antithetical," though sometimes referred to by him as the opposition of subject and object, is really a true contrary. In the "antithetical" mode of thought the opposition of subject and object is denied; in the "primary" mode the opposition is affirmed. In the "primary" mode, the objective world (Locke's "primary" qualities of experience) dominates the subjective (Locke's "secondary" qualities). In this case subjectivity is really declared to be unreal, therefore "negated." Blake claims that the same thing occurs historically with the soul–body opposition, which to him is a "negation." The traditional theology of the Blakean "churches" created the soul–body distinction and "negated" the body in favor of the greater reality of the soul. From this act followed sexual repression, the "religion of chastity," and the warfare of spectre and emanation. The true contrary was for Blake not soul–body but reason and energy, as Blake explains in *The Marriage of Heaven and Hell.*

Yeats's difference from Blake on this point comes when Yeats tries to imagine a state in which proper contraries are resolved and blend into the so-called thirteenth cone or sphere, which is introduced in the second version of *A Vision* (1937). The sphere as the symbol of ultimate reality we can trace back into pre-Socratic thought and connect with the traditional Greek aesthetics of harmony. Blake would probably have called Yeats's recourse to the sphere "Grecian worship"; he never allows his contraries to blend into the harmonious sphere, arguing that such blending is always the result of "negating" one side of an opposition. Blake thus maintains the principle of contrariety right into apocalypse. Indeed, it is the principle of apocalypse itself. The intellectual war and hunting that goes on in heaven, which is, of course, a mental state in Blake, not a place beyond the sky, is the proper contrary form of those dreadful "negations" known as war and hunting in nature. Yeats thinks of that symbolized by the sphere as things-in-themselves, which fall into antinomies in experience. Blake's heaven is the life of intellect itself, which proceeds by dialogue and contrariety.

A profound difference in tone between Blake and Yeats accompanies this philosophical difference, and the two tones express quite opposite temperaments—Blake's open, Yeats's ironic and masked. I shall return to this point, adding here only that this difference leads Yeats to an ironic welcoming of violence, while Blake was always horrified by war, which he regarded as the result of the repression of true contrariety.

2. Center and Circumference. Yeats wrote in "Discoveries":

> If it be true that God is a circle whose centre is everywhere, the saint goes to the centre, the poet and artist to the ring where everything comes round again. The poet must not seek for what is still and fixed, for that has no life for him; and if he did, his style would become cold and monotonous, and his sense of beauty faint and sickly, . . . but be content to find his pleasure in all that is for ever passing away. . . .[10]

There are, of course, traditional sources for this paradoxical description of God, the same as those for Eliot's still point of the turning wheel. But there is superimposed on it an idea gotten from Blake and then changed to suit Yeats's purpose. Blake's idea is the expansion or opening of "selfish" centers to circumferences. The opening of a center brings the world inside one's imaginative range and allows for sympathy and communion. A closed center is a situation in which the mind finds itself isolated, surrounded by an alien objective nature. It is an entirely selfish mind with no connection to anything else. The center Blake also calls the "limit of contraction." Contraction means matter, which means Locke's primary qualities of experience, which in Blake are what "nature" is. (This is the reason Blake dislikes nature and regards it as part of a "negation.") To be at a center is to be a subject enclosed in an infinite expanse of matter. Blake sees the expansion of centers as the whole aim of life. At the beginning of *Jerusalem* the Savior tries to coax Albion to expand to a circumference so that they can contain each other. Albion has retreated to a center, thrusting all, including his emanation, Jerusalem, beyond himself into the area of the objective or the "primary" world.

Yeats posits a necessary conflict between poet and saint. The poet is the radical creator who for Blake is every man. He is at the circumference, which is the world of flux, experience, and particulars; and he tries to make everything into his own forms. The saint, on the other hand, gives himself up to an external authority, and imagines that authority to be beyond or surrounding him and himself at a center. The Blakean notion has undergone a considerable change here. All human imaginative activity is not assimilated to a quest for a circumferential vantage. (There is, in the end, of course, a sense in which the saint's imagining himself at the center is itself a sort of circumference, being an imaginative act; but this is at another level of thought.) For Yeats, human beings divide into contrary types, and in the end the centrist condition triumphs over the antithetical circumferential one. Antithetical man suffers the same fate as primary man. Both are gathered up into the great darkness, poet as defeated and thus tragic rebel. The poet's antithetical role is therefore ironic. The irony is carried to the notion that antithetical man must hate God in order to bring his soul to God. His way is a circuitous path at best. God, as a word denoting a "primary," external, far-off deity, is abstract. Yeats claims that antithetical men must hate such a god because that idea of God disembodies and distances the deity from himself.

> At stroke of midnight God shall win.
>
> (CP 286)

Yeats's notion is basically Blakean, introducing the far-off Blakean sky god; but it is filtered through an embattled attitude foreign to Blake, and it comes out in a way that Blake would have objected to. In Blake, what Yeats separates off as the tragic but culturally necessary antithetical role has apocalyptic possibilities; indeed, it is the true source of all culture, upon which reason builds its edifice. Saintliness, on the other hand, is a virtue for which Blake had little respect; for him all truly visionary behavior, rather than acceptance (passively, in his eyes) of an external deity, is artistic circumference-making:

> Prayer is the Study of Art
> Praise is the Practise of Art
> Fasting &c. all relate to Art
> The outward Ceremony is Antichrist
> The Eternal Body of Man is the IMAGINATION. . . .
>
> (E 272)

For Blake, there is an opposition between what he calls "prolific" and "devourer"—a necessary opposition. But these have their intellectual and fallen forms, whereas in Yeats the only opposition is the one before him in the world of conflict itself. A cleansing of perceptions to see the intellectual form would result in annihilation of the contrary.

This whole matter points to a fundamental difference between the two poets. Blake is radically humanistic and is totally devoted to a vision of *this* world as potentially apocalyptic through an improvement in mental power, which includes sensuous power. Yeats is also humanistic, and his antithetical man opts for such a vision. But at the same time Yeats concludes that a humanistic apocalypse is impossible, or at least only momentary, and that the ultimate condition is beyond all who are bound to the antinomies—and all are. Yeats's struggle is always against a superior (primary) force that in time brings around the ruin of antithetical endeavor:

> . . . day brings round the night, . . . before dawn
> His glory and his monuments are gone.
>
> (CP 287)

> No handiwork of Callimachus,
> Who handled marble as if it were bronze,
> Made draperies that seemed to rise
> When sea-wind swept the corner, stands;
> His long lamp-chimney shaped like the stem
> Of a slender palm, stood but a day;
> All things fall and are built again, . . .
>
> (CP 292)

There is a quite conscious irony in Yeats's choice of the term "antithetical" for the humanistic visionary. He cannot fully succeed but instead provides an antithesis that prevents a fall into the chaos of a completely abstract primary world. Such a chaos would be beneath even the world Blake called Ulro. It would be beneath the mathematic starry floor that was given to us till break of day.

Center and circumference in Blake are the Blakean vortex observed from above or below, so to speak. They also make the cone that Yeats adopts, not entirely from Blake, as his central symbol. Blakean closed vortexes are the Cartesian ones that Urizen attempts to create but which give him no visionary aid. They are selfish surrounded centers. Vortexes in Blake's visionary sense are centers of vision opened up to circumferences like that achieved by the farmer in *Milton* I: 15, 28–33. Vortexes or cones (gyres) in Yeats are ironic. The vortex of "The Second Coming" represents a situation both literally and figuratively out of hand. Expansion from such a vortex is not visionary. Still, the poet's stance at a circumference shows that Yeats holds on to some of the visionary qualities that Blake attributes to opened vortexes or expanded centers. He vastly complicates Blake's vortex with his double gyres and ironic theory of history, in which the gyres turn each other inside out, the circumference of one becoming the center of the other, endlessly antinomial.

3. The Religious. Yeats appears to be influenced by Blake's concept of the "religious," probably through John Butler Yeats, who, as I have said, tended to oversimplify Blake's contraries. The term "religious" in Blake is a negating word; it means those who unthinkingly give themselves to an external moral law. For Blake, Jesus came to destroy the moral law and substitute for it the single principle of the forgiveness of sins. Harold Bloom accurately observes that this is one of the few Blakean ideas that Yeats got quite clear in his interpretation. And it influenced him, possibly because the idea also came to him through his father. John Butler Yeats speaks of this matter in a letter to his son; and it is here that we see the Blakean concept of the religious mixed with the idea of poet and saint:

> There are two kinds of belief; the poetical and the religious. That of the poet comes when the man within has found some method or manner of thinking or arrangement of fact (such as is only possible in dreams) by which to express and embody an absolute freedom, such that his whole inner and outer-self can expand in a full satisfaction.
>
> In religious belief there is absent the consciousness of liberty. Religion is the denial of liberty. An enforced peace is set up among the warring feelings. By the help of something quite external, as for instance the fear of hell, some feelings are chained up and thrust into dungeons that some other feelings may

> hold sway; and all the ethical systems yet invented are a similar denial of liberty, that is why the true poet is neither moral nor religious.[11]

But Yeats does not himself quite adopt this stance. For John Butler Yeats, there is nothing admirable to be associated with the religious. For his son, in his earlier years, there is an effort to create his own religion through poetry and, later to make a prolific contrariety out of the opposition of religion and poetry, saint and poet. The saint is respected but intellectually opposed for the sake of culture:

> . . . I—though heart might find relief
> Did I become a Christian man and choose for my belief
> What seems most welcome in the tomb—play a predestined part.
> Homer is my example and his unchristened heart.
> The lion and the honeycomb, what has Scripture said?
> So get you gone, Von Hügel, though with blessings on your head.
> (CP 247)

Yeats's saint is not unthinking and is, contrary to his father's view, conscious of liberty. He freely chooses against it. Blake turns Jesus into an antithetical man, an artist, subsuming what is good in religion under an expanded definition of art. Jesus is a prolific to be devoured by his followers, just as a work of art is a prolific to be devoured by society and its interpreters. The "religious" are those caught in the snare of a fixed interpretation and thus chained and unfree. Yeats's religious man does not necessarily choose law, but he does choose a myth opposite to that of the artist—one of external supernatural power and authority.

4. Forgiveness of Sins. This idea, as I have already indicated, is connected with the idea of the religious. Blake thought of Jesus as the supreme image of human imaginative power. Blake's idea was that sympathy and identity (through taking the so-called "sinner" into one's circumference) was in fact forgiveness. In Yeats, the antithetical man does not find forgiveness to be an attribute of his primary opposite. No one else forgives him; he forgives himself.

In Blake, acts of forgiveness are apocalyptic. In Yeats, they are a defiance of the prevailing external or primary authority, which is ultimately victorious: "At stroke of midnight God shall win." Meanwhile, the antithetical man insists on antithetical blessedness:

> I am content to follow to its source
> Every event in action or in thought;
> Measure the lot; forgive myself the lot!

When such as I cast out remorse
So great a sweetness flows into the breast
We must laugh and we must sing,
We are blest by everything,
Everything we look upon is blest.

(CP 232)

This condition is tenuous. It must be rewon constantly and carries with it a tension greater than that in Blake's remark: "whenever any Individual Rejects Error & Embraces Truth a Last Judgment passes upon that Individual" (VLJ 84). Blake believed in the apocalyptic power of the imagination. Yeats believed in the imagination's power to prevent the fall beneath the starry floor into the void.

5. *Every thing possible to be believ'd is an image of truth* (MHH 8: 38). This Blakean exuberance seems clearly to have influenced Yeats toward what Richard Ellmann has aptly called a stance of "affirmative capability." [12] It is, of course, an assertion that the imagination has the power, working at a circumference, to prophesy a cultural world. The idea takes a different form in Yeats because of his quite self-conscious idea of "stylistic arrangements of experience" as they are called in *A Vision* (V 25). Indeed, in *A Vision*, Yeats abandons the term "belief," which to him implies alienation and doctrine and is thus inappropriate to an antithetical stance. He substitutes antithetical creativity for primary imitation. In the antithetical view the question is no longer what to believe but what is and can be imagined. Antithetical reality is emanation, primary reality is imposition. They are contraries equally true.[13]

6. *Minute Particulars*. In "The Double Vision of Michael Robartes," only the eye and ear can silence the mind, and the reason is that they are the senses through which art plays in antithesis to abstract thought and to the dominant forms of modern culture: "Art bids us touch and taste and hear and see the world, and shrinks from what Blake calls mathematic form, from every abstract thing, from all that is of the brain only, from all that is not a fountain jetting from entire hopes, memories, and sensations of the body" (EI 292–293). This is a relatively early statement, but it actually applies more to the work of the later Yeats than to that of the early. Minute particulars are defended by Blake against Reynolds, who complains of excessive attention to trivial detail in certain kinds of paintings. Minute particulars involve for Blake the bounding line in painting, the idea that the particular embodies universality if clearly enough expressed, the idea that only immediate experience formed through the senses is real and all

else is in "the mind of a fool." The minute particular is also connected to Blake's championing of the body as a spiritual form against the negating power of the soul, the body being always a particular, but not a material object. Material objects in Blake's view are fictions of the system of Locke; they are not material in any solid or minute sense, since Locke's system reduces them to measurement or "mathematic form." Blake's quarrel was with all negations: soul-body, subject-object, thought-sense.

But the early occultist Yeats did not hold the position expressed in the quotation above. Rather, the following seems to have been his stance: "Everything that can be seen, touched, measured, explained, understood, argued over, is to the imaginative artist nothing more than a means, for he belongs to the invisible life. . . ." (EI 195). This interpretation of the poet as occultist or mystic Yeats later abandons when he comes to see that on his own terms he has confused the issue. Later he opposes touch to measurement, recognizes that they are not qualities of things but of human intercourse with things. They are contrary modes of such intercourse. Only then does he come fully to understand Blake's use of the term "mathematic form." When he does, however, he does not attack it, as Blake does, but claims it as a formative element, an expression of human creative power, parallel to but also opposite to art: "Measurement began our might," he asserts. Abstract thought, the creator of externality as objective form, gave humankind primary cultural power. Yeats's reading of philosophy later than the quotations I have offered here—particularly works of Berkeley and Kant—helps account for the development of a stance that took him past Blake yet back to him too—to an idea of contrary, parallel cultural forms.

7. The Bright Sculptures of Los's Halls. The idea in Blake of the permanent forms of human imaginative activity and of every moment as a plenitude obviously affected Yeats, but he tended to read the idea through the occultist one of "pictures in the astral light" (V 193). Either he hardens Los's forms into ideas, spirits, or whatever lurks in the *anima mundi* or he interprets Los's halls to be that eternity into which everything goes, there to be preserved in the form of archetypes. Our "daimon" is the condition of seeing all things as present. We ourselves do not achieve that condition: "All things are present as an eternal instant to our *Daimon* (or *Ghostly Self* as it is called, when it inhabits the sphere), but that instant is of necessity unintelligible to all bound to the antinomies" (V 193). Blake insists on the importance of the present as all that there is and the equation of the present moment to eternity. Los's bright sculptures are the totality of imaginative power in the moment—the power, for example, to create a historic past. There is for Blake no *beyond* that we cannot apprehend or penetrate. What is beyond is only that which we have as yet failed to contain because we have not sufficiently "enlarged" or exercised our sensuous powers. But for Yeats antithetical containment is never complete, or at least, when it is, the moment passes and decay sets in. This moment, in Yeats, is always a mystery: "Where got I that truth?" he asks in a poem about such a moment, and only an ironic answer follows (CP 211). The truth breaks in violently upon the antinomies, but, captured by them, can never maintain its purity. For Blake, the moment is not a mystery but a *now* that contains past and future. The bright sculptures are radically created over and over by man. Yeats as antithetical man claims that we even create death, but he gives the attitude of primary man the role of providing a countertruth to this assertion: Death is something that happens to us. From that opposite point of view the bright sculptures were there before man, and their creator is the unknown Gnostic god.

One may say that these seven influences merely introduce differences, that they are not the eyes of Blake, but the eyes of Yeats upon his predecessor's work and upon a good many other things as well. That would be fair enough. I cannot believe these are deliberate misinterpretations made out of anxiety. This would be a view quite foreign to artistic behavior as I understand it. The early Yeats misinterpreted Blake for many of the same reasons that most of the nineteenth century and much of the twentieth did. He was a difficult poet to understand for those who saw things differently. Beyond this, not as an interpreter but as a poet, Yeats did what any good poet tends to do, steal and create. In such activity there is less competition with one's predecessors than the treatment of all one's experience as the material of art. All mature poets know, as Blake did, that competition of the sort implied by Bloom's theory of anxiety is destructive of art and that art does not progress: "If Art was Progressive We should have had Mich Angelo's & Rafaels to Succeed & to Improve upon each other But it is not so. Genius dies with its Possessor & comes not again till Another is Born with It" (E 645). Neither does art necessarily decay.

The overall effect of these two poets, Blake and Yeats, with so much in common, is quite different. Both are poets of exuberance, but of entirely different sorts. Blake's exuberance is open. His humor, of which there is a great deal in the prophecies, is hyperbolic and full of joy. Samuel Palmer's remark that he was a man without a mask seems to me definitive. Blake's form of joy is enthusiastic. Yeats's is tragic. Blake believed he was what he was. Yeats believed his true being to be the mask he sought, more real than his self. He took much from Blake but adapted it to the dominating theme of the mask. Yeats belongs clearly among the ironic humorists of the Anglo-Irish tradition, one of that mode's supreme practitioners. That tradition, and not Blake, must have contributed heavily to his masked ironic manner as surely must have the growing murderousness, the terrible twentieth century, something Blake seems to have been warning us against, though with that strange optimism that, in its idea of the apocalyptic consolidation of error, sees life darkest just before the dawn.

Notes

1. This essay follows twenty-six years upon the publication of *Blake and Yeats: The Contrary Vision* and twelve years upon its second printing with a corrective preface. This essay sets out anew, rather than attempting a retrospective glance at what I said some time ago.

2. *Collected Poems* (New York: Macmillan, 1965), p. 168; hereafter cited as CP.

3. As he does elsewhere. See the quotation on p. 10.

4. See W. B. Yeats, *Memoirs* (New York: Macmillan, 1973), p. 158. "Feb 3 [1909]. Blake talking to Crabb Robinson said once that he preferred to any man of intellect a happy thoughtless person, or some such phrase."

5. *Yeats* (New York: Oxford Univ. Press, 1970), pp. 70–71.

6. *The Works of William Blake*, 3 vols. (London: Quaritch, 1893).

7. *Yeats*, pp. 7, 72.

8. W. P. Witcutt, *Blake: A Psychological Study* (London: Hollis & Carter, 1946).

9. *A Vision* (New York: Macmillan, 1938), p. 72; hereafter cited as V.

10. "The Cutting of an Agate," *Essays and Introductions* (London: Macmillan, 1961), p. 287; hereafter cited as EI.

11. *Further Letters of John Butler Yeats*, ed. Lennox Robinson (Cuala, Ireland: Dundrum, 1920), pp. 22–23.

12. *The Identity of Yeats* (New York: Oxford Univ. Press, 1954), pp. 238–245.

13. Harold Bloom remarks: "Blake asserted that anything possible to be believed was an image of truth. Yeats bettered him in finding it possible to believe anything whatsoever, if it were sufficiently marvelous, and made enough of a gap in nature" (*Yeats*, p. 66). Bloom praises Yeats for this "humane receptivity," but in the end is more critical of him, as the tone of the sentence above suggests. The sentence seems to me, in any case, an oversimplification.

Donald Pease

Blake, Whitman, Crane: The Hand of Fire

To read William Blake is to experience the opposition of great contraries. While such lapsed patrons as William Hayley might bear witness against a certain disturbing contrariness in Blake's demeanor, nevertheless the moment Blake converted his contrary nature into a principle of literary composition, his poetic genius was born. Blake's use of contraries is pervasive enough that some semblance of continuity in his poetic career can be derived by measuring the increasing expansiveness of the contraries he yoked together. He found his measure, then, when he lyricized the fearful symmetry of the worlds of innocence and experience, attained maturity when he subjected the tradition's hallowed but no less hollow description of heaven to a forced marriage with prophetic visions antinomian enough in their import to have been relegated by that same tradition to some lower circle in hell, and reached artistic fulfillment when he harnessed the epic form to his prophetic vision. This final vision, the yoking together of two contrary literary forms, saw Blake through to the end of his poetic career and enabled him to envision the end of the created world in his poetry. Moreover, it is Blake's remarkable capacity in these epic prophecies to incorporate a nation's history into eternal vision, or as he would more eloquently phrase it, to build the ruins of time into the mansions of eternity,[1] that marks him as a precursor for such moderns as Walt Whitman and Hart Crane.

The epic form and the prophetic vision arise from two completely opposed impulses. An epic consolidates a way of life by celebrating the ideals that hold a people together; a prophecy disrupts the institutions honored in a nation's history by delivering a vision of an eternal world still to be attained. An epic reminds a people of who they are and urges that they remain the same; a prophecy puts a people in mind of who they can be and demands that they change. While an epic affirms the continuity between past and future and intones upon the harmony between a nation and a transcendental realm authorizing its activities, a prophecy conflates past, present, and future into a prophetic moment wherein the infinite moves in the same direction as the finite and the world that can end is consumed in a vision of a world without end. In short, an epic brings the ways of the world into a fully realized form while a prophecy returns that actualized world where everything seems complete—even final—back to the status of renewed possibility, where everything seems once again about to begin.

This disjunctive form both enacts and represents a crisis, a confrontation between a nation in the "golden age" of an "ancient time" when its actions coincided with its infinite possibilities, and the same nation at a time in its history recognizable as a fall from its earliest promise. All of Blake's epic prophecies work to intensify this conflict to the point of a dialectical separation between what is irremediably fallen in a nation's institutions and what can be regenerated through prophetic vision, with the dual goals of restoring all Englishmen to their "original" status as prophets and imagining a New Jerusalem for these prophets to inhabit. As soon as Blake envisions such a New World, however, the contrariety constituting the form of the epic prophecy resolves itself into a vision wherein the actual world, recapitulated in the epic formulations, is no different from the world that can be aspired to in prophetic invocations; for, as a result of his efforts, Jerusalem itself will have been rebuilt "In England's green & pleasant Land."

An interpretation of Blake's *Milton* will clarify the contrariety informing the epic prophecy, and the repetition of the same process of contrariety in Hart Crane's *The Bridge* will elucidate the pertinence of such a form in a modern poem. But the choice of *The Bridge* as a modern example will itself necessitate a further expansion, for when Crane returns to Blake to recover the tradition of epic prophecy for American poetry, his return includes America's first true epic poet, Walt Whitman, in the same tradition. Upon reaching that moment in his epic prophecy when the time comes for the poet-voyager to remember America's "golden age," he must do so by recalling Whitman's poetry, a poetry unique in its capacity to fuse epic and prophetic elements.

I

If Whitman begins his poetry with a resolution of the opposition between epic and prophecy, he begins where Blake ends. In Blake's terms, the crisis in British poetry forged the opposition between epic and prophecy. Since

Blake located the apogee of that crisis in the poetry of John Milton, it will be helpful to isolate the epic and prophetic strains in Milton's poetry. And here contemporary Milton criticism can be of help, for something of a schism has opened between those critics who place Milton as the last poet in an epic tradition and those who insist on reclaiming for him a position in the prophetic line of British poetry.

Thomas Vogler in *Preludes to Vision* is the most recent proponent of the first view. He argues with considerable discernment that Milton is the last poet able to write an epic informed by the "accepted spirtual orientation . . . of a shared sense of value," that *Paradise Lost* preserved rather than created an "acceptable collective ideology" and thus "brought to completion different elements of the Christian culture and produced epic expressions of the validity of life" shared by an entire nation.[2] Vogler's argument has been countered by another—that Milton continued a line of poet-prophets whose challenge was not to preserve but to renew a nation by destroying its "specious orthodoxies" and to create a new value system in their place.[3] For Northrop Frye, the major proponent of this latter view, a prophet is recognizable out of his intention to renew values by breaking the bondage of a fallen world and releasing the total human form that lies dormant within the imagination. Such a vision necessitates a psychic reorientation away from the absence of freedom experienced by a self-limited psyche and a reattachment to "the total human body within, the Word that reveals the Eden in the redeemable human soul, and so releases the power that leads to a new heaven and a new earth." [4] Such a revolution in consciousness will obviously not honor any merely diachronic conception of a nation's history and will insist instead on a vision of the total form of all genuine human efforts and achievements as a movement from creation through the fall and the redemption and into apocalypse. Poet-prophets, by way of a common distinction, transcend the epic convention of a brooding subject reflecting on his memories of perception to achieve a fulfilled vision wherein the entire universe articulates a living human form.

Clearly the proponents of a prophetic Milton have, by the very nature of their category, the greater force on their side; but when they explain the epic qualities in Milton's prophetic poems, they are compelled to argue that Milton uses prophetic force *against* his own form. The necessity for this turn derives from the ground terms qualifying the distinction between epic and prophecy: an epic is composed of "conventions," a prophecy of "renovations." When Milton wrote *Paradise Lost*, the epic was a form elemented of diverse conventions defined by such persistent characteristics as a heroism exemplifying the full range of human potential, an encyclopedic knowledge, a narrative structure, a lofty tone, a presentation of some crucial episode in a nation's history, and a justification of the cosmic order as propitious to life. All of these conventions are clearly discernible in earlier epics, but, these critics argue, that is precisely what constitutes their problem; for the prophet in Milton would charge each convention with the burden of presenting things yet unattempted in prose or rhyme, and with the prophetic purpose of asserting Eternal Providence and justifying the ways of God to man.

Consequent to placing the prophetic over the epic mode, such critics as Joseph Wittreich find Milton's poetry to include "more than its traditionally accepted generic limits . . . would allow it to include" and to combine opposed symbolic modes, then hold them "under pressure in a state of high, even ecstatic tension." Thus, in the very act of creating this transcendental form, "Milton pushes beyond the tradition of mimetic art, disrupting the free movement of narration with the mental exertions characteristic of visionary art," [5] thereby causing epic conventions to be superseded by prophetic exertions. The rationale behind these propositions partially justifies the fervor of the argument, for these proponents of a prophetic Milton take quite literally the invocation to the muse when he asks for his "advent'rous Song . . . to soar / Above th' *Aonian* Mount, while it pursues / Things unattempted yet in Prose or Rhyme" (PL I: 13–16). Here, so these critics maintain, Milton clearly reveals his purpose to write an epic that utterly surpasses all previous efforts in the tradition, reducing them to the status of suggestive allusion and then relegating them to the role of background for the one true history of divine Providence of which all previous epics are merely a dim distortion.

To an extent the rest of Milton's invocation to the muse also authorizes this argument.

> . . . What in me is dark
> Illumine, what is low raise and support;
> That to the highth of this great Argument
> I may assert Eternal Providence
> And justify the ways of God to men.
>
> (PL I: 22–26)

With this moving appeal to the spiritual source of his verse, Milton himself stands on a mental pinnacle where he would exchange his egocentric point of view for one that finds everything in the Word of God. Unlike the poet in the conventional invocation to the muse, Milton does not stay separate from his source of inspiration, but struggles with the very spirit of his verse as his means of tempering his own spiritual being.

Since even the conventional address to the muse has thus been made to serve the ultimate purpose of regaining for Milton the status of prophet, these commentators cite the entire invocation as an example of Milton's prophetic purpose; but when they do, they implicitly conflict with William Blake's "prophetic" reading of these lines, for he finds a contradiction insidiously at work in the two different parts of this invocation. This contradiction, moreover, will lead to Blake's powerful revaluation of the fundamental relationship between the epic and prophecy in Milton. Blake echoes the last line of Milton's invocation in his epigraph, "To justify the Ways of God to Men," but he then proceeds in a preface to complain against Milton's need to "soar above" the Greek and Roman models. In Blake's reading, Milton was "curbd by the general malady & infection from the silly Greek & Latin slaves of the Sword. . . . We do not want either Greek or Roman Models if we are but just & true to our Imaginations, those Worlds of Eternity in which we shall live for ever; in Jesus our Lord" (M I: 1). Unlike the more recent commentators, Blake identified Milton's use of the classical tradition not as a strength, but as a source for the error in all of Milton's poetry. Far from proving the superiority of his vision, Milton's use of the classical world as an ideology to be superseded by Christianity instead diminished, in Blake's view, Milton's ability to use the Bible properly, that is, imaginatively. For he treated the "Sublime of the Bible" in the same way that he treated the Greek world, not as true inspiration, but merely as a style to be imitated or as a deed to be remembered. Since, according to Blake, Milton became an epic poet at the expense of his prophetic vision, the drama of Blake's re-vision of Milton's poetry in the epic prophecy entitled *Milton* can be defined by dividing the two different charges to the muse into clear oppositions. In the Blakean reordering of priorities, Milton is "tempted" by the very wish to represent "things unattempted yet in prose or rhyme" and this temptation must itself be "illumined" before Milton can justify the ways of God to man.

Even this stark restructuring, however, cannot bring the issue raised by Milton's poetry clearly into the foreground. The opening scene in Blake's *Milton*, wherein Milton listens to the Bard's Song while contemplating the "intricate mazes" of divine Providence with other similarly blessed eternals in heaven, now requires attention. In this song it is not Christ but Satan who would perform deeds "as yet unattempted"; in this particular case, though, the deed assumes the form not of writing an epic poem, but of taking over a harrow from an immortal named Palamabron and following behind Rintrah's plow. Once Satan leads Palamabron's harrow and Palamabron supervises Satan's mills, terrible confusion results, and Los, the father of all three of the embattled parties, must call an assembly of eternals to adjudicate. In making almost nothing explicit the narrative leaves everything to the imagination; and in the context of the entire scene it is Milton's imagination that must make sense of the action; that is, the action must be understood in terms of the discrepancy between that project and its fulfillment, for when Blake begins with a Milton "unhappy tho' in heav'n" pondering there the same mazes of divine Providence he had earlier reserved for the more cerebral of the fallen in Hell, still waiting and watching for his estranged Emanation and all the while listening to another bard's version of *Paradise Lost* different from his own, a more profound dimension of Milton's vision emerges, still struggling to inspire him by illuminating the motives too dark for even him to address. These dark motives include not only Milton's wish to better the Greek or Roman models, but also to "assert Eternal Providence." The Bard's Song, at the moment in the action when Satan must "justify his ways" against the charges brough by Palamabron, reveals these wishes fused:

> For Satan flaming with Rintrahs fury hidden beneath his own mildness
> Accus'd Palamabron before the Assembly of ingratitude! of malice:
> He created Seven deadly Sins drawing out his infernal scroll,
> Of Moral laws and cruel punishments upon the clouds of Jehovah
>
> . . . .
>
> . . . Saying I am God alone
> There is no other! let all obey my principles of moral individuality
> (M I: 9, 19–22, 25–26)

The passage leads the intent listener, Milton, to renewed aspiration in the etymological sense; it literally "takes away the breath" from the lines of his poetry. Moreover, it does so not because Satan defends himself in echoes from the epic poems, but because it finally exposes Milton's God to be only Satan in disguise. In this single passage, Blake suggests that Milton in *Paradise Lost* did not justify the ways of God to man, but instead justified his own satanic wish to be greater than God, displaced, as in such lines as the address to the Muse, into a wish to be greater than the Greek or Roman models. However disguised the wish to be "original" may be, as long as Milton makes a point of overcoming the derivative themes of Homer and Virgil, the wish continues to resound in the quite literally displaced image of a desperate and vengeful Satan. Imitation (or memory) and revenge thus come together in *Milton* as the dual aspects of a single dark and complex experience, the dual experience of feeling belated, accompanied by a denial of this feeling accomplished by punishing it in another. Milton, in his wish to outsoar the Greeks and Romans, has not surpassed their theme of arms and the man after all, but only continued it at the subtler level of a Christian crusade—sanctioned by Divine Providence—and if he has *continued* their theme, he has not surpassed them but only imitated them after all. Perhaps to defend himself against this recognition above all else, Milton uses Satan (who is not to be believed) as the common foundation for both the feeling of being derivative and the resultant need for revenge. But this resourceful translation, out of its "conventional" associations, represses other recognitions as well, such as that of the essential similitude of the epic form and the feeling of being derivative or that of the unconscious use of God as the means of being revenged against just such feelings.

If Milton's poetry, through its adaptation of epic and theological conventions, forever masks these recognitions, the Bard's Song will not let him recognize anything else. Consequently, in terms generated by Milton's own epic, the Bard's Song functions as the inspiration which would "illumine" the dark and "raise up" the low invoked by Milton in his address to the muse. In other words, the Bard's Song is the inspiration which has not been articulated in Milton's finished poem, or, put still differently, it is a belated *re*-vision of *Paradise Lost*.

Blake's greatest insight coincides with the most profound blind spot in Milton's poetry—his theology. This theology, with its dualistic version of a just God opposed by a tyrannical rebel, could not conceive of a figure like Satan in *Milton*, capable of playing by turns both a just God and a cruel rebel. Blake, on the other hand, could conceive of no character more central to the creation than just such a figure, called Orc when young and rebellious and Urizen when old and tyrannical. Urizen and Orc then are not really opposed, but twin aspects of the same process which Blake, in his remarkable genius for multiple registers, alternately named in political, personal, and cosmic perspectives, respectively: the Orc cycle, jealousy, or the female will. No matter what Blake calls it, though, Milton notices its essential similarity to the same feeling of being derivative which led to the monumental self-deception in all of his poetry; and as soon as he does, this recognition inspires him to proclaim:

> What do I here before the Judgment? without my Emanation?
> With the daughters of memory, & not with the daughters of inspiration[?]
> I in my Selfhood am that Satan: I am that Evil one!
>
> (M I: 14, 28–30)

This time when Milton identifies his selfhood with Satan, he no longer means the Satan endorsed by centuries of theological speculation. In keeping with Milton's personal insight, this satanic selfhood (or "Human Abstract") can be illuminated by treating it as an ongoing psychological process. It begins then, as did Milton, with a sense of loss. This feeling leads to the wish to possess what another has not lost; and, while such a wish begins in jealousy, it soon turns into imitation, for imitation is a means of possessing by proxy the property of another. But as soon as the imitation is recognized as a "mere" imitation and not the "original," self-pity sets in as a means of justifying the loss by "deserving" it, self-pity turns into self-hatred, which out of compensation for having suffered this process of loss in the first place culminates in self-righteous indignation. This whole sequence may initially sound abstract, but it regains plausibility because it is a precise psychological explanation of Satan's complex interaction with Palamabron and Rintrah in the Bard's Song, which, in its turn, is an insight into Milton's unspoken motives for writing *Paradise Lost*.

Blake's vision, however, does not remain at this deep psychological level. Were it to do so, it would, of course, "illumine" what is dark but not yet "raise up" what is low in Milton. "What do I," Milton explains, in the remainder of the poem.[7] Milton brings both the created universe as well as his own created epic poems into a final judgment by ceasing to behold them as outward forms. Before he can *cease* to behold their outward forms, which constitute their imitative, derivative—in a word, satanic—element, he must begin to behold some other dimension in them, which becomes explicit when he takes off the robes of promise of the elect in heaven and descends into the valley of Beth Peor, where he begins molding Urizen into a shape, "Creating new flesh on the Demon cold, and building him, / As with new clay a Human form in the Valley of Beth Peor" (M I: 19, 13–14).

In the context of this perspective on *Milton*, the scene enacts Milton's most profound recognition; for after having described man as a creature made in the image of God in *Paradise Lost*, he here reverses the process and re-creates God in the image of man. Through this reversal, Milton does not limit either God or man to sole responsibility for the creation; instead he dramatizes in this visionary form a profound insight: God becomes as man so man can become as God. The perfect symmetry of these "contrary" clauses establishes the only theodicy Milton can now and Blake could ever accept, for it utterly shatters the psychology of jealousy underpinning the satanic universe and truly justifies, in the sense that it makes equal, the ways of God and man. This justification, moreover, truly constitutes a final judgment; for when man becomes *as* God, he need no longer behold an outward show of creation. Rather he can behold or rather delight in the organized innocence of creating. Neither Palamabron's harrowing nor Rintrah's plowing should be done in isolation, for taken together the "sweep" of their action establishes the full range of the imagination. When Satan, eager to possess the outward show as his own, intervenes between the two, creation appears as an activity separate from revelation. And since John Milton asked in his earliest invocation to the muse that "his" poetry outsoar the "show" of all previous creations, he must, in his renewed understanding of the theodicy, bring his own epic form to a last judgment.

By his "epic form," I mean the organizing principle for his epic poems, which in their very urge to better all other efforts in the epic tradition are no less satanic for all of their claim to be the living Word of Jesus Christ. In the terms of the Bard's Song, when Milton asserts the power of his moral universe *against* the ignorance of the pagans, he is truly reenacting the revenge of Satan while *pretending* to be the all-merciful face of Christ (who in this aspect is Palamabron). Having recognized the error in his creation, Milton must in the remainder of Blake's *Milton* re-cognize each major scene in the context of the double epiphany, "In my selfhood I am that Satan!" and "John Milton is God become as Man." Or, what amounts to the same thing, he must plow and harrow his own creation.

This process is not free of danger, however, as we can readily perceive from these lines:

> Satan! my Spectre! I know my power thee to annihilate
> And be a greater in thy place, & be thy Tabernacle
> A covering for thee to do thy will, till one greater comes
>
> . . . .
>
> . . . know thou: I come to Self Annihilation
> Such are the Laws of Eternity that each shall mutually
> Annihilate himself for others good, as I for thee[.]
>
> (M II: 38, 29–31, 34–36)

Whatever other echoes we hear in these lines, we must not fail to hear in this sequence a revision of Christ's final admonition to Satan in *Paradise Regained* not to tempt the Lord his God, for Milton here has revaluated even that profound utterance as only another satanic threat. But if any contention of wills only perpetuates the work of Satan, all of Milton's epics, based on just such fundamental contests of the will, here expose themselves as satanic. Truly to be free of Satan, Milton must withstand the temptation to smite him, for that would only mean that he had become satanic in his turn; instead he must "annihilate" the satanic element in his own heart, which means he must cease to behold Satan. Since in Blake's economy of vision, ceasing to behold one aspect of creation implies beholding another, Milton's act of turning his vision away from his already created forms immediately brings to consciousness what still remains for him to form, his estranged emanation, Ololon.

Although she represents the total form of Milton's epics, Ololon, as if to reveal the "undeveloped" as well as the willful elements in those labors, has the appearance of a twelve-year-old virgin. But Milton, unlike Adam, who was swayed from his task through idolatry of Eve, does not chasten his vision out of deference to Ololon's inexperience. Instead he thunders at her:

> Obey thou the Words of the Inspired Man
> All that can be annihilated must be annihilated
>
> (M II: 40, 29–30)

> To cast off the rotten rags of Memory by Inspiration
>
> . . . .
>
> . . . imitation of Natures Images drawn from Remembrance
> These are the Sexual Garments, the Abomination of Desolation
> Hiding the Human Lineaments as with an Ark & Curtains
> Which Jesus rent: & now shall wholly purge away with Fire
> Till Generation is swallowd up in Regeneration.
>
> (M II: 41, 4, 24–28)

In this exchange, both the poem and Milton have come full circle, for here Milton not only plays Rintrah to Ololon's Palamabron, thereby repeating the action in the Bard's Song, but this time implicitly "annihilating" the satanic masquerade, he also effectively rescinds that first portion of his invocation to the muse, by asking this time not to "soar above" all previous epics but "to cast off" these "rotten rags of memory" by inspiration. He separates all that is derivation from all that is inspired in his epic form.

In this re-cognition of Ololon, Milton in effect converts the total form of his epic labor from the status of an unsatisfied, hence jealous ghost into an inspired, hence fulfilled emanation. With the appearance of this emanation, the exclamation, "I in my Selfhood am that Satan!" no longer has any referent; with nothing left to say, Milton is fully absorbed in what he beholds:

> One Man Jesus the Saviour. wonderful! round his limbs
> The Clouds of Ololon folded as a Garment dipped in blood
>
> (M II: 42, 11–12)

With Milton, like his epic form, thus utterly transformed into an act of recognition, Blake alone remains to speak these lines, and when he does, he no longer beholds Milton, but sees *with* the power of inspiration that he has seen *through* Milton.

The entire poem has amended Milton's vision and done so through a remarkably just deed. Whereas Milton organized his epic prophecies around the defeat of a misguided figure, Blake's *Milton* is organized around the annihilation of the *need* to defeat such a figure. Whereas Milton's poetry enacted the sacrifice of Satan to attain to its own self-righteous posture,

Milton in Blake's prophecy sacrifices his own desire to be self-righteous, for Satan exists only as such a desire. *Milton* separates the false prophet from the true, the memory from the imagination, the changeable from the eternal, the selfhood from the imagination; and Milton converts himself into the space of transfiguration called *Milton*.

Thus *Milton* exists as the fulfilled wish of the prophet in *Paradise Lost* who asked that what was dark in him be illuminated, for that prophet has become in *Milton* the scene where such an illumination takes place. And if this scene is the only actual scene, however often repeated, in the entire poem, the poem does not describe a sequential narrative, but an ongoing act of revelation, an expanding recognition of the full significance of a single scene. As we move through *Milton*, we are not seeing different scenes, but more and more of the same scene, or rather we are seeing more and more of what we see with, "One Man Jesus the Saviour," for in the end it is this process of the imagination, this visionary form, dramatically revealing itself through everything else.

When the imagination reveals itself working through everything else, the essential distinction between the epic form and the prophetic spirit also breaks down, for the world actualized in the epic form turns out to be no different from the world imagined by the prophet. By the end of *Milton*, an actual world is no longer opposed to a possible one, or a past opposed to a future, or an infinite opposed to a finite. For when all of the actual scenes turn into means of revealing the power of prophecy, the epic form turns out to *mean* the imagination's act of imaging its power, which is to say the epic form is itself raised to the power of prophecy.

II

A century and a half after Blake wrote *Milton* Hart Crane returned to it, not merely as a source of inspiration, but as a fundamental lesson in the techniques of epic prophecy. This is not to say, however, that Crane merely reproduced either the vision or the mechanics of Blake's poem. If anything should be clear from the discussion of epic prophecy thus far, it would be the impossibility of such a duplication, for each poet who undertakes an epic prophecy—which is, after all, a vision of what is possible for a nation at a particular time in its history—must meet the demands of his age. It is the prophet in the poet who intuits both the demands and their solution. Underlying everything else in Blake, then, is a fundamental insight into the primary deficiency of his age and a technique to meet it. In Blake's mind, the need and its solution were interrelated: man had to recover his status as a creator not a creature of nature, and he could do so by deepening perception until it attained to the level of imagination.

Crane's definition of poetry declares his similar faith in the powers of the poet: "poetry . . . may well give you the real connective experience, the very 'sign manifest' on which rests the assumption of the godhead." [6] When he wrote, he found blocking his pathway a precursor whose epic poem provided even more of an impasse than did Milton's conventions for Blake. Indeed he found T. S. Eliot's *The Waste Land* alien to the most fundamental elements in his definition of poetry; the one expereince that poem would not provide was one of connection. Moreover, *The Waste Land* subverted the most basic element in the epic: its capacity to consolidate the ideology, history, and religion of an age into a coherent form. In *The Waste Land*, the poet's power to organize the fragments into a rationale for an epic had come into question. Whereas in Blake's *Milton*, prophetic epiphanies disrupted the sequential line established by Milton's epic descent until the entire poem revealed itself to be a single sustained prophecy, *The Waste Land* provided no coherent sequential line, let alone a prophetic epiphany. Instead of being limited to privileged moments, discontinuity pervades the entire form; consequently, no real distinction can be drawn between a prophetic recognition and just another fragmented perception. The discontinuity inherent in the prophetic mode ushered in a vision of apocalypse; here, on the other hand, it evokes a sense of radical and insuperable disintegration, which does not threaten to end in an apocalyptic vision so much as never to end at all. Thus the strength of *The Waste Land* does not reside in its capacity to return a people to personal power, but to deprive even the most inspiring of quotations of any power whatsoever.

The Waste Land does not provide a vision of order so much as it makes that vision its central, though unfulfillable wish, a wish, moreover, for a reality finally *beyond* or transcendent to it. To begin to see this wish in the poem is to begin to apprehend even here Eliot's need to believe in a realm of faith, myth, and history finally inimical both to the techniques and the substance of poetry. The best a poet could manage from the start for Eliot would be an admission of the inadequacy of both his subject matter and his style so that his poem would not, like Blake's, call forth the "real" world, but point, with quiet despair, to a world beyond the poet's capacity to call forth, until the poet finally seems absorbed in the pointing.

All of which means that Eliot returned man to the status of creature not creator and the poet to the position of impersonal craftsman, more absorbed by the fragments he manipulates than absorbed *in* the act of creation. But his most appalling regression of all, at least in Crane's mind, was his insistence on the poet's adherence to a religious and cultural orthodoxy *in place of* a faith in the regenerative power of poetry. Crane knew he had to come to terms with Eliot. He wrote:

> I have been facing [Eliot] for *four* years, . . . and I have discovered a safe tangent to strike which, if I can possibly explain the position,—goes *through* him toward a *different goal*. . . . I would apply as much of his erudition and technique as I can absorb and assemble toward a more positive, . . . ecstatic goal. . . . I feel that Eliot ignores certain spiritual events and possibilities as real . . . now as say . . . in the time of Blake. (*Letters* 90, 114, 115)

By "going through," Crane obviously does not mean he will ignore Eliot's poetry. Without denying Eliot's poetics of discontinuity, he will nonetheless move through these fragments by regaining the vision behind them. This vision, though, will not be finally distinguishable from a profound wish.

Perhaps this formulation will become clearer if we restate it as Crane's solution to a specific problem raised by Eliot's "epic." If *The Waste Land* frustrates in advance the epiphanic power of any prophetic utterance, the poem can be deprived of its disruptive powers. A dream, once fully understood, is no longer elemented of a chaos of fragments, but of "free associations," all emanating from the variegated demands of a single frustrated wish. If Crane begins *The Bridge* with the wish for a vision Eliot claims to be beyond the ken of poetry, he goes on to expose Eliot's fragments, which Crane would accept as adequate representations of the twentieth-century sensibility, as free associations resulting when Eliot frustrates the wish for a vision. These free associations appear to be fragments only because the wish for a vision has had to descend into the unconscious or dream state for fulfillment. When their *common* wish arises into consciousness, they will turn into emanations (in Blake's sense) rather than fragments.

Crane sees *through* the fragments of *The Waste Land* into the wish behind them, but he acknowledges that in the twentieth century (as Freud tells us) such a wish can be fulfilled only in a dream. Without breaking faith with either the intuition or the acknowledgment, Crane creates a poem which will not awaken modern man *from* this dream, but wake him up *to* this dream so that he can dream it while awake, as a vision.

Such a monumental revision obviously required changes from Eliot's poetic strategy. To effect a change at the most fundamental level, Crane's epic internalized the quest motif Eliot used only as an outline, thereby turning *The Bridge*'s modern quest for the grail into the equivalent of a search for a true epic vision, or, as Crane puts it, a quest "to enunciate a new cultural synthesis of values in terms of our America" (*Letters* 273).

Both the drama and the quest begin to become clear in "The Harbor Dawn" section of *The Bridge*, for here a man awakens to a rather startling experience of the disconnectedness of the twentieth-century street:

> Insistently through sleep—a tide of voices—
> They meet you listening midway in your dream,
> The long, tired sounds, fog-insulated noises:
> Gongs in white surplices, beshrouded wails,
> Far strum of fog horns . . . signals dispersed in veils.[7]

In these lines the disparate noises, whether from ships, trucks, factories, cars, or churches, do not originate in the "real" world outside the dream, but are emissaries *from* the dream world. The gongs remind us of priests in their "white surplices," while the fog-laden atmosphere when connected with "beshrouded" and "veils" brings associations of the incense in a benediction service wherein a sacred world blesses a profane one. Through these associations even the potentially chaotic welter of dispersed noises comes together as "signals" of some ceremony we do not know—for we have awakened from it—but which all the sounds and activities of our day *unconsciously* serve and strive to regain.

It is not just in this section, though, that a dream vision threatens to break into the world. The very beginning of the poem, "To Brooklyn Bridge," establishes this action as a motif central to the structure of the entire poem. After a rather bored office worker daydreams around the free flight of a seagull, he finally loses sight of the bird, and when he does, the bird, by becoming "As apparitional as sails that cross / Some pages of figures to be filed away" (CP 45), brings to mind still another dream of adventure in a daily routine marked by as many dreams as duties.

Crane, however, has an even more profound reason for organizing *The Bridge* around the opposition between dream and daily activity than merely providing a unifying context for the multitude of fragmented activities. If such "flashing scenes" as these continually disrupt twentieth-century existence, that existence can with almost equal certitude be labled either a reality principle *or* a distortion of a dream. It was the latter description, however, that Crane turned into his principle for the composition of *The Bridge*. Having comprehended this disruption as his poetic principle, however, we are faced with an imperative to understand what dream has been distorted.

Here the discussion of *Milton* proves quite helpful; for in that poem, Blake located all the error in Milton's poetry in a single scene—that of the address to the muse, where Milton both asserted his "Selfhood" when he asked to better his precursors and longed to be a prophet when he asked to be truly inspired. Once he separated the prophet in himself from the selfhood, Milton was able to revise prophetically every other scene in his epic poetry. Similarly, Crane organizes *The Bridge* around a single scene, that of Columbus in the "Ave Maria" section as he longs to return to the Old World with his vision of the New, but a third world "of water, tests the word." After suffering from mutiny, doubt, bewilderment, derision, and stormy seas, Columbus looks out on the "vast rondure" of the sea and, while in the midst of his most profound expereince of despair and longing, envisons God as an "incognizable Word," who searches "cruelly with love" his "parable of man." Having discovered, in other words, a new geographical world, Columbus finds on his way back with the news of this discovery a new kind of faith and vision, one which does not replace doubts with the platitudes and conventions of religious orthodoxy—all that he now finds to belong to an *Old* World—but which will see beyond doubt, even beyond despair, into the "kingdoms naked in the trembling heart."

Whereas Blake used Milton's invocation as his means of prophetically revaluating the orthodoxy inherent to the other scenes in Milton's epic poetry, Crane uses Columbus's vision as the "dream text" twentieth-century reality distorts. Throughout the poem whenever one level of the seeker's reality conflicts with another—whether through daydreaming, slip of the tongue, chiasmus, talking at cross-purposes, cacophonous quotation—Crane registers the suggestion that the giant form of Columbus is attempting to awaken within the consciousness of the seeker. Consequently, this single scene runs implicitly *through* all the others.

Crane, moreover, uses the historical figure of Columbus in a way similar to Blake's use of Milton; that is, as a giant mental form whose creative efforts summarized the aspirations and wishes of a people—in short, as an epic hero. Crane, nevertheless, adds an innovation to Blake's conception, for after he envisions Columbus about to return to the Old World having conquered space and time, he is in a position to correlate all of America's technological efforts directed at mastering space and time with "catching up" to Columbus. Crane, in other words, organizes *The Bridge* around America's repetition throughout its history of Columbus's initial historical adventure. Each of the seven sections following "Ave Maria," from "Harbor Dawn" through "Cape Hatteras," either intimates or adumbrates a different aspect of America's conquest of time and space, through the railroad (in "The River"), the sailing ships (in "Cutty Sark"), the covered wagons (in "Indiana"), the highway systems (in "Van Winkle"), or the airplane (in "Cape Hatteras").

Only two of these sections fail to represent such a conquest; they are bridges for further connections, for that is what true expansion was for Crane, "a sign manifest of a connective experience." "Harbor Dawn," then, does not represent a technological conquest of either space or time, but nonetheless bridges between the fifteenth and twentieth centuries through the medium of the dream. As the poem moves from the time of Columbus in the "Ave Maria" section to the "Harbor Dawn" section quoted above, only the devotional language used in the "Ave Maria" section provides a proper context for the religious images analyzed in the dream sequence. The implications here are no less remarkable for being obvious: when the man who wakes up in the twentieth century continues to hear sounds from the fifteenth, it is the man from the fifteenth century who is trying unsuccessfully to wake up. Furthermore, if the chaotic "reality" of the twentieth-century street interferes with the "waking up," it is not fundamentally different from the "third" world of water which tested Columbus's faith four centuries earlier.

The association of modern America with the ocean becomes important in the "Atlantis" section, because the kingdom of Atlantis also disappeared under an ocean. But not even this notion of a dream-bridge will account for "The Dance" section of the poem, wherein a medicine man named Maquokeeta, after being sacrificed by his tribe, turns into the morning star, "twilight's dim perpetual throne" and looks each day upon the body of America, which is what his beloved Pocahontas has become. In Blake's terms, Maquokeeta, the sachem medicine man who gave America the name and genius of his beloved, is a native of the "golden age" of America, and the confrontation between his "golden age" and the present age, now recognizable both as the period of "The Flood" and an iron age, constitutes the "crisis" between the world that is and the one that ought to be, which marks the distinguishing trait of an epic prophecy.

Before Crane can recover the vision of America's golden age, or rather before he can intensify the conflict between the Golden Age and modern America to the point of a dialectical separation, he must regain the voice of America's first epic prophet, Walt Whitman.

III

As the "ghoul mound" responsible for wrecking so many ships, Cape Hatteras represents a natural pause to reemphasize the impasse in *The Waste Land*, a "disconnection" in the action of *The Bridge*. By its very nature, it impedes bridging or free passage. Moreover, when Crane the voyager watches the airplanes fly above this mound, he arrives at the insight that America, in the invention of the plane, has entered into the final conquest of time and space. With this recognition, Crane secures the "complete" correlation with Columbus in the "Ave Maria" section, for "The seas all crossed, weathered the capes, the voyage done . . ." the traveler must return home.

But the difficulty of returning home indicates a mission for the new voyager somewhat different from Columbus's. Columbus had to return to the Old World with a vision of the New; Crane, now, has to turn the "old" world of America back into the New World by returning her to her original vision, and that means bringing back up into consciousness the "mythic soil" drowned beneath the twentieth century's "dream of fact." Returning to the original vision of America means turning away from the poetry of T. S. Eliot and turning to Walt Whitman. Eliot felt modern poetry had been compromised by the imperial personality in Whitman's line, and he felt, as Roy Harvey Pearce has pointed out, a personal responsibility to subject that line to the deadening influence of his own impersonality.[8] When in the "Hatteras" section Crane harkened back to Whitman, he took true delight in hearing Whitman's voice shake Eliot back out of America's poetic line:

> O Walt!—Ascensions of thee hover in me now
>
> . . . .
>
> Years of the Modern! Propulsions toward what capes?
> . . .—O, something green,
> Beyond all sesames of science was thy choice
> Wherewith to bind us throbbing with one voice. . . .
>
> (CP 93, 94–95)

However much he wanted Whitman's voice, he certainly needed the "twin" of that voice, Whitman's vision, even more; for the "Hatteras" section marked the "turning point" in *The Bridge*, the moment when the voyager could no longer nostalgically recall figures from bygone days or daydream about adventures. Instead when he experienced "ascensions" of Walt "hover" in him, he had to prove that Whitman's poetry was actually the "vision" that Eliot's epic so desperately wished to attain (*Letters* 261). Whitman, then, in every sense prepared the traveler on Hatteras for the descent into the dark world of *The Waste Land.*

In Whitman's work, however, there exist none of the mythological figures of Blake's epic prophecies. Blake invented a mythological system of his own to deliver the consciousness of England from the "conventional systems" which had entrapped it for centuries. His mythological system, centered as it was on the action of the Orc cycle, was of a peculiar kind: it was a mythology designed to expose the dangers of pitting one myth against another. But Whitman, writing, as he was, for a democratic country, did not even want to do combat with mythologies long enough to expose their error. For Whitman, mythology meant feudalism or master–slave relationships, and he wanted equality. But if he did not subscribe to Blake's mythological system, he nevertheless set for himself the same central task Blake did. Like Blake, Whitman in his lifelong labors on the epic prophecy *Leaves of Grass* wanted to make prophets of all God's flock; or, as he worded it in his "Preface" to the 1855 edition:

> The messages of great poets to each man and woman are, Come to us on equal terms. . . . We are no better than you. . . . Did you suppose that there could be only one Supreme? We affirm there can be unnumbered Supremes . . . and that men can be good or grand only of the consciousness of their supremacy within them.[9]

Without the benefit of a traditional mythological system, Whitman in *Leaves of Grass* gave the impression that he was beginning everything afresh, or rather that everything was finding a new beginning in him. When Whitman wrote that he was "the age transfigured," that to him "opened the eternity which gives similitude to all periods and locations and processes and animate and inanimate forms, and which is the bond of time . . . and makes the present spot the passage from what was to what shall be . . . ," he ceased to be the empirical ego Walt Whitman and turned into the visionary consciousness of America.[10] He did not, however, lead up to this conversion as did Blake in *Milton* through a dramatic recognition scene. Instead, throughout *Leaves of Grass*, he "democratizes" rather than dramatizes recognitions of immortality, which then take their place beside others as perceptions of equal value:

> Is it wonderful that I should be immortal? as every one is immortal;
> I know it is wonderful, but my eyesight is equally wonderful, and
> how I was conceived in my mother's womb is equally wonderful.
>
> (WCP 278)

But if Whitman refuses such a "drama" of vision, he presents a formidable problem for a literary criticism geared to discover the "development" or "structure" of an act of self-discovery. James E. Miller, Jr., in his "*Song of Myself* as Inverted Mystical Experience," reads the poem as a reversal of the traditional path leading up to and away from an experience of godhead. And though its scope is expanded to include Whitman's entire life of writing, Roger Asselineau's *The Evolution of Walt Whitman* still insists on reading the epic in terms of a progressive attainment and then loss of the power of poetic vision. Charles Feidelson in *Symbolism and American Literature* certainly establishes a point of departure from the other two views when he writes that Whitman's "long poems generally lack [a] stabilizing factor . . . the nominal subject . . . is lost in the process. . . . When the subject is endless, any form becomes arbitrary." [11] Not even Feidelson's exquisite formulation that Whitman's poetry "instead of referring to the completed act of perception, constitutes the act itself, both in the author and in the reader," [12] however, quite captures the magnitude of Whitman's epic. Feidelson's account still maintains a subject–object dualism in the act of perception, but Whitman, like the consciousness in a dream, manages to create for himself a being equally identifiable with subject, object, act of perception, and the stage on which all of this action transpires.

Whitman raised an important issue in *Democratic Vistas*: "What is the fusing [relation] between the (radical, democratic) Me . . . on the one side" and "the whole of the material objective universe and laws . . . on the other side?" [13] The answer to this question is Walt Whitman in *Leaves of Grass*, who ceases to be a subjective identity and becomes instead a democratic relation. In a simple but profound solution to the problem of writing a democratic epic, Whitman settles on the *relation between* one person and another, persons and objects, even objects and objects as the truly equalizing experience. Everything else exists to realize this experience, not the reverse. For Whitman, a subject is not a gain in identity but a loss of relation. Whitman equates the relation with the traditional notion of "soul," and as Quentin Anderson notes, in Whitman "body and soul, image and beholder, are correlative. If they truly are, then eternity is what you truly see now, not what you hope for, remember, or try to imagine." [14]

In *Leaves of Grass* Whitman replaces the usual conception of an identity standing apart from his experience with a view of a subject who is enough part of a continuum to seem indistinguishable from it, or, if an agent at all, an agent within a process as in "Your vapors I think have risen with you." All of *Leaves of Grass* takes the form of a repetition, however brilliantly varied, of this single experience from Section 5 of "Song of Myself":

> I mind how once we lay such a transparent summer morning,
> How you . . . plung'd your tongue to my bare stript heart
> And reach'd till you felt my beard and reach'd till you held my feet.
>
> (WCP 28)

Although the passage ostensibly describes the union of body and soul, of "I" and "you," the body and soul are interfused enough to have exchanged their traditional roles. If soul recognizes itself through union with the body, which body experiences itself *as* this union with the soul, a consciousness identifiable with neither body nor soul but with their union arises. Thus the fusing relation between body and soul releases an "I" in between both, an "I," however, whose consciousness requires much more than merely man's physical body to satisfy its awareness of being in relation. Instead of stopping with this merger with the body, then, "I" proceeds to realize

> . . . that the hand of God is the promise of my own. . . .
> And that a kelson of the creation is love,
> And limitless are leaves stiff with drooping in the fields. . . .
> And mossy scabs of the worm fence, heap'd stones, elder, mullein and poke-weed.
>
> (WCP 28)

The catalog, though, need not stop here, for this democratic "body electric" is as much in relation to all the objects in the universe as it is to man's physical body. All the world, subjects and objects alike, exists in *Leaves of Grass* to reveal and endlessly repeat the consciousness with its "merger," then its "outlet again" of being totally and utterly in relation.

But if in Whitman the actual or physical world exists only for the sake of revealing the purely possible eternal world of original relation, his poetry never represents the crisis between epic and prophetic elements in Blake's *Milton* and Crane's *The Bridge*. In *Leaves of Grass* epic and prophecy are as interfused as the body and soul in the scene just described, so that every moment of this poem enacts the final moment of Blake's: that the world that *is* is swallowed up in the vision of the world that *can be* and time is enclosed by eternity. Whitman has not just called forth the golden age that is his true home, he abides in it as the only world there is.

IV

If Crane, standing on the "ghoul mound" of Hatteras, preparing to descend into Eliot's world of utter fragmentation, returns to Whitman, he turns from an experience of alienation to an experience of being "in connection." Whitman, for Crane, is a visionary "bridge" to his true home, the golden age of America. Moreover, as he prepares to descend into the Old World of *The Waste Land*, it is the Word of Whitman's New World that he hopes to bring home.

In reestablishing a relation with Whitman's vision, Crane did not intend to write in Whitman's style or even about Whitman's subject. In fact, the reverse is true. His rediscovery of Whitman only replicates Columbus's discovery of the New World; he does not bring that world back with him, only news of it. And he must still get across the ocean to do even that. Crane's recollection of Whitman, then, is used more as a "contrast" to the experience of estrangement in the modern world than as a living part of his experience. Remembering Whitman increases rather than abates his despair as he passes through "Three Songs" and "Quaker Hill," for in recalling Whitman's vision, he knows how far America has fallen.

The entire second half of *The Bridge* from "Three Songs" through "The Tunnel" heightens the crisis between the epic elements in *The Bridge* (its recapitulation of events in American history, its encyclopedic synthesis of everyday life) and the prophetic visions of Columbus, Whitman, and Maquokeeta. These two different aspects of the poem have conflicted from the beginning, but they enter into high, even ecstatic tension in "The Tunnel" section.

If *The Bridge* was Crane's response to the fragmentation of everyday life represented in *The Waste Land*, and if he effected this response by exposing these fragments as free associations of a dream, *The Bridge* as its final action must reveal the dream *The Waste Land* has distorted. In distinguishing a dream from "reality," the dream becomes the place where wishes, unfulfillable in reality, descend for fulfillment. In Crane, then, the dream must entail the experience of an "unfulfilled wish." Not just any wish, however, will do. The wish in *The Bridge* must approach the magnitude of either Columbus's wish to return to the Old World with the vision of the New in "Ave Maria" or the repetition of that wish in the voyager's desire to return to modern America with the news of Whitman's golden age. Neither in "Ave Maria" nor in the second half of *The Bridge* does the traveler's wish get fulfilled; and precisely because it cannot be fulfilled it must descend to a much more profound level of consciousness. Only after his desire deepens to the point of despair can Columbus rise to a lyric vision of "Kingdoms naked in the trembling heart" in "Ave Maria," and only after the traveler in "The Tunnel" despairs of ever returning home with a "Word that will not die" can he have a vision of "Atlantis." It is not the fulfillment of the desire that confers the visions, it is a despair over their never being fulfilled which finally opens into vision. In other words, Crane increases the distance between the actual and the possible, the desire and its object until only the span of longing between them remains, and this longing itself generates a world.

This profound longing renders even the unconscious state of the dream useless and instead reduces all the scenes from American history, recounted in the previous section of the poem, into the span of a single prophetic moment, whereby the epic world that America was is consumed in the prophecy of the New World she can become. Thus "Atlantis" is quite literally a kingdom of the heart's desire, not a world we fall asleep to dream, but a dream world we awaken into. And when this real world appears, *The Waste Land* disappears as if it were only a bad dream.

Both Blake and Whitman were instrumental in the act of transcending

The Waste Land. In "The Tunnel," the traveler fully accepts the challenge of Eliot's vision by adopting the persona, sensibility, and style of J. Alfred Prufrock. Crane relocates Prufrock in a subway system reminiscent of that in Eliot's later poem "Burnt Norton." After establishing these surface correlations, however, Crane's traveler undergoes a profound experience of self-transformation that Eliot claimed was beyond the reach of poetry. Eliot's "Burial of the Dead" only alluded to the Eleusinian mystery as an unassimilable vegetative ritual, but Crane's traveler goes through all the steps in the ritual from burial to resurrection as a "Lazarus" figure who feels "the slope / The soil and billow breaking." But, upon reflection, this traveler in the twentieth-century subway, sitting across from a "Genoese washer woman" and praying for passage home, is a repetition of Columbus, who underwent the same ordeal four centuries earlier. Columbus, though, in his turn is Crane's version of one of Blake's giant mental forms who, like Blake's Milton, is able to reduce all of a nation's history into a single act of consciousness. Thus, when Crane's traveler is resurrected from *The Waste Land*, he also fulfills Blake's prophecy of man's potential. Nonetheless, by the time we enter into Crane's "Atlantis," his difference from Blake's epic prophecy becomes clear. Whereas Blake's *Milton*, for example, reduced all the scenes in his epic poetry to a single act of the Christian imagination, Christopher Columbus in *The Bridge* converts all of American history into the "free associations" of visionary longing. Thus, while Blake's *Milton* introduces the epic prophecy of Jerusalem, a kingdom reserved for true Christians, Crane's *The Bridge* ends in a vision of "Atlantis," which like America calls forth the natives of all countries who long for a return to the kingdom of the heart. Columbus's epiphanic act of longing puts him in as profound a relation with all the mystic figures in the epic tradition (he is able, after all, to shout at Jason of *Argonaut* fame in "Atlantis") which Whitman proclaimed was the true duty of the American poet. The central distinction between Whitman and Crane then resides in the differing intensity of their epic prophecies more than in their content, for while Whitman greeted the golden age with as much ease as he accepted the weather, Crane had to overcome an entire world to call it back into being.

V

While Blake, Crane, and Whitman all wrote in the same fiery hand of the tradition of epic prophecy, their finished poems are as different as their times and countries. In eighteenth-century England, Blake attempted to redirect the consciousness of England away from a scientific investigation of physical nature and onto the process of imagination which confirmed nature's true form. To effect this reversal, he returned to the last English poet who envisioned nature as a loss of paradise and by isolating the prophetic moment in Milton's poetry, renewed all of Milton's epics and, by extension, all of England in the vision of that moment. When Crane wrote for twentieth-century America, he found the problem different; America had lost, through a diminution of her desire, all sense of connection with the original vision of a land of promise. To effect a cure of her will, he recalls the epic prophecy of the American-poet who sang of her golden age. He then correlates a series of central moments in the epic history of America as common efforts to sing that song until—as Blake did for England—Crane conflates all of American history into that single moment when the total form of America's epic turns into the prophetic act of Atlantis rising from the sea.

Notes

1. Northrop Frye, *Fearful Symmetry: A Study of William Blake* (Princeton: Princeton Univ. Press, 1947), p. 318.

2. Thomas A. Vogler, *Preludes to Vision: The Epic Venture in Blake, Wordsworth, Keats, and Hart Crane* (Berkeley: Univ. of California Press, 1971), pp. 8–9. Brian Wilkie's opening chapter in *Romantic Poets and Epic Tradition* (Madison: Univ. of Wisconsin Press, 1965) offers the fullest treatment of the transformation of epic conventions.

3. For further discussion of Milton's place in the epic tradition, see Joseph Wittreich, "Opening the Seals: Blake's Epics and the Milton Tradition," in *Blake's Sublime Allegory: Essays on "The Four Zoas," "Milton," and "Jerusalem,"* ed. Stuart Curran and Joseph Anthony Wittreich, Jr. (Madison: Univ. of Wisconsin Press, 1973), pp. 23–58.

4. Northrop Frye, *The Return of Eden: Five Essays in Milton's Epics* (Toronto: Univ. of Toronto Press, 1965), p. 59.

5. The first quotation is from Angus Fletcher's *The Transcendental Masque: An Essay in Milton's "Comus"* (Ithaca: Cornell Univ. Press, 1971), p. 43; for the sake of argument, however, I have included it in Wittreich's definition in "Opening the Seals," p. 27.

6. Crane's definition appears in a letter to Gorham Munson (March 17, 1926), *The Letters of Hart Crane*, ed. Brom Weber (New York: Hermitage House, 1952), p. 237; hereafter cited as *Letters.*

7. All quotations from Crane's poetry are from *The Complete Poems and Selected Letters and Prose of Hart Crane*, ed. Brom Weber (New York: Anchor Books, 1966), p. 54; hereafter cited as CP.

8. Pearce writes that in Eliot's poetry, "the Whitmanian mode is made to negate itself and generate its opposite: a wholly personal style takes on a grand impersonality." *The Continuity of American Poetry* (Princeton: Princeton Univ. Press, 1961, p. 304.

9. Citations from Whitman's prose and poetry are from *Complete Poetry and Selected Prose by Walt Whitman*, ed. James E. Miller, Jr. (Boston: Houghton Mifflin, 1959), p. 418; hereafter cited as WCP.

10. Quentin Anderson, *The Imperial Self* (New York: Random House, 1971), p. 149.

11. James E. Miller, Jr., *A Critical Guide to "Leaves of Grass,"* (Chicago: Univ. of Chicago Press, 1957), pp. 256–261; Roger Asselineau, *The Evolution of Walt Whitman* (Cambridge: Harvard Univ. Press, 1960); Charles Feidelson, *Symbolism in American Literature* (Chicago: Univ. of Chicago Press, 1953), p. 25.

12. Feidelson, p. 18.

13. See Whitman's "Specimen Days," *Prose Works, 1892*, vol. 1, ed. Floyd Stovall (New York: New York Univ. Press), p. 258, for Whitman's discrimination of himself from the too-"subjective" William Blake.

14. Anderson, p. 129.

LEROY SEARLE

Blake, Eliot, and Williams: The Continuity of Imaginative Labor

Though very much a man of his own time, Blake was almost invisible in it, in part because he addressed himself to a world of "eternity" that depends on a thorough commitment to imagination. As poet, painter, printer, and publisher, Blake could provide exactly what he thought necessary for his work to be understood; but he necessarily left to faith the reader-viewer's own imaginative activity, without which the "minute particulars" of his art may seem, in his phrase, a "mill with complicated wheels."

This is the central difficulty of Blake's "system." As modern Blake studies attest, attention to particulars yields rich ambiguities, especially in Blake's use of tradition and contemporaneous events, but no degree of diligence in exploring sources and tracking influences can replace the specific kind of imaginative apprehension that Blake requires.[1] Blake's art is "systematic" because he took the whole domain of human experience as his field, in the radical faith that imagination could disclose its meaning. To see Blake in the context of "eternity" depends less on cracking a set of codes than on understanding, in detail, the workings of imagination as an indispensable human power. Similarly, Blake is a paradigmatic artist not so much because his work can be schematized, but because it reveals an intimate, consistent understanding of imagination as a generative process.

Blake's example is of particular interest because he sought, through that process, total intelligibility; and though we will see that the expectation of a unique totalizing form breaks down as imagining goes on with its labor, Blake's exemplary desire for comprehensiveness is the major source of the vitality of his art. This goes far to explaining Blake's importance to later artists, and his special place in the development of modern literature. Through Yeats and Joyce, Blake became a part of the literary environment early in this century, so it is not difficult to find indirect connections between Blake and many other writers. Yet Blake's importance exceeds the mere tracing of resemblances, mediated through curious contingencies. As an exemplary artist, he exhibits imaginative labor itself as a system, belonging to no one in particular, save the person who takes it up with total dedication.

Thus to compare Blake, Eliot, and Williams, who seem to have only the word-hoard of the language in common, does not involve arguing a case of "influence." Eliot at least read Blake (though with scant sympathy), while Williams shows only a casual acquaintance with him, appearing to think of Blake primarily as a mystic.[2] Just so, these three poets offer an ideal occasion for examining the consequences of art pursued with total dedication, all the more so because their work cannot be accommodated to a single scheme without a violent reduction of the particularity on which all three insisted.

For Blake and Williams, trust in the imagination takes precedence over any other claim upon the artist's loyalties, and it led both to seek the source of artistic value in their native places and persons. As Blake loved his "green and pleasant land" with a justifiable prophetic rage, he devoted his life to revealing in it what Williams called the "universality of the local"; while Williams, seeing no reason to leave the place where he was born, did the same in the environs of Rutherford and Paterson, New Jersey. While contemporaries might dismiss the one as mad, the other as a minor talent outside the traditionary mainstream, both poets sustained themselves in the grace of fleeting moments like the Lark's Song in *Milton* (M II: 31, 35), or the brief visions of the "beautiful thing" in *Paterson*, missing which we put ourselves "in the way of death." [3] To stake so much on such apparently fragile moments may seem either desperate or naïve, but it reflects a belief that without imagination, there is no life worth living, and no human place in which to live it.

Covering two continents and twenty centuries in his supremely articulate raid on Western culture, Eliot seems much nearer the mainstream, but he shows perhaps more clearly than any other poet his awareness that a faith in imagination entails great risks. With a certain uneasiness, Eliot admitted that Blake was a "poet of genius," though terrifying in his honesty; but complained that Blake's energetic genius made only "formless" compositions betraying a certain "meanness of culture":

> Blake was endowed with a capacity for considerable understanding of human nature, with a remarkable and original sense of language and the music of language, and a gift of hallucinated vision. Had these been controlled by a respect for impersonal reason, for common sense, for the objectivity of science, it would have been better for him. What his genius required, and what it sadly

> lacked, was a framework of accepted and traditional ideas which would have prevented him from indulging in a philosophy of his own, and concentrated his attention upon the problems of the poet.[4]

As a sometime philosopher himself, it might have been better for Eliot to have considered this case more closely, but even this ironically self-revealing appraisal calls attention to the fundamental problem of the poet: Where can he place his trust, and with what consequences? Given Eliot's commendation of "accepted and traditional ideas," which Blake and Williams alike blamed as forms of artistic bad faith, the issue appears to divide quite neatly, yet in Eliot's concern for poetic form lies a basis for a common "tradition," with its owm implicit "philosophy" stemming from the process of vision and revision which brings imaginative possibilities to light.

Without this vital labor, there could never be a tradition of any sort, for it is an eternal activity of intelligence—as Williams put it, "to refine, to clarify, to intensify that eternal moment in which we alone live. . . ." [5] We may mark its "beginning" as Williams did in *Spring and All*:

> I let the imagination have its own way to see if it could save itself. Something very definite came of it. I found myself alleviated but most important I began there and then to revalue experience, to understand what I was at— (I 116)

With this inaugural gesture, Williams shows how very definite are the consequences which come from letting the imagination have its own way.

I. Imagination, the Corrosive Power

In a notebook entry of 1803, Coleridge complained that "Without Drawing I feel myself but half invested with Language," [6] a remark Blake would have savored. As an augmented "language" of art, Blake's illuminated poetry begins a process of construal which is not exhausted in a single act. Rather, it makes us participants in the activity which produced the art, and the mental consequences which follow. To use Blake's metaphor for his craft, we apprehend structure in a way resembling the action of acid etching a plate, seeing patterns at once created and disclosed, which gain depth with each succeeding look. In composition, the artist is led forward into his material and backward to reflect on results, just as the activity of reading returns upon itself to measure the coherence of insights against the expanding range of their implications.

The Frontispiece and "Introduction" to the *Songs of Innocence* supply a paradigmatic illustration. In playing "songs of pleasant glee," a piper sees a laughing child in a cloud—which, in the Frontispiece, surrounds the head of the piper. The child dictates a subject for a song, a lamb; the piper plays it twice, and the child weeps at the repetition. Presumably, the song "piped" is not verbal (just as the poem we are reading is not about a lamb); thus, for a third performance, the piper is enjoined to "Drop thy pipe thy happy pipe" to sing a cappella, at which the child "wept with joy to hear." Then the piper is bid "sit thee down and write / In a book that all may read"; but as he starts to comply, the child vanishes, leaving the piper alone to pluck a "hollow reed" and repeat the song a fourth time. But in writing, he finds that he has "stain'd the water clear" in order to preserve songs which "Every child may joy to hear" (E 7).

In five equal stanzas, Blake takes us from unreflective action to a high degree of self-reflexive consciousness, making sure that we notice how the *record* of vision displaces the vision itself, not once but four times. The laughing, weeping, and joy of the visionary child echo and reverberate, in a poem about recording a vision which has vanished, pertaining to a song we have not yet heard. Thus Blake sends us back for second thoughts: we are being told about "songs" of "innocence," but what is the character of this "song," or the character of "innocence" itself?

We cannot suppose that "the *Innocence* poems were the products of a mind in a state of innocence and of an imagination unspoiled by the stains of worldliness," [7] for as soon as the "Introduction" was penned, the waters of vision are already "stained" with self-reflexive consciousness, in which being "innocent" and *knowing* it are not contrary but incompatible. When we look at the piper in the Frontispiece, we see that he has his head in the cloud, attending to the child, not the sheep behind him, and sheep in a forest are sheep lost. The piper may be ignorant of pastoral care, but the child can scarcely represent "innocence," since in weeping when the song is repeated, but weeping with joy when it is made articulate, he already knows what the piper and reader have yet to discover: "innocence" is a passing state of fragility and peril, to be celebrated but not sentimentally retained.

What these two plates show is that the "experience" of "innocence" invariably displaces it; but as they present a complex relation which comments on itself, they determine a state of mental vision which is permanent just as it systematically transforms itself. This is no paradox, for it is the central principle of imaginative activity, unfolding in the process of vision, loss, and recovery focused by the plates themselves. Nothing is missing nor is there anything indeterminate: the precise structure of the plates constitutes a mental field that is inexhaustible, so long as there is a reader-viewer sufficiently alert to see that the "state" in question is his or her own imagination.

Even though it may come as a shock, we are thus prepared for the consequences which follow when we turn to the matching Frontispiece and "Introduction" to the *Songs of Experience*. The figures from *Innocence* are preserved, through pervasive transformation. The sheep are out of the woods, but *we* are being watched by both man and child. The cloud has given way to a halo around the child's head, now a conventional winged cherub, sitting (and being held) on the man's head as if rooted there—specifically, by a diminutive penis appearing to penetrate the man's forehead, while his own genitalia are now clearly evident beneath draped clothing. This transformation preserves and explicates the implications of "innocence," but when we recall Blake's work between *Songs of Innocence* (1789) and *Songs of Experience* (1794), we recover perspective to see that this expansion of imaginative horizons has been repeated in two complementary directions, linking the most allegorical and "mythic" of Blake's early work (as in *Thel* and *America*) with the most familiar and immediate (in *Experience*).

Yet it is somewhat misleading to claim (as Northrop Frye does) [8] that the much more dense "Introduction" to *Experience* leads directly to the intricate networks of Blake's "myth," without explicitly acknowledging that the "myth" in 1794 presents a different shape than it had assumed by 1815. The more crucial issue is that myth, viewed as a body of existing stories, may provide a poet with material, but myth as a structure of relationships emerges in transactions between vision and experience which are evident only retrospectively. Thus we may say that at any stage of elaboration, the possibility of "mythic" consciousness does not presuppose a finished "vision," but rather a recognition of structural connections which link diverse experience in an expanding context of significance. When we are enjoined to "Hear the voice of the Bard! / Who Present, Past, & Future sees," the poem itself unfolds by exploiting a potent ambiguity of relationship among the voice of the bard, the "Holy Word" that he has heard, and the "lapsed Soul," all of which may walk "among the ancient trees," weep "in the evening dew," control "the starry pole," and "fallen light renew!" While the language of the poem does not restrictively locate the agent, the action (being conditional) is unambiguous: though in a fallen state, it is possible to renew the fallen light.

Through the voice of the bard, the movement toward "myth" in *Experience* is the expansion of context which permits the most intimate personal experiences to be linked to momentous public events, and even projected on a cosmological scale in familiar themes of sexuality and repression, revolution and religion. The bard's visionary transversal of time and space in the "Introduction" to *Experience* is systematically important not merely because it anticipates the elaborated cosmogony of Blake's later poems, but because it is the same journey Blake (or the reader) could take through his own house, workshop, or the streets of London.

In this expanding, self-transforming process, the movement from loss to recovery mediated only by the active imagination is generalized as it repeats itself, but the consequences do not simply take us forward. The loss of felicity and joy which appears characteristic of the ordinary "fallen" world (as in the "Introduction" and "Earth's Answer" in *Experience*) is inextricably bound to the fate of imagination itself: if imagination falters, self-recovery fails. For the reader-viewer, Blake's art succeeds as it opens the doors of perception; but a feeling of personal "crisis" may follow, since the effect is to make the reader responsible for his or her own imagination, engaging themes which cannot be quarantined in the pages of books.

For the artist, expanding implications and increasing coherence carry still more potential for uneasiness. In the persistence of a formal record of vanished visions, the artist is likewise responsible for what he has created, particularly as it affects the self-recovering power of imagination itself. The momentum of his journey forces Blake, like Los in *Jerusalem*, to "Create a System, or be enslav'd by another Mans," with the intent of "Striving with Systems to deliver Individuals from those Systems" (J I: 10, 20; 11, 5); [9] but it also creates the risk that the artist may become the slave of his own "system." While writing songs "Every child may joy to hear," the artist may lose every joy himself, the more deeply imagination "bites" into the opaque surfaces of ordinary experience, until he may not only desire deliverance from the unfolding process of his own imaginative development, but come to fear that imagination, by its own operation, can lose its way and become self-enslaved. Imaginative labor begins again, in a sterner phase as imagination discovers the need to revalue itself.

II. Changing Forms of the Eternal

In the expansion of his work to encompass the intimate and the mythic, Blake's decision to develop an epic cosmogony makes him both a paradigm and an anomaly among the Romantic poets, writing in an interval between a vanishing heroic tradition and a not yet articulated world of the modern common man. From the lucidity of his earliest poems to the penetrating mastery of his latest, Blake's path led into an endless project, at least partially recorded in *The Four Zoas*.[10] Though Blake evidently spent at least ten years on this manuscript without arriving at a form he saw fit to publish, it is an extraordinary illustration of the elliptical unfolding of second thoughts, partially abandoned plans and strategies through which imagination comes to maturity. As Helen T. McNeil and others have argued, this poem represents an essential (though perhaps unwelcome) "experiment" in generative form.[11]

Blake did not set out to "experiment," but to tell a story, following from situations already familiar in his earlier poems.[12] From the text and illustrations, it is clear that explicitly sexual themes were dominant at some time, evidently while the poem was still called "Vala"; but in letting dramatic action unfold in familiar experiential terms, the cosmogonic premise of a "Fall" enters the orbit of the ordinary to precipitate an extreme narrative and conceptual difficulty, centering on creativity in general. While the experience of reading the poem is affectively coherent, the emerging pattern of action as the "Four Mighty Ones" that are in every person fall into sexual division cannot be told in a linear "story," since these multiple divisions are replicated over and over, changing and deepening the implications of dramatic situations as they follow an immanent course of generation. It is not, then, as McNeil claims, that "*The Four Zoas* operates without a context, even a Blakean one" (p. 374); we might say that this manuscript, as a unique record of imagination trying to understand its own development, *is* Blake's context.

The action of the poem "begins" with Tharmas, the last of Blake's Zoas to be named, being sexually divided from his emanation, Enion. Ironically, the problem with these first few pages of the manuscript, more heavily revised than any other portion of the poem, is that they *almost* make sense. Enion flees from Tharmas when she finds "secret sins" (i.e., other females) in his soul, only to be further divided in isolation between her desire to return and her fear of Tharmas as a "terror." Tharmas feels the same way, and the two attempt independent creation—Tharmas, by building a "Labyrinth"; Enion, by weaving a "Garment"—in the attempt to hide an interior "anatomy" full of "Death Despair & Everlasting brooding Melancholy." Everything goes awry. Tharmas's "Labyrinth" turns into a "circle of Destiny," before whose awful turning Tharmas divides again into an exhausted form and a "Spectre," which in turn falls into Enion's loom, animating her "Garment" as a creature with a "Will of its own / Perverse and wayward." This monster rises up to assault Enion, who then "divides" again, giving birth to two willful and perverse "infants," Los and Enitharmon (FZ I: 3–10).

This elaborate "bootstrap" operation is confusing, but it is not confused. It represents Blake's effort through countless revisions to match the "beginning" of his poem with subsequent developments, making this episode an exceedingly compact model of the action and interpenetrating themes that dominate the poem—and particularize Blake's entire career.

It fuses the initial fall into sexual division with a demonic repetition, attending the creation of containing forms, paradoxically meant to compensate for something absent or lost. The created "form," in turn, exerts its own will, leading to still more divisions in a recursive pattern, encompassing all the Zoas since it is immanent in "creation" itself.

As a model, it locates the two main issues which thematize action: Who can (or does) create living form; and who (or what) governs it? Throughout the poem these issues are the springs of dramatic action, as each Zoa awakes in ruins, reflecting on a vanished paradise, and then proclaims himself "God" over the desolate world he beholds.[13] Such narrative continuity as there is in the poem depends on the Zoas' encounters with each other, appearing after the fall as mutually deadly terrors that must be suppressed; and the brutal conflicts that ensue constitute a pervasive dilemma: How can form be created which is both generative in itself and compatible with the life of free individuals?

In this respect *The Four Zoas* anticipates Hegel's "master–slave" dialectic,[14] but the process of immanent development in Blake's poem becomes demonic for two connected reasons. There can be no cosmogony without a "beginning," nor a traditional "epic" without an end; but in the self-generating drama of *The Four Zoas*, Blake's "Eternal Forms" are forever at war with themselves and each other, leaving everything stubbornly *in medias res*. Every attempt at a start or finish only further unhinges the narrative line, just as every revision generates the need for more revisions. The second problem generally determines the logic of Blake's revisions. In his earlier, more allegorical prophecies, Blake could partly finesse the question of narrative continuity by leaving a "hero" who advances action implicit in the voice of the poet or bard; but in a more directly visionary mode, with creation as its subject, the problem of the creator as hero is inescapable.

This adequately explains Blake's decision to cancel the title "Vala," to examine the dilemmas of generation with all "Four Zoas," but in trying to tell the story of this recursive process, the problem which invariably emerges is how to domesticate the imagination. Thus, in the last stages of revision, the poem declares it will be a "song" of "Los." We see why only in the middle of the poem, when Tharmas finally takes his turn at being "God."

Seeing Urizen in ruins, Tharmas commands Los to take up the work of constructing a universe, but Los refuses, thinking he is "God" himself. Following the pattern of previous "falls," Tharmas subdues Los by tearing Enitharmon away, which further divides Los from the "Spectre of Urthona." Tharmas compels them both to bind Urizen down, "Lest he should rise again from death in all his dreary power" (FZ IV: 51, 4). With this "success," Tharmas finds what the others found: to be "God" is to despair:

> And I what can I now behold but an Eternal Death
> Before my Eyes & an Eternal weary work to strive
> Against the monstrous forms that breed among my silent waves
> Is this to be A God far rather would I be a Man
> To know sweet Science & to do with simple companions
> Sitting beneath a tent & viewing sheepfolds & soft pastures
>
> (FZ IV: 51, 26–31)

So far from the *Songs of Innocence*, pastoral ambitions are doomed when all one's companions are either "monsters" or "Gods," who become terrors when they forget that these "forms" do indeed have a life and will of their own—a point that applies with redoubled force to Blake, the maker of all these "Gods" and "monsters."

By the end of Night the Fourth, all the other Zoas have fallen at least once, tried their hand at creation and made a terrible mess, leaving it all to Los—and Blake. Blake's revisions, furthermore, do not help matters, since the basic outlines of events remain the same, while all the implications change, as Blake, recalling Enion's celebrated lament, finds "My heavens are brass my earth is iron my moon a clod of clay. . . ."

> What is the price of Experience do men buy it for a song
> Or wisdom for a dance in the street? No it is bought with the price
> Of all that a man hath. . . .
>
> (FZ II: 35, 11–13)

In returning again and again to revise the scenes of creation, it appears that Blake suffered a loss of faith in what he was doing, for on a second look, Los begins his work in "binding" Urizen, but he actually creates a separate form for reason, free to wander gloomily, through Blake's poems at least.

While this still implies that imagination creates the forms within which reason operates, the ensuing consequences are so devastating that it is tempting to assign blame rather than take responsibility. Where Los works on Urizen, we find in the manuscript an unrealized note to "*bring in here the Globe of Blood as in the B of Urizen*"; and a much later addition, invoking the "Council of God" as a deus ex machina to explain why Los is doing what he is doing. But the first is irrelevant, the second redundant: the "Globe of Blood" bears on the creation of the female, already created here, but the dangers of a female will cannot explain all the strife of the poem; while Los's work itself is already fully explained by the preceding action, without the insurance clause of a "Council of God." (FZ IV: 55). Either way, Blake could not leap to a transcendent perspective in "eternity" nor go back to earlier work without incurring the obligation to revise still again everything he had written in a "prophetic" visionary mode. There was nothing for it but to take Los through his special hell.

His "creation" is demonic not just because it is Urizen; for as Los works, "terrified at the shapes / Enslavd humanity put on," it is now inescapable that Los is the shaping agent who "became what he beheld"—a parody of his own creation, stonified into "one stedfast bulk." Furthermore, in being "transformed" he "became what he was doing" (FZ IV: 55 [second portion], 20–23)—namely, forging chains and setting formal limits—and does it with a vengeance to Orc, whom he binds with an unbreakable "chain of Jealousy" (FZ V: 60, 22). Thus when Orc rages against his chains, drawing Urizen to find out what is the matter, we see that Los is the one who has created all these forms and set in motion the whole pattern of action that culminates in the deadly war of Orc and Urizen, leaving himself powerless to prevent it or ameliorate its terrors.

Here we see the "Orc cycle" described by Northrop Frye[15] contained within a larger pattern, a Los cycle, as everything Los does produces a greater terror than the one he has just labored to contain, while the vision which prompts him to act (or to resist) becomes a "visionary form" containing his action and paralyzing him as agent. We will see the same pattern with Eliot and Williams, because the Los cycle is an entirely general process of "loss" intrinsic to the journey of any artist whose work expands contextually until there is nothing stable outside it. He displaces his own identity into the forms of his art, as distinctions between art and life, the man and his writing vanish, and everything depends on invention.

Blake's is an extreme case, for having anticipated the loss of vision, he had followed the route of imaginative invention with an unprecedented faith, only to find a more total demand for invention staring back at him like a spectre from his own pages, an accusation embodied in his own artistic strategies, generating the same deadly pattern over and over again with always one more degree of "loss" than all previous recoveries.

McNeil raises the question whether "so dialectical a poem can ever arrive at the unity of an apocalyptic conclusion" (p. 390); but that is not exactly the issue. The "story" Blake was trying to tell portends an "apocalyptic" finale only because the epic and dramatic conventions he employed presuppose it, while the content of his poem implies that such a strategy would only mean an end to human life or a return to a moment before the fall with nothing to prevent it from happening again in exactly the same way.

Whatever plans Blake may have entertained for this manuscript, the crucial fact remains that it makes no *formal* innovations, staying entirely within the temporal and narrative categories and conventions appropriate to and privileged by the classical and Christian traditions of heroic myth. Thus Blake's problems are no mere "writer's block," for in following the immanent development of those conventions, *The Four Zoas* systematically subverts them. As McNeil notes, the poem "bluntly abandons the associative obligations of major poetry, and by so doing threatens the mimetic mode itself" (p. 379); but it does so by showing that the "associative obligations" are not, after all, obligatory but conventional; and by staying within its categorical conventions, Blake does not merely threaten the mimetic mode, he demolishes it.

Here the demands Blake made on himself and his reader escalate: in trying to engineer an apocalypse in *The Four Zoas*, it was Blake's conventional strategies that broke down, not his mental powers nor his artistic faith. Having come to an apparent impasse in the image of Los paralyzed and Urizen prowling, Blake followed out the implications, beginning with the inversion of mental and dramatic "action" which makes it possible for Los to understand, at least, what Urizen does. We find the most sympathetic portrait of Urizen anywhere in Blake's work, as Urizen goes through the "Los cycle" to become his writing, undertaken to recover his own lost paradise:

> . . . the books remaind still unconsumd
> Still to be written & interleavd with brass & iron & gold
> Time after time for such a journey none but iron pens
> Can write And adamantine leaves receive nor can the man who goes
> The journey obstinate refuse to write time after time.
>
> (FZ VI: 71, 39–42; 72, 1)

Following the fine ambiguity of the last line, a scribal error on this page required the erasure of seven and a half lines, producing perhaps the most penetrating ironic moment in the whole poem when Blake writes, "Oft would he sit in a dark rift & regulate his books" (FZ VI: 72, 6; cf. E 754). As Donald Ault has argued, Blake opposed traditional reason because it could parody imagination in the pursuit of "system";[16] but imagination can parody itself when it is reduced to "regulating its own books." When Urizen cries, "Can I not leave this world of Cumbrous wheels? . . . I thought perhaps to find an End a world beneath of voidness / Whence I might travel round the outside of this Dark confusion" (FZ VI: 72, 22; 26–27), he also speaks for Blake, finding himself of "Urizen's party" without quite knowing what to do about it. Eventually, he wrote *Milton*, having to confront his own heritage in a more profoundly critical spirit to prevent his own creative powers from becoming a self-destructive parody of themselves. Yet the enabling discovery in *The Four Zoas* is that a mind divided against itself can see nothing but a need for power and dominion;

while reason is demonic only when it is isolated from imagination, just as imagination turns perverse when it is isolated from reason.

In this light, the impasse of the Los cycle is in actuality the moment in the imaginative process when the demands of creativity and criticism intersect; but in order to resolve the opposition between Los and Urizen, Blake had to penetrate still further into the "Dark confusion" by further divisions of these mental powers, reflected in the most notorious textual crux of this mitotic poem, the doubling of Night the Seventh.

At the end of Night the Sixth, Urizen is traveling toward confrontation with Orc, while Los, pinned down by an insensible Enitharmon on his knees, can only watch and brood on what he sees. Directly, Urizen's incapacity to do the work of imagination becomes clear: he is unable to recognize *living* form (e.g., his own daughters, FZ VI: 67–68), turning all his works to testaments of death. Thus, when he confronts Orc, he fails to recognize his brother Luvah until it is too late, while Orc, in the sheer energy of his resistance, assumes a "serpent form" intelligible to Los, but utterly baffling to Urizen. A "tree of Mystery" springs from Urizen's heel, and Orc begins to writhe up its branches, presenting to Los's horrified gaze the figure of the crucifixion, while Urizen codifies his books into moral law and Orc fights his chains in self-justifying frenzy (FZ VIIA: 80).

While this image is a primary locus for the unmediated conjunction of passion and reason in which Blake perceived the inherent corruption of conventional religion and politics, presenting death as life, repression as liberty, responsibility for it falls here to the imagination. Like Tharmas, Los laments the fate of his work, warring with "secret monsters of the animating worlds" which return to haunt him just when he is most alienated from Enitharmon (FZ VIIA: 81). Thus the imperatives for action have already divided, between what is occurring before Los's eyes and what is happening on his lap; but by this point in *The Four Zoas*, nothing can be done to patch the poem together again, since its conventional heroic-narrative strategy has already been thoroughly deconstructed. Having penetrated to the center of "Death Despair & Everlasting brooding Melancholy" in his own imaginative praxis and the tradition which informs it, it is evident that any hero who takes arms against this sea of troubles becomes a murdering despot. Blake's problem is less a matter of finishing his "story" than of explicating this fatality of heroic narrative, which always issues in such violence.

In perhaps his most courageous gesture, Blake takes one more step in the divisive logic of the poem to have the "Shadow" of Enitharmon divide from her sleeping form, while the spectre of Urthona abandons Los to pursue her. Twice removed from their "eternal" state, these spectral forms "confer" below in the "intoxicating fumes of Mystery," to bring forth "shadows of the dead," as "male forms without female counterparts," resembling cancer cells "ravening with Enmity & Hatred & War" (FZ VIIA: 85, 5, 19, 20). In horror, what they see is just the action represented in Night the Seventh *b*, the contagious war of Orc and Urizen—itself the inner form of the crucifixion represented in Night the Seventh *a*.[17] This radical formal division of the poem thus mediates a radical identification of Blake's themes in a single act of comprehension, seeing those "spectres of the dead" as males without females, men without women. But with both male and female spectral forms to reflect the ultimate consequences, the shadow and spectre then achieve a restoration of memory in the clearest consecutive account of the fall in this poem, culminating in the spectre's prediction to Los, "If we unite in one[,] another better world will be / Opend within your heart & loins & wondrous brain" (FZ VIIA: 85, 43–44).

In the fourfold reconciliation that follows, Los and Enitharmon revive, and imagination returns to work not as a "God" or "hero," but merely a faithful worker, understanding that the fate of the work does not depend on victory but on absolute attention to *form*. With this understanding, Los accomplishes an "apocalypse" without overt action beyond the purely mental action implicit in poetic composition, representing an inner world of human form that dissolves "Urizen's war" by "dividing the powers of Every Warrior." Working together (like William and Catherine Blake), they "fabricate embodied semblances in which the dead / May live before us," providing each male form with a female counterpart:

> And first he drew a line upon the walls of shining heaven
> And Enitharmon tincturd it with beams of blushing love
> It remaind permanent a lovely form inspird divinely human
>
> (FZ VIIA: 90, 35–37)

In this mild episode the continuity of Blake's work is most profoundly confirmed, but it marks a vital threshold of critical awareness, in which "vision" is the *life* of individuals, as Blake affirmed in *Milton* understood only by distinguishing it from the changing "states" through which that life passes (M II: 32). From a nadir of confusion, Los rises to see

> . . . his Enemy Urizen now
> In his hands. he wonderd that he felt love & not hate
> His whole soul loved him he beheld him an infant
> Lovely breathd from Enitharmon he trembled within himself
>
> (FZ VIIA: 90, 64–67)

Neither the poem nor the problem ends here, for there still remains the spectral form of Urizen, reasoning power separated from imagination (cf. J

III: 74), lurking wherever imagination sets to work. Having found it at the heart of his own art, Blake found not only the dominant theme for *Jerusalem*, but a compelling motive to pursue that spectre in Milton and to hunt it down wherever it appeared from Homer to his own time.

In this concluding phase, Blake completes a whole cycle of transformations, as the revaluing of experience leads to the revaluing of tradition; but it is no wonder that when he once again brought his "Giant Forms" before the public, Blake felt the need to explain himself, sometimes darkly, by calling very special attention to the *form* of his later work. As Eliot observed, Blake's longer poems, especially *Milton* and *Jerusalem*, are obviously prone to expend structural energy on allegorical explanations and intricate philosophical perplexities, but not at all because Blake neglected the "problems of the poet" for a "philosophy of his own." It is precisely the reverse, as Blake provides an ideal paradigm for the dynamic relation between tradition and the individual talent, being led by the intrinsic problems of the poet to the critical problems of literary history. Yet Eliot's failure to see this reflects a major problem in Blake's formal strategy in his later works, for they are not just "poems" in any familiar sense, but *inventions* that incorporate explicit criticism—not merely of Milton and other predecessors, but most particularly of his own "unregulated" poem, *The Four Zoas*.

That his later compositions can be read independently of *The Four Zoas*, moreover, gives rise to misunderstandings to which the critic is much more prone than the poet. While there can be no question that Blake wanted compatriots of the imagination, this in no way implies that he wanted disciples. No poet could possibly "imitate" Blake's later work—and it would be only madness to try, since it is a sustained, impassioned attack on "imitation" as a self-defeating perversion of the mind. The critic, however, may be irresistibly tempted to imitate Blake's "system," since Blake so clearly adopts the stance of the teacher-critic himself. In his later years Blake's composite art increasingly divides, with more painting and less poetry, conceived as visual commentary on the great literary art of the past; but the point of this encompassing gesture is not to get the "last word," or create "Blakean" doctrine, but to teach the public how to *see*.

Blake's critical authority is grounded precisely in the intimacy of his own understanding of the perils of imagination trying to make its way without critical reflection on the path itself; but just so, his most "visionary" inventions, *Milton* and *Jerusalem*, are not just visions but instructions on how to see a vision. For good reason and to good effect, Blake addressed *Milton* to the "Young Men of the New Age," imploring them to listen to him, but to be "just & true" to their own imaginations—before turning his own to the past (as Milton did before him) to revive an eternal vision always in danger of lapsing into conventionality.[18] Turning to all segments of the public in *Jerusalem*, the appeal has increased in urgency, until we find Los literally screaming at the spectre, the very type of the unimaginative critic, "Go! put off Holiness / And put on Intellect" if he ever expects to see what art can show:

> He who would see the Divinity must see him in his Children
> One first, in friendship & love; then a Divine Family, & in the midst
> Jesus will appear; so he who wishes to see a Vision; a perfect Whole
> Must see it in its Minute Particulars; Organized & not as thou
> O Fiend of Righteousness pretendest; thine is a Disorganized
> And snowy cloud: brooder of tempests & destructive War.
>
> (J IV: 91, 18–23)

This lecture by Los applies perhaps most pointedly to *The Four Zoas*, where the collapse of poetic form and the perpetuation of "destructive War" are a single fact. For poets of a new age to take Blake as their master would be only to make themselves slaves, but to take Blake at his word ensures a revival of imagination, creating form that can follow the unpredictable "bounding line" (E 540) of life itself and see it whole. Blake spoke quite literally in *Jerusalem* when he said, "Poetry Fetter'd, Fetters the Human Race!" for when poetic form is reduced to the limiting shapes of inherited practice, a fall from a vision of human life follows and a failure to invent anew carries that fall to a point of despair. Blake's most finished work is retrospective; his least finished offers his best prophecy: a trust in convention leads to the chaos of a "dark rift," but a trust in imagination leads to renewal.

III. Charting the "Dark Rift": The Modern Map as Palimpsest

Like many other unfinished or heavily revised "epic" projects of its period, problems of form in *The Four Zoas* have a strong thematic correlate in the experience of a hero or self who in seeking liberty discovers alienation—and the need for imagination to reflect critically on itself and its own heritage. While this is a perennial issue, the relative uniformity of the discovery in such writers as Rousseau, Goethe, Wordsworth, Coleridge, Poe, and Emerson suggests that the most important characteristic of "Romanticism" may be the realization that literature, even culture itself, cannot thrive without authentic criticism; and that until imagination is experienced as an actual, personal need, it cannot be understood critically as a real but vulnerable power.

By taking the imagination as his hero, Blake integrates these issues into a single formal, thematic, and historical project, making *The Four Zoas* an especially revealing index of problems common to "Romantic" and "modern" writers alike. Under conditions of accelerating historical change, pressure to establish new ways to read and write places an immense burden on literary form as a mediating instrument of culture, commonly leading to irony or ideology[19] But as Blake's example suggests, many of the most vexing problems of literary form since the Romantic era arise from trying to work out the relationship between creative and critical functions within the scope of single texts. Thus when poetry masquerades as criticism, criticism as poetry, each becomes the other's spectre reducing the notion of authenticity to a pious wish, increasingly subject to ironic deconstruction or coercive dogmatism.[20]

Whether it takes the form of poets attempting to make literature into religion, or critics seeking some privileged "approach" to justify their own activity or defend the value of literature, the question of poetic faith has remained a constant dilemma. We may say that the issue is "political," insofar as the intentional horizon of imaginative labor is always the same: the need to participate as an individual in a common life; but for a modern "self," the impasse Blake encountered in *The Four Zoas* comes to seem a constant condition of existence, when every imagined form of life not only divides the "self" from others but from its own desires. Any claims of "authenticity" or "authority" are immediately suspect as covert assertions of power, and the very idea of a politics of the imagination may seem a self-defeating exercise in distraction.[21]

Between Eliot and Williams, these issues are clearly delineated. In his desire to escape the alienation of "personality," Eliot adopted the strategy of embracing tradition as the potential locus of an elite community—later conceived as his "Community of Christians," composed of "both clergy and laity of superior intellectual and/or spiritual gifts"; while Williams, also seeking to escape alienation, rejected "tradition" as the cause of it. Williams followed an avowedly personal strategy in which the artist is answerable to an open society but responsible to the imperatives of his own perceptions of human needs. In the place of an elite, whether of creed or education, Williams appealed to the "function of the imagination," as an "order" which is "in its vigor the process of ordering," both arising from and returning to one's immediate, local community.[22]

From these opposing strategies, highly symmetrical ironies flow. By adopting so many verbal masks that he sometimes seems a literary everyman, Eliot's poetry seems all the more "personal," in affect and implication, since the practice of wearing masks not only raises questions of the masker's identity, but may enforce a loss of identity itself.[23] Williams by contrast, strips himself so bare of traditional associations that he sometimes seems a nonliterary anyman, who becomes effectively invisible in the literary community that already exists.[24]

Similarly, Eliot's attempt to embrace Western literary tradition led to perhaps the most self-enclosed vision in modern literature; while Williams's early rejection of tradition evolved into an open and generous acceptance of it. Yet the essential point is that literary strategies generate content and have practical consequences far beyond conventionally "literary" concerns, which become evident only in following the conviction that a rigorous concern for poetic form and composition is a necesary response to the pervasive experience of alienation and loss. These three poets, sharing this conviction, reveal a more general pattern immanent in the process of honoring it.

Like many of his essays, Eliot's remarks on Blake are more revealing about Eliot. Finding that Blake's "method of composition" is "exactly like that of other poets," Eliot praises his poetic form as "one illustration of the eternal struggle of art against education, of the literary artist against the continuous deterioration of language" (SE 276–277). While it follows that unless his education has already won the struggle the poet will develop a "philosophy of his own," Eliot merely remarks Blake's clarity in presenting his own interests and feelings, "unclouded by current opinions," as a man "naked," who "saw man naked, and from the centre of his own crystal." There is "nothing of the superior person about him"; and "this," says Eliot, "makes him terrifying," in his uncompromising honesty.

Perhaps Eliot's sense of "terror" was more surprise at a poet so different from himself who worked in the same way, but it reflects a subtler recognition that by turning to "tradition" to prevent the deterioration of language, the content of Eliot's education generates the structure of his poetry, leaving it an open question whether there is a naked man or a fragmentary encyclopedia at the center of his own crystal. In either case, Eliot's poetry starts with a "vision" that ironically reverses the pattern we have seen with Blake. There is no visionary child in a cloud, vanishing before the poet's pen, but a multitude of spectres from literary history that refuse to vanish, becoming more insistent and more personal as Eliot continues.

Prufrock and Other Observations, for example, offers no desultory song, but a well-planned, mappable journey, by a much-diminished and uneasy descendant of traditional "heroes," confronting a life "composed so much, so much of odds and ends" that it is necessary to "borrow every changing shape / to find expression" (CP "Portrait of a Lady," 8, 12). Taking only tradition as his guide, the speaker of these poems reads a pattern which does not change, a palimpsest structured by epigraphs, allusions, and analogs of the speaker's situation:

> The memory throws up high and dry
> A crowd of twisted things;
> A twisted branch upon a beach
> Eaten smooth, and polished
> As if the world gave up
> The secret of its skeleton,
> Stiff and white
>
> (CP "Rhapsody on a Windy Night," 16–17)

In these exquisitely polished poems, the skelton is a violently compressed design, comprising at once a brief, formal, and folk "epic" in twelve poems that correspond sequentially with the twelve chapters of *Ecclesiastes*, telling a unified story of failed desire that matches episodes in literary history with ordinary events in the street, in rooms, in family albums and intimate experiences. "The Love Song of J. Alfred Prufrock" starts literally with a "spectre of the dead," quoting Dante's Guido de Montefeltro, a soldier turned monk condemned as a faithless counselor, speaking in confidence that no one ever returns from hell to tell its secrets. As the "Love Song" begins, Prufrock sees that hell keeps no secrets, recalling Dante's reply to Guido which Eliot does not quote: "your Romagna is not and never was / without strife in the hearts of its tyrants." [25]

With all this allusive apparatus, it is easy to forget that the Romantic "quest" in the "Love Song" is for a woman; but the speaker only mounts a stair and stands outside a room, finding no woman at all, certainly not a Beatrice and no *Paradiso*. Instead, he sees hell's secrets made visible in a pattern of faithless counsel and strife, repeated in literature, history, his own mind, and even "spread against the sky." Guided by ghosts, he descends the stair to resume his journey, making "observations." Through the book, what the speaker sees explains the reluctance of Prufrock to "force the moment to its crisis," for the crisis is already a universal fact in the tradition the book exploits, and endless repetition of "formulated phrases" sufficient to stop any originary action by pointing to traditional "heroes"—Odysseus, Aeneas, Romeo, Hamlet, Lear. No wonder he is afraid. Everything he sees is love denied, lost, or perverted, with deadly war taking its place.

Terror in these poems is generally attenuated by their urbane diction, but the speaker comes closest to crisis in "Hysteria"—significantly, the only poem in the collection without allusions, composed in prose—where a young man watches a woman laugh uncontrollably, drawing him in until he feels "lost finally in the dark caverns of her throat, bruised by the ripple of unseen muscles." The real hysteria of the poem, however, is not the woman's laughter but the speaker's response. Instead of laughing or wooing this woman to bed, he decides that "if the shaking of her breasts could be stopped, some of the fragments of the afternoon might be collected," and concentrates his "attention with careful subtlety to this end" (CP 24).

In this synecdoche of Eliot's whole career, we may see the overwhelming question as a search for redemptive wholeness in a world that has it not; but the concluding poem in *Prufrock*, "La Figlia che Piange," shows from the beginning the circularity of the wholeness Eliot reached at the end in *Four Quartets*. Composed in Italy, "La Figlia" returns us to Dante, by way of Virgil his guide, in an epigraph from the *Aeneid* where Aeneas asks Venus, "Maiden, by what name shall I know you? " According to Grover Smith, the occasion of the poem was a promise by an Italian friend to show Eliot a beautiful image of a pair of young lovers, but the image was lost.[26] In the poem the maiden remains shadowy and nameless, all the more effectively to recall Aeneas and Dido, Romeo and Juliet, Dante and Beatrice; and all the more effectively to distance the speaker from the tragedy of love lost by permitting him to be the stage manager of a scenario:

> So I would have had him leave,
> So I would have had her stand and grieve,
> So he would have left
> As the soul leaves the body torn and bruised,
> As the mind deserts the body it has used.
> I should find
> Some way incomparably light and deft,
> Some way we both should understand,
> Simple and faithless as a smile and shake of the hand.
>
> (CP 26)

The poem itself, incomparably light and deft, concludes with the imagination of the speaker "compelled," his repose troubled by "cogitations" as he wonders "how they should have been together! " He drops the matter, saying, "I should have lost a gesture and a pose." But the central image of the poem is a grim prophecy, combining Descartes and Christianity to sum up a faithlessness inherent in Eliot's approach to "tradition." It is the identity of conventional religion and reason when love is blocked or denied, a condition of strife at the most intimate core of experience when imagination fails to invent a form to mediate desire. Eliot's craft effects only a transition from hysteria to resignation, all the more corrosively confirming Blake's discovery: by reposing one's faith in tradition, one does not revive it but discovers that it is dead, suffering a loss of faith for a self that sees its own spectre everywhere and despairs.

In this book a warrior turned priest and a lover turned warrior carry the young poet back to Rome, implicating all traditions that passed through the eternal city, whether Caesar ruled there or the Church, in a common, timeless cycle: the denial of love and the renewal of war. Finding himself in just the impasse Blake discovered in the middle of *The Four Zoas*, more intense for having an objective correlative in concrete world affairs, Eliot did not follow the critical imperative for more radical invention but persisted in the same direction, using tradition judiciously but not presuming to alter it.

The way led to a sterner, more personal hell in *The Waste Land*, where his strategy of composition is informed by authorities whose very proximity to the condition of the speaker intensifies his agony without relief. Though later, Eliot could rediscover Milton, it was not as Blake had done in the joy of recovering a compatriot of the imagination, but more a matter of admitting the great Christian poet into the "Community of Christians." In *The Waste Land*, the chorus of dead voices "singing out of empty cisterns and exhausted wells" (CP 68) culminates in the strained effort to hear the song of the hermit thrush and the cock crowing in the rooftree, auguring and echoing a distinctly Buddhist thunder "high in the air," bringing not the satisfaction but the extinction of desire. Ending the poem with a repetition of the formula from the Upanishads, that "peace which passeth understanding" is all too understandable in the question contained in Eliot's allusions to Canto XXVI of the *Purgatorio*, the *Pervigilium Veneris*, to Kyd and Verlaine and Tennyson: Shall the poet who sings of love end like raped Procne, the swallow, with her tongue cut out? Or shall he simply give up song? (cf. CP 67–69; 75–76.)

Through "Ash Wednesday" to *Four Quartets*, the same question persists as Eliot follows the same allusive strategies, seeking what was blocked and denied from the start: a faith in imagination. But as Eliot turned to the Church for authority, the faith reduces the imagination to the "still point of the turning world," a reduction which will suffice only by implication if love, "the unfamiliar Name / Behind the hands that wove / The intolerable shirt of Flame / Which human power cannot remove" (CP 207), is at least imagined. Eliot's personal recovery from devastation leads him to a note of renewal in "Little Gidding," where he sounds very like Blake and Williams, finally hearing

> The voice of the hidden waterfall
> And the children in the apple-tree
> Not known, because not looked for

But heard, half-heard, in the stillness
Between two waves of the sea.

(CP 208–209)

Urgently, Eliot points forward, "Quick now, here, now, always— / A condition of complete simplicity / (Costing not less than everything)"—but it is, for the poet, already too late. All he can affirm is a condition of personal belief that does not require the creation of poetic form to attract the unhappy soul, for it comes to rest in a self-enclosing vision, a "crowned knot of fire," that supports the poet with doctrine, a fixed pattern of repetition that points beyond itself only to a realm of silence.

It is much easier to see in this light why Williams was so violently opposed to Eliot from the start. Writing *Kora in Hell* when *Prufrock* was published, Williams expressed his outrage at Eliot's success not from envy but with foresight that, being imitative, Eliot would be imitated to everybody's woe. "La Figlia," singled out by reviewers for lavish praise, Williams damned as the work of a "fumbling conjurer," evincing a profound failure of nerve by perhaps the most talented man of his generation, content to write "rehash, repetition," following the "connotations of [his] masters" (I 24–25). *The Waste Land* deepened Williams's opposition—he called it the "great catastrophe to our letters" [27]—because its technical mastery in composition parodies the dialogical relation between tradition and the individual talent by fracturing both. In his devotion to the "new," Williams did not oppose tradition but the parodic use of it, hiding what he called "the strange phosphorous of the life" [28] by which tradition can be recovered and renewed. *The Waste Land* merely conjures the literary past in disarticulated verbal bodies that will not lie quietly, and, like the corpse Stetson planted in the garden, will not grow. They simply rise up like the uneasy ghost in *Hamlet*, or Lear's heart, when the Fool says to him:

> Cry to it, nuncle, as the cockney did to the eels when she put 'em i' th' paste alive. She knapp'd 'em o' th' coxcombs with a stick and cried "Down, wantons, down!" (II. iv. 118)

Williams followed a strategy from the beginning only vaguely suggested by Eliot's end: in "Tract," for instance, he instructs his townspeople on how "to perform a funeral," stripping away the ornaments which vainly try to "shut grief in," when to "sit openly— / to the weather as to grief" puts the fact which imagination must raise to vitality undeniably before us. His early experiments with open form, particularly in *Spring and All* or *Kora in Hell*, reflect an acute diagnosis of modernist distress, expressed years later in "Against the Weather: A Portrait of the Artist": "We are stopped in our tracks by the dead masquerading as life." [29] As Williams insists, the only way to value tradition is to recall that it once was new; and it is a desecration of the spirit to refuse to bury a corpse. For the poet, the way to perform a funeral is a rebirth, giving the living spirit a new body, a new form, which may be naked and vulnerable but must be integral and open to growth.

In *Spring and All*, published a year after *The Waste Land*, Williams followed a plan of alternating prose comment and poetry, utterly different from Eliot's nervously appended footnotes, as a way of reflecting on the demands of poetic form and contemplating his own generative experiments as they gradually assumed the force of an emergent "myth," which in no particular is set against "reality." For Williams, as for Blake in *The Marriage of Heaven and Hell*, a disjunctive strategy of composition, having the effect of satire, opens to the poet the immanent vistas of his own work. Understanding the point of Blake's aphorism, "We are led to Believe a Lie / When we see not Thro the Eye," Williams renews it with a significant difference:

> The inevitable flux of the seeing eye toward measuring itself by the world it inhabits can only result in himself crushing humiliation unless the individual raise to some approximate co-extension with the universe. This is possible by aid of the imagination. Only through the agency of this force can a man feel himself moved largely with sympathetic pulses at work— (I 105)

To be raised to a "perception of the infinite," as Blake put it, does not require the literal eating of dung, but rather, valuing the commonplace as it is imaginatively expanded, as Williams says, "by revealing the oneness of experience." Imagination "rouses rather than stupefies the intelligence by demonstrating the importance of personality, by showing the individual, depressed before it, that his life is valuable—when completed by the imagination" (I 107). Williams demonstrates his point, not by a memorable fancy, but by poems which disclose the structure of familiar things, not as prose, treating only "the fact of an emotion," but as poetry effecting "the dynamization of emotion into a separate form" (I 133). In apparently simple poems—about flowers on the road to the contagious hospital, a "girl with one leg / over the rail of a balcony," a red box, or a red wheelbarrow—Williams performs what he describes. In "The rose is obsolete," for instance, the contemplation of its literal shape where it meets and cuts the air extends the rose beyond itself till it "penetrates / the Milky Way / without contact—lifting / from it—neither hanging / nor pushing—"; thus, "to engage roses / becomes a geometry—" (I 107–109).

The consequences in Williams's career are comprised, like Blake's before him, in the remarkable power of imaginative recovery, and a continuous extension of themes disclosed early to an encompassing articulation of their implications in an open, ever-changing field of action. Yet Williams has even less need than Blake for metaphysical or religious doctrines, and suffers less vitiating anxiety than Eliot, by eliminating redundancies which undermine the health and vitality of imagination. In "Against the Weather" Williams articulated his position in a sentence, written "with all the art [he could] muster":

> A work of art is important only as evidence, in its structure, of a new world which it has been created to affirm. (I 196)

This plain, precise sentence refuses to flirt with the self-protective notion that works of art create a "world," and so is liable to be misread. The new world is already, always there: it is the world complete with changing "weather" which the poet occupies, but he must create a *structure* to *affirm* it. Turning to the favorite example of both Eliot and Pound, Williams illustrates his point by comparing the structure of the art in Dante's *Commedia* with the less polished, anonymous *Book of Love*. In the elegance of terza rima, Williams saw "the craftsman skilfully following orders," whereas Dante, the artist, sought much more: fulfilled love. The same quest, the same generosity of desire, Williams found in the *Book of Love*, since the essential quality of the art is the same in both cases, its sensual exuberance. Dante's craft runs the greater risk, for without "sensuality the dogmatism of the *Commedia* would have killed all attempts at a work of art—as it limits it and, except for the skill of the artist . . . would have submerged it" (p. 206).

In conceiving artistic structure as an affirmation of a new world, the work of the imagination becomes, for Williams, a praxis, a way of being and acting in the world. It is the artist's business to write books but to live in the world in order to avoid irremediable confusion about what is alive and what is not. Vision, without a transcendent metaphysics, places the faithful imagination in an active relation to what it sees:

> The imagination is the transmuter. It is the changer. Without imagination life cannot go on, for we are left staring at the empty casings where truth lived yesterday while the creature itself has escaped behind us. It is the power of mutation which the mind possesses to rediscover the truth. (I 213)

In *Kora in Hell* Williams had written that "the slave and the despoiled of his sense are one" (I 18); the imagination occupies the leading edge of understanding, continuously mediating our perceptions and supplying a basis for action. Whether we see the world as alive or dead depends on whether imagination supplies affirmations. As Williams put it: "By a mere twist of the imagination, if Prufrock only knew it, the whole world can be inverted (why else are there wars?) and the mermaids be set warbling to whoever will listen to them" (I 25). The trajectory of the "twist" Williams effected led him, in 1939, to this radical claim:

> . . . the artist is dealing with actualities, not with dreams. . . . [But he is not] a popular leader in the Rousseauian sense. Rather he builds a structure of government using for this the materials of his verse. His objective is an order. It is through this structure that the artist's permanence and effectiveness are proven. (SE 213)

Such a "structure of government" does not rely on any church or party, just a faith in ordinary humanity and the life-affirming power of imagination. To repeat the point, "order is in its vigor the process of ordering" (SE 188); and unless poetic form is generative it becomes tyrannical. For Williams, the dynamic basis of order lies in learning to speak gently to the earth itself and not get back an angry denunciation as in Blake's "Earth's Answer"; and poetry which refuses this challenge only haunts itself and its readers by reviving war and warlike problems of dominion, without finding a human domicile. For Williams as for Blake, this condition can only be met by a continuous act of creation, a full exercise of intelligence, not in mimicry of tradition but in the continuation of its life. For both poets, the "order" lies immanent in the artist's dedication, in Blake's words, to "an improvement of sensual enjoyment," expunging the "notion that man has a body distinct from his soul" (MHH 14). Sounding still more like Blake, without his prophetic metaphors, Williams points to the minute particulars of the "eternal" world of here and now, waiting in judgment according to the quality of our imaginative care:

> Those who permit their senses to be despoiled of the things under their noses by stories of all manner of things removed and unattainable are of frail imagination. Idiots, it is true that nothing is possessed save by dint of that vigorous conception of its perfection which is the imagination's special province but neither is anything possessed which is not extant. A frail imagination, unequal to the tasks before it, is easily led astray. . . . Although it is a quality of the imagination that it seeks to place together those things which have a common relationship, yet the coining of similes is a pastime of very low order, depending as it does upon a nearly vegetable coincidence. Much more keen is that power which discovers in things those inimitable particles of dissimilarity to all other things which are the peculiar perfections of the thing in question. (I 18)

Williams says, "On this level of the imagination all things and all ages meet in fellowship." Whether the signal phrase is Williams's "no ideas but in things," Blake's "minute particulars," or even Eliot's "objective correlative," the poet's quest for form leads back to a common world, a common language, waiting to be renewed, as Williams concretely proved in *Paterson*. More specifically, the generative development of Williams's whole career shows that the continuity of imaginative labor is never static nor does it consist in a return to any single privileged structure of content, information, or imagery. While Blake had reached his highest point of mastery by exemplifying systematic principles in schematic imagery, the achievement is self-limiting if the generating principles are mistaken for their merely illustrative product; and Eliot, coming to rest on the still point of a structure of religious doctrine, willingly limits the movement of imagination to a circular repetition that leads to parody or renunciation as the "end" (but not the *telos*) of the power for self-recovery. But in affirming the generative principles by which art maintains contact with the ordinary world and raises it to imaginative vitality, Williams demonstrates the continuity in principle by showing that every moment of vision is new, renewable, and possessed of a perfection in the here and now which is everywhere the same as it is perfect and unique. For Williams, the authentic *telos* of that process is to preserve a human vision in any place and any circumstances where people live.

IV. Paying Attention: The Continuity of Imaginative Labor

The process of imagination as we have traced it here might seem a cycle of "visionary weariness," [30] but perhaps no poet since Blake trusted the power of self-recovery inherent in the process more throughly than Williams. For this reason Williams's benign influence on other poets is pervasive and obvious, even as it is hard to document precisely, just as the influence of other poets on him is typically diffuse. Eliot, who seems more masterly, can be more easily imitated than Blake or Williams, both of whom invite us, in deceptively simple language, to participate in a liberating dialogue not just between poet and reader, or one poet to another, but between the person and his or her own immediate circumstances. Williams particularly makes it look easy, but in working to develop an authentically open and generative form, he liberates the imagination by showing a way in the very process of finding it, not by calculation or "prophecy" but by radical attention to particularity. To follow Williams is to find one's own voice in a new world.

In *Paterson* V, Williams says, "I have told you, this / is a fiction, pay attention" (P 275), as he calls our notice to the individual flowers in the unicorn tapestries, some of whose "names and perfumes I do not know." In this simple invitation to participate, Williams expects us to listen and look attentively, in order to renew the process wherever one happens to be and so learn to "Music it for yourself" (P 141). Unlike Blake, who left it to the reader to perceive the heuristic quality of any artistic "system," Williams embraces the principle explicitly in a "plan" for *Paterson* that is self-transforming, a "*dispersal and a metamorphosis*," which answers "*Greek and Latin with the bare hands*" (P 10). The result is no easier to follow than Blake, but *Paterson* more clearly exemplifies the generative principles which also underlie *The Four Zoas* by explicitly bringing imagination into alignment with the actual, not to copy it but to illuminate it and learn its value.

Parallels between Blake and Williams are exceptionally rich for many reasons. Like Blake (and Eliot), Williams's decision to write an "epic" involved him in the contextual expansion of a "Los cycle," with the important difference that the "world outside" *was* the world outside. To enter and engage it inaugurated for Williams possibilities of meaning that not only temper the severity of the experience of loss, but augment the meaning of recovery from it. Starting from his "improvisations" in the teens and twenties, Williams's journey corresponds with Blake's in what Thomas Whitaker calls "a characteristic rediscovery" [31] that a free imagination generates structure, which in turn generates responsibilities and needs for careful composition. The general principle of continuity also applies, for in working out a provisional plan for *Paterson*, Williams's decisions reflect his earlier work (notably "The Wanderers"), the contemporary context (notably the work of Hart Crane, Pound, and Eliot), and a response to tradition. As Whitaker shows, Williams's avowedly self-transforming strategy of composition creates rich internal patterns in the poem in "assonances" and "homologues" that accumulate in significance as the poem unfolds, following a path from the Falls of the Passaic to the sea in Books I to IV. For Blake, however, the immanent expansion of "epic" led to a trauma of revision, which for Williams proved a self-renewing release, in the transformation of his whole plan in Book V, cmbracing a whole world of art which "HAS / SURVIVED!" (P 244).[32]

In starting out with a literal "fall," the crashing water of the river in a continuing descent to the sea ("What common language to unravel? / . . . combed into straight lines / from that rafter of a rock's / lip" P 15), the most remarkable similarities between Blake and Williams are evident in thematic analogies with mythic resonance that mark the passage from beginning to end in a cycle of transformations that does not terminate.

These analogies stem in both cases from a strategy which links the mythic to the actual, but from different directions. In *The Four Zoas*, for example, Blake gives us a "Nameless Shadowy Female," emerging in the jealous "Female will" of Enion, Enitharmon, or Vala; Williams supplies from the other side "A man like a city and a woman like a flower," becoming "Two women. Three women. / Innumerable women, each like a flower" (P 15)—proliferating until it seems (as Tharmas says) all have "a root growing in hell" (FZ I: 4, 38), flashing out in the "Lightnings" that "stab at the mystery of a man / from both ends . . . to destroy him at home" (P 22–23). With both poets, this concern with themes of sexuality, desire, and jealousy brings personal and artistic life into direct entanglement—which for Williams includes suffering the accusations of Edward Dahlberg and the anonymous woman poet (called Cress after Chaucer's Criseyde)[33] that all he cares about is turning life into literature.

But as Williams says at the end of Book III, "this rhetoric is real!" (P 173), since it brings into the life of the writer the whole register of frustrations, "blockages," and devastations which characterize the whole (fallen) human economy. Thus Blake gives us the confrontation between snowy Urizen, the writer of books, and fiery Orc, the spirit of passionate revolt, locked in a cycle until Los can transform it by means of art; while Williams gives us "The Library," catastrophically but redemptively burning, as "Dead men's dreams, confined by these walls" go up in "a dark flame, / a wind, a flood—counter to all staleness" from which the poet must learn "to beat fire at its own game," finding "in all things an opposite / that awakes / the fury, conceiving / knowledge / by way of despair" to create a "Beautiful thing" in a refining flame (P 121ff.). And just as Blake saw conventional reason and religion as alienated parodies of imagination, only to find his own imagination growing stale in the same patterns, Williams presents the poet, in "Sunday in the Park," making the same discovery when "the poem / the most perfect rock and temple" is rivaled by the graceless words of an evangelical preacher, in a society everywhere blocked by failures of invention—in economics, politics, sexuality, even down to petty restrictions against roaming dogs—where "no poet has come" (P 99; cf. 81ff.).

Though these thematic analogies are rich, they are but symptoms of a more coherent underlying correspondence between Blake and Williams, in specific functions of mediation that approximate a generative "grammar" of imaginative labor. The fellowship between these two poets is a single epic project to keep a human vision alive "in the middle of things," subject to perpetual change. In *Paterson* we can see a continuation of the process Blake also followed, unfolding in a rich but simple logic of progressions and renewals, returning upon itself to recover the ground of human meaning.

Literary texts do not privilege the truth of discrete propositions; rather, they enact a logic of continuous qualification, creating their own context by the composition of particulars self-reflexively conceived. The most primitive and enduring motive is simply expressed in the desire to find "one phrase that will / lie married beside another for delight" (P 167); a motive for making a comprehensive harmony. Thus as Blake's piper started with liquidity of sound, "stained" by the discreteness of writing, *Paterson* begins with the sound of filthy water, carrying over the brink of the falls "The multiple seed / packed tight with detail." In both cases the first gesture of composition is to measure the otherwise meaningless flux of experience, articulately, for as Williams says, the "seed" is "soured" and "lost in the flux" if "the mind / distracted, floats off in the same scum" (P 12). What is present to the mind is "a mass of detail / to interrelate on a new ground, difficulty" (P 30); and the relation between the continuity of the flux and the discreteness of the word is what Williams might call the "supple" domain of poetic *predication.* As a mediating function, predication generates those phrases that lie married beside each other, by establishing not merely a relation between subjects and predicates, but between speech and vision in a particular place for a person affectionately attending to it.

The consequences of this relation are not dialectical, but dialogical;[34] taking shape as a dialogue not dependent on presumed logical primitives (such as concepts of subject and object, thesis and antithesis), but rather, to use Whitehead's terms, on the "prehension" in an "occasion of experience"[35] of relatedness between "subject" and "object," anterior to concepts of either. More simply, attention itself is organized by identifications, recalling Emerson's definition of imagination as a "sort of seeing, which does not come by study, but by the intellect being where and what it sees; by sharing the path or circuit of things through forms, and so making them translucid to others."[36] To make that "path or circuit" articulate, Blake's piper sings about a lamb; in *Paterson*, the same function of *identity* is fulfilled through the whole of Book I, locating not the topics for argument but the "homologues" that link the animate to the inanimate in "Paterson" as a poem, a person, a double pun, and a place with its own special perfections and peculiarities. In this phase of the process, myth and commonplace merge, as the poet and his subject interpenetrate "both ways" (P 12), with "the grace and detail of a dynamo" (P 139); but the result is a quickening sense of loss as one occasion of contact gives way to the next. As the poet observes the "thoughts" of Paterson, "listed in the Telephone Directory," but walking "incommunicado" (P 18), language itself becomes the primary theme or stem, liable to become a stale flux as these "thoughts" of Paterson "may look at the torrent in / their minds" to find it, "foreign to them" (P 21). Thus, as Blake's piper of *Innocence* gives way to the bard of *Experience*, Book I of *Paterson* descends into a painful examination of language failing, from the wife of the Rev. Hopper Cumming to Same Patch, to the poet himself.

This linguistic investiture, placing the poet, his subjects, and the language on the same ground, is the essential initiative of myth—which, as Paul Valery succinctly notes, is the "name of everything that exists and abides with speech as its only cause." [37] For Blake the path led to the vexed nightmare of *The Four Zoas*; for Williams it leads more directly to Book II, "Sunday in the Park," taking the poet into an equally vexed world "subject to [his] incursions" (P 47). For both poets the discovery of an articulate "way of language" [38] is generalized by its own repetition, establishing as a function the *process* of correlating self and world, found to be more vulnerable and more valuable than the beginning of the way foretold. A deepening sense of loss or immanent loss connects Williams's discovery of lovers in the park, "so flagrant in desire" but blocked (P 88; 78ff) with Blake's dilemma of Zoas alienated from their emanations; but each follows the way to find the poet himself is most subject to the blockage. In a moment where his resemblance to Blake is most powerful, Williams finds himself in the "dark rift," a poet "in disgrace" as he is tempted to "borrow from erudition (to / unslave the mind); railing at the vocabulary / (borrowing from those he hates, to his own / disfranchisement)," trying to "induce his bones to rise into a scene / . . . above the scene, (they will not)" that "history may escape the panders" (P 99).

The very possibility of generalizing imaginative process to tell a universal story becomes for both poets an occasion to articulate their own despair; for Blake it is Los paralyzed and parodied by Urizen, needing a "system" when all systems seem deadly and coercive, while for Williams the moment comes in a search for "the N of all equations," which would bring "the death of all / that's past / all being" (P 95). But at this moment of epic aporia, Williams does not "sit in a dark rift and regulate his books," but regulates his attention (and ours) by the invention of an open form in a revived vulgate idiom:

> The descent beckons
>   as the ascent beckoned
>   Memory is a kind
> of accomplishment
>   a sort of renewal
>   even
> an initiation, since the spaces it opens are new
> places

inhabited by hordes
heretofore unrealized,
of new kinds—
since their movements
are towards new objectives
(even though formerly they were abandoned)

(P 96)

This relaxation of the will by tightening attention on particulars effects the same "twist" of imagination which Los employed, turning the monstrous world of Urizen and Tharmas into the illuminations of art as a human vision, living and permanent through all loss. But for both poets, this critical threshold discloses the spectres of the dead, the subtle lapse of the imagination into conventionality which makes the past a burden to the present. For Blake, the generalization of artistic process leads to this discrimination of historical *structure* mediating between past and present in a search for the spectre in the whole of Western tradition, while for Williams, that structure is disclosed in the burning of the library where "Texts mount and complicate them- / selves, lead to further texts and those / to synopses, digests and emendations," blocking the living (burning) spirit of transformation that made them (P 156). To revive the "wind or ghost of a wind / in all books echoing the life / there" (P 118), the function of literary structure is to create a community of imagination, beginning with the poet's own power to affirm a living spirit which is constantly passing away.

Thus, as Blake follows the war of Orc and Urizen to its end, Williams completes the provisional plan for *Paterson*, following the river to the sea and the failure of language to a public hanging on Garrett Mountain; but for neither poet is this the "end." For in coming to know the way of imagination by traveling it, measuring the consequences of failure by enacting them, both poets come to an understanding of structure, over time, as the affirmation Williams claimed it had to be. Everything depends on a completing but not terminating mediation, a *choice*, to be freely made in the knowledge that imagination *is* the power of self-recovery intending a vision of that "beautiful thing," the fulfillment of love, "locked in the mind past all remonstrance" if the imagination refuse its labor. As Blake found his way out of the dark rift of *The Four Zoas* to the magnificently humanized world of *Jerusalem*, Williams returns to his own work and the world of art in Book V to reaffirm that through "the cavern / of death, the imagination / escapes intact" (P 247); finding an augmented meaning in his claim that "The province of the poem is the world, / When the sun rises, it rises in the poem" (P 122).

Yet more clearly than Blake, Williams demonstrates the continuity of imaginative labor by choosing "Not prophecy! NOT prophecy! / but the thing itself" (P 242). Whether it be a "basalt grasshopper," tumbling from the core of the awakened mind, or a juniper bush, frantically quaking in a gale, the truth imagination "rediscovers" in choosing the world is a truth of praise, always new and hence eternal. To the end of his career Williams continued to bring forth the new, by more forthrightly embracing transformation as the condition of the artist's faith. In *Pictures from Breughel* Williams renewed his poetry in a gesture complementary to Blake's, uniting it with painting from the past, affirming a world of the senses which survives because art survives, as Williams aims to say clearly what he sees, as Breughel before him saw when he "faithfully recorded it." At the last, Williams's poetry became simpler and more eloquent still, for in affirming transformation what most survives the "corrosive power" is desire itself transformed to a modest but encompassing demand:

> Sing me a song to make death tolerable, a song
> of a man and a woman: the riddle of a man
> and a woman.
> What language could allay our thirsts,
> what winds lift us, what floods bear us
> past defeats
> but song but deathless song?
>
> (P 131)

This was Blake's abiding design, from *Innocence* to *Jerusalem*, and Williams sings it in "Of Asphodel, That Greeny Flower," his profoundly moving love song to his wife, in old age. The poem celebrates a revival of love when least expected, just as it maintains that war, even the ultimate weapon of war, the atomic bomb, is containable in and through imagination if we affirm it, with Blake, with Williams:

> If a man die
> it is because death
> has first
> possessed his imagination.
> But if he refuse death—
> no greater evil
> can befall him
> unless it be the death of love
> meet him
> in full career.
> Then indeed
> for him
> the light has gone out.
> But love and the imagination

are of a piece,
swift as the light
to avoid destruction.

(PB 179)

The claim of this passage is encompassing but modest; it tells us simply that the power of imagination is actual and consequential; but what it shows is that poetic form is a form of life, an affirmation of its value, precisely suited to its circumstances, and noble in its simplicity. It is the grace of imagination in which we acknowledge a common life; the condition under which we continue it.

Notes

1. See especially Joseph Wittreich's "Preface" to *Blake's Sublime Allegory: Essays on "The Four Zoas," "Milton," and "Jerusalem,"* ed. Stuart Curran and Joseph Anthony Wittreich, Jr. (Madison: Univ. of Wisconsin Press, 1973); and V. A. DeLuca, "How We Are Reading Blake: A Review of Some Recent Criticism, *University of Toronto Quarterly* 50 (1980–1981): 238–247.

2. T. S. Eliot, "William Blake," *Selected Essays* (New York: Harcourt, Brace, 1950), pp. 275–280 (hereafter cited as SE); William Carlos Williams, *Selected Essays* (New York: New Directions, 1954), p. 125; and *The Autobiography of William Carlos Williams* (New York: New Directions, 1967), pp. 63, 241. See also Francis E. Skipp, "Eliot's Prufrock and Blake's Lithe Lady," *Notes on Modern American Literature* 4: Item 23 (1979).

3. *Paterson* (New York: New Directions, 1963), p. 31. Citations from *Paterson* here refer to the first edition, second printing; hereafter cited as P.

4. *Selected Essays*, pp. 279–280.

5. *Imaginations*, ed. Webster Schott (New York: New Directions, 1970), p. 89; hereafter cited as I.

6. *Notebooks*, Vol. 1, ed. Kathleen Coburn (Princeton: Princeton Univ. Press, 1957), #1554.

7. Geoffrey Keynes, *The Songs of Innocence and of Experience* (New York: Orion Press, 1967), p. xiv.

8. "Blake's Introduction to Experience," in *Blake: A Collection of Critical Essays*, ed. Northrop Frye (Englewood Cliffs, N.J.: Prentice-Hall, 1966), pp. 119–126.

9. Cf. Jerome McGann's "The Aim of Blake's Prophecies and the Uses of Blake Criticism," in *Blake's Sublime Allegory*, pp. 3–21; and Donald Ault, *Visionary Physics* (Chicago: Univ. of Chicago Press, 1975), esp. pp. 28–29, 45–56.

10. For this study, I have used Erdman's transcription, and G. E. Bentley's indispensable *Vala or The Four Zoas* (London: Oxford Univ. Press, 1963). Erdman's textual notes in *The Poetry and Prose of William Blake* provide a good descriptive account of revisions, partially recoverable or canceled lines, and the important caution that the "complexities of the manuscript . . . continue to defy analysis" (E 739). As I shall argue briefly here, however, the nature of the problem is not descriptive but explanatory, for without some hypothesis bearing on the motivation of revisions, analysis simply remains incoherent. For this reason, I have not found

H. M. Margoliouth's *Vala: Blake's Numbered Text* (London: Oxford Univ. Press, 1963) persuasive, but quite useful for a preliminary sorting out of obvious additions. The reading of *The Four Zoas* developed here does not attempt to provide more than a framework within which a fuller analysis of the manuscript is possible.

11. I am especially indebted to Helen T. McNeil's "The Formal Art of *The Four Zoas*," in *Blake's Visionary Forms Dramatic*, ed. David V. Erdman and John E. Grant (Princeton: Princeton Univ. Press, 1970), pp. 373–390; subsequent references will be incorporated in the text in parentheses. I am also indebted to John E. Grant's careful description of illustrations in the manuscript (and infrared photographic reproductions published with his essay); cf. "Visions in *Vala*: A Consideration of Some Pictures in the Manuscript," in *Blake's Sublime Allegory*, pp. 141–202.

12. For an important contrast to the argument developed here, see Northrop Frye's contention in *The Stubborn Structure* (Ithaca: Cornell Univ. Press, 1970), p. 162, that Blake did not engrave any of his poems where the narrative element is strongest, in systematic preference for a mode of simultaneous thematic presentation. The persistent critical problem is that Blake obviously wanted to write a continuous narrative, but his difficulties in doing so have been consistently interpreted by reading *The Four Zoas* from the perspective of *Milton* and *Jerusalem*. See especially Harold Bloom, *Blake's Apocalypse: A Study in Poetic Argument* (Garden City, N.Y.: Doubleday, 1965), pp. 208–225, and Frye's *Fearful Symmetry: A Study of William Blake* (1947; reprint ed., Boston: Beacon Press, 1962), pp. 269–309, for the putative "standard" treatments of this issue; and, more recently, Mary Lynn Johnson and Brian Wilkie, *Blake's Four Zoas: The Design of a Dream* (Cambridge: Harvard Univ. Press, 1978).

13. In Night the First, additions and revisions present all of the Zoas in this state of delusion; for the "fall" of Luvah, see especially FZ II: 25–29; for Urizen, FZ III: 37–43; and for Tharmas, FZ III: 44–46; IV: 47–48.

14. Cf. G. W. Hegel, *The Phenomenology of Mind*, trans. J. B. Baillie (New York: Harper & Row, 1967), pp. 229–240.

15. *Fearful Symmetry*, pp. 185–268. Cf. *The Stubborn Structure*, p. 197.

16. *Visionary Physics*, p. 45ff.

17. For this reason it is a mistake to suppose that either of these can be regarded as definitive. Cf. Bloom, *Apocalypse*, pp. 266–280. Night the Seventh *b*, presumably the earlier version, establishes important links with earlier work, especially in *America*; and the conduct of this Armaggedon between Orc and Urizen figures prominently in Night the Eighth. There are (as Bloom points out) many details in these two versions which are not supplied elsewhere.

18. It should be noted particularly here that the Bard's Song in *Milton*, where we told repeatedly to "Mark well my words, they are of your eternal Salvation" (M IV: 20; M VII: 16; M IX: 7; M XI: 31), are not "prophetic" concealments to lead the righteous to vision, but quite direct references to events in *The Four Zoas*. Cf. James Reiger, "The Hems of Their Garments," in *Blake's Sublime Allegory*, pp. 273–280; and Bloom, *Apocalypse*, p. 340ff.

19. See especially Paul de Man, "The Rhetoric of Temporality," in *Interpretation: Theory and Practice*, ed. C. S. Singleton (Baltimore: Johns Hopkins Univ. Press, 1967); Frederic Jameson, *The Prison House of Language* (Princeton: Princeton Univ. Press, 1972), especially p. 101ff., and *Marxism and Form* (Princeton: Princeton Univ. Press, 1971).

20. It would be inappropriate to argue this controversial issue here; but see Harold Bloom, *The Anxiety of Influence* (New York: Oxford Univ. Press, 1973); Gerald Graff, "Fear and Trembling at Yale," *American Scholar* 46 (1977): 467–478;

and especially the exchange between Geoffrey Hartman and Wallace Martin in *Critical Inquiry* 4 (1977): 397–416.

21. See in this context Charles Altieri, "Northrop Frye and the Problem of Spiritual Authority," *PMLA* 87 (1972): 964–975.

22. T. S. Eliot, *The Idea of a Christian Society* (New York: Harcourt, Brace, 1940), especially pp. 32–37; Williams, "The Basis of Faith in Art," *Selected Essays*, pp. 175–195, especially pp. 188, 194–195; *Collected Poems and Plays* (New York: Harcourt, Brace and Co., 1950), hereafter cited as CP.

23. Cf. Hugh Kenner, *The Invisible Poet* (New York: Ivan Obolensky, 1959); and for an illuminating study of the related problem of solipsism, A. D. Nuttall, *A Common Sky: Philosophy and the Literary Imagination* (Berkeley: Univ. of California Press, 1974), especially pp. 201–209, 238ff. See also Charles Altieri, "Steps of the Mind in T. S. Eliot's Poetry," *Bucknell Review* 22(2) (1976): 180–207.

24. This overstates the case, for Williams did, of course, maintain contact with the literary community which mattered to *him*; but see Yvor Winters's "In Postscript: [1965] " to "Poetry of Feeling," in *William Carlos Williams: A Collection of Critical Essays*, ed. J. Hillis Miller, (Englewood Cliffs, N.J.: Prentice-Hall, 1966), p. 69. More recent criticism has contributed substantially to the clarification of the literary community in which Williams was, and is, central. See especially Hugh Kenner, *A Homemade World: The American Modernist Writers* (New York: Alfred A. Knopf, 1975); and Reed Whittemore, *William Carlos Williams: Poet from New Jersey* (Boston: Houghton Mifflin, 1975).

25. *The Divine Comedy*, trans. H. R. Huse (New York: Holt, Rinehart & Winston, 1954), "Inferno," canto 37, 11. 37–38, p. 129.

26. *T. S. Eliot's Poetry and Plays: A Study in Sources and Meaning* (Chicago: Univ. of Chicago Press, 1956).

27. *Autobiography*, p. 146. But see also Everett A. Gillis, "T. S. Eliot and the Classical Tradition," *Proceedings of the Comparative Literature Symposium* (1979) 11: 215–231.

28. *In The American Grain* (New York: New Directions, 1956), p. v.

29. *Selected Essays*, p. 204.

30. I adapt the phrase from Yeats's *Mythologies* (New York: Macmillan, 1959), p. 340.

31. Whitaker, *William Carlos Williams* (New York: Twayne, 1968), p. 130. I am particularly indebted to Whitaker's chapter on *Paterson*, pp. 129–151; and his superb introductory chapter, "Attention," pp. 17–33.

32. Cf. Whitaker, pp. 147–151.

33. See Williams, *Selected Letters*, ed. John C. Thirlwall (New York: McDowell, Obolensky, 1957), p. 233; Whitaker, p. 142.

34. For a fuller discussion of the critical model in use here, see my "Tradition and Intelligibility: A Model for Critical Theory," *New Literary History* 7 (1976): 393–415; on the distinction between "dialectical" and "dialogical" see also Whitaker, p. 131, and "On Speaking Humanly," in *The Philosopher Critic*, ed. Robert Scholes (Tulsa, Okla.: Univ. of Tulsa Press, 1970), pp. 67–88.

35. *Adventures of Ideas* (New York: Mentor Books, 1955), pp. 178–179.

36. Ralph Waldo Emerson, "The Poet," in *Selected Writings*, ed. William Gilman (New York: New American Library, 1965), p. 318.

37. "A Fond Note on Myth," *History and Politics*, trans. Denise Folliot and Jackson Mathews (New York: Pantheon Books, 1962), p. 40.

38. Cf. Whitaker, *Williams*, pp. 132–136.

Jay Parini

Blake and Roethke: When Everything Comes to One

> Not all the dead are used: we must take
> what we can from them.
>
> Roethke, *Notebooks*[1]

In an essay entitled "How to Write like Somebody Else" Theodore Roethke said that in a time when "the romantic notion of the inspired poet still has considerable credence, true 'imitation' takes a certain courage. One dares to stand up to a great style, to compete with papa." [2] Implicit in this statement is a distinction between false imitation, which comes down to mimicry of certain stylistic effects, and true imitation, which involves a confrontation, an appropriation and *re*-creation of the precursor's visionary stance. This latter kind of imitation occurs in the case of Blake and Roethke. For Blake remains the single most important poet for Roethke, not so much on the level of style (though I shall point to similarities at this level) but at the deeper level of mythopoetic action. Both poets were intent upon making a system or a personal *mythos* (in Northrop Frye's sense of the term as a shaping principle of literary form), and this *mythos* moves beyond allegory to anagogy, so that the characters in the system do not simply represent another stage or level of reality but move toward embodiment. This is the stage often called "mystical," when (as Roethke said) "The mind enters itself, and God the mind, / And one is One, free in the tearing wind." [3] Here Roethke seems close to the heart of Blake's visionary stance; as Frye has said, "the true God for such visionaries is not the orthodox Creator . . . but an unattached creative Word. . . . Unity with this God could be attained only by an effort of vision which not only rejects the duality of subject and object but attacks the far more difficult antithesis of being and non-being as well." [4]

It is mostly in his last volume, *The Far Field*, that Roethke comes to express his visionary sense of wonder, particularly in the *Sequence Sometimes Metaphysical* and the *North American Sequence*. Here Roethke approaches the apocalyptic identification of the kingdom with his own body that was Blake's culmination in *Jerusalem*. When one is one, free in the tearing wind, Blake's vision has been accomplished, although his imagery is drawn from the New Testament and Roethke's is taken from the Old Testament. It was Blake's method, especially in the later phase, to outleap the world, to claim the transcendental vision directly; whereas Roethke, fascinated by the spirit *as manifest* in nature, ascends the ladder of creation by gradual —indeed loving—steps. But the influence of Blake on Roethke can be detected much earlier, in the *Lost Son* sequences. In these poems Roethke set out to create his *mythos*, the struggle of the lost son in his quest for identity and his efforts to overcome Papa. Blake proposed the same process in his "Orc cycle," which occupies a central position in his work as a whole. Orc represents the natural man, and his struggle to resolve the contraries of Los and to overcome the opposing spectres of Urizen and Urthona becomes the equivalent *mythos* in Blake. Orc, like the lost son, moves through various stages of maturation; he opposes the old man, Urizen, until he naturally becomes an old man himself (at which point regeneration occurs and the cycle begins again). "Implicit in the myth of Orc and Urizen," Frye comments, "is the allegory of the young striking down the old, the most obvious symbol of which is the son's revolt against a father" (FS 5, 214). The Oedipal myth resides at the base of Blake's cycle, and it is this same myth that links Roethke's sequences to Blake.

Orc, says Martin Price, "embodies the rebellious principle of renewed and independent life." [5] He is the son of Los, the redeeming power of imagination, and Enitharmon, the "first female now separate." But Orc is fallen man as well. Los and Enitharmon chain their son to a rock, and the matter of Blake's cycle involves Orc's struggle for freedom, especially against Urizen (who is a negative aspect of Los). Urizen represents pure rationality and lifeless order, a version of Roethke's Papa, who represents *ordnung* in *The Lost Son*. Blake does not oppose intellect in its complete form, where it combines with freshness of perception and feeling, but in this fallen (Urizenic) aspect he condemns it. "Like Milton," Price says, "Blake sees all human existence as shot through with moments of fall and moments of redemption, and one fall provides an archetype for all others." [6] Blake's myth, ultimately, like Roethke's, looks forward to a redemptive vision, to the restoration of that primal unity lost in the fall. But Blake's protagonist, Orc, must first release himself from the treadmill of desire; as Frye puts it, "The natural tendency of desire (Orc) in itself is to find its object. Hence the effect of the creative impulse on desire is bound to be restrictive unless the release of desire becomes the inevitable by-product of creation." [7]

The body of Roethke's work focuses on the single *mythos* that begins in *The Lost Son*, Roethke's second book (1948). This volume provides the key to the rest of his work, for all the essential symbols of his system are present here in one form or another. Papa, the Urizenic father, is Otto Roethke, the greenhouse owner. Otto is at times seen as God; he is terrifying and powerful. Roethke's mother, Helen, is present but in the background. Like Enitharmon, she is passive, sometimes conflated with nature itself in its passive aspect. The greenhouse is a cultured Beulah-world apart from the harsher nature outside, Roethke's "symbol for the whole of life, a womb, a heaven-on-earth" (SP 39). In his notebooks of the forties Roethke tried to understand this luminous symbol occupying the center of his work: "what was this greenhouse? It was a jungle, and it was paradise, it was order and disorder. Was it an escape? No, for it was a reality harder than the various suspensions of terror." [8] There is also the open field, a place of illumination and, sometimes, mystical experience. "The Lost Son" itself, the title poem, contains the primary symbols; it is the text which informs the rest of his work, reiterating the elementary hero-myth with its classic pattern of flight (separation from the tribe), testing in the wilderness, descent into the underworld, and return (atonement, transfiguration). This cycle, like the Orc cycle in Blake, recurs in successive volumes—though it finds fullest expression in *The Lost Son, Praise to the End*! (1951), and *The Waking* (1953), of which the initial poem, "O, Thou Opening, O" completes the *Lost Son* sequence per se.

In "The Lost Son" Rothke invokes the Blakean dialectic of innocence and experience. Scattered through his working notebooks of the period (1943–1953) is the famous proverb from *The Marriage of Heaven and Hell*: "Without Contraries is no progression," which could serve as an epigraph to Roethke's *Collected Poems*. In Blake's system, the mind pulls into its own orbit those forces which might exist outside of its control; the dialectic absorbs all resistances; necessities become internal. Hence the lost son journeys toward identity, self-affirmation and, later, self-transcendence; but his path remains tortuous, marked by detours and culs-de-sac as in Section 3 (of five sections), which begins:

> Where do the roots go?
>   Look down under the leaves.
> Who put the moss there?
>   These stones have been here too long.
> Who stunned the dirt into noise?
>   Ask the mole, he knows.
>
> (CP 55)

In the last line above Roethke alludes directly to *The Book of Thel* and Blake's epigraph: "Does the Eagle know what is in the pit? / Or wilt thou go ask the Mole . . . ? " (E 3). The lost son is instructed to look downward, to dig into nether regions of psychic history for answers to his questions.

The Book of Thel concerns the failure of a heroine, Thel. She fails to progress from innocence, from Beulah (an earthly paradise, associated with unfallen sexuality) to Generation (fallen sexuality, but a necessary condition, the phase at which Orc begins his struggle). By failing to make this "fall," Thel refuses to exercise one of the vital powers of the soul, the *will*. She is timid, afraid of incarnation and the terrors of sense experience. By staying a virgin for too long, she forfeits the opportunity of progress and final redemption. As a result, she cannot remain static—Blake does not admit of this possibility—rather, she is destined to fall back into the solipsistic state of Ulro, the lowest condition in Blake's scheme. Her fear recalls the moment in Section 4 of "The Lost Son" where the boy says "Fear was my father, Father Fear" (CP 56). But unlike Thel, the lost son passes from the world of the greenhouse and his family cloister into the dangerous zone of Generation, here represented as a swampy bogland:

> Hunting along the river,
> Down among the rubbish, the bug-riddled foliage,
> By the muddy pond-edge, by the bog-holes,
> By the shrunken lake, hunting, in the heat of summer.
>
> (CP 54)

At this stage of his journey the boy-hero enters into the cyclical *process* of nature; the summer (which Blake associates with Generation) gives way to late autumn or early winter in the last section of the poem, a time when

> It was beginning winter,
> An in-between time,
> The landscape still partly brown:
> The bones of weeds kept swinging in the wind,
> Above the blue snow.
>
> (CP 58)

"The Lost Son" cannot be said to conclude; conclusion goes against the cyclical grain. Instead, the hero reaches an "irresolute resolution," an ending which is as well as beginning. This parallels the movement of Blake's cycle, where each poem achieves a partial conclusion, as in *The Book of Urizen*:

> 8. So Fuzon call'd all together
> The remaining children of Urizen:

and they left the pendulous earth:
They called it Egypt, & left it.

9. And the salt ocean rolled englob'd . . .

(U 28: 19–23)

This ending prepares for the opening of *The Book of Ahania*, where the Orc cycle is resumed: "Fuzon, on a chariot iron-wing'd / On spiked flames rose" (BA II: 1).

The last section of "The Lost Son" seems a long way from the seasonless paradise of Eden, the uppermost estate in Blake's overall scheme; but a partial cleansing of the senses certainly occurs: "The mind moved, not along, / Through the clear air, in the silence" (CP 58). *The Book of Thel*, on the other hand, ends with an unredemptive thud as Thel is shown "the secret of the land unknown" but has not the courage to make an adequate response; indeed, "The Virgin started from her seat, & with a shriek, / Fled back unhindered till she came into the vales of Har" (E 6). She will doubtless lapse into the condition of nonparticipation characteristic of Ulro, where desires go perpetually unsatisfied; having failed to make the journey *through* desire which can lead to freedom from desire. Her destiny is the "single vision" Blake reviled, a dreadful retreat from the "threefold vision" of Beulah or the ideal "fourfold vision" enjoyed by those in Eden. Roethke's "lost son," and this again has parallels in the Orc cycle, lacks none of the required courage; just as Orc has the dual aspect of Adonis, the dying and reviving god, and Prometheus, the thief of fire, the protagonist of the *Lost Son* sequence is dismembered, psychologically, in the wilderness, buried (Section 2 of "The Lost Son"), and revived; like Prometheus, he accepts the responsibility of fire: "I'll take the fire" (CP 61). The fire, in this case, is sexual desire; the lost son sees that he must face up to his passion if he will control it.

The contraries of innocence and experience, so crucial to Blake's system, operate in the whole of Roethke's work, but they have a special place in *The Lost Son*, which concerns the hero at the point of maturation where sexuality must be repressed (Thel's choice) or accepted (the option taken by Blake's later heroine, Oothoon). The "married land" of Beulah from which Roethke's hero is "lost" appears once again in the lyric "The Waking," which precedes the *Lost Son* sequence in the 1948 volume. The poem recalls the opening of Blake's lyric from *Poetical Sketches*, "How sweet I roam'd from field to field, / And tasted all the summer's pride" (E 404)—although Roethke avoids the harsh ironies into which Blake falls:

I strolled across
An open field;

The sun was out;
Heat was happy.

This way! This way!
The wren's throat shimmered,
Either to other,
The blossoms sang.

The stones sang,
The little ones did,
And flowers jumped
Like small goats.

A ragged fringe
Of daisies waved;
I wasn't alone
In a grove of apples.

(CP 51)

Roethke's lyric invokes the world of *Songs of Innocence*, a place where the glowworm gives counsel ("A Dream"), the sun "make[s] happy the skies" ("The Ecchoing Green"), and "the green woods laugh, with the voice of joy / And the dimpling stream runs laughing by" ("Laughing Song"). The last lines of Roethke's poem recreate the bliss of "Infant Joy," where Blake writes:

Pretty joy!
Sweet joy but two days old.
Sweet joy I call thee:
Thou dost smile.
I sing the while
Sweet joy befall thee.

(E 16)

In much the same way does Roethke conclude:

My ears knew
An early joy.

And all the waters
Of all the streams
Sang in my veins
That summer day.

(CP 51)

But neither poet has yet dramatized the separation of subject and object which follows inevitably as the realm of innocence gives way to experience. In Roethke as in Blake, the fall of man is coincident with the creation; both poets posit a condition of unity, a golden age, prior to the fall. And both look ahead to the restoration of that unity, a state raised above "the hateful siege of contraries" (in Milton's phrase). "Blake gives us," says Price, "a world conceived as the manifestation of imaginative energy, hardened into opacity as energy fails, raised through intense and confident assertion to the image of One Man, containing all powers within himself and exercising them in the creation of works of art." [9] Likewise Roethke, in "The Far Field," envisions "the end of things, the final man" whose "spirit moves like monumental wind / That gentles on a sunny blue plateau" (CP 201). But this is to look well beyond Orc and the lost son.

The poems of Roethke's sequence, individually and as a whole, recapitulate the journey from disorganized innocence through Generation, the crucible of summer, to organized innocence. As Bloom observes, "the only road to creativity and apocalypse lies through the realm of summer, the hard world of experience." [10] Roethke's dialectic exacts a share of pain for each portion of joy in this summery woodland where

> Small winds made
> A chilly noise;
> The softest cove
> Cried for sound.

Or where the hero

> Reached for a grape
> And the leaves changed;
> A stone's shape
> Became a clam.
>
> (CP 62)

Not until the end of summer, "Along the low ground dry only in August," does the hero catch a glimpse of Eden, and that only after an intimation of mortality ("Was it dust I was kissing?"):

> I could watch! I could watch!
> I saw the separateness of all things!
> My heart lifted up with the great grasses;
> The weeds believed me, and the nesting birds.
> There were clouds making a rout of shapes crossing a windbreak of cedars,

And a bee shaking drops from a rain-soaked honeysuckle.
The worms were delighted as wrens.
And I walked, I walked through the light air;
I moved with the morning.

(CP 63)

The intensity of the lost son in his moment of ecstasy contrasts sharply with the infantile joy of "The Waking," although the sense of oneness with the natural world remains constant. Having come through the harsh world of experience, where the division of subject and object is underscored, the boy-hero enters this momentary flash of vision. It is the dramatic context which provides the intensity.

One self-contained sequence of brief lyrics within *The Lost Son* has come to be known as the Greenhouse Poems; it contains some of Roethke's most widely anthologized pieces. These tough, sensual, and concrete poems recreate the texture of experience in the manner of *The Songs of Experience* and serve as a prelude to the *Lost Son* sequence in the way Blake's *Songs* adumbrate the Orc cycle. Roethke's lyrics establish the mythopoetic context necessary for the *Lost Son* sequence to work and prepare the ground for the symbolist methods characteristic of the later poems. In short, he invents a sequence of natural fables; his poems exploit various mythic structures and allude to such standard hermetic symbols as the rose and the worm. "Cuttings" is the first fable:

Sticks-in-a-drowse droop over sugary loam,
Their intricate stem-fur dries;
But still the delicate slips keep coaxing up water;
The small cells bulge;

One nub of growth
Nudges a sand-crumb loose,
Pokes through a musty sheath
Its pale tendrilous horn.

(CP 37)

The human parallels (the metaphor) are submerged; the sticks are "in-a-drowse," and the slips "coax" up water: both figures suggest a form of consciousness above the level commonly associated with the plant world. Roethke's cuttings are primordial nerve ends, low on the phylogenetic scale, but they prefigure something higher. The poem calls up a state of beginnings, a condition where the life-force is reduced to an urge, an importunate breathing. Again, the poem derives its force from the tacit myth of awakening.

Still, it is in the *Lost Son* sequence as it stretches over three books that Roethke accrues his largest debts to Blake. The lost son gropes toward self-awareness and separate identity in the manner of Blake's "fierce child," Orc, born in *The Book of Urizen* and struggling through many of the major poems against his various opposing spectres. The apocalyptic imagery and associational logic of both poets operate within a consistent, albeit difficult, symbol system. These systems are closed, and full of internal references. The lost son engages in the cycles of nature, advancing slowly toward his goal of identity and self-transcendence; his way out of nature is *through* it. Blake, by contrast, does not himself identify with Orc or suggest that his involvement with the natural cycles is a good thing. For him, the cycles of nature were a kind of death, a grinding down. As Frye explains, "the vision of life as an Orc cycle is the pessimistic view of life. . . ." (FS 225). In Blake's system, Orc is equivalent to the giant Albion in his fallen aspect. At the end of the cycle, Orc comes face-to-face with Urizen and the spectre of Urthona, who represents clock time (an aspect of the grinding down effected by the natural cycles). Orc's destiny is, of course, to become Urizen himself; then the cycle must begin again. Roethke's "lost son"—on the other hand—goes beyond these cycles, transcending the self-consciousness which leads into Ulro and the fate of Orc. Nonetheless both Roethke and Blake were aiming toward a myth of creation and destruction, a poetics of redemption.

The *Lost Son* sequence resumes in *Praise to the End*! with the hero-as-infant; the language of these poems suggests the process of disintegration which accompanies the fall into creation, akin to the breakup of the giant Albion into the four Zoas in Blake's system. Both poets reformulated the myth of disintegration at several stages in their careers. La Belle finds this myth in Blake emerging in the *Songs of Innocence* and compares the "Little Boy Lost" to Roethke's "lost son": "For both poets, the physical condition of the little boy lost in the Stygian darkness and trapped in the mire is an emblem for a state of psychological disorientation and for a loss of the true vision of innocence." [11] In Blake's companion piece, "The Little Boy Found," the child is restored to innocence by God, who is "ever nigh," and who "Appeard like his father in white" (E 11). In a similar way the lost son encounters Papa, who represents *ordnung* or authority (in its negative Urizenic aspect, however), upon his return from "The Pit" and the terrifying journey into experience. Throughout the *Lost Son* sequence Papa reappears at crucial moments as a "beard in a cloud" to provide (or force) order.

Praise to the End! opens with a birth poem, "Where Knock Is Open Wide," in which the poet reconstitutes the dreamworld of infancy. The poem opens with the infant-hero in some confusion over what is happening to him; he cannot distinguish cause from effect: "I know it's an owl. He's making it darker" (CP 72). He still thinks he is in Beulah-land, the state of primal unity, where God answers to every need within the instant: "God, give me a near. I hear flowers." This world is absolutely self-centered, and all sexual pleasure is onanistic: "Hello happy hands." But the truth of his new condition, which is postlapsarian, occurs to him rather suddenly: "I fell! I fell! " he cries, "The worm has moved away. / My tears are tired." He complains, "God's somewhere else," and darkness seems to have come for "a long long time" (CP 73).

"I Need, I Need" follows immediately and reviews the condition of loss. The title derives from the ninth design of Blake's series *For Children: The Gates of Paradise* (1793) with its inscription, "I want! I want! " The poem chronicles the infant's first encounters with unsatisfied desire, the terror of Blake's Orc as well. "I can't taste my mother," Roethke's infant cries. For the first time, the hero feels cut off from his source, separate. His consciousness has been divided, which leads him to wish for a prior state. And so unsatisfied desire leads necessarily to the habit of wishing:

I wish I was a pifflebob
I wish I was a funny
I wish I had ten thousand hats,
And made a lot of money.

(CP 75)

Through this section Roethke uses the language of schoolchildren without being condescending; he enters into the child's consciousness by imitating verbal patterns that are thought to be childlike, a technique used by Blake in his *Songs of Innocence*. As S. Foster Damon has written: "Blake does not contemplate children, in the manner of Wordsworth, Hugo, and Longfellow; he actually enters into their souls and speaks through their own mouths." [12] So Roethke, in the above passage, uses the most basic of childhood tropes, a series of wishes. In Blake's engraving there are three figures, one of whom is a naked child, poised for climbing a moonbeam and, clearly, destined to failure. The child here has yet to move from innocence to experience, although the picture itself contains within its perimeter both contrary states. As La Belle says, "The viewpoint and the final significance of many of Blake's and Roethke's poems about childhood become very complex because the two contrary states of innocence and experience are not mutually exclusive and can exist in the same child or the same poem at once." [13]

In Roethke's sequence, the states of innocence and experience alternate, and nature is by turns sympathetic and antagonistic. In "I Need, I Need," a poem about the fall into experience, nature appears unresponsive:

Went down cellar,
Talked to a faucet;
The drippy water
Had nothing to say.

(CP 74)

But nature responds with robust sympathy in the next poem, "Bring the Day," which begins with a nursery rhyme-like chant:

Bees and lilies there were,
Bees and lilies there were,
Either to other,—
Which would you rather?
Bees and lilies were there.

The green grasses,—would they?
The green grasses?—
She asked her skin
To let me in:
The far leaves were for it.

(CP 77)

Similar rhythms occur in many of Blake's *Songs*, such as "The Ecchoing Green"—though Roethke remains more tentative than Blake throughout:

The Sun does arise,
And make happy the skies.
The merry bells ring
To welcome the Spring.
The skylark and thrush,
The birds of the bush,
Sing louder around,
To the bells cheerful sound.
While our sports shall be seen
On the Ecchoing green.

(E 8)

Both poets use what Hopkins called "sprung rhythm," a meter familiar to readers of Mother Goose; other devices common to the nursery rhyme are used, such as repetition, short lines, internal rhyming, and alliteration. Roethke, in his essay "Some Remarks on Rhythm,' comments on Blake's "A Poison Tree": "The whole poem is a masterly example of variation in rhythm, of playing against meter. It's what Blake called 'the bounding line,' the nervousness, the tension, the energy in the whole poem. And this is a clue to everything. Rhythm gives us the very psychic energy of the speaker, in one emotional situation at least" (SP 79). True enough; but more than meter is involved. The underlying pattern of gradually sharpened antitheses which force the hero of Roethke's sequence into a moral choice works as a principle of organization in much the same way as it does in Blake's Orc cycles and the later prophetic books.

The progress of Roethke's infant-hero in *Praise to the End*! is steady but not linear. "By snails, by leaps of frog, I came here," he says. The hero treks a landscape of few comforts, a *paysage moralisé* where "Eternity howls in the last crags. / The field is no longer simple." As he says, "It's a soul's crossing time" (CP 89). This setting resembles the familiar testing ground of most quest literature; Roethke's woodlands, far from being the enchanted forests one associates with childhood, come closer to Dante's *selva oscura*: "It's a dark wood, soft mocker" (CP 85). These dark woodlands resemble in character the Urizenic "dens / Mountain, moor, & wilderness" that trap Orc in the *Book of Urizen* (U 22: 46–47). The path through these dark woods which leads to transcendental vision is beset with crossroads and detours. Sometimes the hero makes a wrong turn and finds himself in a place of total disaffection:

Touch and arouse. Suck and sob. Curse and mourn.
It's a cold scrape in a low place.
The dead crow dries on a pole.
Shapes in the shade
Watch.

(CP 80)

Yet later the hero can say with pride: "I've crawled from the mire, alert as a saint or a dog; / I know the back-stream's joy, and the stone's eternal pulseless longing" (CP 88). In general, the speaker arrives at some temporary conclusion near the end of each poem, slipping back again at the start of the next one, but never back quite so far. "I go back because I want to go forward," Roethke says in his notebooks.[14] The lost son accepts his difficult quest with a certain equanimity: "What grace I have is enough" (CP 91).

What Roethke's "lost son" and Blake's hero, Orc, have in common is a belief in the powers of intuition; "Knowledge," Blake writes, "is not by deduction but Immediate by Perception or Sense at once" (E 653). Conceptual discourse bears no interest. In *Jerusalem*, Blake's last prophetic book, the contraries of rational and emotional discourse find mythic equivalents:

Rational Philosophy and Mathematic Demonstration
Is divided in the intoxications of pleasure & affection

Two Contraries War against each other in fury & blood,
And Los fixes them on his Anvil, incessant his blows:
He fixes them with strong blows. placing the stones & timbers.
To Create a World of Generation from the World of Death:
Dividing the Masculine & Feminine: for the comingling
Of Albions Luvahs Spectres was Hermaphroditic

(J III: 58, 13–20)

Los, the terrifying artificer, creates out of these contraries a better world; however, the act of submitting to these contraries, to the sublunary world of Generation, requires genuine courage. Those without this courage, like Thel, must slip back inexorably into the sleep of Ulro.

The naïve Romantic sides with "feeling" against "reason" in a simpleminded way. Blake does not do this; for his ultimate goal, Jerusalem, is a vision of the giant Albion restored. Head (Urizen), body (Tharmas), loins (Orc), and legs (Urthona) come together in the end. The imagination subsumes both "feeling" and "thought." "The act of creation," says Frye, "is not producing something out of nothing, but the act of setting free what we already possess." [15] Nevertheless Blake, with some justice, attacks the "single vision" of Locke, Newton, and other rationalist thinkers of his time:

I turn my eyes to the Schools & Universities of Europe
And there behold the Loom of Locke whose Woof rages dire
Washd by the Water-wheels of Newton. black the cloth
In heavy wreathes folds over every Nation; cruel Works
Of many Wheels I view, wheel without wheel, with cogs tyrannic
Moving by compulsion each other: not as those in Eden: which
Wheel within Wheel in freedom revolve in harmony & peace.

(J I: 15, 14–20)

Roethke says, in a much less complex way, the same thing in the last poem of *Praise to the End*! entitled "I Cry, Love! Love!" (itself a quotation from Blake):

Reason? That dreary shed, that hutch for grubby schoolboys!
The hedgewren's song says something else.
I care for a cat's cry and the hugs, live as water.

(CP 92)

The lost son is learning to begin, as Blake suggests, with perception and sense.

The title of this poem comes from the *Visions of the Daughters of Albion* (1793) in which the character of Oothoon answers to the feckless virgin, Thel. Oothoon attempts to move beyond innocence into experience, from

Beulah into Generation; she is "a virgin fill'd with virgin fancies / Open to joy and to delight where ever beauty appears" (E 49). Her failure to do as she wishes comes as no fault of her own; rather, the object of her desire, Theotormon, is utterly self-enthralled, sitting "Upon the margind ocean conversing with shadows dire" (E 50). The central passage in *Visions* gave Roethke his theme:

> I cry, Love! Love! Love! happy happy Love! free as the mountain wind!
> Can that be Love, that drinks another as a sponge drinks water?
> That clouds with jealousy his nights, with weepings all the day:
> To spin a web of age around him. grey and hoary! dark!
> Till his eyes sicken at the fruit that hangs before his sight.
> Such is self-love that envies all! a creeping skeleton
> With lamplike eyes watching around the frozen marriage bed.
>
> (E 49)

Oothoon makes the crucial distinction between narcissism and "that generous love" which attaches itself to another person; the first is nugatory, even destructive, denying the reality of anything beyond the self. It brings on the dread sleep of Ulro. But this "happy happy love" does not drink another "as a sponge drinks water," merely feeding on the other person's energies. It exults in the other, celebrating itself in the process; it knows how "everything that lives is holy"—a phrase which Roethke liked to quote (SP 24).

The hero in "I Cry Love! Love!" says, "Delight me otherly, white spirit" (CP 92), playing on "utterly" to gain a double sense. The maturing speaker now sees that he can discover his own identity only through another. "Bless me and the maze I'm in!" he says, accepting the siege of contraries and the world of objects: "Hello, thingy spirit." He has now fully accepted the fall into creation and will try to use this misfortune to his best advantage. He accepts Blake's sacramental view of nature, that everything alive is holy: "Behold, in the lout's eye, / Love." The last stanza of the poem brings this realization to its conclusion:

> Who untied the tree? I remember now.
> We met in a nest. Before I lived.
> The dark hair sighed.
> We never enter
> Alone.
>
> (CP 93)

The question "Who untied the tree?" shows how mature the boy has become; it is equivalent to "Who made me and turned me loose in this fallen world?" He recollects a spirit who was present with him in the womb, the nest. And he takes great comfort merely in the fact that someone other than himself exists. The narrow self-consciousness of Ulro is denied, and the possibility of self-transcendence through love seems within the hero's reach.

But such optimism proves short-lived. As Roethke later notes: "From me to Thee's a long and terrible way" (CP 246). His last three books, from *The Waking* (which brings the *Lost Son* cycle to a close) to *Words for the Wind* (1958) and the posthumous *The Far Field* (1964), record the steady movement toward self-transcendence on "the long journey out of the self" (CP 193). The myth of the lost son, with its attendant symbols, remains at the center of his work, but the myth widens. A similar pattern occurs in Blake as he recapitulates his personal myth in *Milton* and *Jerusalem* (both written and etched between 1804 and 1820). As Frye says, "*Milton* describes the attainment by the poet of the vision that *Jerusalem* expounds in terms of all humanity" (FS 356). It is the same myth, the story of the fall of man, his struggle through the cycles of nature, and his redemption, which occupies him almost from the beginning. Similarly, *Words for the Wind* describes the transcendence of the self through love of another, the major theme of Roethke in his middle years (1953–1959). *The Far Field* represents his *Jerusalem* or *Paradiso*; it recounts his hero's attainment of "the imperishable quiet at the heart of form" (CP 188).

North American Sequence, in particular, moves toward a fullness of vision characteristic of *Jerusalem*. Blake's identification of the New Golgotha with the body and his daring to look directly into the fierce light of the godhead find an analog in Roethke's last meditations. In "The Longing," for instance, he writes:

> I would be a stream, winding between great striated
>   rocks in late summer;
> A leaf, I would love the leaves, delighting in the
>   redolent disorder of this mortal life. . . .
>
> (CP 188)

The meditations all contain passages where the poet wishes to identify with the world outside himself, to enter the body of nature and move with his "body thinking," thereby extending human consciousness, perhaps indefinitely. The mortal self, as in *Jerusalem*, is destined for extinction: "Annihilate the Selfhood in me." Nothing will come of retaining the old self but the dreaded sleep of Ulro. Los, the heroic figure in Blake's epic, confronts the spectres which threaten him, saying:

> I know that Albion hath divided me, and that thou O my Spectre,
> Hast just cause to be irritated: but look stedfastly upon me:

Comfort thyself in my strength the time will arrive
When all Albions injuries shall cease, and when we shall
Embrace him tenfold bright, rising from his tomb in immortality.
(J I: 7, 52–56)

The great themes of *Jerusalem*—the restoration of the God in man and the triumph of imagination and fourfold vision—occupy Roethke as well in his last poems. In a moment of summary vision he declares:

My eyes extend beyond the farthest bloom of the waves;
I lose and find myself in the long water;
I am gathered together once more;
I embrace the world.
(CP 198)

Roethke, unlike Blake in method, embraces the world to find redemptive vision; yet both poets discover themselves transfigured, sloughing off the old self for the new one, the Self, to be born.

But the quest, even in this last book, remains antithetical. The hero often lapses into self-doubt as he proceeds. He reenters the jungle world of "The Lost Son" in "The Long Waters," which begins the *North American Sequence*:

I return where fire has been,
To the charred edge of the sea
Where the yellowish prongs of grass poke through the blackened ash,
And the bunched logs peel in the afternoon sunlight
(CP 196)

In these "unsinging fields where no lungs breathe," the old fear returns, and the poet cries out for help to Blake's nurse, Mnetha, the guardian of Beulah: "Mnetha, Mother of Har, protect me / From the worm's advance. . . ." As in *Jerusalem*, the poet in *The Far Field* sharpens the antitheses, moving gradually toward illumination, restoration. In these last poems Roethke is working out an *analogia visionis* not unlike Blake's; he reads the world as "A steady storm of correspondences!" (CP 239) and approaches that apocalypse where "one is One, free in the tearing wind." This comes very close to Blake's "mysticism," which "is to be conceived neither as a human attempt to reach God nor a divine attempt to reach man, but as the realization in total experience of the identity of God and Man in which both the human creature and the superhuman Creator disappear" (FS 431). Roethke puts it this way in "A Walk in Late Summer":

It lies upon us to undo the lie
Of living merely in the realm of time.

Existence moves toward a certain end—
A thing all earthly lovers understand.

(CP 149)

This end toward which all existence moves is the restoration of that primal unity of perception sought after by Blake; it also involves a resolution of contraries and a rejection of temporal or clock time (the spectre of Urthona) in favor of an eternal present. For Blake, this condition is represented, finally, by Golgonooza, the city of art. For Roethke, in his final mystical sequences, the rose becomes his symbol of eternity (as it had for Dante, Rilke, Eliot, and Yeats before him): "this rose, this rose in the sea-wind, / Rooted in stone, keeping the whole of light" (CP 205).

The Far Field gives final evidence of Roethke's continuing dialogue with Blake; the *North American Sequence* with its search for "imperishable quiet at the heart of form" parallels Blake's "fearful symmetry." For it is in the city of art that fallen man is restored in the New Golgotha (Golgonooza). As God and man come together in the figure of the visionary poet, the apocalypse occurs, and the mythopoetic action moves from allegory to anagogy: the level where spiritual truth is embodied. It is, at last, at the level of mythic structure that Blake affected Roethke most significantly. This structure, according to Frye, has its fittest analogy in music: "The beauty of *Jerusalem* is the beauty of intense concentration, the beauty of the Sutra, of the aphorisms which are the form of so much of the greatest vision, of a figured bass indicating the harmonic progression of ideas too tremendous to be expressed by a single melody" (FS 359). It is this same "harmonic progression of ideas" which underlies Roethke's mystical sequence, too. Commenting on "The Longing," which opens the *North American Sequence*, Hugh B. Staples writes:

> In a manner that suggests counterpoint in music, the principle of alternation controls the elaborate pattern of contrasting elements in the poem: body and soul, the sense of self and the release from subjectivity, earth and water, past and present, motion and stasis. . . . The sequence, then, can be regarded as a tone poem consisting of an overture ("The Longing"), in which the major themes appear, followed by four movements in which the tensions and oppositions of the whole sequence are summarized and move toward a resolution.[16]

Roethke's sequence, then, moves in the manner of *Jerusalem*—via a series of gradually heightened antitheses—toward its resolution, the resurrection of Roethke's "final man" or Albion restored.

The last poem in Roethke's last book is "Once More, the Round," and here the poet provides more than could be wished for, a final summary of his complex relationship to Blake couched in Blakean terms, a poem in celebration of the cosmic dance and visionary mode:

> What's greater, Pebble or Pond?
> What can be known? The Unknown.
> My true self runs toward a Hill
> More! O More! visible.
>
> Now I adore my life
> With the Bird, the abiding Leaf,
> With the Fish, the questing Snail,
> And the Eye altering all;
> And I dance with William Blake
> For love, for Love's sake;
>
> And everything comes to One,
> As we dance on, dance on, dance on.
>
> (CP 251)

Notes

1. Unpublished manuscript quotations are from the *Theodore Roethke Papers* of the University of Washington's Suzzallo Library; references include box and file number and, where available, the date which Roethke marked on the notebook. The present reference is TRP 34–38, April 2, 1943.

2. *On the Poet and His Craft: Selected Prose of Theodore Roethke*, ed. Ralph J. Mills, Jr. (Seattle: Univ. of Washington Press, 1965), pp. 69–70; hereafter cited as SP.

3. *Collected Poems of Theodore Roethke* (New York: Doubleday, 1966), p. 239; hereafter cited as CP.

4. Northrop Frye, *Fearful Symmetry: A Study of William Blake* (Princeton: Princeton Univ. Press, 1969), p. 431; hereafter cited as FS.

5. Martin Price, "The Standard of Energy," in *Romanticism and Consciousness*, ed. Harold Bloom (New York: W. W. Norton, 1970), p. 257.

6. Ibid., p. 255.

7. Northrop Frye, "The Keys to the Gates," in *Romanticism and Consciousness*, p. 253.

8. TRP 35–66, August 13, 1945.

9. Price, p. 273.

10. Harold Bloom, *The Visionary Company* (Ithaca: Cornell Univ. Press, 1971), p. 25.

11. Jenijoy La Belle, *The Echoing Wood of Theodore Roethke* (Princeton: Princeton Univ. Press, 1976), p. 99.

12. S. Foster Damon, *William Blake: His Philosophy and Symbols* (London: Constable, 1924), pp. 40–41.

13. La Belle, p. 60.

14. TRP 34–41, January 8, 1944.
15. Frye, in *Romanticism and Consciousness*, p. 254.
16. Hugh B. Staples, "The Rose in the Sea-Wind: A Reading of Theodore Roethke's 'North American Sequence,'" *American Literature* 36(2) (May 1964): 192–193.

Robert J. Bertholf

Robert Duncan: Blake's Contemporary Voice

A literary tradition delineates direct influences as well as spiritual affinities.[1] The case of William Blake and Robert Duncan calls in both lines, producing a complex of affinities and modifications which declare the vitality of the tradition itself. Just as Blake reached backward to Dante and to Milton to bring forward the poetic vision of the salvational fall of mankind, so Duncan has searched out in conscious maneuvers the texts which immersed him in the continuous contention of universal contraries. He has announced himself a derivative poet; and in the sense that Dante (and for Duncan, Shakespeare), Milton, Blake, Whitman exemplify a tradition, Duncan joins them. He, in fact, declares: [2]

> With Blake, the poet's sense of his primordial inspiration, his coexistence in the original time of spiritual beings and in the very presence of powers, appears in his actual life itself. He does not write poems as ways into the mythological; he writes poems *from* the real of that reality. (T&L 40)

For both poets the creative act involves participation in the first energies of existence, and a projection of a mythological pattern in poetry which describes the spiritual genesis and a possible salvation of mankind. For Blake that required the healing of an unholy separation, as he laid it out in *The Marriage of Heaven and Hell*, and the regaining of the stupendous visions of the Last Judgment: "This World [of Imagination] is Infinite & Eternal whereas the world of Generation or Vegetation is Finite & [for a small moment] Temporal. There exist in that Eternal World the Permanent Realities of Every Thing which we see reflected in this Vegetable Glass of Nature" (VLJ 69). Duncan not only takes off from Blake's poems, his vision of eternity and his mythic studies, but he regards Blake as a poetic companion of the sacramental imagination who has gone before him in exploring the difficulties of revealing the holiness of existence, and the integration of existence in the larger spiritual dimensions of cosmic orders. As Duncan writes: "Poems then are immediate presentations of the intention of the whole, the great poem of all poems, a unity, and in any two of its elements or parts appearing as a duality or a mating, each part in every other having, if we could see it, its condition—its opposite or contender and its satisfaction or twin." [3]

Both poets are visionaries. But while Blake takes the figure of Christ as the imagination—"Human Imagination / Which is the Divine Body of the Lord Jesus" (E 96)—and sees in him the fulfillment of man in communion with God, Duncan takes Eros, the god of love and the first form in the Orphic mysteries, as his guide into the realms of the wholeness of primal creation where all things exist in the purity of first appearances.

> Eros is a primal authority, a cosmic need. . . . Love, desire, and beauty, in the poet's Theogony, precede mankind. They were once forces that came to be forms. We experience something, the meaning of things seems to change when we fall in love, as if life were a language we had begun to understand. It is the virtue of words that what were forces become meanings and seek form. Cosmic powers appear as presences and even as persons of inner being to the imagination.[4]

For Duncan, Christ is a transformation of Eros who releases a new possibility of generative love for a new age. Chirst as Eros is the source of cosmic creation men follow and praise in their mythological inventions. While Blake sees the climactic arrival of Jerusalem as the teleological achievement of imaginative freedom to perceive in the unity of eternity, Duncan proposes a field of poetry in whch his imagination defines no *telos*, derives its formulations through immersion in primal energies, and then projects outward poetic inscriptions of that immersion. For him there can be no terminus in his poetry, because there can be no end to the possibilities of new creations in the fertile center of all creativity. He regards his poems as part of a larger whole that is still incomplete, in the same way that he regards the body of his work as part of Blake's "Grand Poem," existing in the energies of the universal imagination in which all poets participate. Blake's poems come into his field of poetry because he finds in Blake a poet of the imagination: a poet, in the Gnostic sense, who possesses a spark of the eternal mind, and who, in his way, contributes to the same grand poem coming out of the universal mind that he contributes to. Both poets claim a membership in a universal poem which reveals itself, and so also the nature of mankind, through the interaction of contending powers of good and evil, or what Blake called contraries.

"Following lines of alliteration and rime or the rhythms of an entranced voice," [5] Duncan writes, he senses an attunement with the creative powers.

In his world of poetry, the musical measures of language—what he calls in "The Venice Poem" "the tone-leading of vowels" (FD 91)—or the interplay of sounds and meanings—awakens the mythological reality, which for him is the presence of the central, generative source from which all morphologies of reality and the mind proceed.

> Poems come up from a ground so
> to illustrate the ground, approximate
> a lingering of eternal image, a need
> known only in its being found ready.
>
> (OF 60)

And the immediacy of original time, spiritual beings, and powers produce in the body of his work many poems which take as their subject the beginning of things, or the vision and re-vision of the original energies coming into form.

> The design of a poem
>   constantly
> under reconstruction,
>   changing, pusht forward;
> alternations of sound, sensations;
>   the mind dance
> wherein thot shows its pattern:
>   a proposition
>   in movement.
>
> (D 9)

Incessantly the poems attempt to reconstruct the energies of original time and powers. Like Blake he writes from the middle of a mythological reality. However, while Blake evolves a complicated system with a cast of characters, divisions of those characters, a symbolic landscape, and a host of derived associations which define, in mythological form, his vision of mythological reality, Duncan evolves a poetry of process in which the drive of the imagination to propose approximations of eternal images takes precedence over the approximations which illustrate that process. "O, to release the first music somewhere again, / for a moment," he writes in "Night Scenes," "to touch the design of the first melody! " (R&B 6). From this mythological center of process and the first melody the figures and images of previous myths become available to him, not as fixed figures, but as illustrations of the process of creation itself, as testimony to his immersion in the energies he enacts in his poetry. Figures such as Eros/Aphrodite (and the avatars, as in "The Maiden" [OF 27]) appear many times, as does

Christ, as an emblem of personal suffering, and the lion, as an aspect of sexuality, but Duncan does not cast a unique company of players to demonstrate his sense of primordial reality. His system of freedom is the process of the imagination realizing its affinities with the wisdom of existing fictive mythologies.

"Men's visions and fictions as well as their facts move their histories and belong to the reality principle," Duncan tells us, and then continues, "To take Blake or Dante as gospels of Poetry, as I do, is to testify to and in that to enter into the reality of divine history within what man calls history" (T&L 58). Before 1950 Duncan wrote two series of poems, *Domestic Scenes* and *Medieval Scenes*, which have the general configuration of the *Songs of Innocence and Experience* in that each is a sequence of poems connected to a central theme. The two series recognize the isolation caused by the lack of human love, but also the barriers produced by selfhood. "I sleep a serpent-sleep in slough of human skin," Duncan writes in "Breakfast," the first of *Domestic Scenes*. Like Blake, Duncan knew well the spectral substance of isolated self-possession and like Blake at the beginning of *Jerusalem*, wants to "Annihilate the Selfhood in me" (J I: 5, 22). Duncan writes at the end of *Medieval Scenes*:

> I would come unto the source of light unsung.
> The Golden Ones move in invisible realms.
> If we could know their chastity. We strive to touch.
> The consoled of God die away from life.
> We reach, we reach to hold them back.
> They grow invisible to our lust.
>
> (FD 63)

Jealousy in these poems promotes the spectre of selfhood and prevents the entrance into the community of love. "The Golden Ones" of the dream vision then are transformed companions, now, in a sense, installed in Jerusalem with the isolation of selfhood dissolved. The contest between self and community appears again in the "Coda" of "The Venice Poem": but while Duncan wants to occupy the same divine history that Blake occupies, he does not want to imitate Blake's poetics and mythology (imitate in the sense of following the master blindly). Blake becomes a presence in his poetry who provides entrances to new mythic territory.

In the prose piece "A Lammas Tiding," for example, Duncan describes how the poem "My Mother Would Be a Falconress" was written. He says he took off from the line "With what sense is it that the chicken shuns the ravenous hawk" from *Visions of the Daughters of Albion* (E 46). Blake's lines are transformed in his own dream into the poem. "My Mother Would Be a

Falconress" deals with another version of contrariety, the mother–son relationship, in its tender and brutal aspects:

My mother would be a falconress,
And I, her gay falcon treading her wrist,
would fly to bring back
from the blue of the sky to her, bleeding, a prize,
where I dream in my little hood with many bells
jangling when I'd turn my head.

(BB 52)

The poem revolves around the conflict between the homosexual poet ("her gay falcon") and the dominant mother who seemingly controls the young falcon, directs his flights. Pride and domination enter the relationship in opposition to freedom, until after the death of the mother:

My mother would be a falconress,
and even now, years after this,
when the wounds I left her had surely heald,
and the woman is dead,
her fierce eyes closed, and if her heart
were broken, it is stilld .

I would be a falcon and go free.
I tread her wrist and wear the hood,
talking to myself, and would draw blood.

(BB 53–54)

With Freud as the guiding factor here, and Blake as a serving text, Duncan samples the primal melody; he advances a version of the melody with a dream, and that statement announces too that he acknowledges that daily event and night dreams are perceptions of a universal primal reality. Like Blake he takes the imagination of the household to be equal to the imagination of the cosmos, so even the contentions between mother and son, freedom and domination can be understood as a projection of dipolar emanations, of a struggle of Blakean contraries. The struggle must never be fully resolved; it must remain as an instigation to bring forth insights.

And so in the poem "Variations on Two Dicta of William Blake"—"Mental things alone are real" (*A Vision of the Last Judgment*) and "The Authors are in Eternity" (letter to Thomas Butts, July 6, 1803)—Duncan recognizes that authentic perception destroys manufactured dualisms—here rifts between lovers—and that as a poet who acknowledges the existence of divine history he too is a scribe on an infinitely wonderful poem. The poem begins with a statement of the situation:

The Authors are in eternity.
Our eyes reflect
prospects of the whole radiance
between you and me

where we have lookd up
    each from his being.
And I am the word "each".
And you are the word "his".

(R&B 48)

The lovers are part of the greater whole of love, as Blake's "The Divine Image" puts it, and of "love, the human form divine" (E 12), with that form an aspect of the human form divine of Jesus, as the highest manifestation of the imagination. The poet/lover is engaged in the universality of love and poetry, and writes out in his actions versions of that universal impulse. But the revelation of that impulse comes only from an inner contention, in the poem whether to "reach up, / restore our hands touching." (R&B 48)

    Each his being
a single glance the authors see
    as part of the poetry of what is, what
we suffer. You talkd of "freedom",
    and I saw
how foreign I am from me.

(R & B 48)

While the certainty of the author of the immediate poems is itself authored by the forces of eternity, there is a resistance to entering that presence of eternity that would come with touching. There is a simultaneous longing for and fear of the engagement that will reveal the sparks that Blake speaks of in *Jerusalem*:

In Great Eternity, every particular Form gives
    forth or Emanates
Its own peculiar Light, & the Form is the
    Divine Vision
And the Light is his Garment. This is
    Jerusalem in every Man[.]

(J III: 54, 1–3)

Duncan stops the third section of the poem with:

> What I am is only a factor of what I am.
> The authors of the author
> before and after
> wait for me to restore
> (I had only to touch you then)
> the way to the eternal
> sparks of desire.
>
> (R&B 50)

Love is the manifestation of the eternal mind in human behavior and the lines of poetry.

The revealing statement comes in the central fourth section (there are seven sections to the poem):

> Come, eyes, see more than you see!
> For the world within and the outer world
> rejoice as one. The seminal brain
> contains the lineaments of eternity.
>
> (R&B 50)

A major proposal of Duncan's poetry is the pushing aside of the epistemological complications and diversions of the subject-object split. He is not a Cartesian annotator, and neither was Blake. Duncan rejoices in "the Jerusalem in every Man," though he would never cast aside the sexual passions as restrictive forces. He does not in any way foster the limiting reason of Urizen, but celebrates the freedom of the divine spark alive in all men as Man. "To be a man—but we are men / who are of one mind" he writes in the way to a main point in the sixth section, again praising the poet Charles Olson:

> —the poet's voice, a whole beauty of the man Olson,
>   lifting us up into .
>
> where the disturbance is, where the words
>   awaken
> sensory chains between being and being,
>   inner acknowledgements
> of fiery masters—there
>   like stellar bees my senses swarmd.
>
> (R&B 51–52)

In response to Duncan's poetry and essays, Olson published an essay "Against Wisdom as Such" (1954), in which he took Duncan to task for his use of wisdom and learning in his writing. Duncan responded, not with personal anger, but with a shout of joy that Olson, by entering into a controversy about writing, had given Duncan back his poetry with a higher energy. In Blakean terms, Duncan and Olson were now contraries, and from the contrasts between them would come a new poetry informed by inspired energies and thus new insights. The poem, as the love affair, thrives on these inner contentions to reveal the wholeness of the eternal nature.

The vision, the dream, is alive in the events of the daily, and the events of the daily alive in divine history. The same processes operate in "Figures of Speech," a section of the book *Letters*, which Duncan says could have been dedicated to the poet Helen Adam. In 1954, at a poetry workshop at San Francisco State College, Helen Adam had read from *Songs of Innocence* and *Songs of Experience*. Her dedication to the realms of the mysterious, and her devotion to Blake caused Duncan to realign his thinking about literary history to include more of European literatures. This was an important turning because it came at a time when Olson and his thinking in "Projective Verse" were having a profound impact on Duncan's thinking and poetry. Duncan writes in "Figures of Speech":

> It were a good thing to begin a book with Blake's beginnings: HEAR THE VOICE OF THE BARD! for it is the imagination who listens then—but the Bard is the voice of the listener, who hears, sees, the ancient trees, the Holy Word walking there, crying. And if Present, Past & Future were to appear then, three daughters of Chronos, sisters, in neo-classical gowns, were his personifications, it were a good thing. (D 102)

Knowing full well he is distorting Blake's view, Duncan changes present, past, and future into the daughters of Chronos, goddesses and personifications of time; then he announces with the line "RETURN . . . THE MOON RISES FROM THE SLUMBEROUS MASS":

> Then: and this is for me the full splendor of poetry in which we blindly see—the fallen light is renewed and the universe of Otherness is entire. Earth rises out of Earth, and angelic personification, being of light. The throngs of Beings rise up, vapours of daybreak as from the dewy grass, and this is a choir of voices. Above old Nobodaddy: below, three young girls, Seasons, or Hours, or Graces, or what they will. But beyond, and sweeping the mind clear—the image of Truth new born. The heart springs up, and we see Him, a babe in flames of joyous liberation. 'YOUTH OF DELIGHT COME HITHER, AND SEE THE OPENING MORN' Blake cries.
>
> We see the cut by Blake. Two maidens bend over a form, a naked man's. It is the Adam, and the Ancient of Days revives him with a pitcher of water; but it

> is THE Baptism, not a baptism, it is THE Water, not water. And on the Maker's robe Blake has inscribed "IT IS RAISED A SPIRITUAL BODY." (D 103)

Switching from the illuminations for the "Introduction" to *Songs of Innocence*, to the illuminations for "Infant Joy," to "The Voice of the Ancient Bard" for a quotation, and finally to "To Tirzah" near the end of *Songs of Experience*, Duncan again illustrates the process of moving into attunement with Blake's vision, modifying it, and then projecting his own version outward as an illustration that "it is thru language that we can imagine the universe" (D 103). Furthermore, as the following poem, "Metamorphosis," which enacts the changes discussed in "Figures of Speech," shows, the universe imagined in language is not, for him, an absolute truth, "but imagined, bogus eternities of the poetic mind" (D 104), or fictive versions of the grand poem.

In creating his visionary world, Blake, avoiding the confinements of previous systems, set a limit to the imagination as Jesus, "the Divine / Humanity" (J III: 70, 19–20): Duncan, rejecting final limits, allows his imagination free interplay with every variety of order—scientific, poetic, natural—because all are aspects of a cosmic order which he both makes and discovers. He agrees with Blake in "All Religions Are One": "The Religions of all Nations are derived from each Nation's different reception of the Poetic Genius which is everywhere call'd the Spirit of Prophecy" (E 2). All versions of the poetic genius have imaginative validity, but none stands as the definitive system. Each is an approximation, a version of the poetic genius entertained as valid with the later full awareness that its validity rests in the authenticity of the imaginative processes flowing in tune with primal energies. "We must make it up," Duncan tells us, "in order to make it real." [6] Making (in the sense of *poiein*) sanctifies the office of the poet, who, in the discharge of his duties, issues propositions rising out of the cosmic design. "The Fictive proposition," Duncan reminds us, "is also visionary reality" (T&L 39). And the visionary reality reveals itself to Duncan, as for Blake, "in minutely organized Particulars" (J III: 55, 62). The daily events of the household, the garden, the kitchen come into his poetry as participants in a grand drama of emerging designs that he lives in and reveals. He is the lover of reality, and the creator of the reality he loves.

> The Imagination raises images of what a man is or what a woman is again and again in order to come into the shape of our actual life; or it seems in order that we come to live in terms of imagined being where we act not in our own best interest but in order to create fate or beauty or drama.[7]

While Blake saw in Dante's *Divine Comedy* a betrayal of the spirit of prophecy for political purposes and a debased use of the structures of

Thomistic logic as a means of arriving at a logical visionary truth, Duncan takes Dante's poem as one of his gospels of poetry. He writes in *The Sweetness and Greatness of Dante's Divine Comedy*:

> With Dante, I take the literal, the actual, as the primary ground. We ourselves are literal, actual beings. This is the hardest ground for us to know, for we are *of* it—not outside, observing, but inside, experiencing. It is, finally, I believe, the only ground for us to know; for it is Creation, it is the Divine Presentation, it is the language of experience whose words are immediate to our senses; from which our own creative life takes fire, *within which* our own creative life takes fire. This creative life is a drive towards the reality of Creation, producing an inner world, an emotional and intellectual fiction, in answer to our awareness of the creative reality of the whole. If the world does not speak to us, we cannot speak with it. If we view the literal as a matter of mere fact, as the positivist does, it is mute. But once we apprehend the literal as a language, once things about us reveal depths and heights of meaning, we are involved in the sense of Creation ourselves, and in our human terms, this is Poetry, Making, the inner Fiction of Consciousness.[8]

Creating an inner fiction of consciousness out of actual reality is a central proposition in Duncan's poetry. To allow the appearance of this consciousness the imagination must be free from "the mind-forg'd manacles" (E 27) of man's solidification of the orders of thinking, poetics, and politics. "If the doors of perception were cleansed," Blake tells us, "every thing would appear to man as it is, infinite" (MHH 14), and Duncan agrees, adding that the process of breaking down determinations of sight and feeling, of struggling with restrictions to seek openness, energizes one with the vital processes of poetry itself. After the mind has cleared away its hindrances, creation begins. "Form," he says, "to the mind possessed by convention, is significant in so far as it shows control. What has nor rime nor reason is a bogie that must be dismissed from the horizons of mind. It is a matter of rules and conformities, taste, rationalizations and sense." [9] Conventional literary structures found in handbooks of poetics untransformed by a new imagination predetermine thought and feeling, forcing the life out of the poem and leaving only a Urizenic tablet. "Poetry Fetter'd, Fetters the Human Race! " (J I: 3) Blake tells us, and Duncan:

> The poem
> feeds upon thought, feeling, impulse,
> to breed itself,
> a spiritual urgency at the dark ladders leaping
>
> This beauty is an inner persistence
> toward the source

striving against (within) down-rushet of the river,
 a call we heard and answer
in the lateness of the world
 primordial bellowings
from which the youngest world might spring.

(OF 50)

Duncan emphasizes the idea that the poet struggles with and against the emergencies of the poem. "But there remains the deepest drive of the artist, a yearning to participate in the pedagogy again and again. In the orders of the poem the poet is commanded by necessities of a form that will not be turned to exemplify moral or aesthetic preconceptions" (T&L 22). As he writes in "Passages 32," "The Four Directions / must be let loose make it new, / the Human Mind loose" (T 6). The poet, as Blake says, must cast off "the rotten rags of Memory by Inspiration . . . Bacon, Locke and Newton" (M II: 41, 4–5) and announce the spiritual urgency to live without external or abstract restrictions in the particularity of the emergence of a divine vision and form. His business is to create.

The urgency to keep imaginative freedom led both Blake and Duncan to condemn abstraction in religion and tyranny in politics. Blake denounced the Deists at the beginning of Chapter 3 of *Jerusalem* because they neglected the mysteries of the supernatural, and replaced the inspiration of the New Testament with sterile reason and a regulated universe following fixed natural laws. "The deceits of Natural Religion" (M II: 36, 25) removed God from nature and suggested "Worshipping the Material / Humanity" (J IV: 90, 65–66) in his place. In his own time Duncan cries out against a similar attack on the Scriptures. In his championing of old tales from myth and folklore he says: "Rationalizing scientists have conducted a war against fairytales and phantasies. Myth can be allowed as an element of personal expression in creative art, but myth as an inherited lore of the soul-way of Man has been put aside" (T&L 27). He specifies Rudolf Bultmann's manifesto *New Testament and Mythology* as the most egregious example of "demythologizing" the Bible, which is now "cleared of those gnostic and fictional elements in which man's intuitions and imaginations of his relationship to the cosmic myth are embodied" (T&L 12). Ruled by reason man loses the immediacy of God; directed by a purely humanistic message in the New Testament man loses touch with the myths that make immediate the primal drives of existence.

As Blake thought political tyranny a result of the fallen state, and war religion gone mad, so Duncan sees in contemporary politics, especially the war policies of the Johnson and Nixon administrations, the imagination gone rotten, the surfacing of ancient Mithraic cults, and satanic aggression.

Blake hoped in *America: A Prophecy* and *The French Revolution* that liberty would overthrow political bondage and announce a new age of freedom. Duncan too longs for freedom and "the community of every thing . . . in the great household" (BB 79) in the series of poems "Of the War (Passages 22–27)," while he deplores the horrible domination of the present political and economic systems:

> In the streets of Santo Domingo Herod's hosts again
>
> to exterminate the soul of the people go
>
> leaving behind them the dirty papers,
> torn books and bodies . . .
>
> (BB 78)

And the soldiers have gone to Southeast Asia under the burden of lies and the betrayal of freedom, for profit and greed:

> The monstrous factories thrive upon the markets of the war,
> and, as never before, the workers in armaments, poisond
> gasses and engines of destruction, ride
> high on the wave of wages and benefits. Over all,
> the monopolists of labor and the masters of the swollen
> ladders of interest and profit survive.
>
> The first Evil is that which has power over you.
>
> (BB 115)

But especially in "Up Rising, Passages 25," Duncan invokes Blake:

> As Blake saw America in figures of fire and blood raging,
> . . . in what image ? the ominous roar in the air,
> the omnipotent wings, the all-American boy in the cockpit
> loosing his flows of napalm
>
> (BB 81)

And later he comments:

> Blake looking into the beginning of the American Revolution saw the Revolution of the States as belonging to the drama of the deep sickness of Europe "where the horrible darkness is impressed with reflections of desire." Blake's vision is of confusion in intents and powers that strikes true to the confusion in which America was born. At first seeing Washington, Franklin, Paine as heroes rising in the flames of unfulfilled desire, rising to liberate Man from his bonds

> of repression, Blake came in his lifetime to see Washington as he saw Napoleon, as a "heroic villain," for following the subsidence of the American and French Revolutions came no liberation of Man's nature from the external repressions of social law or the internal repressions of the superego, as we would call it.[10]

In calling up Blake, Duncan reaches toward the point that "a new order is a contention in the heart of existing orders," or that he sees the forms of his poetry as growing out of cosmic orders and existing in them. He proposes the evolution of social and political forms in the Darwinian sense of continual struggle and adaptation, and understands, as he thinks Blake did of an earlier period of American history, the present condition of tyranny as an event in the universal struggle of contrary states which will give rise to new orders of the imagination. "This," he concludes, "is the grievous impatience and the ecstatic patience we are fired by as we apprehend in all the disorders of our personal and social life the living desire and intent at work towards new orders." [11] But like Blake, Duncan realizes that war and corruption are the necessary contraries which not only reveal man's true nature but also engage him in the empowered contraries of universal energy.

In both Blake and Duncan, the tensions between contrary states motivate the shift from formless life of the vision to the mythological formulations that contain the vision in poetic form. The main difficulty of the visionary poet is how to transcribe into the morphology of language the wonder seen in the instantaneous flash of perception. From the early presentation in *The Book of Thel* and *Songs of Innocence*, Blake cast and recast portions of his myth in changing relationships until he propounded Albion as a humanizing center in the perfected form of *Jerusalem.* And in the process of repetition in poem after poem, he transformed simple figures into multiphasic symbols of both the original impulse and the historical characteristics of cosmic reality. Blake evolved, out of the process of searching for an adequate expression of the vision that always existed in the grand universal poem but had no form, a complex mythology which is internally coherent, referentially consistent, and founded on the interaction between the states of innocence and experience.

"In my Brain are studies & Chambers fill'd with books & pictures of old," Blake wrote to John Flaxman, "which I wrote & painted in ages of Eternity before my mortal life; & these works are the delight & Study of Archangels." [12] To a mind which had penetrated to the origins of mythological genesis, all books and pictures were simply variations and modifications of the origins. In the major prophecies, features from many fields can be identified. The New Testament is as present as the influence of alchemy in the furnaces of Los (the athanor), in Urizen's gold and Tharmas's silver. Albion resembles the Adam Kadman of the Kabbalah; the dispersion of the energy of the stars in the minds and affairs of men can be found in the writings of Jacob Boehme; the distinction between the states of eternity and materiality (generation) is a commonplace of the Gnostic mysteries, as is the division into the sexes as a sign of the fall. This is to say nothing about the appearances of Plato, Swedenborg, Milton, Newton, Bacon, and Locke as either positive or negative forces in the poems. In his re-vision of the literature of the mysteries, Blake appropriated to himself images and ideas that were coincident with his visionary attunement, and when he recast them into his poetry, the visionary literature was not so much a deposit of sources as it was a confirmation of his own position. These images and ideas were not his, actually, but eternal projections from cosmic origins, fictive presentations of the grand poem. In collecting the divergent parts of this universal language of the mysteries, and fixing it to the centrality of his vision of the fall and redemption of Albion, Blake performed the basic mythopoetic act. In this visionary world, which is eternity, all images and ideas exist simultaneously. Blake tried to assimilate and compress as many of these as he could, giving them the special organization of his personal feelings and relationships. The stunning message of *Jerusalem* comes in the first two lines: "Of the Sleep of Ulro! and of the passage through / Eternal Death!" (J I: 4, 1–2). In the first three chapters of the poem Blake enacts the process of evoking eternity by repeating three times the central sacrifice of Luvah and death (division) of Albion, in different contexts; and by the contextual variations demonstrates the process by which this vision of the fall counts for all visions of the fall. The fourth chapter presents the final integration and the appearance of Jerusalem, the union of divine vision. And this occurrence is given a very bold habitation in the geography, politics, and society of England.

> O lovely mild Jerusalem! O Shiloh of Mount Ephraim!
> I see the Gates of precious stones: thy Walls of gold & silver:
>
> . . . .
>
> Thy Bosom white, translucent coverd with immortal gems
> A sublime ornament not obscuring the outlines of beauty
> Terrible to behold for thy extreme beauty & perfection
> Twelve-fold here all the Tribes of Israel I behold
> Upon the Holy Land: I see the River of Life & Tree of Life
> I see the New Jerusalem descending out of Heaven
> Between thy Wings of gold & silver featherd immortal
> Clear as the rainbow, as the cloud of the Suns tabernacle
>
> (J IV: 85, 21–22; 86, 14–21)

In this highly scriptural poem the actual geography of England and the spiritual geography of the Bible are combined. The poem achieves its form by demonstrating the process of bringing together elements of great diversity in the visionary mix of the imagination, and then projecting outward into the known locality of English shires the new version of the sequence of the fall and redemption as the central act of the human condition.

Blake's prophecy of mythological reality reaches into the core of Duncan's vision and practice of poetry. His early poetry turned on the continuing struggle between the longing for love—the jealousy and tormenting selfhood involved in that longing—and the full possession of love's company—the loss of selfhood and the union involved in that company. In such poems as "The Years as Catches" (FD 15), "An Apollonian Elegy" (FD 25), and "An Imaginary War Elegy" (FD 132), Duncan plays the part of Psyche, who, like a forelorn poet, searches after this form of love, performs the drama of Los-Enitharmon, in his unsuccessful search for love. For being possessed by love releases him into the energies of primal love, as "The Venice Poem" shows. In the Orphic theogony, Eros is the first form, and the creator of all forms; and in the visionary ambience of this god of love, Duncan's imagination moves with the first energies, from which all forms spring. "A Poem Beginning with a Line by Pindar" (OF 62) describes the entrance into the visionary core, which becomes a return to the Palace of Eros, a habitation for the visionary self in the presence of the highest achievements of the creative imagination. The Palace, with its inexhaustible display of magnificent images and sounds, is the imagination's storehouse, its reservoir of memory. He finds there a full supply of images and figures to weave into the designs of his poetry, for he combines the occupations of Los and Luvah. Living in the Palace represents a return to the state of innocence, to the period of his own childhood when fairy tales and the old stories were as real as daily events. Dreams and memory have high places in Duncan's poetry because they bring from the unconscious mind images and areas of experience he thought impossible or lost, and return them to the conscious mind. And in praising memory as the matrix of fictions, Duncan departs from Blake:

> Mnemosyne, they named her, the
>   Mother with the whispering
>   feathered wings. Memory,
> the great speckled bird who broods over the
>   nest of souls, and her egg,
>   the dream in which all things are living,
> I return to, leaving my self.

(BB 10)

But, in another sense, Mnemosyne could be taken as a metaphor for positing the origin and genesis of poetry in the universal mind. When Duncan enters the power of memory as a place of genesis, he leaves himself, he avoids the terrible restrictions of possessed selfhood and enters a holy realm of poetry and love.

But form remains the preeminent concern of Duncan's poetry. He says, again asserting the force of contraries, "I have come to think of Poetry more and more as a wrestling with Form to liberate Form" (T&L 16). For him the form of the poem is inherent in the melody and meaning of the words. The poem achieves its form by projecting its energy outward; the form is never imposed from the stock of convention. Duncan refuses to be enclosed in the fixed structures of tradition as he follows out the message of dreams, visions, and memory, all of which inform not control the flow of sound and association into the poem. The indigenous tension between the recalcitrance and the willingness of the music and associations forcing themselves up in the poem move the impulse into the area of language forms.

> It is not that poetry imitates but that poetry enacts in its order the order of first things, as just here in the consciousness, they may exist, and the poet desires to penetrate the seeming of style and subject matter to that most real where there is no form that is not content, no content that is not form.[13]

To contain his unique vision Blake created his multiphasic myth and a method of presentation in the prophecies which is neither epic nor narrative, but a composite organization which discovers its own structures. And so Duncan, following the line of the rebels against convention, designs a notion of form which eliminates the terrific problems of the split between form and content, and which declares itself as a projection of primordial energies.

The vision of the mythological reality and the drive to create a fiction of consciousness inform Duncan's poetry. And here Duncan becomes Blake's contemporary voice. While Blake saw certain *truth* in the vision of the imagination as Jesus, and redemption, which trumpets the end of time, as the principal event of human existence, Duncan sees this pattern as only one example of many possible explanations of man's part in the cosmic household. In Duncan's play, "Adam's Way," for example, he puts forward the Altantean dream of the perfect time before the fall as a basis of presentation. The fall occurs, and then it is necessary to repair the divisions and separations, in a Gnostic sense, brought on with the state of experience, the state when materiality appears. Change enters and becomes dominant. Erda's speech summarizes the central concerns of the play.

I heard the names of Man
ring down the chambers of a dream,
as if from round to round
of that great shell Time is, where
elves and shadows build eternal halls,
Moon and Man and Woman out of Man
rang Change and Change
and Night was figured with a soul.

His name is Hell
and Heaven too. I heard the names of Man
boom in every cell as if it were
a waiting room where frightend creatures
stood at bay before
a door in creation or at
the breaking of some day, a dragon's egg.

His name is Love.
And, What is Love? I said.
I heard the creaking of a step
and heard the beating of a heart.
All innocence from its shade had fled.
All single being was torn apart.

(R&B 142)

The thinking here is very close to the Orc cycles set out by Blake in "The Mental Traveller," for both poets understand the processes of the universal contraries as appearing and reappearing in multiple variations, and in cycles.

In another way, Duncan is aware, as Blake was, of the major scientific, literary, and religious achievements of his time, and, while retaining a sense of the holiness of all creation, incorporates these achievements into his poetics. But unlike Blake, Duncan has the privilege of greater freedom: where Blake struggled against the codified doctrines of Newton, Locke, or Swedenborg, Duncan assumes that these doctrines are no longer codified, and that they have become possibilities of imaginative fictions not threats to the imagination itself. Especially in "The Passages Poems"—a sequence without closure—he champions a kind of poetry which entertains multiple perspectives, multiple possibilities of explaining the genesis of myth, and multiple meanings without seeking a final solidity of belief. He writes: "I number the first to come one, but they belong to a series that extends in an area larger than my work in them. I enter the poem as I entered my own life, moving between an initiation and a terminus I cannot name" (BB v). In this series of poems, which Duncan calls "grand collage" (BB vii), he sorts through a startling variety of mythological lore, classical literatures, Gnostic, Orphic, and theosophical texts, and modern literatures, to find the fitting examples of his vision of form. Duncan has gone to the same sources Blake did and found the same vitality there—the records and images of the manifestations of the universal imagination. But Duncan, following the leads of Ezra Pound in *The Spirit of Romance*, also finds affinities in nineteenth- and twentieth-century writing, so his mixture becomes thicker. "The Passages Poems," as significant an assertion of open form as Blake's closed form in *Jerusalem*, give a local habitation for Duncan's vision of the emergence of form out of the contrary tensions of patience and impatience by spreading out a chrestomathy composed of gleanings from his reading and from his imitations of past poetries—of Dante, Shakespeare, Milton, Shelley, Blake, Boehme, H. D., Gertrude Stein, for examples. And in this fictive, mythological design, Duncan acknowledges the possible salvation of mankind, for in the imaginary geography of his poetry which he has created as a habitation for his perceiving self amid the struggles of holy powers, he, like Blake, reaches out to a prophecy of a state when corruption, tyranny, and convention will give way to the union of all men in blessed communion:

> Children of Kronos, of the Dream beyond death,
> secret of a Life beyond our lives,
> having their perfection as we have
>
> their bodies a like grace, a music, their minds a joy, abundant
>
> foliate, fanciful in its flowering
>
> come into these orders as they have ever come, stand
>
> as ever, where they are acknowledged,
> against the works of unworthy men, unfeeling judgments and
> cruel deeds.
>
> (T 24)

Notes

1. This essay, of course, relies on a great deal of previous Blake scholarship: Northrop Frye, *Fearful Symmetry: A Study of William Blake* (Princeton: Princeton Univ. Press, 1947); David Erdman, *Blake: Prophet against Empire* (Princeton: Princeton Univ. Press, 1954); E. D. Hirsch, Jr., *Innocence and Experience: An Introduction to Blake* (New Haven: Yale Univ. Press, 1964); Harold Bloom, *Blake's Apocalypse: A Study in Poetic Argument* (Garden City, N. Y.: Doubleday, 1963); Robert F. Gleckner, *The Piper and the Bard: A Study of William Blake* (Detroit: Wayne State

Univ. Press, 1959); Hazard Adams, *William Blake: A Reading of the Shorter Poems* (Seattle: Univ. of Washington Press, 1963); Milton O. Percival, *William Blake's Circle of Destiny* (New York: Columbia Univ. Press, 1938); David V. Erdman and John E. Grant, eds., *Blake's Visionary Forms Dramatic* (Princeton Univ. Press, 1970); Stuart Curran and Joseph Anthony Wittreich, Jr., eds., *Blake's Sublime Allegory: Essays on "The Four Zoas," "Milton," and "Jerusalem"* (Madison: Univ. of Wisconsin Press, 1973).

2. References to the following books by Duncan will appear in the text under the appropriate abbreviations: *The First Decade: Selected Poems 1940–1950* (London: Fulcrum Press, 1968) as FD; *Derivations: Selected Poems 1950–1956* (London: Fulcrum Press, 1968) as D; *The Truth and Life of Myth: An Essay in Essential Autobiography* (1968; reprint ed., Freemont, Mich.: Sumac Press, 1972) as T&L; *The Opening of the Field* (New York: Grove Press, 1960) as OF; *Roots and Branches* (New York: Scribner's, 1964) as R&B; *Bending the Bow* (New York: New Directions, 1968) as BB; *Tribunals* (Los Angeles: Black Sparrow Press, 1970) as T.

3. Robert Duncan, *The Years as Catches: First Poems (1939–1946)* (Berkeley: Oyez, 1966), p. x.

4. Robert Duncan, "Two Chapters from H. D.," *Triquarterly* 12 (Spring 1968): 69, 70.

5. Robert Duncan, "Man's Fulfillment in Order and Strife," *Caterpillar* 8/9 (1969): 237.

6. Robert Duncan, *Caesar's Gate: Poems 1949–1950 with Paste-Ups by Jess* (Berkeley: Sand Dollar, 1972), p. xii.

7. Robert Duncan, "The H. D. Book. Part Two: Nights and Days, Chapter 9," *Chicago Review* 30(3) (Winter 1979): 39.

8. Robert Duncan, *The Sweetness and Greatness of Dante's Divine Comedy* (San Francisco: Open Space, 1965), n.pg.

9. Robert Duncan, "Ideas of the Meaning of Form," *Kulchur* 4 (1961): 61.

10. Duncan, "Fulfillment," p. 243.

11. Ibid., pp. 229, 249.

12. *The Letters of William Blake*, ed. Geoffrey Keynes (London: Rupert Hart-Davis, 1968), p. 42.

13. Robert Duncan, "Towards an Open Universe," in *Poets on Poetry*, ed. Howard Nemerov (New York: Basic Books, 1966), p. 138.

Alicia Ostriker

Blake, Ginsberg, Madness, and the Prophet as Shaman

> The central activity of the shaman is ecstasy at the wish of his clients, and some have inferred from this that he is a psychopath.[1]

In 1948, while a student at Columbia, living in Harlem, and depressed over a failed love affair with Neal Cassady, Allen Ginsberg experienced a series of visions precipitated by reading William Blake's *Songs of Innocence and of Experience*. The first began with an auditory hallucination of Blake's voice reciting "Ah Sunflower" and "The Sick Rose," modulated into a blissful sense of God's omnipresence, and concluded with Ginsberg's promise to himself that he "never forget, never renege, never deny" what he had seen,[2] coupled with a certainty that his vocation had been confirmed: "from now on I'm chosen, blessed, sacred poet . . . and I'll be faithful for the rest of my life." [3] "Almost everything I've done since has those moments as its motif," Ginsberg told one interviewer in 1965,[4] and another ten years later that "the voice of Blake . . . is the voice I have now." [5] A second vision took place in the Columbia bookstore. While leafing through Blake, "I was in the eternal place once more." The other people in the store appeared to him initially as animals, grotesque and absurd, but then as secretly enlightened beings. He realized that everyone was subject to "a hardening, a shutting off of the perception of desire and tenderness which everybody *knows* and which is the very structure of . . . the atom," and again experienced a sense of resolve: "the problem then was, having attained realization, how to safely manifest it and communicate it" (WW 308–310). Ginsberg's third vision was one of terror, God turned devil, which he associated with Blake's phrase "gates of wrath," and from which he spiritually retreated (WW 311).

During Ginsberg's travels in India in 1962–1963, "a lady saint . . . told me to take Blake for my guru." A guru, living or dead, is the figure by whom one is initiated into the spiritual life, and "I apparently was initiated by

Blake. . . ." (WW 300). At approximately the same time, the attachment to Blake seems to have become a sort of captivity, as Ginsberg indicates when explaining the renunciation experience recorded in "The Change," written in 1962:

> There was a cycle that began with the Blake vision which ended on the train in Kyoto when I realized that to attain the depth of consciousness that I was seeking when I was talking about the Blake vision . . . I had to . . . renounce it . . . give up this continual churning through process of yearning back to a visionary state. (WW 316–317)

But renunciation does not prevent him subsequently from recording his own settings of *Songs of Innocence and of Experience*, singing them at poetry readings, referring to Blake as a major influence in interviews, and employing Blake as a gloss to explain other artists. Cézanne's concern with optics, for example, the *petite sensation* of which Cézanne wrote in a late journal and which in part inspired the telegraphic style of "Howl,"

> has something to do with Blake: *with* not *through* the eye—"You're led to believe a lie when you see with not through the eye." He's seeing through his eye. One can see *through* his canvas to God, really, is the way it boils down. (WW 296)

What exactly does Ginsberg, who calls himself a "Buddhist Jew" and who acknowledges dozens of influences, from Whitman, Williams, and Pound to Kerouac and Snyder, from Cézanne to jazz, from Hebrew lamentation to Sanskrit prayer to haiku and tanka, take from Blake? One might run through Ginsberg's work and find innumerable allusions, quotations, borrowings of images, some more trivial, some more profound. An initial attempt to assimilate his visions by writing transcendental mystic verse in rhymed stanzas failed; the shallow rhymed poems of 1948–1950 later collected under the title *The Gates of Wrath*—poems to which Williams administered the fatherly rebuke "in this mode perfection is basic," which sent the young Ginsberg from poeticisms to prose jottings and from lyric to breath-rhythms—imitate a manner, not an essence.[6] Ginsberg's temporary belief that "Blake's instructions meant delve right into the terror . . . annihilate the ordinary consciousness by death" [7] is skewed Blake, or at any rate Blake with a heavy overlay of post-Rimbaud matter. Decades later, such bits as the catch-reference to "Beulah" or "Princeton in Eternity" in *The Fall of America* are space-filling throwaways. On the other hand, for example, the transformation by imagination of an ashen sunflower into "a perfect excellent lovely sunflower existence," and the understanding of its parallel to the self, is genuinely Blakean work—conflation of the earlier poet's sunflower image with the moral behind "To the Accuser Who Is the God of This World." Ginsberg's "revolution of the sexy lamb" set against the illusion-grinding "mills" in "Death to Van Gogh's Ear" authentically illustrates another set of Blakean contraries.[8]

Like Blake, Ginsberg freely uses the term "prophecy" to refer to his own work or to work which he admires, and it is on this point that I want to concentrate. The idea of the prophetic role clearly forms the core of Blake's influence on Ginsberg, and he is the only one of Blake's modern disciples who publicly assumes such a mantle or burden; doubtless Yeats would have if he could have. Moreover, to investigate the parallels between Blake's and Ginsberg's interpretations of the prophetic role sheds new light on the older poet as well as the younger—which is itself a sign of the validity of their relationship. The eye altering alters all: as Milton undergoes a metamorphosis when we see him through Blake's eyes, so Blake alters in the perspective of Ginsberg's discipleship.

To say that William Blake and Allen Ginsberg are poet-prophets means a few rather precise things. First, it means that they experience personal visions of a potential divine life for humanity, while in a state which normal persons in our society would call trance or hallucination, and which in other ages has been called revelation or illumination; second, that they commit themselves as writers to the establishment of such life on earth, and dedicate their work to this end rather than to what is usually understood as literary success.[9] Ginsberg's "vow to illuminate mankind" parallels Blake's "I will not cease from Mental Fight" as a declaration of vocation (K 13; M I: 1, 13). Third: their writings fall in radical opposition to conventional religious, political, and social institutions, as well as defying literary decorum. But both poets deviate radically from the traditional prophetic mode, and in the same direction.

The fourteen canonical prophets of the Old Testament, as well as the vast majority of Christian evangelists and religious writers before our century, employ two persuasive strategies. If the children of God will return, God through the tongue of the prophet promises blessing, His love, a redeemed land. If they persist in evil, God condemns, curses, and will destroy them. Blake and Ginsberg, committed to the promise, avoid the threat. Like Isaiah, they hate and despise our offerings—the human sacrifices by which we propitiate deities of church and state. Yet they fail to announce imminent punishment, to divide mankind into good and evil, or to accept the validity of moral terms which have been the consistent weaponry of Western religion. The powerful rhetoric of a just and angry God rests unused, as it were, at their feet, and they are alike in considering the violence and destructiveness in history to be man's work, not God's. Yet if the prophet's inspiration and hence correction of the world cannot rely on the *curse*, on what can it rely?

Blake, and Ginsberg after him, pursues a more primitive and mysterious strategy than that of moral division, the intent of which is the healing and integration of mankind. In Blake this strategy occurs in a somewhat oblique form. In Ginsberg it finds more open declaration. In both, the key to healing appears to be madness, and the prophet appears to behave like a shaman. I do not suggest that Blake ever heard of the term "shamanism," or that Ginsberg uses it in any strict anthropological sense. I shall delineate a pattern.

I

The idea of madness takes three distinct forms in Blake's writings. At times it is a purely negative term, but falsely applied by the world to men of vision. At other times, madness signifies mental illness in a more or less modern sense, but everyone is mad. On still other occasions, ambivalently related to the first two, madness may be a necessary route to sanity.

Early in *The Marriage of Heaven and Hell*, Blake's visionary tourist drops a casual remark on "the enjoyments of Genius; which to Angels look like torment and insanity" (MHH 5). This is a jab at the angels, and at Swedenborg, who made the mistake of conversing with them. Several parallel jabs occur in Blake's Notebook epigrams: "Thou callst me Madman but I call thee Blockhead" is typical (E 499). In the marginalia to Reynolds, Blake comments: "Reynolds's Opinion was that . . . all Pretence to Inspiration is a Lie & a Deceit . . . if it is a Deceit the Whole Bible is Madness" (E 632). *Public Address* asserts, to an invisible antagonist, "It is very true what you have said for these thirty two Years I am Mad or Else you are so. . . ." (E 562). And one of the inscriptions in *The Laocoon* says simply enough, "There are States in which all Visionary Men are accounted Mad Men. . . ." (E 271).

The idea that what the world considers mad is really the expression of inspiration, "the enjoyments of genius," becomes a major issue in *Milton*, which deals with the visionary man's struggle to combat doubt, from within and without, of vision's validity:

> . . . Whitefield & Westley; were they Prophets
> Or were they Idiots or Madmen?
>
> (M I: 22, 61–62)

> Calling the Human Imagination: which is the Divine Vision & Fruition
> In which Man liveth eternally: madness . . .
>
> (M II: 32, 19–20)

It comes to a head in Milton's ultimate oration:

> To bathe in the Waters of Life; to wash off the Not Human
> I come in Self-annihilation & the grandeur of Inspiration
> To cast off Rational Demonstration by Faith in the Saviour
> To cast off the rotten rags of Memory by Inspiration
> To cast off Bacon, Locke & Newton from Albions covering
> To take off his filthy garments, & clothe him with Imagination
> To cast aside from Poetry, all that is not Inspiration
> That it no longer shall dare to mock with the aspersion of Madness
> Cast on the Inspired, by the tame high finisher of paltry Blots,
> Indefinite, or paltry Rhymes; or paltry Harmonies.
>
> (M II: 41, 1–10)

These passages are transparently autobiographical. Their author burns with the personal anger of one who, according to *The Examiner* and general opinion, was "an unfortunate lunatic, whose personal inoffensiveness secures him from confinement." [10] These are the passages to which Blake's modern critics refer when they argue that Blake demonstrates "the sanity of genius and the madness of the commonplace mind." [11] But the question is not so clear-cut.

In a second sense, madness for Blake is an actual condition which, like the poet's metaphors of sleep, death, or disease, or "opacity" and "contraction," indicates mankind's pathological distance from divinity. It is a commonplace phenomenon throughout Blake's prophetic poems—that is, throughout the work in which the poet as narrator names and analyzes the sickness of humanity—and is not confined to commonplace minds. It strikes inspired and uninspired, just and unjust, alike. The early tyrant-figure Tiriel is possessed by "madness and dismay" (E 276). Women are driven to madness in *Visions of the Daughters of Albion* by loveless marriages (E 48). In *The French Revolution*, the last of seven prisoners in the Bastille is "Mad, with chains . . . and his ravings in winds are heard over Versailles" (E 284–285). Later in this poem we have an image of "Strength madden'd with slavery," and in one of the most rhythmically vivid lines in *America*, the fires of revolution suffer a counterattack of spiritual plagues, in which "Fury! rage! madness! in a wind swept through America" (E 55).

The Book of Urizen portrays Blake's tyrant God as tormented by "howlings & pangs & fierce madness" (U 5: 24) when he attempts to build mountains and hills to protect himself from his own void. To Los, Urizen is formless:

"the Perturbed Immortal mad raging" (U 8: 4). In *The Four Zoas*, the cities say their sons "are Mad / With wine of cruelty" (FZ I: 14, 19–20), and in both *The Four Zoas* and *Jerusalem*, the spectre—a figure for man's rationalism—"is in Every Man insane" (FZ VIIA: 84, 36; J II: 33, 4). Indeed, the spectre of Los, as he attempts to thwart Los's creative love for Albion, is a magnificent capsule portrait of paranoia. In *Milton* the usurping false artist Satan maddens the horses of the true artist Palamabron. And in *Jerusalem*, Blake shows what it means to be driven to madness by his portrait of the eponymous heroine, who in the poem's opening movements is beautifully lucid, and defends love and forgiveness against the hysteria of Albion and the self-righteousness of Vala. Subjected to numberless rejections and insults, falling into Babylonian captivity, Jerusalem too becomes "Insane" and "raves upon the winds hoarse, inarticulate" (J III: 60, 44).

In each of these cases, Blake represents madness as the inevitable result of proud reason attempting to impose itself repressively over energy. Man's rationality provokes and precipitates man's insanity, and his condition is treated by Blake with the utmost seriousness as one of wildness, chaos, and dislocation. We should remark that modern psychology from Freud to Laing, insofar as it treats mental disorder as psychological rather than chemical in origin, consistently explains it as Blake does: pressure of a "higher" principle of order causes outbursts of a "lower" principle of disorder. For Blake, madness in this sense is an essential condition of life in a fallen world.

For hints of a third sort of madness in Blake, we turn back to his first known work on this theme, the lyric called "Mad Song" in *Poetical Sketches*, where a singer in a Lear-like climate of "roaring winds" and "tempests," burdened with unexplained "griefs," "sorrow," and "howling woe," rejects the comforts of east and daylight, and "Like a fiend in a cloud" crowds after night (E 407). Why does he do so? Bloom sees the poem as "intellectual satire" and the singer as a wilfully deranged, self-deceiving escapist somewhat like Cowper or Collins;[12] yet the subjective rather than third-person rendering of madness, and the element of voluntary choice suggested in the poem, are unique.

Another curiosity is Blake's own vision of Cowper, recorded in the Annotations to Spurzheim's *Observations on Insanity* late in his life, around 1819. Cowper told Blake: "You retain health & yet are as mad as any of us all—over us all—made as a refuge from unbelief—from Bacon, Newton & Locke." In the same vision, Cowper declares: "O that I were insane always. . . . Can you not make me truly insane? . . . O that in the bosom of God I was hid" (E 652). Is it excessive to note that this has the rhythmic ring of "Would to God that all the Lord's people were Prophets"?

"Mad Song" does not explain itself, and the Cowper vision was a private statement, not intended for publication, whose directly positive view of madness recurs nowhere in Blake's writings. However, another anomaly appears at the opening of Night V in *The Four Zoas*. Los the eternal prophet, Blake's figure for man's imagination, has just finished in Night IV creating a body for the fallen and chaotically insane Urizen. In all Blake's versions of this story, as Los becomes a blacksmith who binds Urizen down to a solid and limited body, and simultaneously by the beat of his hammer creates both time and the meter of poetry, the tone is obsessive. Fixing a limit to Urizen's decline, Los himself declines. "Frightened with cold infectious madness," he "became what he beheld." Blake repeats with emphasis at the close of Night IV:

> terrifid at the shapes
> Enslavd humanity put on he became what he beheld
> He became what he was doing he was himself transformd
> (FZ IV: 52, 28; 53, 24; 55, 21–23)

The opening line of Night V is: "Infected Mad he dancd on his mountains high & dark as heaven." Both Los and Enitharmon become solid, opaque, and unexpansive. The fires of Los's exhausted creativity go out. But soon after, in a dismally midwinter scene, Enitharmon gives birth to a fiery Orc; revolution, child of prophecy, has been born.

The line "Infected Mad he dancd on his mountains high & dark as heaven" has not been explained. Stevenson suggests that the infection might be rabies.[13] A more interesting observation would be that Los, at this initial moment of his prophetic career on earth, resembles a shaman. He is performing as, in a multitude of primitive societies before religious specialization, the figure who is at once a priest, a poet, and a witch doctor performs, when he heals a diseased person by entering a state of autointoxication in which he dances wildly, chants ecstatically, and by so doing, retrieves a fugitive soul.

If Blake intends such an idea, he does not develop it further. Los does many other things, in *The Four Zoas, Milton,* and *Jerusalem*, but he does not again go explicitly mad. However, he builds furnaces, and his furnaces *rage*.

Rage, in the early nineteenth century, was among the richest words available to a poet. It could mean madness, mania; anger, indignation; sexual passion; unchecked violence (e.g., as in a raging battle, sea, or disease). Since 1600 the term had also been used to signify poetic or prophetic inspiration. Various forms of the word appear over 150 times in Blake's writings, usually in contexts which allow resonances of most or all of these meanings, although as a rule the central sense is either anger—as "the just man rages in the wilds"—or violence—as in "the raging of the stormy sea" which in *The Marriage of Heaven and Hell* is one of the "portions of eternity too great for the eye of man" (MHH 33, 36). This is an important and systematically used term in *The Four Zoas*. When Tharmas falls in Night I he becomes a raging sea, and is to be understood as continuing so, sometimes in the poem's foreground, sometimes in its background. Orc at birth has the form of a raging fire. In Night VIII Urizen lets loose "his mighty rage" in the form of war (FZ VIII: 100, 26), and almost simultaneously Los's furnaces begin to rage (FZ VIIIB: 113, 3)—as they will do throughout *Milton* as well. Thus at the outset of Night IX of *The Four Zoas*, subtitled "The Last Judgment," all four Zoas have become involved in "rage." The turning point of man's recovery comes when Urizen, amid cosmic upheaval, realizing his error, says, "Rage Orc Rage Tharmas Urizen no longer curbs your rage" (FZ IX: 121, 26). Nothing happens here to Orc and Tharmas, who have been raging without Urizen's permission. Instead, Urizen himself arises in radiant youth, shedding his snows and his aged mantle, and becomes what he originally was, not doubt but faith. Urizen's last judgment is a decision not to judge. The moment of mental capitulation to disorder and madness becomes the moment of regeneration from it.

Does the foregoing imply that the inspired man functions in Blake like a shaman to this world: that he absorbs its insanity, its mental disease, taking on the madness of fallen life as Christ takes on its sin? Blake does not overtly invite us to such a conclusion. Given the necessity of defending himself against "the aspersion of madness," he could not easily have done so. Nevertheless, he does what no prophet before him had done: not Isaiah, not Ezekiel, not Milton. Each of his three major epics is a descent into the sickness of our life, which is its mental sickness. In each, insanity is fully and completely imagined by the poet, in the activity of giving Error a body. In each, moreover, the poet violates normal laws of prosody and punctuation, normal expectations about time, space, and the consistency and distinguishability of characters, and normal rules of rational discourse. Blake announces in his explanation of the meter of *Jerusalem* that "every word and every letter is studied and put into its fit place; the terrific numbers are reserved for the terrific parts—the mild & gentle, for the mild & gentle parts, and the prosaic, for inferior parts. . . ." (J I: 3). We may note that the moments of poetic lucidity and order, in *The Four Zoas, Milton,* and *Jerusalem*, are consistently associated with visions of reintegration, while the ground tone remains one of psychic turbulence. It appears that like Los, the poet of these books must, in order to write them, become what he beholds. Blake observed of Milton that he was a true poet and therefore of the devil's party. We might observe of Blake that he is a true poet and therefore of the party of madness. Of course, each of these poems concludes—at the point when madness is most deeply realized—in healing. But if we ignore the texture of Blake's poetry, and its force, which is the force of irrationality, we ignore not only Blake's chief means of representing the human dilemma, but also the mode he chose for its solution.

II

Allen Ginsberg has written three major poems about insanity. "Howl," whose title is one of Blake's favorite words, deals with the insanity of "the best minds of my generation"; "Kaddish" with that of his mother; "The Fall of America" with that of his nation. The poet-prophet's activity follows a similar pattern in all these works. I shall examine the first, as I think it most clearly represents this activity in outline form—and is also most evidently Blakean—and discuss the others more briefly.

Part I of "Howl" opens:

> I saw the best minds of my generation destroyed by madness, starving hysterical naked,
> dragging themselves through the negro streets at dawn looking for an angry fix,
> angelheaded hipsters burning for the ancient heavenly connection to the starry dynamo in the machinery of night,
> who poverty and tatters and hollow-eyed and high sat up smoking in the supernatural darkness of cold-water flats floating across the tops of cities contemplating jazz,
> who bared their brains to Heaven under the El and saw Mohammedan angels staggering on tenement roofs illuminated.
>
> (H 9)

The poem moves here into its litany of "who's"—"who chained themselves to subways . . . who disappeared into the volcanoes of Mexico . . . who bit detectives in the neck and shrieked with delight . . . who plunged themselves under meat trucks looking for an egg." Ginsberg's anonymous heroes are social pariahs and criminals, guilty of sexual deviance and excess, self-destructiveness, drug use, political peculiarity, and habitual craving for hallucination. They have been "destroyed" by the vulnerability of their vitality, the insistence on impossible desires. As Ginsberg wrote to Richard Eberhart in 1956, when Eberhart had heard "Howl" recited and was impressed by its "spiritual quality":

> I am saying that what seems "mad" in America is our expression of natural ecstasy (as in Crane, Whitman) which suppressed, finds no social . . . validation from the outside and so the "patient" gets confused thinks he is mad and really goes off rocker.[14]

In Blakean terms we might say that these figures combine the chaos and self-destructiveness of Tharmas, the thwarted and distorted passion of Luvah-Orc, and the potential visionary imagination of Los—all the capacities of man, with the exception of reason, "raging" in an urban and national wilderness. As Part I nears its close, there are clustered references to the visual, verbal, and musical arts, and the litany concludes "with the absolute heart of the poem of life butchered out of their own bodies good to eat a thousand years."

For most of this section, after the initial "I saw," the first-person singular pronoun evaporates. The "I" releases itself, or is released, into its material. While the litany-structure and the long accretive periods imply, by association with liturgy, that the poet is a sacred figure, we have no sense of him as a controlled being apart, capable of observing, interpreting, judging, explaining. Instead of shaping, he appears to let himself be shaped, spontaneously and irrationally, by his visions. In other words, Ginsberg "becomes what he beholds." The madness of this reveals itself as a manic rush of language without logic, a dramatic violation of rules of prosody, punctuation, grammar, and syntax (e.g. "paint hotels," "purgatoried their torsoes"), and a violent (or casual) yoking together of elements which our reasonable mental habits keep asunder: the sacred and the profane, the realistic and surrealistic, a sense of comedy and a sense of tragedy:

> who threw their watches off the roof to cast their ballot for Eternity outside of Time, & alarm clocks fell on their heads every day for the next decade,
> who cut their wrists three times successively and unsuccessfully, gave up and were forced to open antique stores where they thought they were growing old and cried.
>
> (H 13–14)

Part II of "Howl" opens with a question:

> What sphinx of cement and aluminum bashed open their skulls and ate up their brains and imagination?
>
> (H 17)

The question's answer is "Moloch": the Canaanite god of fire to whom children were offered in sacrifice, and whose worship is condemned in *Leviticus*, 1 and 2 *Kings, Jeremiah, Amos*, and *Ezekiel*. In Blake, Moloch represents the obsessive human sacrifice of war, especially as connected with perversely suppressed sexuality. Ginsberg's Moloch likewise has this aspect, and is a broadly Urizenic figure for the inhumanity of a modern industrial and military state, exuding from reason:

> Moloch! Solitude! Filth! Ugliness! Ashcans and unobtainable
> dollars! Children screaming under the stairways! Boys
> sobbing in armies! Old men weeping in the parks!
> Moloch! Moloch! Nightmare of Moloch! Moloch the loveless!
> Mental Moloch! Moloch the heavy judger of men!
> Moloch the incomprehensible prison! Moloch the crossbone soulless jailhouse
> and Congress of sorrows! Moloch whose buildings are judgment; Moloch
> the vast stone of war! Moloch the stunned governments! . . .
> Moloch whose love is endless oil and stone! Moloch whose soul is electricity
> and banks! Moloch whose poverty is the specter of genius! Moloch
> whose fate is a cloud of sexless hydrogen! Moloch whose name is
> the Mind!
>
> (H 17)

Again the tone is at once hieratic and hysterical, as the source of madness is madly defined, and the definition becomes at once invocation and exorcism. In Blakean terms, Ginsberg is "giving a body to Error."

To do so, we find, is cathartic. After the manic clamor of Part I and the agonized roar of Part II, Part III of "Howl" brings us quite suddenly, like calm after storm, a normal speaking voice:

> Carl Solomon! I'm with you in Rockland
> where you're madder than I am
> I'm with you in Rockland
> where you must feel very strange. . . .
>
> (H 19)

And we realize that the poet who vanished from his poem after the opening "I saw," has coherently returned. "I'm with you." The voice is no longer wildly mad but calmly mad, tender, generous, loving, sympathetic, intimate, and joking: "I'm with you in Rockland / Where you've murdered your twelve secretaries / I'm with you in Rockland / Where you laugh at this invisible humor." Blake, for whom rock was a symbol of mental barrenness, would doubtless smile at the invisible humor of the name of New Jersey's state mental hospital.

The enactment of personal intimacy with a friend is crucial in "Howl" as it is in Blake. "I am in you and you in me," says the savior to Albion at the opening of *Jerusalem*. "I am a brother and friend" (J I: 4, 7, 18). But just as a reunion of the disunited can never be accomplished in Blake's poems until all the miserable consequences of division—between man and woman, man and man, man and God—are actualized, so in Ginsberg one must submit to Moloch in order to be released from him. And as Urizen's acceptance of "rage" in Tharmas and Orc is restorative, so is Ginsberg's smiling acceptance of his friend's madness. Having performed this act, Ginsberg can go on to the "Footnote to Howl," which begins:

> Holy! Holy! Holy! Holy! Holy! Holy! Holy! Holy! Holy!
> Holy! Holy! Holy! Holy! Holy! Holy!
> The world is holy! The soul is holy! The skin is holy! The nose
> is holy! The tongue and cock and hand and asshole holy!
> Everything is holy! everybody's holy! everywhere is holy!
> everyday is in eternity! Everyman's an angel!
>
> (H 21)

As in Blake, everything normally considered base or common must be celebrated as divine. More, what has previously been interpreted as monstrous by the poet himself may now be reinterpreted:

> Holy the solitudes of skyscrapers and pavements! Holy the
> cafeterias filled with the millions! Holy the mysterious
> rivers of tears under the streets!
>
> (H 21)

In a spurt of hilarity, even Moloch can now be included:

> Holy time in eternity holy eternity in time holy the clocks in space
> holy the fourth dimension holy the fifth International holy
> the Angel in Moloch!
>
> (H 21)

And finally,

> Holy the supernatural extra brilliant intelligent kindness of
> the soul!
>
> (H 22)

"Holy" is "howly," inverted. The act of the poet is complete. As in the conclusion of Blake's *Marriage*, "every thing that lives is Holy" because the poet has made himself, by a certain process, able to say so:

> The poem itself is an act of sympathy, not rejection. In it I am leaping *out* of a preconceived notion of social "values," following my heart's instincts, and

> exposing my true feelings—of sympathy and identification with the rejected, mystical, individual even "mad." . . . The criticism of society is that "society" is merciless. The alternative is private individual acts of mercy. The poem is one such.[15]

While neither "Kaddish" nor the *Planet News–Fall of America* sequences are as conspicuously Blakean as "Howl," Ginsberg continues and maintains his role as poet-prophet in these works, and extends its range. "Kaddish," the poet's poem of mourning and homage for his mad dead mother, conveys throughout its long narrative of humiliations—his mother's sickness and helplessness, his own, his family's, the half-truths of her Hitler-Hearst-Capitalists-Franco-Mussolini fantasies, her physical grossness, her flutterings among violence, idealism, and apathy, her hospitalizations, lobotomy, stroke—a paradoxical joy, which we can identify as the poet's joy in being able to identify with Naomi Ginsberg. Communist, madwoman, Jewish mother—as he draws her, she is, even more that his peers in "Howl," the prototype of an American nightmare. Neither does he romanticize Naomi as he does his friends. Nevertheless, he celebrates. Naomi remembered on the verge of death is addressed:

> O glorious muse that bore me from the womb, gave suck first
> mystic life & taught me talk and music, from whose pained
> head I first took Vision—
> Tortured and beaten in the skull—What mad hallucina-
> tions of the damned that drive me out of my skull to seek
> Eternity till I find Peace for Thee, O Poetry—and for all
> humankind call on the Origin
>
> (K 29)

It is she whose letter from her last hospital tells of the key in the window which is the poem's talismanic symbol for our ability to touch the divine world, as well as she who a few pages back was

> Naomi, Naomi—sweating, bulge-eyed, fat, the
> dress unbuttoned at one side—hair over brow, her
> stocking hanging evilly on her legs—screaming for
> a blood transfusion—one righteous hand upraised—
> a shoe in it—barefoot in the Pharmacy—
>
> (K 18)

The "Hymmnn" section after Part II of "Kaddish," like the footnote to "Howl," has been made possible by all that has come before. It includes God, "the world which He has made according to his will," the horrors of Naomi's life, and death itself, in its exclamatory "Blessed be . . . Blessed be!"

As in Blake's major poems, and as in "Howl," to accept is to redeem. There is also a resemblance between "Kaddish" and the most personal of Blake's long poems, *Milton*, a poem concerned with the passing on of prophetic inspiration from the dead to the living, during privileged revelatory moments. In "Kaddish," such a moment appears at the conclusion of Part III. The poet imagines his mother's death, and there is a possible echo of "O Earth O Earth return":

> only to have come to that dark night on iron bed by stroke when
> the sun gone down on Long Island
> and the vast Atlantic roars outside the great call of Being to
> its own
> to come back out of the Nightmare—divided creation—

He has "no tears" for this imagination of her death:

> But that the key should be left behind—at the window—the
> key in the sunlight—to the living—that can take
> that slice of light in hand—and turn the door—and look
> back see
> Creation glistening backwards to the same grave, size of universe,
> size of the tick of the hospital's clock on the archway over the
> white door—
>
> (K 33)

Part III concludes here, and the final two movements are movements of relinquishment, the "farewell" to his mother's body and soul, and the graveyard scene in which the shrieking crows—one remembers the larks in *Milton*—and the name of the Lord are one.

The "Poem of these States," which became *The Fall of America*, was planned by Ginsberg as an epic chronicle continuing the vein of *Planet News*,

> a poem including history . . . *dis*sociated thought stream . . . newspaper headlines and all the pop art of Stalinism and Hitler and Johnson and Kennedy and Vietnam and Congo and Lumumba and the South and Sacco and Vanzetti—whatever floated into one's personal field of consciousness and contact. And then to compose like a basket . . . (WW 317–318)

The two writers Ginsberg mentions in his *Paris Review* interview as sources for the "method" of this work are Blake and Burroughs, the former for his treatment of contemporary politics in *The French Revolution*, the latter for techniques of narrative dissociation. Both volumes are dark in tone, and *The Fall of America* is less "composed" than it is a series of notebook-written and tape-recorded footnotes to Ginsberg's spiritual and political travels during the bleak war years 1965–1971. Its formlessness constitutes a kind of surrender to what it records, the hydra of a debased political life expressed physically by a killing technology, spiritually by a poisoned mass media. Ginsberg acknowledges in at least one interview that his writing of late involved "Principally no cutting out":

> I do a lot of writing like that, so not all of it is as good, because not all of it is focussed, not all of it is tied together by some emotional feeling-center.[16]

Among the few critics who writes seriously of Ginsberg as a poet, Eric Mottram criticizes the repetitiousness, the "sloppy utterances," the insufficient concern for "rhythmic flair and language interest" of his '60s compositions, making exception only of "Wichita Vortex Sutra" and a few other pieces.[17] In another sense, one might argue that "no cutting out" is an extension of Ginsberg's characteristic insistence on compassion, the refusal to judge, the refusal to reject, simultaneous with the geographical extension of his subject.

In "Wichita Vortex Sutra," Ginsberg's most important single antiwar poem, he comes close not to the Blake of *The French Revolution*—who is confident and unambiguous both in his political sympathies and in his plot line—but to the Blake-Los of *Jerusalem*. Like Blake in that poem, Ginsberg finds himself identifying with, loving, and desperately desiring to save from its error, his nation, engaged in an unjust war which appals him. Like Blake, he dwells on places and place-names, personifying the heartland states of Kansas and Nebraska as Blake does the cathedral cities of Albion. His analysis of the pathos behind imperialist cruelty, like Blake's, stresses the rejection of sex and the dominion of what Blake calls the spectre and Ginsberg calls "television language" or "black language": the technology-oriented use of words without imagination, which enables "Vietcong losses leveling up three five zero zero / per month" to exist abstractly as a set of numerals (PN 117). His journey is a "search for the language" which will undo error, and the climax of the poem is Ginsberg's consciously "magic" declaration of the end of the war:

> this Act done by my own voice,
>   nameless Mystery—
> published to my own senses,
>   blissfully received by my own form
>   approved with pleasure by my sensations . . .
>
> . . . .

The War is gone,
Language emerging on the motel news stand,
the right magic
Formula, the language known
in the back of the mind before, now in black print
(PN 128–129)

Although the headlines in fact continue to print war news, for Ginsberg "the war is over now," and the understanding of the poem is that such declarations have the power to change the world, as white magic has power over black, and as imagination has power over illusion.

A typical piece in *The Fall of America* is called "A Vow":

I will haunt these States
with beard bald head
eyes staring out plane window,
hair hanging in Greyhound bus midnight
leaning over taxicab seat to admonish
an angry cursing driver
hand lifted to calm
his outraged vehicle
that I pass with the Green Light of common law.

Common Sense, Common law, common tenderness
& common tranquillity
our means in America to control the money munching
war machine, bright lit industry
everywhere digesting forests & excreting soft pyramids
of newsprint, Redwood and Ponderosa patriarchs
silent in Meditation murdered & regurgitated as smoke,
sawdust, screaming ceilings of Soap Opera,
thick dead Lifes, slick Advertisements
for Gubernatorial big guns
burping Napalm on palm rice tropic greenery.[18]

The imagery of destruction continues, but the promise to "haunt these States . . . decoding, deciphering" concludes the piece, dated 1966. Though diffused rather than focused, the emotional center of *The Fall of America* is still the poet-prophet's obligation to encounter spiritual ills intimately, graphically, and nonetheless tenderly. It would be difficult to find a document of equivalent political engagement in which the writer sympathizes as thoroughly as Ginsberg with forces which he conceives to be both horribly powerful and inhumanly evil—unless one turned to *Jerusalem*, and the portrait of Blake-Los struggling to save an Albion who is devoted to

"Eternal Death." America's Vietnam years mean to Ginsberg much what the years of the Napoleonic wars mean for Blake: a challenge to give a body to Error, a mental fight against self-doubt, the stubborn use of poetry to maintain a saving image of humanity.

III

The prophet of Old Testament tradition and the shaman of primitive culture have in common the capacity for visionary experience and the gift of verbal expression of it. Blake and Ginsberg alike deviate from the role of the prophet in their avoidance of the rhetoric of curse and punishment, their rejection of a god of wrath. By the same token, they approach the pattern of the shaman in their stress on healing rather than punishing, in their perception of their roles as *direct* agents of a healing which appears to be magically accomplished through the ecstatic personal engagement of the poet, and, finally, in their willingness to identify with the ills which they attempt to cure, even to the point of madness.

When the phenomenon of shamanism, which figured in religious life throughout primitive societies in Asia, North America, and Indonesia, was first discovered by Western investigators, the shaman was classified as a hysteric or epileptic—a person unfit for normal life. Mircea Eliade's exhaustive and pathbreaking study *Shamanism: Archaic Techniques of Ecstasy* insisted, to the contrary, that shamans were healthy, energetic, intelligent men, or that their possible psychic disorders were self-cured and transformed by their vocation; in other words, that "madness" was, for the shaman, converted to valuable social purposes. Eliade emphasizes the shaman's mystical capacities, his function as "the great specialist in the human soul,"[19] and the significance of the healing ceremony, during which the shaman "goes in search of the patient's fugitive soul, captures it, and makes it return to animate the body that it has left" (S 182), to the accompaniment of self-generated music, dance, and usually flamboyant narration:

> in order to extract the evil spirits from the patient, the shaman is often obliged to take them into his own body; in doing so, he struggles and suffers more than the patient himself. (S 229)

> he is free to leave his body, to transport himself to great distances, to descend to the underworld, to scale the sky, and so on. This "spiritual" mobility and freedom . . . make him vulnerable, and frequently, through his constant struggling with evil spirits, he falls into their power. . . . (S 236)

This is not far from the drama of *Milton* and *Jerusalem*, or that of "Howl" or *The Fall of America*, in which the struggling, suffering, and vulnerability of the poet vis-à-vis "evil spirits" is a central theme. Moreover, although Eliade dwells on the shaman's spirituality as a subject of interest in itself, more recent studies have suggested that the shaman may be particularly valuable in periods of cultural crisis:

> The shaman is a kind of social safety valve who dramatizes [social] disequilibrium and employs techniques to reduce it, not the least of which is the dramatization itself . . . the shamanistic seance and ritual make the unknown visible and palpable, transforming anxiety into something manageable by giving it form—a name, a shape, and a way of acting as a consequence of this embodiment.[20]

That cultures as well as individuals may be ill or insane is of course assumed by both Blake and Ginsberg, and for both poets, there is a method in madness, of which the logic is essentially quite simple. To the world, the inspired man is mad, because he is unworldly. But to him, it is mad, because it is unpoetic and uninspired; and the symptoms of its madness are the facts of human suffering. Therefore, if the duty of the poet-prophet is restoration of unity—rather than the division of the saved from the damned—then the necessary act of the poet is to enter into the madness of this world, descending into its hell to suffer it, to respond to it, trace it to its source, become what he beholds, and by so doing heal both himself and it. The program of a future prophet-shaman seems to have been stated by Blake, who had a habit of stating his programs early, in the "Mad Song" of *Poetical Sketches*:

> Like a fiend in a cloud
> With howling woe,
> After night do I croud,
> And with night will go;
> I turn my back to the east,
> From whence comforts have increas'd;
> For light doth seize my brain
> With frantic pain.
>
> (E 407)

What comforts the world can never comfort him. He chooses otherwise. Just such a program for the poet is stated by Ginsberg in the piece which gives the title to *Reality Sandwiches*, written to William Burroughs:

> we eat reality sandwiches.
> But allegories are so much lettuce.
> Don't hide the madness.[21]

There is a single character in English literature whose example may have touched the young Blake, who read Shakespeare early. That is the old king who admonishes himself "to feel what wretches feel." The king meets a young man who feigns madness, feigns it perhaps himself, and in a fit of what his friends presume to be insanity, in a mock trial where all are guilty, cries:

> None does offend, none—I say none! I'll able 'em.

It is an extraordinary statement in *Lear*, and an extraordinary undertaking in the career of William Blake. Following Blake's, the one poetic career cut after the same pattern, assuming comparable obligations, has been that of Allen Ginsberg.[22]

Notes

1. *Encyclopedia Britannica Macropedia*, 16th ed., S. V. "shamanism."

2. Ginsberg interview in *Writers at Work: The Paris Review Interviews*. 3rd series (New York: Viking Press, 1967), p. 303; hereafter cited as WW. This interview contains Ginsberg's fullest discussions of his Blake visions and their importance for him, although some important supplementary details are available in Jane Kramer, *Allen Ginsberg in America* (New York: Random House, 1968), pp. 72–73. Paul Portugés, in *The Visionary Poetics of Allen Ginsberg* (Santa Barbara, Calif.: Ross-Erikson, 1978), treats the Blake-Ginsberg connection as central to Ginsberg's work, using primarily the *Paris Review* account, supplemented by interviews in the mid-seventies; valuable here are the descriptions of the biographical context in which the visions took place, and the inclusion of hitherto unpublished pre-"Howl" poems illuminating Ginsberg's early struggle to assimilate Blake and follow his poetic "instructions."

3. Portugés, p. 23.

4. Edward Lucie-Smith, *Mystery in the Universe: Notes on an Interview with Allen Ginsberg* (London: Turret Books, 1965), p. 6.

5. Ginsberg, "Notes Written on Finally Recording Howl," in *A Casebook on the Beat*, ed. Thomas Parkinson (New York: Thomas Y. Crowell, 1961), p. 28.

6. Allen Ginsberg, *The Gates of Wrath: Rhymed Poems 1948–1952* (Bolinas, Calif.: Grey Fox Press, 1972), p. 55.

7. Portugés, p. 43.

8. "Sunflower Sutra" is in *Howl and Other Poems* (San Francisco: City Lights, 1956), pp. 28–30; hereafter cited as H. "Death to Van Gogh's Ear" is in *Kaddish and Other Poems* (San Francisco: City Lights, 1961), pp. 61–65; hereafter cited as K. *Planet News: 1961–1967* (San Francisco: City Lights, 1968), is hereafter cited as PN.

9. It should but does not go without saying that to be "smit with the love of sacred song" and to define oneself as belonging to a prophetic tradition does not preclude the writing of poetry. The poet-prophet inclines to believe that all poetry is originally visionary, and that "literature" represents a decline from that high estate insofar as it settles into orthodoxy. The antagonistic critic who prefers orthodoxy to heterodoxy will, if well educated (e.g., Eliot, Babbitt, Ransom), tend

to evade the issue and state his position as one of classicism versus romanticism, implying that only the former has ethical weight and formal merit. If naïve, he will use the terms "poetry" and "prophecy" to mean something like a composed work versus a spontaneous gush; see, for example, Thomas F. Merrill's innocent volume *Allen Ginsberg* (New York: Twayne, 1969), pp. 152–155.

10. G. E. Bentley, Jr., *Blake Records* (New York: Oxford Univ. Press, 1969), p. 216.

11. Northrop Frye, *Fearful Symmetry: A Study of William Blake* (Princeton: Princeton Univ. Press, 1947), p. 13.

12. Harold Bloom, *Blake's Apocalypse: A Study of Poetic Argument* (New York: Doubleday, 1963), pp. 19–20.

13. W. H. Stevenson, *The Poems of Blake* (New York: W. W. Norton, 1971), p. 351.

14. Allen Ginsberg and Richard Eberhart, *To Eberhart from Ginsberg* (Lincoln, Mass.: Penmaen Press, 1976), p. 18. This volume contains a detailed discussion by Ginsberg of both the morals and the poetics of "Howl."

15. *To Eberhart from Ginsberg*, pp. 18, 32.

16. Mark Robson, ed., *Improvised Poetics: Conversations with Ginsberg, Michael Aldrich, Edward Kissan, Nancy Blecker, taperecorded in 1968* (San Francisco: Anonym Books, 1971), p. 15.

17. Eric Mottram, *Allen Ginsberg in the Sixties* (Seattle and Brighton: Unicorn Bookshop, 1972), p. 6ff.

18. *The Fall of America: Poems of These States 1965–71* (San Francisco: City Lights, 1972), p. 46.

19. Mircea Eliade, *Shamanism: Archaic Techniques of Ecstasy*, trans. Willard R. Trask, Bollingen ser. 76 (Princeton: Princeton Univ. Press, 1970), p. 8; hereafter cited as S.

20. Eleanor Wilner, *Gathering the Winds: Visionary Imagination and Radical Transformation of Self and Society* (Baltimore: Johns Hopkins Univ. Press, 1975), p. 15. See also, on the subject of shamanic mental instability as channeled into solutions to social problems, Weston La Barre, *The Ghost Dance: Origins of Religion* (New York: Doubleday, 1966); George Devereux, "Shamans as Neurotics," *American Anthropologist* 63(5) (1961): 1088–1090. On the shaman as poet and guardian of poetic tradition, see Eliade, p. 30. On shamanism as a major source of sacred art, see Andreas Lommel, *Shamanism: The Beginnings of Art* (New York: McGraw-Hill, 1966).

21. "On Burroughs' Work," *Reality Sandwiches* (San Francisco: City Lights, 1963), p. 40.

22. Ginsberg's most recent volume, *Mind Breaths* (San Francisco: City Lights, 1977), includes a "Blakean Punk Epic" entitled "Contest of Bards" which appears to constitute an entirely new sort of approach to Blake on Ginsberg's part. *Mind Breaths* is a collection predominantly lyric rather than prophetic. Most of the poems are personal, and the recurring themes are sexuality and death; social and political commentary is comparatively minimal, and the intense moral strenuousness which characterizes most of Ginsberg's poetry appears to have relaxed. "Contest of Bards" deals with the challenge of a bearded old bard by an arrogant youthful poet. In the course of their encounter the two make love, and ultimately approach becoming "One friend." The poem employs a loose derivative of Blake's fourteener line, and seems obviously related to *Milton* thematically, although the exuberance of tone, and the evident enjoyment taken by both bards in their verbal and sensual contest, suggest the entertainment of a Blakean Eden rather than the struggles of prophecy in a fallen world. Both figures are clearly derived from Blake's iconography—"the youth free stripling bounding along . . . And the old man bearded, wrinkled,

browed in his black cave" (*Mind Breaths*, p. 93) are types which will be instantly recognizable to any student of Blake's art. Possibly Ginsberg's work will in future provide as interesting a commentary on Blake as a visual artist as his past work has done for Blake the poet.

PART II

Robert F. Gleckner

Joyce's Blake: Paths of Influence

In 1899 Joyce was seventeen years old, in 1912 he delivered his Trieste lecture on William Blake, in 1915 he began *Ulysses*, and from 1922 to its publication in 1939 he worked steadily on *Finnegans Wake*. While these dates are obviously not all the landmarks in his career, they are the most salient in understanding his lifelong relationship with Blake. There has been a good deal written piecemeal about this relationship, but its history has never been charted thoroughly nor indeed has its nature been adequately analyzed. What has been done ranges widely in its estimate of the importance of Blake in Joyce studies—from L. A. G. Strong's flat assertion that Blake was one of only three writers who most influenced Joyce (though his own proofs of this influence are remarkably brief) and Frances Boldereff's even more extreme conclusion that Blake represented "Joyce's closest alliance to another human being," to Frank Budgen's cautionary admission that he had "never heard Joyce pretend to be a Blake adept" and James S. Atherton's view that there are "few signs" of Joyce's use of Blake in *Finnegans Wake* since by then "Joyce had left Blake and gone on to other mystics, for whom Blake had prepared him." [1] While a complete chronicle of all the critical discussions of the Blake-Joyce relationship is impossible in an essay of this kind, I propose here to review some of the central features of those discussions and thereby to try to account for the wide divergence of opinion—as well as to suggest a view of Joyce's acquaintance with Blake that has not, to my knowledge, been advanced before.

When Joyce was "a seventeen-year-old student," C. P. Curran recalls, "his interest lay in Yeats and Blake and the French Symbolists." [2] Stanislaus Joyce corroborates this: "In early youth, my brother had been in love, like all romantic poets, with vast conceptions, and had believed in the supreme importance of the world of ideas. His gods were Blake and Dante." [3] In 1893 the monumental, and monumentally careless and strange, edition of *The Works of William Blake, Poetic, Symbolic, Critical*, edited by E. J. Ellis and W. B. Yeats, was published by Quaritch. Curran says categorically that Joyce "read Blake closely in the Ellis-Yeats edition," [4] but I have found no other evidence for this in Joyce's letters, Ellmann's biography, or the numerous accounts of his life and habits by Joyce's close friends. Stanislaus Joyce claims that "it was Yeats's edition of Blake's poems that directed my brother's attention to him," but it is unclear whether he meant the Ellis-Yeats edition or Yeats's 1893 Muses Library edition, *The Poems of William Blake* (reprinted in 1905).[5] I am inclined to the latter myself for two reasons—though the first is hardly compelling. The three-volume Ellis-Yeats was both cumbersome and extremely difficult to read (because of the unhappy method by which the plates of the prophetic books were reproduced). More to the point, in Joyce's Blake lecture in Trieste he quotes six lines from "Auguries of Innocence" but identifies the source as Blake's "Proverbs." [6] In his Muse's Library edition Yeats assigns the title "Auguries of Innocence" only to the opening quatrain of the poem, the famous "To see a World in a Grain of Sand" (which he misquotes as "the world," although the line is correct, except for Blake's original capitalization in the Ellis-Yeats edition), the rest of the poem, including the lines Joyce quotes, appearing six pages later under the title "Proverbs." In Ellis-Yeats the entire poem is entitled "Auguries of Innocence." It is also possible that Joyce had seen Yeats's two essays on Blake in *Ideas of Good and Evil*, which was published in 1903, or even perhaps in their earlier journal appearances, "William Blake and the Imagination" (under the title "William Blake") in *The Academy* in 1897 and the three-part "William Blake and his Illustrations to 'The Divine Comedy' " in *The Savoy* of July, August, and September of 1896. These contain, among other things, Blake's statement about poetry not admitting "a letter that is insignificant," his "road of excess" and "Bring out number, weight and measure" proverbs of hell, the "globule of man's blood" and the "pulsation of the artery" passages, and the distinction between vision and imagination on the one hand and fable and allegory ("formed by the daughters of Memory") on the other—all materials that Joyce used very early on in his career.

Although the earliest evidence for Joyce's actual use of Blake's work in his own writing is said to be *Chamber Music* (most of these poems were written probably in 1901 and 1902), I find little of Blake here. W. Y. Tindall's guess that, if Joyce was attracted to the older poet's "union of contemporary and Elizabethan elements," presumably in Blake's *Poetical Sketches* and perhaps some of the *Songs of Innocence and of Experience*, the differences between the two poets' handling of such material was "that Blake's is better," [7] seems to me to argue little real impact of the one on the other. More interesting are Joyce's direct references to Blake in his early critical essay on "James Clarence Mangan" (1902). If Stanislaus Joyce is correct in identifying the phrase "the most enlightened of Western poets" as a reference to Blake,[8] that is high praise indeed, but of greater interest is Joyce's quotation from Blake's "Proverbs of Hell" ("To create a little flower is the labour of ages") and his reference to "history" as "fabled by the daughters of memory"—an idea that was obviously a favorite of Joyce's since he used it in *A Portrait* as well as *Ulysses*. He also paraphrases Blake's lines from *Milton* (which he could have found either in Yeats's Muses Library edition or in Yeats's Blake essays):

> Every time less than a pulsation of the artery
> Is equal in its period and value to six thousand years.
> For in this period the poet's work is done, and all the great
> Events of time start forth and are conceived in such a period,
> Within a moment: a pulsation of the artery.
>
> (Yeats's version; Gandolfo notes this connection, p. 216)

And, like the "daughters of memory" phrase, also from Blake's essay on Chaucer's Canterbury pilgrims is Joyce's idea that "the ancient gods, who are visions of the divine names, die and come to life many times, and, though there is dusk about their feet and darkness in their indifferent eyes, the miracle of light is renewed eternally in the imaginative soul" (C W 82–83). Blake put it this way: "Visions of these eternal principles or characters of human life appear to poets in all ages. The Grecian gods were the ancient Cherubim of Phoenicia, but the Greeks, and since them, the Moderns, have neglected to subdue the gods of Priam. These gods are visions of the eternal attributes or divine names. . . ." (Y 245). Joyce then adds to this what Blake has to say of Chaucer's parson, who is the kind of character "sent in every age for its light and warmth" and who "in every age sends us such a burning and shining light" (Y 243–244); and also Blake's idea that the "eternal image" of everything "never dies, but renews by its seed. Just so the imaginative image returns by the seed of contemplative thought" (Yeats 250).

We have here, then, in Joyce's early years a particular interest in *The Marriage of Heaven and Hell*, especially the proverbs, and in two other major Blakean ideas: (1) the poet's annihilation of time, and (2) the imaginative realities that are the "eternal attributes" of man and God, and that are perceivable only by the true poet. Both of these are supported by Joyce's adoption of Blake's distinction between imagination and fable or allegory, the former produced by the daughters of inspiration, the latter by the daughters of memory—Joyce adjusting the distinction to his own interest of opposing history and poetry. To this may be added the only reference to Blake in *Stephen Hero*, stemming from approximately the same time as the Mangan essay. In Chapter 16, very early in the incomplete manuscript as we now have it, Stephen is said to have "read Blake and Rimbaud on the values of letters. . . ." [9] This refers pobably to Blake's statement in *A Vision of the Last Judgment* that "as poetry admits not a letter that is insignificant, so painting admits not a grain of sand or a blade of grass insignificant"—though Joyce may have had in mind the prefatory "Address to the Public" of *Jerusalem*: "Every word and every letter is studied and put into its fit place. . . ." While all these materials were available to Joyce in the Ellis-Yeats edition, they (except for the preface to *Jerusalem* passage) were also ready at hand in the likelier sources, Yeats's one-volume edition of Blake and his essays on Blake. Thus Joyce's own later portrait of Blake "flying from the infinitely small to the infinitely large, from a drop of blood to the universe of stars" (*CW* 222) is a fair summation of his own early interests in his predecessor. That these evidences of Blakean usage are indicative of Joyce's either wide or intense early reading in Blake seems to me to overstate the case. That he read around in Blake and read Yeats on Blake is far more credible. Frank Budgen's testimony that he "never heard Joyce pretend to be a Blakean adept" is probably right, at least at this time. "But," Budgen goes on, "I knew that he was familiar with the interpretations of Blakean mysteries of Yeats and his circle." [10] I shall return to this point later in my discussion of E. J. Ellis's *The Real Blake*.

In *A Portrait of the Artist as a Young Man* the Blake that Joyce invokes, if indeed he invokes him at all, wears the masks of Shelley and the early Byron. The only unequivocal reference to Blake is Stephen's recollection of two lines from "William Bond": "I wonder if William Bond will die / For assuredly he is very ill," followed by an ambiguous comment, "Alas, poor William! " [11] There seems to me little in the book that capitalizes on or extends the earlier Blake references I have been talking about. That Stephen "wanted to meet in the real world the unsubstantial image which his soul so constantly beheld" (65) is straight out of Shelley's "Alastor," the "Hymn to Intellectual Beauty," or perhaps the essay "On Love"; that Stephen "did not know where to seek it or how" but that "this image would, without any overt act of his encounter him" (65) merely pursues the line of development of the "Hymn." Stephen once quotes Shelley directly (96), the tone and substance of the famous passage on the "winged form flying above the waves and slowly climbing the air" (169) are both Shelleyan, Stephen's resolve "to live, to err, to fall, to triumph, to recreate life out of life" (172) echoes the end of *Prometheus Unbound*, and the "Defense of Poetry" becomes part of Stephen's definition of *claritas* or *quidditas*:

> This supreme quality is felt by the artist when the esthetic image is first conceived in his imagination. The mind in that mysterious instant Shelley likened beautifully to a fading coal. The instant wherein that supreme quality of beauty, the clear radiance of the esthetic image, is apprehended luminously by the mind which has been arrested by its wholeness and fascinated by its harmony is the luminous silent stasis of esthetic pleasure. . . .
>
> (213)

The Byron references and allusions are only somewhat less persistent, lending even greater credence than we might allow otherwise to Stanislaus's point about Joyce's "boyish hero-worship of Byron" and his advancing "through Shelley" ultimately to Blake.[12] What Blake there is in *A Portrait* is interesting, however, partly because it is so unobtrusive, seemingly buried by the rush of panting flights, luminous wings, and inconsolable sorrows. Stephen's efforts to escape "the house of prayer and prudence" (225) and, even more important, "those nets" of "nationality, language, religion" (203) are, in essence, Blake's strivings to annihilate father, priest, and king and their respective modes of enslavement. And yet Blake's image of the artist is rarely, if ever, one of flight, the metaphor that informs virtually all of the key aesthetic passages in *A Portrait*. The closest Joyce comes to Blake in the book, it seems to me, is in part of his conception of *integritas*, "the first phase" of which ("apprehension") "is a bounding line drawn about the object to be apprehended" (212). Blake wrote:

> The great and golden rule of art, as well as of life, is this:—That the more distinct, sharp, and wiry the bounding line, the more perfect the work of art. . . . The want of this determinate and bounding form evidences the idea of want in the artist's mind. . . . Leave out this line, and you leave out life itself; all is chaos again, and the line of the Almighty must be drawn out upon it before man or beast can exist. (Y 254)

What is particularly interesting about Joyce's use of the idea, however, is that he translates it into a conception of "universal beauty," an idea quite foreign to Blake's aesthetics. Even here, then, Shelley triumphs over Blake in *A Portrait* and it remains for *Ulysses* and *Finnegans Wake* to substantiate the full impact of Blake on Joyce.

Before we turn to those two major works, however, we must pause here to examine more thoroughly than it has been before what is (aside from, perhaps even greater than, Yeats's 1893 Muses Library edition of Blake) the single most important source of Joyce's knowledge of Blake, E. J. Ellis's *The Real Blake* (London: Chatto & Windus, 1907). Four years after this book's appearance Joyce was invited to lecture at the Università Popolare Triestina and in March 1912 he gave two lectures, one on Defoe, one on

Blake. The first remains to us only in a very small fragment, the latter in more complete form, though it is impossible to tell whether it is "almost the whole" [13] or not. While Ellsworth Mason and Richard Ellmann, in their edition of *The Critical Writings of James Joyce*, note three borrowings from Ellis, the fact is that virtually the whole of the lecture is taken from Ellis's book, often verbatim. Much of the material in it, it is true, was also available to Joyce either in the Ellis-Yeats edition or in Yeats's introduction and text of his one-volume edition, but on close scrutiny Joyce's phrasing is clearly recognizable as having its origin in *The Real Blake*:

JOYCE	ELLIS
[On Blake's association with Mary Wollstonecraft, Tom Paine, the publisher Joseph Johnson, and other "revolutionaries"]	
Even among the members of this circle, Blake was the only one with the courage to wear in the street the red cap, emblem of the new era. He soon took it off, though, never to wear it again, after the massacres in the Paris prisons that occurred in September 1792. (215)	He . . . walked out from them into the streets of London with a cap of Liberty on his head. . . . We do not hear that any other of Johnson's guests defied public opinion in this way. (120) . . . when the September massacres in 1792 came . . . Blake . . . took off the red cap of Liberty. . . . (155)
In 1799, he was offered the position of drawing master to the royal family. Afraid that in the artificial atmosphere of the court his art might die of inanition, he refused it; but at the same time, in order not to offend the king, he gave up all the other lower-class students that formed his major source of income. (215–216)	. . . he was even offered the post of drawing-master to the Royal Family. . . . But he refused, for he feared that his art would languish in the Court atmosphere, and . . . in order not to seem insulting to the Sovereign he gave up all his pupils. . . . (184)
After his death, Princess Sophia sent his widow a private gift of a hundred pounds sterling. Mrs. Blake sent it back, thanking her politely, saying that she was able to get along on little, and that she didn't want to accept the gift because, if it were used for another purpose, the money might help to restore the life and hopes of someone less fortunate than her. (216)	. . . a gift of £100 was sent to Blake's widow by the Princess Sophia. . . . "She sent back the money with all due thanks, not liking to take or keep what, as it seemed to her, she could dispense with, while many to whom no chance or choice was given might have been kept alive by the gift." (235)
The frail curtain of flesh as he calls it in the mystical book of *Thel*, that lies on the bed of our desire. (216)	. . . the flesh, that "curtain on the bed of our desire," as we are told in the *Book of Thel*. (175)

. . . he gave forty pounds to a needy friend. (216)	He gave away a lump sum of forty pounds . . . to an unfortunate young fellow. (185)
Having seen a poor, phthisic art student pass his window each morning with a portfolio under his arm, he took pity on him and invited him into the house, where he fed him and tried to cheer his sad and dwindling life. (216)	He noticed a pale-faced young man with a portfolio under his arm, who passed his house every day. . . . He was a poor art student on his way to death. . . . Blake visited him frequently, taught him, nursed him, and evidently to the last fed him. . . . (185)
For many days before his [Blake's brother Robert] death, he watched over his sickbed without interruption, and at the supreme moment he saw the beloved soul break loose from the lifeless body and rise toward heaven clapping its hands for joy. Then, serene and exhausted, he lay down in a deep sleep and slept for seventy-two hours in a row. (216)	During the last fortnight he watched day and night by his brother's bed without sleeping. He had his reward. He saw the soul spring from the suddenly still, blind body, and ascend upwards, clapping its hands for joy. Then taking this sight with him Blake went to bed, and slept continuously for three days and nights. (100)

[Joyce's summary of Blake's early love affair with a "Polly Woods" is an inaccurate précis of Ellis's account on pages 37–38. It is apparently Joyce's invention that "this girl's face appears in certain drawings in the prophetic book of *Vala*" (217), though his description of Vala as "a soft and smiling face, symbol of the sweet cruelty of woman, and of the illusion of the senses" comes directly from Ellis 160–161.]

To recuperate . . . Blake left London and went to live in the cottage of a gardener named Bouchier. (217)	His parents . . . arranged with a friend of theirs, a market-gardener named Bouchier, that he should go and live at the garden-house . . . in the hope that he might recover. . . . (38)

[Catherine's "heart . . . filled with compassion at hearing of the young man's misfortune in love" and "The affection born from this pity" (217) constitute Joyce's version of the rest of Ellis's story (39).]

[Joyce's assertion that "Mrs. Blake was neither very pretty nor very intelligent" (217) contradicts Ellis's view that she was "pretty" but "simple." I do not know the source of Joyce's ideas here, unless he was thinking of Nora, whom Ellmann describes as seeming "ordinary" probably "to any other writer of the time. . . . She had only a grammar-school education; she had no understanding of literature, and no power or interest in introspection." Even Ellmann, however, describes Nora, finally, as "handsome" if "untutored" (*James Joyce*, pp. 163, 165). That Mrs. Blake "was illiterate, and the poet took pains to teach her to read and write" (217) is straight from Ellis.]

Elemental beings and spirits of dead great men often came to the poet's room at night to speak with him about art and imagination. Then Blake would leap out of bed, and, seizing his pencil, remain long hours in the cold London night drawing the limbs and lineaments of the visions, while his wife, curled up beside his easy chair, held his hand lovingly and kept quiet so as not to disturb this visionary ecstasy of the seer. (218)	She would get up in the night, when he was under his very fierce inspirations . . . sketching and writing, and so terrible did this task seem to be that she had to sit motionless and silent *only to stay him mentally*, without moving hand or feet, this for hours, night after night. (435)
. . . Blake, radiant with joy and benevolence, would quickly begin to light the fire and get breakfast for the both of them. (218)	. . . he was in the habit of lighting the fire and putting on the kettle for breakfast before his Kate awoke. (435)
Blake almost followed Abraham's example of giving to Hagar what Sarah refused. (218)	He claimed the right of Abraham to give to Hagar what Sarah refused. (90)
The vestal simplicity of his wife . . . (218)	[her theory of matrimony] was preposterously vestal. (90).
In a scene of tears and accusations that occurred between them, his wife fell in a faint, and injured herself in such a way that she was unable to have children. (218)	[Joyce's opening phrase is an exact summary of Ellis 90–91 . . . crying out in her desolation, she fell down in a heap by the bed. . . . In that cry and that heavy fall . . . we have the sad knowledge why this vigorous and unstained young couple lived childless all their lives. (91)
In his old age . . . he began to study Italian in order to read the *Divina Commedia*. . . . (219)	He learned Italian in order to read him [Dante] in the original. . . . (403)
. . . recall his spirit from the twilight of the universal mind. . . . (219)	. . . reading of his thoughts in Blake's "Universal Mind." (172)

His brain did not weaken. . . . Death came to him in the form of a glacial cold, like the tremors of cholera. . . . (219)	If Blake had not been the sanest of men, the nerves more closely connected with the brain . . . would have been wrecked. . . . Deathly chill, and symptoms resembling the sort of cholera that is said to be produced by *fear* . . . (430)
He died singing in a strong, resounding voice that made the rafters ring. (219)	He began to sing aloud. . . . His voice was powerful. In his ecstasy he "made the rafters ring." (436)
"My beloved, the songs that I sing are not mine," he said to his wife, "no, no, I tell you they are not mine." (220)	He said of these songs, "My beloved, they are not mine! no, they are *not* mine." (436)

[Joyce's distinguishing Blake from Eastern mystics and aligning him with Paracelsus, Jacob Behmen (Joyce uses Blake's habitual spelling), and Swedenborg is largely taken from Ellis 421.]

[Blake] has in one corner the words: *Michelangelo pinxit*. (221)	Blake put "Michelangelo *pinxit*" on his plate. . . . (22)
It is modelled after a sketch made by Michelangelo for his *Last Judgment*, and symbolizes the poetic imagination in the power of the sensual philosophy. (221)	. . . this design may possibly have been made from a sketch prepared by Michael Angelo for a figure . . . in *The Last Judgment*. (22) Blake . . . meant the "hard, cold, restrictive" portions of mind that forbid imagination and say that the five senses are the only gates by which truth can reach man. (23)
Eternity, which had appeared to the beloved disciple and to St. Augustine as a heavenly city, and to Alighieri as a heavenly rose, appeared to the Swedish mystic in the likeness of a heavenly man. . . . (221)	He seemed (Crabb Robinson goes on . . .) to consider . . . the visions of Swedenborg and Dante as the same kind. (400)
. . . he always insists on the importance of the pure, clean line that evokes and creates the figure on the . . . uncreated void. (221)	The great and golden rule of art . . . is this;—that the more distinct, sharp, and wiry the boundary line, the more perfect the work of art. . . . Leave out this line, and you leave out life itself. All is chaos again, and the line of the Almighty must be drawn out upon it again before man or beast can exist. (291–292)

Eternity . . . appeared to the Swedish mystic in the likeness of a heavenly man, animated in all his limbs by a fluid angelic life that forever leaves and re-enters, systole and diastole of love and wisdom. (221–222)

Inasmuch as God is a Man, therefore the universal Heaven in the complex is as one man, and it is distinguished into regions and provinces according to the members, viscera, and organs of a man. . . . The angels who constitute heaven are the recipients of love and wisdom. . . . (115)[14]

In addition to this extraordinary array of exact (or near-exact) quotations, precise paraphrases, and summaries, either Ellis's *The Real Blake* or Yeats's Muses Library edition is also the source for the references on page 215 of Joyce's Blake essay to "The Chimney Sweeper," "London," and the "Proverbs of Hell," the references on page 217 to "Infant Sorrow" ("the demon . . . hidden in the cloud"), the almost exact quotation on page 222 of the entire passage (partially quoted in the Mangan essay) entitled by Yeats "Time" and "Space," the misquotation (perhaps from memory) of Blake's distinction between seeing *with* the eye as opposed to *through* the eye (Y 99; Joyce has "beyond" instead of "through"), the almost exact quotation on page 222 of Blake's "the eye, / Which was born in a night to perish in a night, / When the soul slept in beams of light" (Y 99), and, finally, Blake's proverb of hell, "Eternity is in love with the productions of time," which Joyce misquotes on page 222 as "eternity was in love with the products of time."

Despite Curran's statement, then, it seems to me clear that if Joyce owned (or saw) the Ellis-Yeats edition of Blake's works, he rarely if ever opened it.[15] The reason seems to me fairly obvious. While Joyce was interested enough in Blake's poetry to read at least some of it, remember (or write down somewhere) certain things from it, of greater interest to him was Blake's life. As he writes, revealingly, in the 1902 Mangan essay, "the life of the poet is intense," as opposed to that of "the philosophic mind"—"the life of Blake or of Dante—taking into its centre the life that surrounds it and flinging it abroad again amid planetary music" (*CW* 82). This accounts in some measure, I think, for the paucity of Blake material in *A Portrait*. For while Joyce was obviously attracted in some ways to Blake's works, it was Blake's personal battle against father, priest, and king that informs Stephen's thoughts.[16] Yet, as Hugh Kenner points out, Stephen "does not . . . become an artist by rejecting church and country." [17] As I suggested earlier, the Shelleyan and early Byronic versions of Blake that *A Portrait* dramatizes emerge not in Stephen as artist but in Stephen as aesthete:

> "Signatures of all things I am here to read," (*Ulysses*, p. 38) he says truly; but in the *Portrait* he shows no inclination even to look at them. He imagines that "the

> loveliness that has not yet come into the world" (p. 297) [Modern Library ed.] is to be found in his own soul. . . . The genuine artist reads signatures; the fake artist forges them, a process adumbrated in the obsession of Shem the Penman with the most famous of literary forgeries, "Macfearsome's Ossian," studying "how cutely to copy all their various styles of signature so as one day to utter an epical forged cheque on the public for his own private profit" *Finnegans Wake*, p. 180) [i.e., 181]. This accords with Stephen's interest in Blake, who, as Northrop Frye tells us, looked forward to a world "no longer continuously perceived but continually created." The mature Joyce of *Finnegans Wake* confidently labels this process "forgery," and holds up its exponent, Shem, to continual ridicule. . . . The Joyce who wrote the *Portrait* was equally enlightened . . . but the exigencies of his immediate task make it difficult for him to "place" Stephen as explicitly as he was later able to "place" Shem.[18]

Kenner's conclusion that *A Portrait*, therefore, "arises from vision without matter" [19] seems to me not only quite right, but it lends additional support to my own point about a Shelleyan and Byronic Blake, whose biography, especially as fancifully presented in Ellis and Yeats, not his poetry, "stirred [Joyce] deeply [in] that in an age of self-satisfied materialism, Blake dared to assert the all-importance of the imagination and to stake his long life on its affirmation." [20] The quotation from Blake's "William Bond," then, toward the end of *A Portrait* is Stephen's recollection of Blake's life, not the poem. His mind is on "E— C—," the kind of poeticized vague figure of woman to whom his idea of the "greatest poet," Byron,[21] wrote sentimental lyrics similar in tone to Mangan's "romantic" lamentations. Accordingly, Ellis's relating of Blake's apocryphal early love affair with a Polly Woods to the lines of "William Bond" surely popped into Joyce's mind as apropos:

> "Are you a fool? " said she [Polly]. "That cured me of jealousy," said Blake afterwards. . . . The shock, however, was a severe one. Blake's temperament being ardent, his character confident, and his heart affectionate and trustful, the whole woof and warp of his emotional fabric was torn to scraps at once. Love, self-regard, and hope were wounded. Such a fit of extreme wretchedness came upon him that, strong as he was, or rather precisely because he was strong, he became seriously ill. Like "William Bond" in the ballad, he "came home in a black, black cloud, took to his bed, and there lay down." (38)

"Alas, poor William! " Stephen writes in his diary (249). Alas, poor Blake; alas, poor Stephen! But, unlike Blake's William Bond, who falls in love with another (whom Ellis persistently identifies as Blake's future wife Catherine), Stephen desires "to press in [his] arms the loveliness which has not yet come into the world" (251):

> The spell of arms and voices: the white arms of roads, their promise of close embraces and the black arms of tall ships that stand against the moon. . . . They are held out to say: We are alone. Come. (252)

Similarly William Bond, who "thought Love lived in the hot sunshine," finds that "O he lives in the moony light! " If, as Kenner suggests, the "indigestibly Byronic" Stephen of the last section of *A Portrait* is severely satirized in the beginning of *Ulysses*,[22] perhaps we can also see the beginnings of his transformation in his diary jotting for "26 *April*: Mother . . . prays now, she says, that I may learn in my own life and away from home and friends what the heart is and what if feels. Amen. So be it. Welcome, O life! I go to encounter for the millionth time the reality of experience. . . ." (252–253). "William Bond" concludes on the same note:

> Seek Love in the pity of others' woe,
> In the gentle relief of another's care,
> In the darkness of night and the winter's snow,
> With the naked and outcast,—seek Love there.
>
> (Y 133)

Ulysses and *Finnegans Wake* are, whatever else they may be, such seeking—and to them we must now turn to see what Joyce makes of Blake there.

Following up S. Foster Damon's early essay, "The Odyssey in Dublin," [23] with its footnote listing of eleven references to or quotations from Blake in *Ulysses*, Weldon Thornton and Don Gifford have exhaustively combed *Ulysses* for Blake appearances, running Damon's total to some twenty-five or so.[24] While from one point of view this seems impressive evidence of an increasing intensity and range of allusion to Blake, perhaps even arguing that Joyce carefully reread Blake with *Ulysses* in mind, that evidence is considerably less compelling than it appears. For the allusions are, in general, the same ones that we have already seen in Joyce's Trieste lecture—or if not the same ones, they are allusions to the same works: *The Marriage of Heaven and Hell* (more particularly the "Proverbs of Hell"), "Auguries of Innocence," *A Vision of the Last Judgment*, the May 6, 1800 letter to Hayley (containing the proverb "The ruins of Time build mansions in Eternity"), and "London." Furthermore, *all* of the Blake usages in *Ulysses* may be found in Ellis's *The Real Blake*.

What has changed, however, is the manner in which Joyce employs the Blakean material, blending it into the texture and thematic structure of his work. Damon has said that the concentration of *Ulysses* into one day, one place, and one action was "made possible" by Blake: "Blake enlarged the epical vision until extremes met: the largest of things were contained in the smallest. Concentrate as hard as possible on the Minute Particulars, and Eternity will appear. A wild flower contains heaven, a grain of sand the world." [25] Similarly, but with greater caution, Stuart Gilbert writes: "For such exact and scientific use of symbolism the nearest parallel to *Ulysses* is in the prophetic books of Blake." [26] Both of these claims seem to me excessive. While it is clear that from his reading of Ellis Joyce could have learned a great deal *about* Blake's mythology, there is very little in *The Real Blake* (or for that matter in Yeats's one-volume edition) of the prophetic poetry itself. As a result Joyce scatters his Blakean material throughout *Ulysses*—to deepen the implications of certain scenes, thoughts, or details, to underscore his own essential meaning, to help to universalize his theme, and, perhaps more simply, to mimic certain striking locutions of an artificer whose life he sympathized with intensely and whose work he saw as an emanation of that life. This is not to say that the Blake references are there, as it were, for their own sakes, honorifically. Joyce rarely, if ever, merely bows. On the other hand, more often than not those references are neither crucial nor indispensable—with the exception of the Circe episode.

Many of the occasions of their arising are the thoughts of Stephen, not Joyce, the Stephen whose "attendant ghosts" were "Swift, Shakespeare, Blake, Thomas Aquinas and a motley horde of medieval philosophers." [27] Frank Budgen seems to me more nearly right than others when he said that "if Joyce at one time steeped himself in Blake he never accepted the Blakean or any other ready-made symbols." [28] We should remember better than we do Joyce's unequivocal criticism of Blake's later work in his Trieste lecture:

> . . . the continual strain of these voyages into the unknown and the abrupt return to natural life slowly but inexorably corrode his artistic power. The visions, multiplying, blind the sight; and toward the end of his mortal life, the unknown for which he yearned covered him with the shadows of vast wings, and the angels with whom he conversed as an immortal with immortals hid him in the silence of their garments. (*CW* 215)

This is an extraordinary "rejection" of what Joyce finally regarded as Blake's "idealist premises" (CW 222). Though he could in *Ulysses* adapt Blake's notion that "fable or allegory is formed by the daughters of memory" for Stephen's mental commentary on the difference between history, the world of time and space, and the world of art, it is Joyce, not Stephen, who rudely paraphrases Blake's proverbs and thereby transforms them into the position Joyce took in his lecture. "The road of excess leads to the palace of wisdom" and "No bird soars too high if he soars with his own wings" (Y 179–180) are transmuted into "thud of Blake's wings of excess." [29] The implication is both startling and instructive: Blake flew too often and too far into the beyond, and that excess led finally not to wisdom but to a thud against the unyielding hardness of reality—for Joyce the reality of Dublin and, in *Finnegans Wake*, of all human history.

And this is precisely what happens in the Nighttown episode of *Ulysses*, where Joyce calculatedly reuses Blake's distinction between fable or allegory and vision or imagination. Just as Bloom, who is a most intensely human, palpable, and earthly reality, "*stops on the fringe of the noisy quarrelling knot*," Stephen with "*elaborate gestures*" includes all of those standing around (including Bloom, who is not yet *of* the group but certainly *in* it) in his thought: "The uninvited. . . . History to blame. Fabled by *mothers* of memory" (572; italics added for "mothers"). That is, simply they are all born of woman, of Molly and, later, ALP, flesh and blood, reductively human and fleshly and gross, the very palpable reality Blake and the early Stephen sought to escape or fly from. Jostling in Stephen's mind throughout this part of the Nighttown episode (572–574) are thoughts of what is "Poetic" and "Neopoetic," myth ("Sisyphus") and reality ("*Kitty's and Lynch's heads*"), Blake and Swift ("Doctor Swift says one man in armour will beat ten men in their shirts"), the "noble art of self-pretence" and Private Carr's threat to "bash" him in the jaw, "retaining the perpendicular" (as Bloom comes forward to hold Stephen upright) and (as "*He taps his brow*") killing "in here . . . the priest and the king" (i.e., the reality of this world versus Blake's mental reality, which for him was "alone real"). Stephen concludes this phase of the episode with a revealing espousal of life's realities:

> You [Private Carr] die for your country, suppose. . . . Not that I wish it for you. But I say: Let my country die for me. Up to the present it has done so. I don't want it to die. Damn death. Long live life! (576)

And this is followed immediately by the incarnate Edward the Seventh (history) levitating "*over heaps of slain*" (a sustaining of the warfare theme that runs throughout the episode as the major leitmotif, along with sexuality, for the world of the flesh), saying:

> My methods are new and are causing surprise.
> To make the blind see I throw dust in their eyes.
>
> (576)

The lines are an adroit reversal of Blake the visionary. As Ellis quotes him in his Chaucer essay, Blake wrote:

> I found them blind: I taught them how to see;
> And now they know neither themselves nor me.
>
> (284)

And in the poem Yeats entitles "Scoffers" Blake wrote:

Mock on, mock on, Voltaire, Rousseau,
  Mock on, mock on; 'tis all in vain;
You throw the dust against the wind,
  And the wind blows it back again.
And every stone becomes a gem
  Reflected in the beams divine;
Blown back, they blind the mocking eye,
  But still in Israel's paths they shine.

(Y 108)

Shrewdly omitting any reference to the first two lines of the second stanza, Joyce has the new prophet, "Joking Jesus," say that while this dust may become gems that shine in Israel's paths as well as in the mind of the imaginative visionary, it is finally the dust of the earthbound man that, thrown into the blind eyes of the idealist visionary, opens his consciousness to the fullness of reality.

Stephen's "war" with Private Carr, then, is (as Paley has pointed out) [30] properly taken from Blake's own experiential battle with one of the king's dragoons. And again the reversal is startlingly apt. Whereas Blake the visionary evicts the king's soldier from his "garden of delight," the realm of vision and imagination, and returns him symbolically to the world in which he belongs, and of which he is the symbol, namely, the "Fox Inn" (a perfect anticipation of the drunken orgy at Burke's public house), in *Ulysses* it is Private Carr who clobbers the visionary and thereby delivers Stephen into the hands of Bloom, the common man. The "mocking eye," though closed, can now see. Levin makes the same point in a somewhat different way, unrelated to the sequential uses of Blake: Molly "incarnates the fertility of earth. She is the compliant body as Stephen is the uncompromising mind, and as Bloom—torn between them—is the lacerated heart. To Stephen's everlasting nay, she opposes a final affirmation." [31] But perhaps it is more proper to say that Bloom, as "fabulous hero" as well as "childman weary, the manchild in the womb," is both Stephen and Molly, the head and the heart, the imagination and the senses, eternity and time, infinity and space, the forger "in the smithy of [his] soul" and the "reality of experience" with which *A Portrait* concludes. As Levin again says, "Bloom's final page [graphically illustrated by the solid dot of ineluctably real punctuation] harks back to Stephen's awakening page, at the beginning of the *Portrait of the Artist*, and looks forward to the drowsy pages of *Finnegans Wake.*" [32] Perhaps, indeed, it is not too much to see part of Joyce's inspiration for Shem and Shaun in Blake's letter to Butts in which he recounts the incident with the dragoon (Joyce no doubt read it carefully in *The Real Blake*):

> O why was I born with a different face?
> Why was I not born like the rest of my race?
> When I look, each one starts; when I speak, I offend,
> Then I'm silent and passive and lose every friend.
> Then my verse I dishonour, my pictures despise,
> My person degrade, and my temper chastise;
> And the pen is my terror, the pencil my shame;
> All my talents I bury, and dead is my fame.
> I am either too low, or too highly prised,
> When elate, I'm envied; when meek, I'm despised.
>
> (Ellis 227)

In 1962 I tried to demonstrate that there was "overwhelming evidence that Blake was seldom out of Joyce's thoughts when writing *Finnegans Wake*" and that his "intimate knowledge of Blake's life and the Blake canon, and his intense sympathy with Blake's vision, were controlling elements in his own vast undertaking." [33] In the same year Clive Hart made a similar claim, but centered his not on the entire Blake canon or life but on one of Blake's poems: "Chief among the non-Viconian cycles which help to mould the lines of *Finnegans Wake* are the world-ages of Indian philosophy and the opposed gyres of Yeats' *A Vision* and Blake's 'The Mental Traveller.' " [34] Five years earlier, Northrop Frye more cautiously advanced the notion of "major parallels" existing "between Blake's myth of Albion and Joyce's myth of Finnegan," but he too bases his parallels on Blake's "Orc-Urizen cycle." [35] While both Hart and Frye are engagingly persuasive in their establishment of parallels between the myths of the two writers, Frye seems to me now more nearly correct in suggesting Blake's as a parallel rather than a source. "We may be tempted to speak of 'influence,' " Paley wrote in 1962, "but there is something more important and alive at work here. It would be more to the point to say that Joyce, in the process of choosing—and thereby creating—a tradition, as every great artist must, realized that Blake participated in that tradition." [36]

In this light what is most striking about the relationship of *Finnegans Wake* to Blake is Joyce's inability or disinclination to incorporate into his "tradition" or myth Blake's four Zoas, who are at the core of his "system." [37] It is they, finally, who are the basis for all of Blake's fours—the senses, the points of the compass, the geographical reference points, the four rivers of life, the four levels of vision, and so on. They are not associated in any way with Matthew, Mark, Luke, and John, and, unlike Joyce's four old men, they are in no sense historians or chroniclers, nor are they judges, censors, lawgivers, or voyeuristic leerers "at all mating."[38] Finding the basic source for his own many foursomes in Vico, Joyce, who was obviously aware of Blake's Zoas through Ellis's and Yeats's accounts of them, *did* think about amalgamating them into his plan. In David Hayman's "Draft Catalogue" we find these revisions by Joyce: "From the urizen of the speeches" (to be inserted at 386.12 after "Johnny"); "Tharmuz syphon Mark" (to be inserted at 388.10 after "Marcus"); "For the luvah the lands Lucas" (to be inserted at 390.34 after "Lucas"); and "the grand old Urthonian?" (to be inserted at 392.14 after "Matt Emeritus").[39] What is of particular interest in these notes is that they are very late (July 1938) and hence perhaps an afterthought, that they were intended for the most extensive section of *Finnegans Wake* that deals with the four old men (the "Mamalujo" section), and that Joyce finally did not use them in the finished work. Why not?

As I have suggested above, it is, I think, because Joyce has finally rejected what he understood to be Blake's idea of the artist-visionary as an adequate model for what he was about in *Finnegans Wake*, that rejection being enunciated and dramatized in the Circe episode of *Ulysses*. Frye makes the same point.[40] At the end of *A Portrait* Stephen's appeal to the "old father, old artificer" is essentially an appeal to Blake's Los, for him a symbol of the artist who escapes from the labyrinth of father, priest, and king and the earth into the realms of imagination. In *Ulysses* Stephen returns to earth, to Dublin (to Blake's "London," a poem remarkably prefigurative of the harlotry, warfare, disease, weakness, and woe of the Circe episode), away from Los and Stephen's vision of him as the timelessness and spacelessness of eternity, Blake's "imagination." *Ulysses*, then, appropriately closes with Marion Bloom's "weaving of her never-finished web" of space and time—the web being also one of Blake's symbols

> for female sexuality. The drowsy spinning of the earth, absorbed in its own cyclical movement, constantly affirming but never forming, is what Marion sinks into, taking the whole book with her. Blake, if he had read *Ulysses*, would probably have recoiled in horror from its celebration of the triumph of what he calls the "female will," the persistence of the sleep of externality.[41]

It is no surprise, then, to find that although Los's name appears several times "there is no Los figure in *Finnegans Wake*" (unless he is Joyce, the creator of it all, which seems to me apposite), just as there are no four Zoas.[42] As Budgen put it, "Joyce deals with elemental shapes rather than [Blake's] elemental forces," those "creative elements" which are "for ever forging and building, groaning and howling." In *Finnegans Wake* "things are. They are not in a state of clamorous and painful becoming."[43] The "thingness" or "areness" of Joyce's final vision, then, are the very grounds on which Blake's mythological pantheon must, for the most part, be absented from it. "The visions," to repeat what Joyce said of Blake in his lecture, "multiplying, blind the sight." Rather than being apocalyptic, the end toward which all of the efforts of Blake's Los successfully tend (not the least aspect of which is the reunion of the four Zoas), "breaking clear of the natural cycle altogether," Joyce's final form is precisely that cycle (and to that extent alone his "version" of "The Mental Traveller" perhaps), the cycle that contains but finally overpowers the Blakean quest.[44] As Goethe said of Kant to Eckermann, "although you have never read him; now you need him no longer, for what he could give you, you possess already."[45]

But Blake *is* there, after all, in the *Wake*—in some of the old familiar ways: the proverbs, a few striking phrases, and above all the life, the man. For example, we find in *Scribbledehobble*, which Connolly dates "between 1922 and 1923,"[46] the beginnings of what will be the pattern of Blake usage in the finished work. The jotting "that's enough, too much" and "the contempt of the contemptible" echo the proverbs of hell "Enough! or too much" and "As the air to a bird, or the sea to a fish, so is contempt to the contemptible."[47] Why the proverbs? Because, I believe, they sounded ringingly in Joyce's sharp ear as well as articulating splendidly a kind of wisdom different from those proverbs that were "of an ethical and practical interpretation . . . moral aphorisms."[48] Joyce's own "proverbs" (and *Finnegans Wake* is filled with them) are clearly his emulation of Blake's tune and rhythm, the mesmerizing operation of a heretical mind. For example, in *Scribbledehobble* we find:

> Give that to me & be a fool yrself
> Catch the pig by the leg: asking a goat for wool: how to brush a hare
> from a bush where she isn't
> Men may meet but mountains never part
> Rent to a lord like pap to a child
> Better sit beside it than in its place
> A fool's word like a thorn in hand
> Woe to him who has a stranger's spancel on him
> A greyhound finds its food in its feet
> What I'm afraid may be said to me I had better say first myself
> A dog's snout, a man's knee, a woman's breast
> Labour of bees, flow of tide, mind of woman
> Every hound is a pup till he hunts[49]

The closest we come to this passage in *Finnegans Wake* itself is on page 505.16–25. Other possible references to what was apparently Joyce's favorite Blake work are on pages 43.10.25–26; 175.1; 315.30–31; and

318.33–35. That the proverbs especially stuck in his mind is attested to also by Stanislaus Joyce[50] and echoed in the fact that in 1926 his friend Eugene Jolas's *Manifesto: The Revolution of the Word*, which Joyce obviously saw (though, unlike a number of other modern writers, did not sign), was punctuated by no less than six of the Proverbs of Hell.[51]

Despite this seeming "proof" that Joyce very early on intended to make wide use of Blake's work in the *Wake*, and despite my own earlier "proofs" of that use, I am not now willing to maintain my brief for Joyce's intimate and extensive knowledge—or even interest in—a wide range of Blake's poetry. Even "allowing for error, for overreading and overeagerness," [52] I find now much of what I "established" as Blake references to be severely strained. Oh, Albion is still there to be sure, and Los and Thel, a few of the *Songs of Innocence and of Experience*, and Nobodaddy—in addition, of course, to *The Marriage of Heaven and Hell.* But, most important, Blake is there in propria persona, the historical Blake, or, more accurately, "the real Blake" as Joyce had finally decided he was in *Ulysses.* Perhaps taking his cue from Yeats's phrase, "Blake the penman," [53] and Blake's own poem, cited above, in his letter to Butts about the quarrel in the garden with the king's dragoon, Joyce transforms Ellis's Blake into Shem the Penman as well as into Shaun. He is blake, black, blac, blak, bleak—black and white alternatively and simultaneously,[54] finally a sham.[55] Shem, is, as Adaline Glasheen points out, whatever else he is, "a sort of burlesque of Joyce, or rather, of Stephen Dedalus, the impotent artist," [56] and, we might add, the visionary Blake. The Blake of *Finnegans Wake*, then, is both Ellis's *The Real Blake* and Joyce's "the real Blake"—and the *Wake* is filled with Joyce's absorption of the central charcter in Ellis's novelized biography. It is surely not mere coincidence that Ellis, on information attested to as fact by Yeats, records that Blake's grandfather was a John and his father a James, John the O'Neil from whom Blake's side of the family was supposed to have descended, James the one who, born of a previous wife or mistress, took John's new wife's name, Blake, and moved to London to become (how marvelous for Joyce!) a draper, or hosier as it was then called (Ellis 5). The Swift-Blake alliance in *Finnegans Wake* is thus set neatly and early. Compounding the relevance of the names, Blake's oldest brother was a John, "the evil one, / In a black cloud making his moan" (Ellis 4; the quotation is from Blake), the second son a James who took over his father's business at the latter's death.

Ellis next tells us that "Blake was, in blood and spirit, an Irish chieftan" (15) whose "great ancestor of Elizabethan days, Shawn O'Neil" had such a terrible temper that when the fit was on him he was buried to his neck in sand until he cooled off (20). Though it is impossible to tell whether Joyce had read Ellis (whose book was published in 1907) before writing his 1907 essay, "Ireland, Island of Saints and Sages," the coincidence of this passage from Ellis and Joyce's own account of the Elizabethan O'Neil is too striking to write off. Here is Joyce: "The Irish prince, Shane O'Neill, was so strongly blessed by nature that they had to bury him up to his neck in his mother earth every so often, when he had a desire for carnal pleasure" (CW 167). If Joyce had seen Ellis's book (though the different spelling of the name seems to argue against this), he has rather neatly conflated Ellis's account of Shawn with his frequent references to Blake's temper and to his "masterful appetite," his "confident demands of rapture" from his wife, and his uncommon sexual prowess. In any case, clinching Blake's Irishness for Joyce, O'Neil or not, was his discovery that the fourteen ancient tribes of Galway included not only the Joyces but the Blakes, and that like Ellis's Blake the old inhabitants even had raven hair, "Titian red." [57]

It is in precisely these terms that we can understand, for example, Joyce's line, "O'Neill saw Queen Molly's pants: and much admired engraving" (FW 495.26–28)—the Molly of *Ulysses*, of course (whoever else she may be here), whose monologue, as we have seen, erased the value of Blake's visionary art for Joyce. Similarly, in what is one of the two most open admissions of Blake to the *Wake*, Joyce capitalizes on the same misinformation (and at the same time encourages my earlier identification of all, or most, of the "blacks" in *Finnegans Wake* with "Blakes"):

> No later than a very few fortnichts since I was meeting on the Thinker's Dam with a pair of men out of glasshouse whom I shuffled hands with named MacBlacks—I think their names is MacBlakes. . . . (409.20–23)

Here we have the son of the Blakes of Galway (and hence implicitly the son of "Neil"), the two Blakes (Shem and Shaun), and Joyce's absorption in the figure of Blake himself, his grandfather and father, as well as his two older brothers. In fact, the relationship of son to father, explored in Joyce from *A Portrait* on, is neatly adumbrated by Ellis (93).

The other indisputable occurrence of Blake's name is in Joyce's identification of him with Jerry (one of Shem's alter egos). Originally Joyce labeled him here "the little devil" (printer's devil?), but then deleted the phrase, and continued: "He is one to be of the [blake *deleted*] blakes tribe big already. Blake? Whatever do you mean with blake? With blake I mean ink. O, I see now." [58] Allowing for Joyce's awareness of the Blake tribe of Galway, Blake himself is surely here—as Irishman, as writer-engraver-printer, as seer and visionary. Not only does the passage solidify further the black-Blake interchangeability in *Finnegans Wake*, but also my earlier suggestion that the many references to ink also call up Blake's image. The final version of the passage is even richer in Blakean matter:

> He will be quite within the pale when with lordbeeron brow he vows him so tosset to be of the sir Blake tribes bleak while through life's unblest he rodes backs of bannars. Are you not somewhat bulgar with your bowels? Whatever do you mean with bleak? With pale blake I write tintingface. O, you do? And with steelwhite and blackmail I ha'scint for my sweet an anemone's letter with a gold of my bridest hair betied. . . . In the ink of his sweat he will find it yet. . . . But they are two very blizky little portereens after their bredscrums, Jerkoff and Eatsup. . . . What folly innocents! . . . I will to leave my copperwise blessing between the pair of them. . . . kerryjevin. (563.11–37)

"Bleak" (Danish for ink, as well as "Blake" with only a slight Irish accent), tintingface (German *Tintinfass*, inkpot), and Blake's etching on copper plates have now been added to black and Blake, who like the Byron of *A Portrait* rides through life "sun-blest" under the banners of chivalry and romance and writes the poetry of flowers. He is, then, precisely the Blake "rejected" by Joyce in *Ulysses* as too idealist, too visionary. But he is also the "undisciplined and visionary heresiarch" (*CW* 216)—like those other favorites of Joyce, Bruno of Nola, Pelagius, Duns Scotus, Macarius, and Vergilius Solivagus[59]—and is thus a Shem-sham (Jerry), laboring "in the ink of his sweat" to finally "see and see," as well as a Shaun (the pale, the "steelwhite" of the law and conscience). Blake, then, is at least in part remade by Joyce in his own image, a "kerryjevin," a whole man with his feet very much in this world, but not less an artist (perhaps even a greater artist) for that.

Blake's marriage to the illiterate Catherine Boucher has often been noted as a source of satisfaction to Joyce in connection with his own relationship with Nora. He pointedly remarks on it in his Trieste lecture:

> Like many other men of great genius, Blake was not attracted to cultured and refined women. Either he preferred . . . the simple woman, of hazy and sensual mentality, or, in his unlimited egoism, he wanted the soul of his beloved to be entirely a slow and painful creation of his own, freeing and purifying daily under his very eyes, the demon (as he says) hidden in the cloud.[60]

The last phrase is not used by Blake or Ellis in reference to Catherine at all but to Blake's brother John; the emphasis on sensuality, as well as unlimited egoism, however, clearly contributed to Joyce's growing sense of the Blake-Shem identification. Futhermore, in *Scribbledehobble* Joyce noted: "introduced another woman into the house: completely broke down," which is a neat summation of Ellis's account of Blake's apocryphal claiming of "the right of Abraham to give to Hagar what Sarah refused," after which Catherine was said to have completely broken down, falling "in a heap by the bed." [61] Related to this story is Joyce's "*Why am I not born like a*

Gentileman . . ." (FW 150.26), a line from Blake's poem "Mary" (and, of course, a part of Blake's poetic lament, quoted above, following his accusation of sedition), which Ellis reads (93), along with "William Bond," as an autobiographical account of Blake's relationship to his wife, and which to Joyce was a typically Shaunian lament. He may also have had in mind Ellis's point about Blake's friend Flaxman: "Not having been born a gentleman, he was always peculiarly at the mercy of a superior look from any one above him in position. (189).

The manifesto of ALP has striking connections with Ellis's book as well. Like the letter buried in the garbage heap, Ellis describes Blake's prophecies as buried in a "thick . . . accumulation of the ashes of superciliousness":

> The reputation of madness has come down on him like the cinders of Vesuvius in Pompeii . . . but now that the accumulation is being dug away from the buried town, we at least find fruit paintings and portraits of fair dames upon the walls, as fresh as they were on the day when the master's brush left them. In the same way, misunderstanding is being dug away from Blake, and his prophetic books shine out dear and sweet for us now. (153)

Similarly the "chiaroscuro" of the unearthed letter (FW 107.29) is reminiscent of Blake's attack on this technique: "These pictures . . . were the result of temptations and perturbations, seeking to destroy imaginative power, by means of that infernal machine called Chiaro Osuro. . . ." [62] It should also be noted that Ellis refers consistently to Blake's "Public Address" as his "manifesto," and in the Shem the Penman section of *Finnegans Wake*, Shem as author of the letter is described as having written "some most dreadful stuff in a murderous mirrorhand" (177.31–32), an echo of Ellis's point about Blake's having "learned from . . . the *Book of Thel* even more about the laboriousness of copying out a whole manuscript in reverse, every letter and word written backwards. . . ." (158). In fact the entire two-page description of Shem (FW 182–183) is at least partly based on Blake's life and career. For example, as Ellis writes, Blake "would have seven years of bending over copper plates, with a strong glass fixed in his eye, and his nose nearly touching the square of metal" (12), so Joyce: "but for that light phantastic of his gnose's glow as it slid lucifericiously within an inch of its page" (182.4–5). This is the "house of O'Shea or O'Shame . . . known as the Haunted Inkbottle, no number Brimstone Walk, Asia in Ireland" (182.31–32). Not only does Joyce obviously have Blake's *Marriage of Heaven and Hell* in mind again, in which it is the devil who speaks wisdom and in which also Blake pointedly writes of his own process of corrosive etching, but the reference to Asia may also be based on Ellis's point that "the gods of Asia are the names Blake chose for almost all the mental attributes that he most disliked" (179). Joyce's remaking of Blake in Shem's image (and his own) could not be more patent.

Other aspects of the long Shem passage that are equally Blakean include the "furniture" of Shem's room: "bouchers" (a reference, perhaps, to Blake's wife), "alphabettyformed verbage," "fallen lucifers," "blackeye lenses," "magnifying wineglasses," "limerick damns," "blasphematory spits," "fresh horrors from Hades," "globules of mercury"—"to which, if one has the stomach to add the breakages, upheavals distortions, inversions of all this chambermade music one stands, given a grain of goodwill, a fair chance of actually seeing the whirling dervish, Tumult, son of Thunder, self exiled in upon his ego. . . ." (184.2–7).

Finally, the description of ALP's letter, as well as coincidentally Joyce's magnum opus, conforms with reasonable accuracy to Ellis's description of Blake's prophetic works—with, to use Joyce's language, their "curt witty wotty dashes never quite just right at the trim trite truth letter," the "airy plumeflights" and "indignant whiplooplashes" and "round thousand whirligig glorioles" and "strange exotic serpentine" of Blake's marginal and interlinear designs; the "sudden spluttered petulance of some capjaljsed mIddle" of Blake's erratic capitalization; the "four shortened ampersands" (Blake frequently used ampersands); and the four kinds of stops: "stop, please stop, do please stop, and O do please stop" (paralleling Ellis's description of Blake's erratic punctuation: ". . . a semi-colon or a colon is dropped in without any sufficient cause here and there, sometimes doing duty for a full stop, and sometimes for a comma, or for an even slighter pause. . . .") (182).

Ellis's summary descriptions of the difficulties of reading Blake are a remarkable adumbration of the processes by which *Finnegans Wake* has been deciphered as well as of the way to read ALP's letter:

> It requires reading and re-reading before we track all the symbols down and sort out those that are explained in various passages from those that almost remain mere names (like some of the counties of England that are but loosely joined to any other symbols, and for lack of authoritative punctuation not quite comprehensibly divided under the headings of the tribes). . . . The day when people can be expected to endure a full account of *Jerusalem*, which would necessarily be ten times as long as the poem, has not dawned yet. The few students who really care will find that it interprets itself with a little help from Blake's letters, manifestoes, and maxims. But it is always necessary to beware of being satisfied too soon with any *one* of the four meanings of every symbol, even after the stories of the Zoas are familiar to us and we can even see one *in* the other, and Milton *in* Blake, *in* Christ, *in* his own Shadow, and even *in* Satan.[63]

And again:

> The explanation of most of Blake's seeming errors *about himself* in the use of his own symbols is that he never quite threw off a habit of using nouns, and even proper names, as *adjectives*, or rather in places where adjectives would have seemed more comprehensible; and though this sounds a very wicked thing to do, it is not so if we who read have but the wit to understand; and those who contest this point, and set up a prejudice derived from the prose value of the nomenclature of grammar . . . as a reason for condemning Blake, might learn something if they would try and *say what Blake said* according to their own rules. They could do it, but the weary and verbose volume that would result would by its depressing and unpoetic quality so injure the fresh nerves of its best reader as to *unfit him for seeing the visions and hearing the voices* in his own interior faculties, without which all Blake's works will be to him as those nods or winks which the old proverb tells us are the same to a blind horse. (334)

Although he would have frowned a bit, perhaps, at the "seeing of visions and hearing of voices" idea, surely Joyce would have been proud of his major Irish source for divining the way to read the as yet unwritten *Finnegans Wake*.

And where does all this leave us now? There is simply no doubt that as Frye, Damon, Hart, and others have shown, there are distinct similarities between Joyce's total conception in *Ulysses* and *Finnegans Wake* and Blake's in his prophecies. Indeed one might usefully see in Joyce's progression from the early poetry through *Dubliners* and *A Portrait of the Artist as a Young Man* to *Ulysses* and *Finnegans Wake* a general parallel to Blake's development from *Poetical Sketches* and *Songs of Innocence and of Experience* through the early, shorter prophecies (*Thel, The Marriage of Heaven and Hell, Tiriel, Visions of the Daughters of Albion*, the *Book of Urizen*, etc.) to *The Four Zoas, Milton*, and *Jerusalem*. Surely Joyce was perceptive enough to see it himself. And it is even a striking parallel if we recognize Joyce's absorption of all his previous work in each succeeding work just as Blake subsumed everything into *Jerusalem*. And yet, finally, it is Ellis's Blake, not his works, that Joyce found of greatest moment. In 1901 Joyce wrote a birthday letter to Ibsen, which reads in part:

> What I could discern dimly of your life was my pride to see, how your battles inspired me—not the obvious material battles but those that were fought and won behind your forehead, how your wilful resolution to wrest the secret from life gave me heart and how in your absolute indifference to public canons of art, friends and shibboleths you walked in the light of your inward heroism."[64]

The letter might very well have been written to Blake. But Blake's "road of excess" finally for Joyce did not lead to the "palace of wisdom," instead to a blinding of the sight to the grubby realities of this world, to an "idealism" so absolute that there was no room in it for the Blooms and Mollys, the Finnegans and the Earwickers. As a result, Blake's prophetic poetry, however myth-filled and conceptually attractive, was not a comfortable resting place for the Stephen-Joyce of *Ulysses* or the Shem-Joyce of *Finnegans Wake*. Blake's life was—and most especially, as I have tried to argue—his life as perceived, interpreted, and chronicled by two Irishmen. If Shem was a sham, however heresiarchal, and Shaun the presiding moral conscience, it is as Shem-Shaun that Joyce himself finally emerges, blending Blake's vision and life into his own and thus stabilizing vision with the *quidditas* of fact. Or, to put it another way, it was the *fact* of Blake that he finally adhered to, what he knew *of* him rather than his works that finally mattered. It is predictable, then, that two of Joyce's favorite Blake proverbs were "Eternity is in love with the productions of time" and "The ruins of time build mansions in eternity." For it is in Joyce's own giant forms, consubstantial with the reality they symbolize, in their life, death, and awakening that he "finds all *human* enterprise and aspiration." [65] J. F. Hendry said it with uncommon acuteness: Joyce's "bringing together of all myths and allusions" is "an attempt to describe past, present, and future as it lies co-terminous in the human subconscious: not yet as it lies also, spread out in fields of light in the endless vision of Blake." [66]

Notes

1. L. A. G. Strong, *The Sacred River* (New York: Pellegrini & Cudahy, 1951), pp. 83–89; Frances Boldereff, *Reading "Finnegans Wake"* (New York: Barnes & Noble, 1959), p. 73; Frank Budgen, *James Joyce and the Making of "Ulysses"* (Bloomington: Indiana Univ. Press, 1960), p. 310; James S. Atherton, *The Books at the Wake* (New York: Viking Press, 1960), p. 236. See also Boldereff's tour de force, *A Blakean Translation of Joyce's Circe"* (Woodward, Pa: Classic Non-Fiction Library, 1965).
2. *James Joyce Remembered* (New York: Oxford Univ. Press, 1968), p. 9.
3. *My Brother's Keeper* (New York: Viking Press, 1958), p. 33; see also p. 99.
4. *James Joyce Remembered*, p. 35.
5. *My Brother's Keeper*, p. 99. T. E. Connolly's "The Personal Library of James Joyce" *The University of Buffalo Studies*, 22, 1 (April 1955) lists no Blake books, and the only one Joyce mentions in his letters is Darrell Figgis's *The Paintings of William Blake* (London, 1925), characteristically for Joyce by a fellow Irishman. Ellsworth Mason also interprets Stanislaus to mean Yeats's one-volume edition of Blake ("James Joyce: 'William Blake,' " *Criticism* 1 [1959]: 181n). On the other hand, most recently Anita Gandolfo unequivocally announced that "it can be proven beyond doubt that Joyce relied primarily upon [the] Ellis and Yeats [edition] for his knowledge of Blake," and that the Yeats of this edition (plus the critical essays) "is the only *single* source for all of Joyce's allusions to Blake" ("Whose Blake Did Joyce Know and What Difference Does it Make," *James Joyce Quarterly* 15 (1978): 220n, 216). Her "proof" is largely the testimony of Stanislaus Joyce and Curran.

6. "William Blake," *The Critical Writings of James Joyce*, ed. Ellsworth Mason and Richard Ellmann (New York: Viking Press, 1959), p. 219; hereafter cited as CW. Joyce's original Italian version may be found in *Criticism* 1 (1959): 181–189. The capitalization of Mason's English translation of these lines is taken from a more accurate modern edition (probably Keynes's). Joyce's capitalization in his Italian faithfully reproduced Yeats's inaccuracies. Gandolfo, whose essay (cited in note 5) I did not see until this one was completed, makes the same point about Yeats's one-volume *Blake* and his essays on Blake.

7. Cf. W. Y. Tindall, ed., *James Joyce: Chamber Music* (New York: Columbia Univ. Press, 1954), pp. 29–30.

8. *Critical Writings*, p. 75, and note 1. The subsequent Blake quotations are on pp. 80–81. Here, as elsewhere in this chapter, I give Yeats's version of Blake (unless otherwise noted) since that is the one Joyce used; hereafter cited as Y. Blake's original *Milton* lines are on Plate 28, lines 62–63, and Plate 29, lines 1–3, most easily accessible in David V. Erdman's standard edition, *The Poetry and Prose of William Blake* (Garden City, N.Y.: Doubleday, 1965).

9. *Stephen Hero*, ed. Theodore Spencer, new ed. (New York: New Directions, 1955), p. 32.

10. Budgen, p. 310. Gandolfo goes so far as to say that "Yeats is the only *single* source of all of Joyce's allusions to Blake" (p. 216), but she does go on to reveal the impact of Yeats's "Blakean circle" on Joyce as well.

11. (New York: Viking Press, 1964), p. 249. Subsequent page references in the text are to this edition. The Ellis-Yeats edition properly includes the "And" that begins the first line of the *William Bond* quotation.

12. *My Brother's Keeper*, p. 99.

13. Editors' introduction to the Blake essay, *Critical Writings*, p. 214.

14. The reference to the "universal mind" comes also from Yeats, of course, as Mason and Ellmann note. Joyce's comment on Blake's *The Crystal Cabinet* (which Mason unaccountably spells *The Chrystal Cabinet*, following no edition of Blake that I know of) on pp. 218–219 is interestingly from William M. Rossetti's *The Poetical Works of William Blake* (London: George Bell & Sons, 1875), where in a footnote we find: "This poem seems to me to represent under a very ideal form the phaenomena of gestation and birth" (p. 174n). Since I find no other evidence of Joyce's knowledge of this edition, Joyce's apparent source, contra my own thesis, is *The Works of William Blake* by Ellis and Yeats, II, 22, where the editors mention "a footnote in the Aldine [Rossetti] edition" as explaining that *The Crystal Cabinet* gives "under a very ideal form the phenomena of gestation and birth." What is puzzling, however, is that Ellis and Yeats attack this interpretation severely as "interpretation at its wit's end" and "likely to produce more anger than laughter in any real reader of Blake." Since Joyce surely thought of himself as a "real reader of Blake," despite his apparent antipathy to Rossetti (see Ellmann, *James Joyce*, New York: Oxford Univ. Press, 1929, p. 78—or is this some other "Rossetti"?), he may indeed have read the passage in the Aldine edition. In any case, it is difficult to imagine him flying in the face of these severe comments by two fellow Irishmen. Finally, with respect to the Michelangelo section above, Stanislaus Joyce reports that Joyce thought of appending to the end of *Stephen Hero* the signature "Stephen Daedalus pinxit" (*My Brother's Keeper*, p. 244).

15. I might note here parenthetically that the Ellis-Yeats edition spells Blake's wife's maiden name correctly, Boucher (as does Yeats in the introduction to his

Muse's Library edition), but Joyce persists in Ellis's spelling in *The Real Blake*, Bouchier.

16. Cf. the quotation from Joyce's letter to Ibsen below, pp. 158–159, and my comment on it.

17. "The Portrait in Perspective," in *James Joyce: Two Decades of Criticism*, ed. Seon Givens (1948; reprint ed., New York: Vanguard Press, 1963), p. 150. Gandolfo seriously misreads this aspect of Stephens's development (p. 218).

18. Ibid., pp. 151–152.

19. Ibid., p. 152.

20. Stanislaus Joyce, p. 99.

21. *A Portrait*, p. 80. Tindall (p. 28n) suggests Byron's early poem, "To Emma," as the source of Emma Clery's name. More to the point, perhaps, are the several Byron poems with titles like "To E—," "To D—," "To M—," "On the Eyes of Miss A— H—."

22. "The Portrait in Perspective." p. 173.

23. In *Two Decades of Criticism*, pp. 203–242, originally published in *The Hound and Horn* in 1929. The footnote is on p. 203.

24. *Allusions in "Ulysses"* (Chapel Hill: Univ. of North Carolina Press, 1961); *Notes for Joyce* (New York: E. P. Dutton, 1974).

25. "The Odyssey in Dublin," p. 207.

26. *James Joyce's "Ulysses"* (1930; reprint ed., London: Faber & Faber, 1952), p. 57.

27. Ibid., p. 82. L. A. G. Strong (pp. 56–89) uses the same locution but limits the "ghosts" to Shakespeare, Swift, and Blake.

28. Budgen, p. 310.

29. *Ulysses* (New York: Random House, 1934), p. 25. All pages references in the text are to this edition. Gandolfo, I believe, errs in claiming that all the Blake allusions "in *A Portrait* and *Ulysses* occur *only* in the consciousness of Stephen Dedalus" (p. 216) (author's italics).

30. Morton D. Paley, "Blake in Nighttown," in *A James Joyce Miscellany*, 3rd ser., ed. Marvin Magalaner (Carbondale: Southern Illinois Univ. Press, 1962), pp. 182–185.

31. Harry Levin, *James Joyce* (Norfolk, Conn.: New Directions, 1941), p. 125.

32. Ibid., p. 124.

33. "Joyce and Blake: Notes toward Defining a Literary Relationship," in *A James Joyce Miscellany*, 3rd ser., p. 222.

34. *Structure and Motif in "Finnegans Wake"* (Evanston, Ill.: Northwestern Univ. Press, 1962), p. 49; see also pp. 67–69. Cf. Northrop Frye, "Quest and Cycle in *Finnegans Wake*," *James Joyce Review* 1 (1957): 45–46.

35. Frye, pp. 39, 40.

36. Paley, p. 175.

37. Frye makes this point unequivocally in his "Quest and Cycle" essay, p. 43. Joyce must have been pleased to find, however, that it was Ellis who discovered Blake's system of fours (*The Real Blake* 356).

38. Adaline Glasheen, *A Second Census of "Finnegans Wake"* (Evanston, Ill.: Northwestern Univ. Press, 1963), p. xlv.

39. *A First-Draft Version of "Finnegans Wake"* (Austin: Univ. of Texas Press, 1963), p. 318.

40. Frye, p. 44.

41. Ibid.
42. Ibid., p. 43.
43. Budgen, p. 312.
44. Frye, p. 46.
45. *Conversations of Goethe with Eckermann and Soret*, trans. John Oxenford (London: G. Bell & Sons, 1882), p. 242.
46. *James Joyce's Scribbledehobble*, ed. Thomas E. Connolly (Evanston, Ill: Northwestern Univ. Press, 1961), p. ix.
47. Ibid., pp. 110, 86. The two proverbs are in Yeats, p. 182. So far as I know only the second survived in the finished *Finnegans Wake* (New York: Viking Press, 1939), p. 175.1. All references in the text to the *Wake* will be to this edition by page and line number.
48. "William Blake," *Critical Writings*, p. 215.
49. *Scribbledehobble*, pp. 98–99. I have capitalized the initial letter of each "proverb" and set them in columnar form as Blake did.
50. *My Brother's Keeper*, pp. 154, 248.
51. Richard Ellmann, *James Joyce* (New York: Oxford Univ. Press, 1959), pp. 600–601n. The proverbs are "Prudence is a rich, ugly old maid courted by Incapacity," "Bring out number, weight and measure in a year of dearth," "Enough! Or Too Much!", "The road of excess leads to the palace of wisdom," "The tigers of wrath are wiser than the horses of instruction," and "Damn braces! Bless relaxes!"
52. "Joyce and Blake," p. 222.
53. Ellis and Yeats, *The Works of William Blake*, I, 204.
54. See my "Joyce and Blake," p. 192f.
55. It is interesting to note that the germ of the idea of Blake as "forger" is in Ellis, p. 36 (and ultimately, of course, in Blake's own notion of his work being "dictated" to him).
56. Glasheen, p. 236.
57. "The City of the Tribes," *Critical Writings*, p. 229. While Vico, Swedenborg, and others are obvious sources for Joyce's elaborate correspondences, we should not ignore Joyce's account in this essay of a "Blakean" seventeenth-century map of the city of Galway, which, "full of symbolic expressions and engravings, was the work of Henry Joyce, Dean of the Canons of the city. All the margins of the parchment are heavy with the heraldic arms of the tribes, and the map itself is little more than a topographical symphony on the theme of the number of the tribes. Thus, the map maker enumerates and depicts fourteen bastions, fourteen towers on the wall, fourteen principal streets, fourteen narrow streets, and then, sliding down into a minor mode, six gardens, six altars . . . six markets, and six other wonders" (p. 231). No fours, however.
58. *A First-Draft Version of "Finnegans Wake,"* p. 253.
59. See Joyce's essays, "The Bruno Philosophy" and "Ireland, Island of Saints and Sages," *Critical Writings*, pp. 132, 157, 160.
60. *Critical Writings*, p. 217. Mason and Ellmann properly footnote Joyce's *Exiles* (with its echoes of Ibsen, especially *When We Dead Awaken*, one of Joyce's favorite plays), in which Robert Hand says to Richard Rowan: "You love this woman. I remember all you told me long ago. She is yours, your work. . . . You have made her all that she is" (ibid., p. 217n).
61. *Scribbledehobble*, p. 148 (cf. *Critical Writings*, p. 218); Ellis, *The Real Blake*, pp. 90–91.

62. *The Real Blake*, p. 289. Joyce may also have recalled that like ALP's letter Blake describes his picture in the same paragraph as having been "painted at intervals" over some period of time.

63. *The Real Blake*, p. 331. The reference to Blake's *Jerusalem* is prophetic for it is certainly with that poem that *Finnegans Wake* compares conceptually. It is perhaps significant, then, that in 1920 "Philippe Soupault, who was translating Blake, discussed *Jerusalem* with" Joyce (Ellmann, *James Joyce*, p. 506). I still find it difficult to believe that Joyce had actually read *Jerusalem*, however, though he would have known *about* it from Ellis. Also Joyce would have been delighted to learn that Ellis proposed a Blake society, a Blake index, and a Blake encyclopeida to assist in the elucidation of his works (p. 333). In his own way a shrewd reader of Blake, Ellis was also a prophet: the "full accounts" of *Jerusalem* to date amount to far more than "ten times as long as the poem," much of it, as my next quotation from Ellis puts it, "depressing and unpoetic."

64. Herbert Gorman, *James Joyce* (New York: Rinehart, 1939), p. 70. Cf. Stanislaus Joyce, *My Brother's Keeper*, p. 99.

65. *Critical Writings*, p. 214.

66. "James Joyce," in *Two Decades of Criticism*, p. 447.

Myra Glazer

Why the Sons of God Want the Daughters of Men: On William Blake and D. H. Lawrence

> I saw the limbs form'd for exercise contemn'd: & the beauty of
> Eternity, look'd upon as deformity & loveliness as a dry tree:
>
> . . . .
>
> Every Emanative joy forbidden as a Crime:
> And the Emanations buried alive in the earth with pomp of religion:
> Inspiration deny'd; Genius forbidden by laws of punishment!
> I saw terrified; I took the sighs & tears & bitter groans:
> I lifted them into my Furnaces; to form the spiritual sword.
> That lays open the hidden heart.
>
> (J I: 9, 7–8, 14–19)

When Los, the tempestuous artist of *Jerusalem* utters these words, he is depicting the creative matrix of Blake's own art. That art, Los indicates, is Blake's response to the terrifying vision of the destruction of what is best in life. Eros and imagination have been "buried alive" by sham spirituality and moral and political repression. To be beautiful in this world means to be sterile and lifeless. To be sane means to be ordinary. Earlier in his career, Blake alluded to his art as "corrosives . . . melting apparent surfaces away, and displaying the infinite which was hid" (MHH 14); now his art is more directly assertive, a "spiritual sword" poised to cut through established lies to the reality of feelings.

In his unrelenting rage and impassioned commitment (though scarcely in most of his actual views), Blake recalls the biblical prophets. Looking ahead, he also bears a remarkable kinship to that equally intense, iconoclastic artist of "terrifying honesty," [1] D. H. Lawrence. Blake and Lawrence, as Vivian de Sola Pinto has written, are "the two major prophets

This is a revised version of my essay, "Sex and the Psyche: William Blake and D. H. Lawrence," that will appear in Hebrew University Studies in *Language and Literature*.

of the Other England," the England "outside the pale of the governing class," [2] and consequently, outside the pale of conventional truths. Sensuous, eccentrically intellectual, assertive, and religious, the art of both men infuses what Eugene Goodheart calls "already enacted life" [3] with a vision of intuited possibility. Both Blake and Lawrence are obsessed with revealing the "hidden heart" and naming truths not conventionally perceived. Like Blake, Lawrence argues against the repression of the "primal impulsive body" and sees as a consequence the mutilation of a sensual, imaginative apprehension of reality. "Man has closed himself up," writes Blake, "till he sees all things thro' narrow chinks of his cavern" (MHH 14). Lawrence speaks of man closing himself up, as in the dark of a cabbage: "we dare not even peep forth, but . . . we remain secure till our hearts go rotten, saying all the while how safe we are." [4] The "Children of Man" in Blake's *Four Zoas* see "no Visions in the darksom air" because for them the mind is an unlit place. The light cast by the imagination, the belief in an active, living universe, and the awareness of both the transcendent and immanent sacred, have been lost. "What it will be Questioned," writes Blake,

> When the Sun rises do you not see a round Disk of fire
> somewhat like a Guinea O no no I see an Innumerable
> company of the Heavenly host crying Holy Holy Holy is the
> Lord God Almighty I question not my Corporeal or Vegeta-
> tive Eye any more than I would Question a Window concerning
> a Sight I look thro it & not with it.
>
> (VLJ 95)

And Lawrence:

> Where, for us, is the great and royal sun of the Chaldeans? Where even, for us, is the sun of the Old Testament, coming forth like a strong man to run a race? We have lost the sun. We have lost the sun, and we have found a few miserable thought-forms. A ball of blazing gas! (P 299)
>
> The sun, I tell you, is alive, and more alive than I am, or a tree is. It may have blazing gas, as I have hair, and a tree has leaves. But I tell you, it is the Holy Ghost in full raiment, shaking and walking, and alive as a tiger is, only more so, in the sky.[5]

As if glossing his own lines as well as those of Blake, Lawrence remarks:

> The reality of substantial bodies can only be perceived by the imagination, and the imagination is a kindled state of consciousness in which intuitive awareness predominates. . . . In the flow of true imagination we know in full,

> mentally and physically at once, in a greater, enkindled awareness. At the maximum of our imagination we are religious. And if we deny our imagination, and have no imaginative life, we are poor worms who have never lived. (P 559)

Both Blake and Lawrence thus embark on rescue missions: their aim is to reawaken humanity by reasserting imaginative consciousness, and redeeming that "religious state" in which "we know in full, mentally and physically at once, in a greater, enkindled awareness." For both men, the enemy to begin with is what Lawrence calls "mental consciousness," Blake's fallen Urizen, the "Reasoning Power" or "Spectre" of man. Man's tendency to intellectualize all reality leads eventually to the atrophying and chaotic perversion of all his other faculties. Instead of a vivid, fructifying awareness of one's sensuality, intuition, and imagination, one falls under the dominion of an "Abstract objecting power, that Negatives everything" (J I: 10, 14). To live from one side of one's self only is to forget that "Without Contraries is no progression" (MHH 3), as Blake writes, or as Lawrence insists, "in the tension of opposites all things have their being" (P 67). One becomes trapped in one's own partiality. And the first victim of what Lawrence called "the partial soul," the soul poisoned by the mentalized psyche, is sexuality.

In Blake's myth, when Urizen seizes control of the psyche, Los loses his home in the generative loins and thus his identity as Urthona, the "Earth-owner" [6] able to shape reality to accord with imaginative perception. Similarly, Lawrence writes that as "mental consciousness" came to dominate man, he "began to suppress with all his might his instinctive-intuitive consciousness, which is so radical, so physical, so sexual" (P 552). To cripple imagination by allowing mental consciousness to dominate means one dams up passion and sexuality. The partial soul loses touch with his body. Blake and Lawrence both believe in the liberation of the body. But both artists also see sexuality as a "vehicle for exploring wider relationships," in the words of Mark Kinkead-Weekes, including relationships "*within* people, between them, throughout society" and involving, too, "the connection of man to the universe." [7] Each in his own way, Blake and Lawrence both participate in the ancient tradition of regarding male and female as a "primary means of conceptualizing all forms of human reality." [8] For both, the primordial *unalienated* psyche is androgynous—"two-in-one" as Lawrence writes—and the sexes are what Erich Neumann has called "symbolic magnitudes," [9] sources of archetypal, universal principles. Blake embodies those symbolic magnitudes directly in his male Zoas and female emanations; the imaginative goal of his prophetic books is the reconciliation of Albion—container of all Zoas—and Jerusalem, container of all emanations. Lawrence's characters, on the other hand, all possess attributes Lawrence considered archetypally male and archetypally female. The dramatic struggle of his fiction, as H. M. Daleski has shown, is the restoration to each sex of those symbolic magnitudes Lawrence believes properly belong to it.[10] Perhaps because both artists are men, however, and men who reject so many of the predicates of patriarchal culture, it is their encounter with the feminine—as the unknown portion of the psyche, as *anima*, and as woman herself—that is a particular locus of their creative struggle. As Lawrence himself wrote in "Study of Thomas Hardy," sexual conflict "makes the man struggle into articulation." It is the nature of that sexual conflict, and its relationship to their vision of the psyche, that we will be exploring here.

I

Like Carl Jung, both Blake and Lawrence conceive of the psyche in its health as fourfold: "Four Mighty Ones," Blake announces in his introduction to *The Four Zoas*, "are in every Man." For Lawrence, there are "four powerful vital poles which, flashing darkly in polarized interaction with one another, form the four-fold issue of our individual life" (P 628). Blake names his mighty ones—there is Tharmas, Zoa of sensation and the body; Luvah, Zoa of the passional life; Urizen, Zoa of intellection; and Los/Urthona, Zoa of the intuitive and imaginative—and then dramatizes their awesome, intricate, intrapsychic conflict. Like the "integral soul" Lawrence conceives of as "for ever indescribable and unstateable" (P 637), and the totality of the psyche Jungians believe cannot be known or defined, Blake believes his Zoas to be ultimately unknowable by any individual. "What are the Nature of those Living Creatures," he added to the introduction after he was well into the work, "the Heavenly Father only [Knoweth] no individual [Knoweth nor] Can know in all Eternity" (FZ I: 3, 7–8). In fact, that the Zoas exist *at all* is an intuition of what Lawrence calls "primal consciousness," the form of knowledge he believes *issues from* the "four cornerstones of the psyche": "radical knowledge, knowledge non-ideal, non-mental, yet still knowledge, primary cognition, individual and potent" (P 629).

But primary cognition, which is holistic awareness, is precisely what Lawrence believes we have lost, and Blake portrays his Zoas as losing. According to Lawrence:

> In ourselves . . . the primary experience, the vital consciousness grows weaker and weaker, the mind fixes the control and limits the life-activity . . . instead of

> our life issuing spontaneously at the great affective centres, the mind, the mental consciousness grown unwieldy, proceeds to evoke our primal motions and emotions didactically. The mind subtly, without knowing, provokes and dictates our feelings and impulses. . . . We insist over and over again from one mere centre of ourselves, the mental centre. (P 629)

That is the process Blake so minutely and obsessively maps in his prophetic books. Mental consciousness, of which Urizen is a vehicle, abstracts itself from the psyche, assumes the mantle of dominion and autonomy, and throws out of joint all the other functions. Urizen becomes as machine-haunted as Gerald Crich, as insidiously possessive as Clifford Chatterley, and, in his repressiveness, fear of the vital and presumed omnipotence, a Prussian officer. "Make any human being a really rational being," writes Lawrence, "and you have made him," not wise or angelic, but rather like tyrannical Urizen, a "parasitic and destructive force" (P 245).

For Blake, to perceive the world through the eyes of one's rationality alone is to have merely "single vision"—to see the sun only as a "round Disk of fire / somewhat like a Guinea," for example—and not to realize that "The Suns Light when he unfolds it / Depends on the Organ that beholds it" (E 257). In other words, one eliminates one's own subjectivity and in so doing reifies the world. Single vision is inevitably narrow-minded and egoistic; that is what Lawrence thunders against it:

> How gibbering man becomes, when he is really clever, and thinks he is giving the ultimate and final description of the universe! Can't he see that he is merely describing himself, and that the self he is describing is merely one of the more dead and dreary states that man can exist in? When man changes his state of being, he needs an entirely different description of the universe, and so the universe changes its nature to him entirely. (P 300–301)

Blake makes the same point more gently: when man moves "his dwelling-place," he writes in *Milton*, "his heavens also move." Portraying that "dead and dreary state" in its religious, emotional, and sexual aspects, Blake and Lawrence dedicate themselves to transfiguring it into life. Lawrence sees the importance of the novel as leading "our sympathy away in recoil from things gone dead." [11] Blake arms himself with his spiritual sword. And both men, fighting for an authentic life for the human spirit, decide to take on God.

II

Rejecting the "heavens" depicted by the man of single vision, and a psyche dominated by a single function, inevitably brings Blake and

Lawrence in conflict with the concept of a single authoritarian God. God the Father is for both men a bossy moralist "who says *Thou shalt, thou shan't*" (P 528). Blake parodies the God who creates a "Book / Of eternal brass" unfolding

> One command, one joy, one desire
> One curse, one weight, one measure
> One King, one God, one Law.
>
> (U 4: 38–40)

That God, says Lawrence, almost as if he is writing a commentary on Blake's prophetic books, "is the way of egotism, and the One God is the reflection, inevitably, of the worshipper's ego." [12]

Ahania, the feminine portion of Urizen's intellect, offers him her comprehension of man's fall. In "dreams of soft deluding slumber," Man, Ahania tells Urizen,

> ascended mourning into the splendors of his palace
> Above him rose a Shadow from his wearied intellect
> Of living gold, pure, perfect, holy; in white linen pure he hover'd
> A sweet entrancing self delusion, a watry vision of Man
> Soft exulting in existence all the Man absorbing
>
> Man fell upon his face prostrate before the watry shadow
> Saying O Lord whence in this change thou knowest I am nothing.
>
> . . . .
>
> [I] heard the voice of the Slumberous Man & thus he spoke
> Idolatrous to his own Shadow words of Eternity uttering
> O I am nothing when I enter into judgment with thee. . . .
>
> (FZ III: 40, 1–7, 9–12)

Ahania imagines man withdrawing from life into "the splendors of his palace," an ivory tower of pseudorationality where he can enclose himself in his own narrow domain. The weary, isolated intellect of man catapults him between feelings of omnipotence and a conviction of his own worthlessness. Both stances though, says Ahania, are reflections of a "sweet entrancing self delusion," an intellectualized adult version of primary narcissism. The pure, perfect, holy Lord is an image of man's narcissistic self-love whose source is not a liberated, receptive, and assertive imagination, but rather self-pity and self-delusion.

Urizen, predictably, is enraged by her words. His wrath bursts forth like a "black hail storm":

> "Am I not God?" he cries, "Who is Equal to me?":
>
> Shall the feminine indolent bliss. the dulgent self of weariness
> The passive idle sleep the enormous night & darkness of Death
> Set herself up to give laws to the active masculine virtue
> Thou little diminutive portion that darst be a counterpart
> Thy passivity thy laws of obedience & insincerity
> Are my abhorrence. Wherefore has thou taken this fair form
> Whence is this power given to thee! once thou wast in my breast
> A sluggish current of dim waters. . . .
>
> . . . .
>
> And thou has risen with thy moist locks into a watry image
> Reflecting all my indolence. . . .
>
> . . . .
>
> . . . thus I cast thee out.
>
> (FZ III: 43, 6–13, 17–18, 22)

The reaction of Urizen to Ahania's words shows not only the mind perversely twisting back upon itself, but also Blake's brilliant intuition of the sexual fears that underlie mental absolutism. Ahania described to Urizen the dangers of man's withdrawal into pure intellect. Urizen's violent response is to attribute all that she criticized to the *feminine* in the male. *She* is inertia, indolence, and self-indulgence; *she* is trying to take control and destroy "the active masculine virtue." Furious and frightened by her criticism, he casts her out. Blake is suggesting that it is the male intellect's terror of feminine power which drives his reason to assert control and to create a God, whose expression, ironically, is the repressive moral law, in his own image.

Mutatis mutandis, Lawrence portrays a parallel psychological process in *The Rainbow* and, by doing so, explores even further the sexual implications of both male absorption and the monist Absolute. While Will Brangwen feels spiritually consummated in the dark interior of the vast, hushed cathedral where " 'before' and 'after' were folded together [and] all was contained in oneness," Anna Brangwen is impelled toward the defiant, triumphant faces of the gargoyles with their "separate wills, separate notions, separate knowledge." [13] Anna intuits that a monist Absolute suffocates individualized instinct and feeling and the possibility of personal identity. Or as Blake asserts in *The Marriage of Heaven and Hell*: "One Law for the Lion & Ox is Oppression" (MHH 24), and as Lawrence insists, "life is *always* individual, and therefore never controlled by one law, one God." [14]

The gargoyles, as he writes in "Study of Thomas Hardy," deny "the Monism which the Whole uttered" and "declared for multiplicity" (P 454). In focusing on them, Anna destroys the illusion of Absolute Oneness Will had striven to achieve. The experience of Will and Anna is not merely one of monism versus multiplicity, however, for the cathedral is portrayed as a womblike Blakean "Female Space"—one is reminded of Blake's sketch of a woman bearing a Gothic tabernacle on her loins—and in the Hardy essay Lawrence himself claims that the monist is essentially female. Although it is *Will* he portrays as losing himself in the oneness of the cathedral, it is "woman," he writes in the essay, who is "obsessed by the oneness of things, the One Being" (P 451). In *The Rainbow*, indeed, Lawrence is depicting Will's unrealized manhood by portraying the young man's attempt to absorb himself into the archetypal feminine, into the Great Mother whom Anna recognizes as a Terrible Devourer and, simultaneously, as a rival to himself. Will's situation, in short, is exactly that psychic state Urizen acts violently to avoid, as do, in different ways, the feminine-fearing heroes of Lawrence's later fiction. Thus under the image of a psychic tyranny-of-oneness lurks for both artists a distrust of the feminine.

Yet there is, nevertheless, a state of oneness of vital positive significance to Blake and Lawrence, and it is their vision of such a state that serves as a key to their view of the psyche. For both artists, the state prior to the "separation of things" as Jung described it,[15] the state prior to the beginnings of consciousness before "the psyche splits in two, into subjective and objective reality," as Lawrence has written, is of the utmost importance. Lawrence called this state one of the "primal integral *I* which is for the most part a living continuum of all the rest of living things," and he related it, inevitably, both to the world of the infant and to the psychic state longed for in adulthood (P 761). In *The Rainbow*, for example, Lawrence shows the child Ursula living in this state too briefly, unable, "like the other children," to live "at one with the flowers and insects and playthings," for "her father came too near to her . . . wide-eyed, unseeing, she was awake before she knew how to see. She was wakened too soon." [16] As a result, Ursula suffers from her ambivalent, painful consciousness of the masculine throughout the novel. In *Women in Love*, Birkin's fear of the "merging" he thinks Ursula desires is rooted in his belief that the merging of personalities sacrifices the primal integrality of the self. In "St. Mawr," Louise chooses to live at the ranch isolated "deep in America" in the hope of reachieving an integral state; she feels at one with the "wild spirit" there for whom her "sex" is "deep and sacred." [17] Louise abandons men, Aaron Sisson abandons women, and the woman of "The Woman Who Rode Away" is abandoned by and abandons humanity altogether. Lawrence's insistence that one needs to sacrifice "personal consciousness" if one is to connect with one's "passional cosmic consciousness" is expressed in that work by the woman yielding her life itself to the ritual and "mastery" of the Indians. Only in *Lady Chatterley's Lover* does Lawrence again attempt to portray the achievement of integrality through a relationship between the sexes.

Like that of Lawrence, most of Blake's work concentrates on the struggles of the divided world and the task of reintegration. Only the *Songs of Innocence* portrays the psyche "prior to the separation of things." In "Infant Joy," for example, the infant confers identity upon itself and, *because* it names itself, *can* name itself "Joy." The infant is received by the world, embodied in the second speaker of the poem, in precisely the terms in which it experiences itself; no split between self and other, "subjective" and "objective" exists:

I have no name
I am but two days old.—
What shall I call thee?
I happy am
Joy is my name,—
Sweet joy befall thee!

Pretty joy!
Sweet joy but two days old.
Sweet joy I call thee:
Thou dost smile.
I sing the while
Sweet joy befall thee.

(E 16)

In naming itself, however, the infant of this poem avoids conferring upon itself a sexual identity, for Blake, like the early Lawrence, envisions the primal state as both masculine and feminine. "An infant," Lawrence writes in the "Study of Thomas Hardy," "is of no very determinate sex: that is, it is of both. Only at adolescence is there real differentiation, the one is singled out to predominate" (P 459). Just as Ursula's awakening is accompanied, indeed caused, by her awareness of the manhood of her father, so for Blake, sexual differentiation, or division, is a concomitant of the birth into consciousness. *The Four Zoas*, for instance, begins with "Tharmas Parent power darkning in the West," the psychic oneness of preconsciousness experiencing the separation of powers consciousness brings and the crisis of sexual division: "Lost! Lost! Lost! are my Emanations," he cries, creating the troubled psychic ground upon which that work will unfold (FZ I: 4, 6–7).

Blake portrays sexual differentiation as the female, Eve-like, dividing from the male, and not the male from the female. Enion separates from

Tharmas, Enitharmon from Los, Jerusalem from Albion; or the emanations are expelled, like Ahania from Urizen. Blake is concerned with how the male psyche divides and with the assumption of autonomy on the part of the *anima*. He does not offer us a conception of the *animus*. In other words, Blake's psychic ground is the bisexual male psyche and not, as is too often assumed, an androgynous human psyche. Were it the latter, we would expect to meet in his work not only masculine Zoas with feminine emanations (*animae*) but also feminine Zoas with masculine emanations (*animi*). Sexual division would entail the departure of the masculine from the feminine, as well as the other way around; Blake touches this theme only in his portrayals of the birth process, and we shall see later in which light he, as well as Lawrence, regards the feminine capacity to give birth, especially to a male.

I mentioned earlier that it is the early Lawrence who regards the infant as bisexual. In *Fantasia of the Unconscious*, written during the period he was working on *Aaron's Rod*, Lawrence retracts his earlier assertion and insists, rather, that:

> A child is born sexed. A child is either male or female: in the whole of its psyche and physique is either male or female. Every single living cell is either male or female as long as life lasts. And every single cell in every male child is male, and every cell in every female child is female. (F 96)

In *Fantasia*, Lawrence attributes the theory of bisexuality, what he calls the "hermaphroditic fallacy," to the domination of the psychic life by mental consciousness. From his depiction of the sexual confusion such domination wrings, it is not hard to see why Lawrence excluded "mental cognition" from his "four cornerstones of the psyche," envisioning them instead as the "four great nerve centres": the solar plexus, lumbar ganglion, cardiac plexus, and thoracic ganglion, so that "thought and idea," as he says, "do not enter in." Under the domination of the mental consciousness, he writes,

> The great affective centres no longer act spontaneously, but always wait for control from the head. This always breeds a great fluster in the psyche, and the poor self-conscious individual cannot help posing and posturing. Our ideal has taught us to be gentle and wistful: rather girlish and yielding, and very yielding in our sympathies. In fact, many young men feel so very like what they imagine a girl must feel that hence they draw the conclusion that they must have a large share of female sex inside them. False conclusion. (F 96)

Lawrence implies that if the "great affective centres" were to act spontaneously, men would be entirely male and women entirely female (whatever that may mean); but mental consciousness perverts sexuality. The problem is complicated by the conflict Lawrence sees during this period between what he calls "the essentially religious or creative motive" on the one hand, and the "sexual motive" on the other: "In one direction," he writes, all life works up to the "one consummating act of coition," but another, "greater impulse" is the "desire of the human male to build a world . . . out of his own self and his own belief [and out of] his own soul's faith and delight" (F 18). These two impulses, he insists, exist "in great conflict . . . at all periods."

Thus *The Rainbow* portrays men and women dwelling in what Blake called the world of Generation, as if they believe that Generation can be, as Los says in *Jerusalem*, a holy " '[Image] of regeneration!' " (J I: 7, 65); yet Lawrence's men and women in that novel never achieve such Regeneration. Birkin, and after him, Aaron Sisson and Mellors—at the opening of *Lady Chatterley's Lover*—experience Generation in its demonic aspect, as a "swallower" of Regeneration, as Los also describes it (J IV: 90, 37). For these later characters, woman who can be, like Blake's Vala, a "shade of sweet repose" has become "a devouring worm" (J I: 12, 2, 3). They would agree with the speaker of one of Blake's notebook poems:

Till I turn from Female Love
And root up the Infernal Grove
I shall never worthy be
To Step into Eternity

(E 468)

Nevertheless, Lawrence's claim, in *Fantasia*, that "every single cell in every male child is male, and every single cell in every female child is female" is weakened by his suggestion, early on in the work, that each infant contains within itself the "parent nuclei": "every individual has mother and father sparkling within himself." Like the young Anna dancing between the arches of the rainbow formed by her parents, the child exists, says Lawrence, "in the interplay of two great life-waves, the womanly and the male." Lawrence even goes on to say that the home of the knowledge that "I am I," a knowledge "we can know but not think," is the "original nucleus joining male and female at conception" (F 30–35). Thus, even when overtly opposing a bisexual view of the psyche, he implies the latent existence of inherent androgyny. The conviction, voiced in the Hardy essay, that in life "no new thing has ever arisen, or can arise, save out of the impulse of the male upon the female, the female upon the male" (P 44) remains with him.

Lawrence's sexual ethic returns after *Aaron's Rod* and "St. Mawr," in *Lady Chatterley's Lover*. Blake, too, devoted his final prophecy to the immense effort of reconciling Jerusalem and Albion, aggregate of all emanations and the (masculine) human form. For both Blake and Lawrence tacitly recognize that the proper state for the creation of art involves bringing into fruitful relationship the symbolic magnitude "male" with the symbolic magnitude "female."

There is, however, an important difference between the two artists' treatment of sexuality. Whereas Blake creates figures who individually embody masculine or feminine symbolic magnitudes, Lawrence creates personalities who, whatever their sex, possess within them both masculine and feminine attributes. Just as Lawrence himself was (ironically) fundamentally identified with the feminine principle, as H. M. Daleski has shown, so Lawrence's male characters tend to possess qualities he elsewhere asserts to be feminine, and his females possess qualities he elsewhere asserts to be masculine. Though he sees the "Will-to-Motion" as masculine, for example, and the "Will-to-Inertia" as feminine, he describes the generations of Brangwen men in *The Rainbow* as contentedly living "in the drowse of blood intimacy" and the women as "facing outwards . . . to enlarge their own scope and range and freedom." Though he regards the monist urge as feminine, it is, as we have seen, Will Brangwen who longs for an Absolute Oneness and Anna, his wife, who struggles for the diversity of separate individualities. Though he sees "mental consciousness" as masculine and bodily awareness as feminine, it is Hermione in *Women in Love* who wants to *know*, for whom "the pleasure of knowing is *so* great, so *wonderful*," and Birkin who craves the expression of "primal desire"; similarly, it is Connie who begins *Lady Chatterley's Lover* as a developed intellectual sundered from her body, and Mellors who lives at home in his body, close to the sensation-filled world of nature.[18]

Given this exchange of sexual attributes, the ideal "happy end" of a Lawrence novel, as *Lady Chatterley's Lover* evidences, would be the return to the male of his maleness and the return to the female of her femaleness, as Lawrence conceived those states. The novel, in this sense, is a "verbal icon," or isomorphism, of the act of love itself, for as Lawrence writes in the Hardy essay, in the act of love

> that which is mixed in me becomes pure, that which is female in me is given to the female, that which is male in her draws into me, I am complete, I am pure male, she is pure female; we rejoice in contact perfect and naked and clear, singled out unto ourselves, and given the surpassing freedom. . . . (P 468)

On the one hand, then, Lawrence admits the necessity of living, fruitful, essential contact with both the *anima* and with the woman herself; on the other, he fears such contact, and passionately desires a "purification" of both sexes, so that men will be masculine and women, feminine. Although "at times," he writes, "the great female principle does not abide abundantly in woman . . . at certain periods woman, in the body, is not the supreme representative of the Bride" and the "great male principle is only weakly evidenced in man in certain periods . . . the Bridegroom can be hidden away from woman, for a century or centuries," nevertheless, he goes on, the "supreme art" remains that which not only "knows the struggle" between the two conflicting principles, but knows, too, "the final reconciliation" (P 473, 516). Similarly, for Blake, a "Male without a female counterpart" is sterile selfhood: an artist without a muse, time without the space within which to realize its achievements and desires, bridegroom without bride. When the sleeping psyche awakes, the "Crimes . . . Punishments . . . Accusations of Sin . . . Jealousies Revenges. Murders. hidings of Cruelty in Deceit" which in the fallen world distinguish, for Blake, the relationships between the sexes, "vanish & cease" (J IV: 92, 13, 15–16). Male and female arise in renewed, regenerated power. So long as we live under the hegemony of mental consciousness, however, such a purification or regeneration is impossible. Not only is "manhood divided" when Urizen seizes control of the psyche, but the female assumes, for Blake as for Lawrence, a terrible power. Indeed, both Blake and Lawrence concentrate intense artistic energy on portraying the states in which males and females are not mutually fructifying contraries of one another, but rather negations of each other's vitality and strength.

III

The primal division of the male, for Blake, entails dissociation from his "female" side:

> One dread morn of goary blood
> The manhood was divided for the gentle passions making way
> Thro the infinite labryinths of the heart & thro the nostrils issuing
> In odorous stupefaction stood before the Eyes of Man
> A female bright.
>
> (FZ VIIA: 84, 12–16)

The male has rejected his emotional life, his "gentle passions," what Lawrence calls "affective consciousness." His *anima*, for Blake, consequently assumes a psychic independence. The split between "subjective" and "objective" reality widens; the male portion of the psyche becomes dominated by an abstracted rationality, and the female portion by pure will. A demonic parody of the original bisexual state, this conjunction of male rationality and female will is in Blake's terms "hermaphroditic," sterile, negative, incapable of imaginative life or of artistic production. One is reminded of Gudrun and Gerald Crich, as well as the destructive relationship of Romero and "The Princess," though for Lawrence, there as elsewhere, the female, not the male, embodies rationality twisted by emotional repression. Both those relationships, it should be noted, end with the death of the male.

What Blake portrays as an intrapsychic process, Lawrence portrays as a social phenomenon. "Tortured and cynical and unbelieving," he writes, man "has let all his feelings go out of him, and remains a shell of a man . . . nothing really moves him . . ." (P 200). Having lost his "instinctive hold on the life-flow and life-reality," he has also lost his "instinctive hold" over women. Rather than submit to the male with an "instinctive, unconscious submission made in unconscious faith"—as Connie comes to submit to Mellors, as Birkin yearns for Ursula to submit to him—woman begins to fight man "at any cost," like Banford of "The Fox," Winifred of "England, My England," or Mrs. Morel of *Sons and Lovers*, or like Anna Brangwen fighting Will till he is "burned and obliterated" by her power. The result is that the modern world, according to Lawrence, is becoming a "tyranny of women," of mothers "who lust to have absolute power over their children" (F 200, 198, 196, 200). The male child is either arrested, like Paul Morel, "from finding his proper fulfillment on the sensual plane" (F 168), or he grows up to worship women, declaring, like Clifford Chatterley, his "idolatry." Man, says Lawrence, becomes on the one hand "the fetcher, the carrier, the sacrifice, the crucified," devoted, like the desperate Iad in "The Rocking-Horse Winner," to "the great end of Women" (F 98–99), and on the other, overly rational, mechanical, with a mind "curious and cold" like that of Gerald Crich, Lilly, Clifford, the Prussian officer, and, indeed, like that of Urizen after he expels Ahania.

What overwhelmingly concerns both Blake and Lawrence is the *paralysis* of the creative male in such a hermaphroditic state. Blake portrays this paralysis and, with it, what he conceives of as the dangers of a "tyranny of women." In Chapter 1 of *Jerusalem*, for example, Albion's hiding of his emanation in "Jealousy" leads Satan—Blake's symbol of the "Great Selfhood"—to appear before Albion on the "frowning chaos" of his soul. Once he is controlled by his selfhood, Albion worships and idolizes woman, experiencing her as the "Divine Wisdom" just as Gerald Crich worships Gudrun, Clifford, Connie, and then Mrs. Bolton. That is how Hermione aches to be worshipped, and as Aaron Sisson fears he will worship. In

Blake's mythology, the idolized female is "Vala." "Know me now Albion," she declares. "Look upon me":

> I alone am Beauty
> The Imaginative Human Form is but a breathing of Vala
> I breathe him forth into the Heaven from my secret Cave
> Born of the Woman to obey the Woman
>
> (J II: 29 [33], 48–51)

For Vala, the woman-on-a-pedestal is Mother, and it is she who has ultimate control of the imaginative creations of men. Vala conceives of the "Human Divine" as "Woman's Shadow"; for her, the masculine is merely a "breeder of Seed: a Son & Husband" (J III: 64, 13). Vala herself, says Blake, is "Mother from the Womb / Wife, Sister, Daughter to the Tomb" (E 266). Los, the creative male, is horrified by the thought of this ultimate dependency of man upon woman and in words that in a poetic mood Birkin himself might have spoken, he retorts:

> I hear the screech of Childbirth loud pealing, & the groans
> Of Death, in Albions clouds dreadful utterd over all the Earth
> What may Man Be? who can tell! but what may Woman be?
> To have power over Man from Cradle to corruptible Grave.
> There is a Throne in every Man, it is the Throne of God
> This Woman has claimd as her own & Man is no more!
> Albion is the Tabernacle of Vala & her Temple
> And not the Tabernacle & Temple of the Most High
> O Albion why wilt thou Create a Female Will?
> To hide the most evident God in a hidden covert, even
> In the shadows of a Woman & a secluded Holy Place
> That we may pry after him as after a stolen treasure. . . .
>
> (J II: 30 [34], 23–34)

Recoiling from Vala's words, Los hears the "screech of Childbirth" with the "groans of death," for as Blake writes in "To Tirzah": "Whate'er is born of Mortal Birth / Must be consumed with the Earth." To be born of Vala is to be enjoined to that dangerous "Maternal line" that gives birth to the mortal body; it is to be what Blake calls "Adam":

> He repented that he had made Adam
> (of the Female, the Adamah)
> & it grieved him at his heart
>
> . . . .
>
> What can be Created Can be Destroyed
> Adam is only The Natural Man & not the Soul or Imagination
>
> (E 270, 271)

"The question of all time," writes Lawrence in *Fantasia*, is whether man, the "eternal protagonist," was born "of woman, from her womb of fathomless emotion," or whether "woman, with her deep womb of emotion," was "born from the rib of active man, the first created." Though Blake has no such distinction between feminine "fathomless emotion" and male action, and regards Adam not as the "first created" but as the Natural Man born of the Female ("Adamah," or Earth), he and Lawrence agree that to accept the psychological priority of motherhood is to grant divine power to a matriarchy presided over not by a benevolent Great Mother but rather by "the Goddess Nature / Mystery Babylon the Great," the "hidden Harlot" (J IV: 93, 24–25), and therefore to be rendered incapable of imaginative action. For Blake, it is the religious rationalists, the Deists, who worship "the Material / Humanity; calling it Nature, & Natural Religion" (J IV: 90, 65–66), just as it is Lawrence's superrational men who conjoin with the female will. But both men reject "Maternal Humanity" not only because their model of female creativity is confined to the female's capacity to procreate, and not only because under her auspices humanity dies, but also because, for both men, the female as a repository of the divine possesses a disturbing sexual power over the man who conceives her as such.

Whereas in Beulah, portrayed by Blake as a state of psychic relaxation,

> every Female delights to give her maiden to her husband
> The Female searches sea & land for gratification to the
> Male Genius,
>
> (J III: 69, 15–17)

in the state of Generation shaped by Vala and the "Spectre," sexuality is dominated by "Female Space." The male "Organs of Life" become "a little grovelling Root outside" of man (J I: 17, 32), and the "most evident God" is hidden, as Los says, "in a secret covert, even / In the shadows of a Woman" by the female will. That "secret covert" is the womb, now the source of all creation after which man must pry, "as after," in Los's words, "a stolen treasure," man's creativity. Having to enter "Female Space" to search for the creative principle is humiliating, says Blake, because the act of intercourse inevitably entails the loss of potency and power:

> The nature of a Female Space is this: it shrinks the Organs
> Of Life till they become Finite & Itself seems Infinite
>
> (M I: 10, 6–7)

Genital sexuality, for Blake, is "a pompous High Priest entering by a Secret Place" (J III: 69, 44) to commune with a "Female God" who neither discovers nor hides herself[19] and hence keeps man either ever searching and never satisfied, or else at once "satisfied and shattered, fulfilled and destroyed," as Lawrence describes Birkin's feelings after intercourse with Ursula. True embraces, for Blake, are "Cominglings: from the Head even to the Feet" (J III: 69, 43), rather than an assertion of power. But for such "Cominglings" to take place, the female will must disappear. "In Eternity," he writes, "Woman is the Emanation of Man she has no Will of her own There is no such thing in Eternity as a Female Will" (VLJ 85). In *Jerusalem*, he claims that

> Maternal Humanity must be put off Eternally
> Lest the Sexual Generation swallow up Regeneration
> (J IV: 90, 36–37)

Through Birkin as spokesman, Lawrence expresses a similar view of both the female will and genital sexuality. Craving freedom and wholeness, Birkin believes intercourse means the loss of both. In intercourse, he meditates, man is but "the broken-off fragment of a woman" and sex itself is the reminder of "the still aching scar of the laceration." Just as for Blake, the act of intercourse is conceived of as an assertion of *female* power, in love, Birkin believes, "everything must be referred back to her, to Woman, the Great Mother of everything, out of whom proceeded everything and to whom everything must finally be rendered up." [20] In the well-known episode in "Moony," Birkin seeks to annihilate the female will—"the cold white light of feminine independence," as Lawrence calls it in "England, My England" [21]—by destroying the reflection of the moon, "planet of woman," in the water. As the moon's image becomes fragmented and disappears, Ursula, looking on, feels "dazed, her mind . . . all gone." "She felt," writes Lawrence, as if "she had fallen to the ground." Peace comes to the relationship between Birkin and Ursula only later, when Ursula discovers a numinous masculine power in her lover. She experiences him not as the "Tabernacle of Vala," but rather as the "Temple of the Most High," the embodiment of one of the sons of God about which she had fantasized in *The Rainbow*:

> where the sons of God saw the daughters of men, that they were fair. And he was one of these, one of these strange creatures from the beyond, looking down at her, and seeing she was fair. (WL 352)

Birkin's divine maleness becomes manifest to Ursula when genital sexuality is put aside for the erotic pleasure of pure touch.

> Unconsciously, with her sensitive finger-tips, she was tracing the back of his thighs, following some mysterious life-flow there. She had discovered some-

> thing, something more than wonderful, more wonderful than life itself. It was the strange mystery of his life-motion, there, at the back of the thighs, down the flanks. It was a strange reality of his being, the very stuff of being, there in the straight downflow of his thighs. It was here she discovered him one of the sons of God such as were in the beginning of the world, not a man, something other, something more. . . .
>
> She seemed to faint beneath, and he seemed to faint, stooping over her. It was a perfect passing away for both of them, and at the same time the most intolerable accession into being, the marvelousness of immediate gratification, overwhelming, outflooding from the source of the deepest life-force, the darkest, deepest, strangest life-source of the human body, at the back and base of the loins. (WL 354)

Ursula's willingness to abandon the assumed "female power" of genital sexuality and to explore Birkin's body frees her from shame and guilt. Whereas prior to this episode, she had condemned Birkin for the "foulness" of his "sex life" with Hermione, presumably its anality, after her experience of him as a "son of God" she feels only that she and Birkin might now "do as they liked": "She was free, when she knew everything, and no dark shameful things were denied her." That is, once the male is perceived as a "Temple of the Most High," moral inhibition vanishes. That is a possibility for Ursula because she does not identify with the maternal in woman. In *The Rainbow*, she was alienated from Anna whose life was lived in the "violent trance of motherhood"; in *Women in Love*, she constellates the ideal male–female polarity as a "son of God" descending unto the "daughter of man," and thus tacitly rejecting "maternal humanity" altogether.

Lady Chatterley's Lover offers a parallel though not identical psychological and sexual event. For Connie, too, shame is purged. But the purifying act is one of anal intercourse, and the symbolic significance is thus altered. Connie does not glory in the separate being of her lover so much as she physically and spiritually submits to him:

> It cost her an effort to let him have his way and his will of her. She had to be a passive, consenting thing, like a slave, a physical slave. Yet the passion licked round her, consuming, and when the sensual flame of it pressed through her bowels and breast, she really thought she was dying: yet a poignant, marvelous death.[22]

Connie's submission to Mellors releases her from her apparent sense of bondage to "other women": "Ah! " Lawrence shows her meditating, "that in itself was a relief, to be free of the strange dominion and obsession of *other women*. How awful they were, women! " Her refusal to identify with her sex is necessary to Lawrence since he allows her to become Mother. The "maternal line" ceases to be dangerous to the male ego if woman regards her pregnancy as a gift of the male to her.

For Lawrence, females are liberated from the Mother-dominated moral laws when they intuit or experience the sacred, separate power of the male. The same is true for Blake. Bearing "the likeness & similitude of Los" (J IV: 96, 7), *Christ* rends the "Infernal Veil" that grows "in the disobedient Female." Like Birkin or Mellors, Christ liberates eros by removing the law from the "Inner Sanctuary" (the ark, the womb), allowing embraces to become "Cominglings from the Head even to the Feet." Lawrence shares Blake's vision of the son of God. In his essays, he asserts that Christ overcomes feminine power manifested both religiously and sexually. For Lawrence, the Jewish God was the "God of the Body, the rudimentary God of physical laws and physical functions," and the Jew, he writes, was sunk in passive "feminine sensation," keeping his body "always like the body of a bride ready to serve the bridegroom." (One is reminded of Urizen's attack on "feminine indolent bliss.") Antagonistic to "the active male principle, which would deny the age and refuse sensation," the Jew, he writes, "conceived only sins of commission, of change, of transformation," that is, he conceived of only "male sins." Thus, Lawrence contends, "in the whole of the Ten Commandments, it is the female who speaks."

Christ rose, he goes on, "from the suppressed male spirit of Judea": "Out of an over-female race, came the male utterance of Christ" who lived "the male life utterly apart from woman." Christ signifies that a child is born to the spirit and not to the flesh. "The body of Christ," writes Lawrence, "must be destroyed" and "that of Him which was Woman must be put to death, to testify that He was Spirit, that He was Male, that He was Man, without any womanly part" (P 459). Or, as Blake concludes his poem, "To Tirzah":

> The Death of Jesus set me free,
> Then what have I to do with thee?
>
> (E 30)

Thus, the female chosen by Blake and Lawrence for a *hieros gamos* with the male is one whose psychic energy is born of *male* spiritual, imaginative power. Ursula and Connie are reborn through the male; at the end of *Jerusalem*, Enitharmon, the feminine portion of male creativity, dissolves. Blake conceives of Enitharmon as capable of accompanying Los only through the state of Generation, where she creates the "round Womb" to counter the creativity of Los and to defend herself from becoming his "slave." Believing that the universe is "Woman's World," Enitharmon cannot accept the male "Fibres of Dominion." Once Albion is redeemed, however, the powers of Enitharmon fail, for Albion symbolizes in his renewal the separate male who cannot be woven in female looms. Her function is assumed by Jerusalem, the emanation "hidden till time of the end" in "Vala's cloud," and emerging only as the "Poet's Song draws to its period." Jerusalem is the feminine who in beholding "the Maternal Line . . . the Seed of the Woman," perceives it as comprising the "Daughters of Vala" whose creations comprise "the Body of death." "But I, thy Magdalen," she announces to Christ, "behold thy Spiritual Risen Body" (J III: 62, 8, 13–14). In the final moments of the poem, Jerusalem awakes at the call of the redeemed Albion, when "the Night of Death is past and the Eternal Day / Appears upon our Hills" (J IV: 97, 3–4). As she awakes, Albion stretches his hand "into Infinitude" and takes his Bow, "a Male & a Female" whose "Arrows of Love" lay open "the hidden Heart." "And the Hand of Man grasps firm between the Male & Female Loves" (J IV: 97, 15).

IV

For both Blake and Lawrence, the personal ego, abstract reason, and "objectivity" are attributes of a crippled humanity. Both artists are drawn to the undercurrents of consciousness, the "carbon" of being in the words of Lawrence, in quest of a form of intuitive, sensuous, and imaginative knowledge in which the psyche as a whole is free to participate. This position suggests that both artists reject, in the terms of Erich Neumann, qualities of "patriarchal consciousness" in favor of those of "matriarchal consciousness."[23]

The former, according to Neumann, ideally consists of "isolated and abstract conscious contents, free of emotionalism," whereas the latter "conserves the tie with the unconscious realms from which its knowledge springs." Matriarchal consciousness thus surfaces in the psyche of the artist engaged in the creative act; for the male engaged in the creative processes, says Neumann, "accentuated activity" occurs "on the part of the *anima*," the female figure most often identified as the muse.

For Blake and Lawrence, their very opposition to the rigid boundaries of patriarchal consciousness means that both intuit the need for the symbolic magnitudes of the matriarchal. But it also means a meeting with the feminine archetype that can overwhelm their own creativity. They open themselves to "Female Space" and discover by doing so the primacy of the Mother. When the *anima* emerges from the depths of the unconscious to the surface, she declares her separate power to create.

And at that point, both artists resist her with a furious, adamant energy designed to put her in her place. They need to transform her into a helpmate, a midwife to their own creative process. That is the symbolic function of Connie for Lawrence, and Jerusalem for Blake. As Susan Fox points out with reference to Blake, "female separateness is good when it permits communication among males, bad when it corrupts that communication, good when it passively awaits embrace, bad when it actively demands embrace. The more positive Blake's female becomes, the more passive, the more male-circumscribed she becomes." [24]

Susan Fox points out that Blake's character Jerusalem is more "metaphoric than literal," but that the metaphor is "powerful." She quite rightly sees Blake as a "victim" of the same social attitudes toward women he himself intuited as destructive. Lawrence, who began his life's work believing that he should be "sticking up for the love between man and woman," floundered on the shoals of his troubled confusion about his own mother, and his own sexuality. "Teetering always on the edge of homosexuality," as Anne Smith writes,[25] "searching so much of the time for the male in woman and the female in man," Lawrence never quite freed himself from his dread of the feminine. "In his heart of hearts," writes Frieda Lawrence, "I think he always dreaded women, felt that they were in the end more powerful than men. . . . From her man is born and to her he returns for his ultimate need of body and soul. She is like earth and death to which all return." [26]

Lawrence was undoubtedly right when he suggested that the "supreme art," in which male and female were "equal . . . complete," "remains to be fully done" (P 516).

Notes

1. As F. R. Leavis describes both Blake and Lawrence in *For Continuity* (Cambridge: Minority Press, 1933), p. 111.

2. "William Blake and D. H. Lawrence," in *William Blake: Essays for S. Foster Damon*, ed. Alvin Rosenfeld (Providence: Brown Univ. Press, 1969), pp. 106, 87.

3. *The Utopian Vision of D. H. Lawrence* (Chicago: Univ. of Chicago Press, 1963), p. 15.

4. "Study of Thomas Hardy," in *Phoenix*, ed. Edward D. McDonald (1936; reprint ed., New York: Viking Press, 1972), p. 406; hereafter cited as P.

5. "Aristocracy," *Reflections on the Death of a Porcupine*, in *Phoenix II*, ed. Warren Roberts and Harry T. Moore (New York: Viking Press, 1971), p. 482.

6. S. Foster Damon theorizes that Urthona's connection with the earth suggests that his name indicates "Earth-owner," in *William Blake: His Philosophy and Symbols* (Gloucester, Mass.: Peter Smith, 1958), p. 326.

7. See Mark Kinkead-Weekes, "Eros and Metaphor: Sexual Relationships in the Fiction of Lawrence," in *Lawrence and Women*, ed. Anne Smith (London: Vision Press, 1978), p. 102.

8. Purvis E. Boyette, "Milton and the Sacred Fire: Sex Symbolism in *Paradise Lost*," in *Literary Monographs*, vol. 5, ed. Eric Rothstein (Madison: Univ. of Wisconsin Press, 1973), p. 72.

9. Erich Neumann, "On the Moon and Matriarchal Consciousness," in *Fathers and Mothers*, ed. Patricia Berry (Zurich: Spring Publications, 1973), p. 40.

10. H. M. Daleski, *The Forked Flame: A Study of D. H. Lawrence* (London: Faber & Faber, 1965), passim.

11. *Lady Chatterley's Lover* (New York: Bantam Books, 1971), p. 106.

12. "The Crown," *Reflections on the Death of a Porcupine*, *Phoenix II*, p. 380.

13. *The Rainbow* (Middlesex: Penguin Books/William Heinemann, 1974), p. 204.

14. *Fantasia of the Unconscious*, from *Fantasia of the Unconscious and Psychoanalysis of the Unconscious* (Middlesex: Penguin Books, 1971, reprint ed., 1974), p. 131; hereafter cited as F.

15. Quoted by Edward Edinger, *Ego and Archetype: Individuation and the Religious Function of the Psyche* (New York: Putnam's, 1972), p. 184.

16. *The Rainbow*, p. 221.

17. *The Tales of D. H. Lawrence* (London: Martin Secker, 1934), p. 688.

18. For a discussion of Lawrence's concepts of the male and female principles, see Daleski, pp. 18–41. I discuss the consequences of the "exchange of sexual attributes" in "For the Sexes: Blake's Hermaphrodite in *Lady Chatterley's Lover*," *Bucknell Review* (Spring 1978).

19. See Blake's annotations to Dr. Thornton's statement that the "Supreme Being . . . keeps the human race in suspense, neither discovering, nor hiding Himself"; Blake comments, "a Female God" (E 658).

20. *Women in Love* (Middlesex: Penguin Books/William Heinemann, 1974), p. 224; hereafter cited as WL.

21. Quoted by Colin Clarke, *River of Dissolution: D. H. Lawrence and English Romanticism* (London: Routledge & Kegan Paul, 1969), p. 103.

22. *Lady Chatterley's Lover*, p. 267. See also Kinkead-Weekes, p. 118.

23. Neumann, p. 40ff.

24. See Susan Fox, "The Female as Metaphor in William Blake's Poetry," *Critical Inquiry* 3 (1977): 518–519.

25. Anne Smith, "New Adam and a New Eve—Lawrence and Women: A Biographical Overview," in *Lawrence and Women*, ed. Anne Smith (London: Vision Press, 1978), pp. 9–48.

26. Quoted by Judith G. Ruderman, "The Fox and the Devouring Mother," *D. H. Lawrence Review* 10 (1977): 269.

Annette S. Levitt

"The Mental Traveller" in *The Horse's Mouth*: New Light on the Old Cycle

"Degrade first the Arts if you'd Mankind degrade."
William Blake, *Annotations to Reynolds*

I

"The Mental Traveller," only 104 lines long, is, for all its brevity, one of Blake's more puzzling poems. Joyce Cary assimilates this poem within some four chapters of his best-known novel, *The Horse's Mouth*, modernizing and localizing Blake's intricate and ambiguous cycle in his intense mixture of genres. In the process he helps to clarify Blake's vision and to extend our comprehension of both novel and poem.

The Horse's Mouth is commonly appreciated for its humor and for its rich portrait of the irreverent, anarchic antihero, Gulley Jimson. Usually overlooked is the intricacy of the work, its multiple layers of meaning, even the more obvious evocation of the social and political climate in England at the start of World War II. Cary's success at characterization and dramatization enables him to convey complex ideas with such subtlety that they may be lost in the vitality of the narrative. The results both parallel and invert those of Blake, who creates his large landscapes and "allegories addressed to the intellect" in ways which can obscure the presence of a literal level of meaning. Cary obscures the symbolic levels of his novel by setting a realistic scene, and by creating characters so flawed in their human weaknesses that there is little chance to take them seriously, much less regard them or their lives as touchstones in a philosophical commentary.

But Cary's protagonist is an archetypal creator, and the novel is filled with philosophical overtones. The best manifestation of its depth appears in the use of Blake. Cary uses Blake's *Milton* in *The Horse's Mouth*, for example, as an intricate schema for Gulley Jimson's development as human being and as artist.[1] Throughout the novel, frequent quotations focus attention on the *Milton*ic events in Gulley's life, as he moves toward a renewal of his creative potential, culminating in his elaborate painting of the "Creation." This huge mural, filling the entire east end wall of an abandoned chapel, enacts in its imagery the preparations for "the great Harvest and Vintage" at the end of *Milton.* Gulley thus creates what Blake-Milton prepares for. In the modern world, with its greater potential for destruction, creation takes place sooner than in Milton's or Blake's time. Time itself, whose creations are loved by Eternity, is much compressed.

Cary's treatment of *Milton* enacts the universality and timelessness of Blake's archetypal artist, adding possibilities of meaning without destroying the integrity of Blake's masterpiece. He is equally respectful of Blake's artistry in "The Mental Traveller," and similarly imaginative in his unique adaptation of Blake's materials to a twentieth-century setting.

In barest outline, "The Mental Traveller" depicts the Orc cycle of repression and revolt, as a male babe, bound by an aged crone, bursts his fetters, moves through youth to age, and ultimately returns to infancy. While only one male moves through the entire cycle, three different females take part. The first, an old crone, binds the babe, grows younger to become his mistress, then disappears from the poem. As the man ages, a female babe appears and grows up to find her own lover; both disappear after evicting the old man from his home. The final female is the maiden whom the old man takes as a mistress; as he regresses to infancy, she ages, to become another binding crone. The cycle, described by Harold Bloom as "a history of fate of our imagination in the context of natural existence," goes on without foreseeable end; only the narrating Traveller and the second maiden who, with her lover, "escapes from the cycle into creative life," as Hazard Adams puts it,[2] move beyond the cycle. "The Mental Traveller" provides a telling commentary on the world of Cary's protagonist as the events of his life illuminate Blake's poem.

In contrast to the pervasiveness of *Milton*, "The Mental Traveller" appears in one brief section of *The Horse's Mouth*: within thirty pages of the novel are some 21 of its 26 stanzas. The poem functions primarily as a paradigm for Gulley Jimson's life in art. Cary has not, however, simply reduced it to a prescient gloss on the activities of Blake's troublesome descendant. Gulley's running commentary on the poem places it in political and social contexts which parallel Blake's conjunction of artistic freedom with social and political liberty. Moreover, Gulley's review of his own career in art focuses on several of the most important revolutionary figures in modern art—Turner, Manet, and Cézanne. Gulley traces the entire cycle of the poem in his own life, while the individual artists are equated in his mind with specific stages in the cycle. Beyond the novel, moreover, the lives of these artists trace the full creative cycle.

Cary's presentation of Gulley's narrative also parallels the formal strategy of the poem: the narrators of both speak in the first person, and both relay past events. Blake's point of view has a limited impact in this poem, however, since there is much less information on the Traveller than on Thel, for example, or even on the speakers in *Songs of Innocence*. The emphasis in "The Mental Traveller" is on the events of the narrative itself. But Gulley Jimson is a fully developed character, and the telling of his life story and his commentary on the poem reflect his idiosyncratic, pugnacious, art-centered world view. This filter of point of view adds further complexity to a reading of "The Mental Traveller" in *The Horse's Mouth*.

Gulley Jimson at first seems to be the Traveller himself, removed now from the actions he describes. But he is still a participant, one who "has been through [the] whole listing." Now he has "to start again. About 4th time." [3] This explanation comes straight from the horse's mouth—from Cary himself. Voracious and sensitive reader of Blake, prolific (if sometimes illegible) notetaker, he has left voluminous materials for the greater understanding of *The Horse's Mouth*, including detailed charts which trace the events of "The Mental Traveller" and his plans for their enactment in the novel. Cary's charts provide a fascinating glimpse into the novelist's art and his creativity in transforming this enigmatic poem into contemporary and comprehensible terms. Cary's worksheets present images and themes which are not always used explicitly in the narrative, but which contribute to a fuller understanding of both novel and poem. The interweaving of poem and novel, glossed by Cary's charts, clarifies the symbolic world of Gulley Jimson, the world of "The Mental Traveller."

The charts in which Cary plotted his adaptation of "The Mental Traveller" consist of three sheets, 8½ by 14 inches each. One chart is made up of three vertical columns: the first briefly interprets key lines in the poem; the second column suggests, in a word or brief phrase, possible applications of these concepts to Gulley's own or his father's life in art or to the larger framework of art history; the third column elaborates on these cryptic passages. The remaining two sheets are taped together to form one chart six columns wide.[4] In the first column Cary lists crucial phrases from the poem, some of which overlap with the lines interpreted in the one-page chart. The second column applies these images to Gulley's life, at times literally, at others metaphorically. The third column elaborates on these episodes and adds further characters—Gulley's father, Sara Monday (Gulley's former common-law wife), a young couple passing by, and Hitler—as participants in Cary's enactment of "The Mental Traveller." The fourth column adds still more characters—Hickson, Plantie, Young Franklin, Mrs. Ollier, Gulley's mother—and extends some of the incidents of the previous column; the fifth column, which is very sparse, adds detail to only two items on the previous column; the sixth column adds many details inherent in the incidents of the finished novel.

There is some overlapping between the two charts, but there are significant distinctions. The three-column chart is obviously tied to Chapter 13, in which Gulley reviews his life in art. The six-column chart is clearly the basis of Chapters 11 and 12, in which Cary offers the sociopolitical contexts for the poem and introduces various characters to exemplify these concepts. The charts converge in Chapter 14, in their use of the poem's final stanzas and Cary's somewhat startling juxtaposition of the babe, Hitler, and modern art.[5]

II

"The Mental Traveller" first appears in Chapter 11 of *The Horse's Mouth*, after Gulley's brief reunion with Sara Monday; this revitalizing encounter precipitates his first fresh creative impulse since he began work on his painting of "The Fall." [6] But these new images, fish shapes added to the traditional design of Adam, Eve, and serpent, lose their vitality for Gulley after a visit from two "beauty-loving, picture-hating" preachers. Gulley tries not to be affected by their insensitivity, and encourages himself: "Come, I said, you're not one of those asses who takes himself seriously. You're not like poor Billy, crying out:

> I've travelled through a land of men,
> A land of men and women too,
> And heard and saw such dreadful things
> As cold earth wanderers never knew.
>
> [Stanza 1]

"Which probably means only that when Billy had a good idea, a real tip, a babe, some blue-nose came in and asked him why he drew his females in nightgowns" (HM 38). The more vocal preacher is undaunted: "Blue-nose gave another sniff and said, 'I notice that it is the fashion for modern artists to paint the female limbs very large. I must not say that there appears to be a cult of ugliness—I merely stand to be instructed.' " Gulley tries to ignore him, and touches up Adam's big toe, "While old Billy cried:

> And if the babe is born a boy, that is to say, a real vision,
> He's given to a woman old,
> Who nails him down upon a rock,
> Catches his shrieks in cups of gold.
>
> [Stanza 3]

"Which means that some old woman of a blue nose nails your work of imagination to the rock of law, and why and what; and submits him to a logical analysis" (HM 38–39).

By presenting the poem initially in terms of Blake himself, Cary offers it on the simplest level of interpretation: the speaker of the poem is thus the historical persona of the poet, and William Blake is equated with Gulley Jimson, two artists unappreciated by the general public of their respective times—especially the moralizing, religiously oriented segment of that public. The historical Blake soon disappears from Gulley's commentary. Cary gradually adds levels of meaning as he imposes contemporary characters onto the symbolic framework of the poem.

In his discouragement, Gulley temporarily abandons his work, scraping out the new fish shapes, and goes "out to get room for [his] grief. Thank God, it was a high sky on Greenbank" (HM 41). For the next two chapters (12 and 13), during which the bulk of Blake's poem appears, Gulley is out of his studio, free to encounter individuals who suggest meaningful extensions of Blake's poem and to be stimulated by his environment to thoughts about the discipline of art and his own life in its thrall. Chapter 12 alternates the present and the past, Gulley's current adventures and his memories; Chapter 13 takes place entirely in the past, as Gulley reviews his life in art. However, in Chapter 14, which offers only two stanzas from "Traveller,"[7] Gulley is drawn forcefully into the present—a bleak world for artists and other sensitive people in 1939.

The richness of Cary's novel is evident even in his charts. Across the top of one, for example, he gives his interpretations of Blake's babe and crone: "babe equals vision, idea, imagination, love, spiritual insight, modern art, invention, inspiration, life, forgiveness. Old woman equals nature, laws, classical convention, material beauty, tradition, prudence, necessity, laws." While critics have seen these possibilities, Cary alone transforms them into new art.

As Blake uses language at times literally, at others in ironic inversion of normal usage, so Cary varies the symbolic significance of his characters. The very preacher who scorned Gulley's work soon appears to him as a fellow artist, " 'bitten in the backside by a mad dog' " of ideas (HM 39) but restrained to domesticity by his wife, the grocer's rich widow, who does not want him to change his beautiful sermon. In lines prefiguring Gulley's later questioning of his own artistic ability and his search for the elusive maiden of form, the preacher wonders "whether it's a beautiful sermon or a lot of wind, wambling and wallowing among the ruined caves of the British Museum. But the mad dogs keep on singing, 'Speech, speech. More wonderful speech.' And Blue-nose keeps on trying to catch one of them by the tail, but they're always just round the corner" (HM 40).

Gulley's attitude toward the preacher grows more complex as he muses angrily while walking along the Thames, which appears to him like "shot silk," the breeze

> ruffling under the silk-like muscles in a nervous horse. Ruffling under my grief like ice and hot daggers. I should have liked to take myself in both hands and pull myself apart. To spite my guts for being Gulley Jimson, who, at sixty-seven years of age, after forty-five years of experience, could be put off his intentions, thoroughly bamboozled and floored, by a sprout of dogma, a blind shepherd, a vegetated eye, a puffed-up adder of moralities. (HM 41)

Whereas "a vegetated eye" conveys Blake's idea of limited vision, "a blind shepherd" connotes the scorn with which Milton treats the priesthood in "Lycidas" (11. 119–120). The preacher now offends Gulley both in his official capacity and as a fellow artist. Gulley's ambivalence has been reduced to hatred, and Cary has concisely moved from simple character development to the creation of philosophical reverberations which add to his own artist two others with complex attitudes toward religion.

Cary offers another example of ambiguity in Gulley's view of a passing couple:

> Girl going past clinging to a young man's arm. Putting up her face like a duck to the moon. Drinking joy. Green in her eyes. Spinal curvature. No chin, mouth like a frog. Young man like a pug. Gazing down at his sweetie with the face of a saint reading the works of God. Hold on, maiden, you've got him. He's your boy. Look out, Puggy, that isn't a maiden you see before you, it's a work of imagination. Nail him, girlie. Nail him to the contract. Fly laddie, fly off with your darling vision before she turns into a frow, who spends all her life thinking of what the neighbours think.
>
> And if the babe is born a boy
> He's given to a woman old,
> Who nails him down upon a rock,
> Catches his shrieks in cups of gold.
>
> (Stanza 3; HM 41)

To Gulley the girl is at once the female babe of "vision, ideas, imagination" born in Stanza 11 and the maiden of form sought after in Stanza 14; she is also potentially the old woman of "tradition, prudence, necessity." Gulley's description of the young couple also reveals an interesting connection between art and reality. The preacher has asked, in words amusingly evocative of some of the criticism of Blake's art, " 'if—ah—the human form—anatomically speaking, could—ah—assume the position of the male figure. Of course, I know—ah—a certain distortion is—ah—permissible' " (HM 38). The couple, as Gulley sees them, proves that such anatomical distortion exists in nature and is not merely the province of "modern art," as the preacher seems to think. Certainly in our vegetated world we do not see ideal beauty unless we see through, not with the eye, as the boy and girl clearly regard each other.

It is revealing at this point to compare Cary's six-column chart with the novel. After listing symbolic equivalents for babe and old woman, he offers, in parallel columns: (1) "A babe is born in joy"; (2) "The vision of Gully [*sic*], is nailed down to Gods, injustice, material world"; and (3) "The young couple." The entry in column 4 is unclear; column 5 is empty and column 6 offers "Sara . . . imposing laws on his health, and making him take baths." The first entry is a quotation from Stanza 2 of the poem, which Cary omits from the novel—it is an action assumed as the basis of all which follows. The second entry, clearly an application of Stanza 3, is just as clearly connected with the preacher's repudiation of Gulley's apparently anti-naturalistic painting. The third entry is the germ of the rich passage just examined, while the sixth foreshadows later events in the novel.

Cary has carefully annotated the first three stanzas of the poem, using incremental repetition to enrich the levels of interpretation. With much greater concentration than in these four pages, he quickly moves on to assimilate the next four stanzas, those conveying the shift from the mastery of the female to that of the male. Again it is the landscape which prompts Gulley's reflections:

> small red clouds . . . beige pink, like Sara's old powder puffs full of her favorite powder. . . . And I thought how I used to powder her after her bath. I wonder she didn't kill me, the old Aphrodisiac. . . . How I washed and dressed for her, and let her trot me about like her puggy on a ribbon. It was, "Poor Gulley, don't forget your cough medicine. Now darling, what about your socks? I'm sure they're wet." And when I was mad to paint, she was for putting me to bed and getting in after me. Stirring all that fire only to cook her own pot. Growing wings on my fancy only to stuff a feather bed.
>
> She binds iron thorns around his head,
> She pierces both his hands and feet,
> She cuts his heart out at his side
> To make it feel both cold and heat.
> Her fingers number every nerve
> Just as a miser counts his gold;
> She lives upon his shrieks and cries,
> And she grows young as he grows old.
>
> (Stanzas 4, 5; HM 41–45)

Sara's domination is domestic and sexual, subordinating Gulley's creative needs to her own. But Gulley learns that the way to reverse the mastery is simply to hit Sara. And suddenly he is able to have her, on canvas or in bed:

> Yes, I found out how to get Sara on the canvas. Some of her anyhow. And I was always at her, one way or another. The flesh was made word; every day. Till he, that is, Gulley Jimson, became a bleeding youth. And she, that is, Sara, becomes a virgin bright.
>
> Then he rends up his manacles
> And binds her down for his delight.
> He plants himself in all her nerves,
> Just as a husbandman his mould;
> And she becomes his dwelling-place
> And garden fruitful seventy fold
>
> [Stanzas 6, 7]
>
> As Billy would say, through generation into regeneration. Materiality, that is, Sara, the old female nature, having attempted to button up the prophetic spirit, that is to say, Gulley Jimson, in her placket-hole, got a bonk on the conk, and was reduced to her proper status, as spiritual fodder. (HM 42–43)

Cary's chart adds little at this point. Equated with "Till he become a b. youth" are the lines "Sara," "he fights her, uses her" and, in a clear reversal of Stanza 3 and its implications for Cary, "He seizes on the Earth of injustice etc. of Gods, for his delight." Conversely, the chart is extremely useful in clarifying and relating the sections of the novel which follow. One seems entirely removed from "Traveller," while the others explicitly parallel it.

Inexplicably, it would seem, Gulley turns from his reminiscences of Sara to telephone Hickson, his former patron. He plays the role of public official and taunts Hickson with the charge of illegally possessing Jimson's work. This is the game which put Gulley in prison once before. This time he is hurried off the phone by a friendly warning that his ruse has been detected. Shaken by the discovery, Gulley stops to rest. Again the cloud formations inspire thoughts of painting: "I could do that, I thought. Those round clouds and the island in the sky heavy as new melted lead. But what's the good of thinking about it? They've got me. For I saw that they had got me. And I began to feel better. That's that, I thought" (HM 45). The passage seems to allude to Stanza 3, but succeeding events provide an even stronger connection with Stanza 8. Gulley meets "young Franklin," who is "about nineteen, and is just getting his first real worries" (HM 45), and Walter Ollier, whose wife "wasn't on speaking terms with anyone in the world except Walter, and she always abused him" (HM 46). Gulley's friends discuss the frustrations of illnesses and doctors, but Gulley feels too ill to participate in their conversation: "But I felt so old I wondered how my legs kept hanging on to my body. And I couldn't even think of what to do with the blank canvas. My eyes were dead as cod's and my ears only heard noises.

An aged shadow, soon he fades,
Wandering round an earthly cot,
Full filled all with gems and gold
Which he by industry had got.
And these are the gems of the human soul,
The rubies and pearls of a lovesick eye,
The countless gold of the aching heart,
The martyr's groan and the lover's sigh.

[Stanzas 8, 9]

"Well, I thought, I've filled a lot of canvases in my time. Quite enough for any man. It's time I was done for.

"And I remembered my father in the little Normandy farm where we went to live, or starve, because starving was cheaper in the Pas de Calais. Painting still more girls in gardens. And a whole room full of them inside. He wasn't going to be beaten by the wicked world and modern art" (HM 47).

Cary's chart reveals the connection among these stanzas, Hickson, Gulley's father, and Gulley himself, explaining the seemingly inexplicable. The six parallel notations run as follows: (1) "An aged shadow"; (2) "He lives with memories, ancient art, sentiments, old religion"; (3) "As a young man, devoted to Mammon. His papa. The old classical artist"; (4) "Telephone conver[sation] with Hickson. His papa. Himself. He doesn't want to leave life"; (5) "and mommas carrying on so . . ."; (6) "an aged shadow. *Hickson, who loved art.* But now he loves pictures. Benevolent. Papa, the aged shadow. G as the aged shadow." In each case there is a diminution—of powers, of sensibilities—an acceptance of the supremacy of the "earthly" or material over the spiritual. Gulley has said, "They've got me," and, indeed, by regarding his canon as completed, he is more moribund now than he seems at the end of the novel, dying amid his unfinished, crumbling "Creation."

Clearly Blake's "gems and gold" with which Cary equates Gulley's "filled . . . canvases" have been earned by an unhealthy sort of "industry," that which plumbs "the human soul" and enjoys the fruits of unrequited love and martyrdom. This stanza has intrigued Blakeans. Are the "lovesick eye," "aching heart," "martyr's groan," and "lover's sigh" those of the aged shadow himself or of others, whose suffering benefits him? [8] The next lines (from Stanza 10) at first seem to confirm the latter interpretation ("They are his meat they are his drink"), but ultimately add more ambiguity ("His grief is their eternal joy") in the shifting of pronouns. Cary omits these lines from the novel, instead translating their ambiguity into fictional terms. Gulley and his father, as creators, themselves suffer in order to create; Hickson is merely a consumer, "benevolent" though he may be (and Cary portrays him in a sympathetic light), who acquires the fruits of another's passion and suffering. The chart makes clear that Gulley, his father, and Hickson, in differing ways, are all "aged shadows," diminished as artists and as men.

Cary's fictional application of Stanzas 8 and 9 blends past and present, Gulley's memories of his father and his own similar grief. Gulley's sterility of imagination is only temporary. Cary's use of the poem at this point in the novel underlines the artist's search for the means to creation as the central theme in both poem and novel. Cary uses art as metaphor for life itself in a recapitulation of Stanzas 3 to 7, in which Gulley's long-dead mother takes on the roles of both the male babe and the bleeding youth. Chart entry 5, "Mommas carrying on so . . .," now becomes clear:

> And when papa stopped selling pictures and she found herself with five children to feed and no money, and a husband who was already brokenhearted; when, that is, the old woman nailed her down on the rock of necessity and cut her heart open she carried on with duty and devotion. She went on worshipping real art, papa's art, and she even went on having children, or where should I be now? She went on conducting her life in the grand classical style. Yes, that's what it was. And what a technique when you come to think of it. Nothing like the classical. A sense of form. None of your surface tricks; but solid construction.
>
> If I was only fifty or so, I declare I'd go back to school again, to the life class, like Renoir in his forties, and study nothing but form, form in the black and white, for two years. Just charcoal. See what my mother became in the years of misery; a great woman; a person in the grand style. Yes, by God, you need technique to make a good job of life. All you can get. You need to take necessity and make her do what you want; get your feet on her old bones and build your mansions out of her rock.
>
> And she becomes his dwelling-place
> And garden fruitful seventy fold.
>
> (Stanza 7; HM 48)

Gulley's memories of his parents' different responses to the hardships of life are traced in Cary's chart through Stanzas 13 and 14, which portray the aged shadow, or stultified vision, being evicted by the maiden of new vision (modern art, in the case of Gulley's father). This "beggar at anothers door" (Stanza 13) then "wanders weeping" (Stanza 14) until he can find another maiden, the appropriate form, that is, for his ideas. In column 6 Cary equates with these lines "Papa . . . brooding over his old art . . . and mama carrying on . . . a wonderful technique. He didn't know what was happening. A female babe." "Papa" is clearly the old man, grieving and wandering, and Gulley's mother, with her "wonderful technique," is the female babe. Cary has subsumed within the figure of the mother both the male and female babes, each at its most positive point, the male controlling nature, the female newly born from "the fire on the hearth."

The female babe actually appears in the poem somewhat earlier, in Stanza 11. Cary juggles the poem's order to avoid equating Gulley's mother with the rejecting maiden who causes the old man to go off on his pursuit of vision. She is the male babe bound by the old crone, growing into the bleeding youth who binds down and overcomes materiality. When the bleeding youth grows into the aged shadow, however, he is identified with Gulley's father, and his mother changes sex again to become the female babe—here identified less with artistic vision than with the nurturing spirit his father obviously needs. Gulley, an old man himself at this point in the novel, adapts Blake's poem within his memories so that his mother mothers his father at a similar point in the older man's life.[9] Gulley is stronger than his father was; he will manage to transcend this fallow period as he has others.

At this point Gulley is still in the slough of despond, but he is moving toward change. Cary presents the beginning of this shift as parallel to the pivotal section of "Traveller." In Stanzas 11 to 14 two brief cycles of artistic development appear: the artist's grief at his sterility is followed by the sudden birth of the female babe (new vision) which grows up only to reject the old man (stultified vision), who must wander until he finds another maiden. Cary's chart offers fascinating parallels for those stanzas, clarifying this dense section of the novel. Column 4, for example, develops "young Franklin's" surprisingly important role in the novel in conjunction with this segment of the poem. "His grief their joy" and "a little female babe" (the first and last lines of Stanza 11) become "Young Franklin wants to make a new world. Visionary. The small boy victim of the revolution. Creating art." There is greater literalness in the parallels to succeeding lines: "a beggar at anothers door" (Stanza 13) appears as "Franklin drives out the old art," and "He wanders weeping" (a fragment of the first line of Stanza 14) "Until he can a maiden win" (line 4) becomes "Franklin drives out the old art. Who wanders weeping / until he gets the new idea."

The connections between Franklin and Gulley, between revolution and vision, are explained by this section of the chart. Franklin appears in the context of Stanza 4,

> having trouble with boils. . . . The girls he fancies don't fancy him; the ones he fancied last year and doesn't fancy any more are lying in wait for him with kisses and hatchets. Made a bit on the pools and lost a lot on the dogs. And his best friend did him out of a good job, because he wanted to get married. Three years ago he was a happy corner boy, living like a hog in his dirty little mind. Now he's been stabbed alive. He's seeing things. The old woman of the world has got him. Old mother necessity.

She cuts his heart out at his side
To make it feel both cold and heat.

(Stanza 4; HM 45)

Here Franklin is a victim, if not "of the revolution" then of life itself. He also seems to be a realist who knows that "Young Dobson" gets beaten because his mother " 'married again. Got another kid and it's a bit queer in the head. So she wallops young Johnny. She'll murder him some day.' 'Why doesn't somebody do something about it? ' " Gulley asks. " 'Why don't they do something about anything—about Hitler? ' said young Franklin" (HM 46). He is clearly unhappy with the state of the world, and he continues to perform as dour social critic, predicting that Gulley will get two years in prison for his current offense. Gulley cannot resist raising the predicted penalty to seven years, and enhancing his crime as well: " 'Being Gulley Jimson,' I said, 'and getting away with it.' 'It doesn't matter,' said young Franklin. 'Not if you look at what's happening to the Jews in Germany. Nor anybody anywhere' " (HM 49). Gulley does not respond; he merely elaborates further on his own crimes against society: " 'being an artist,' I said. 'For upsetting everybody. For thinking I'd get away with everything at once.' . . . 'It's not what you'd call work,' said Bert. . . . 'It's more of a gift,' said Ollier. 'Like Frankie's boils,' I said. 'To keep him interested' " (HM 50).

Franklin's boils are like the "gift" of art in that both are unwilled irritants, designed to make the bearer itch and then do something to relieve his discomfort. Blake's artist is the prophet, the visionary, the Socratic gadfly, who sees the "Error" in his vegetated universe, and struggles to cast it out and create anew, from his own imaginative vision. Franklin "creates art" by stimulating others—the prophet's essential role. Gulley, on the other hand, is the artist provoked to create himself. Columns 2 and 3 of Cary's chart use Stanzas 11 to 14 to show Gulley's movement toward creation. Thus, "His grief their joy / a little female babe" becomes "Modern art again. . . . Vision / a new idea to Gully" (*sic*) (col. 2) and "Art comes to Gully" (*sic*) (col. 3); "a beggar at anothers door" is translated as "old religion, old law driven out"; and "Until he can a maiden win" becomes "revolutionary idea. Vision / new art" (col. 2) and "He struggles to find the new idea—and takes to art" (col. 3).

These lines are not enacted in Chapter 12. They function both as transitions to Chapter 13, in which Gulley recalls his passage through the various cycles of creation, and as a foreshadowing of what is to come when Gulley actually moves out of his static state. Column 6 parallels "until he can a maiden win" with "He gets the form again. Out of Sara. . . . Drives out the old nature. And the old technique. *He paints Sara and gets back to infancy*." None of this actually occurs until Chapter 15, when Gulley sees Sara again at Plant's religious meeting; by the end of that chapter he realizes "what I've been missing in my Eve, something female, something that Old Cranach had, yes, something from Sara." He then begins to draw "the everlasting Eve, but all alive-oh. She came out strong like Sara, the Sara of twenty years ago" (HM 76). That is still in the future, however. For the moment there is a change only in Gulley's state of mind. This occurs in what at first appears to be merely a description of the landscape:

> On the Surrey side the fire was dead. Clouds in blue and blue-and-soot. Blue-black smoke drifting up like smoky candles, and a blue sky as blue as blue spectacles with long pieces of sooty cobweb floating high up. . . . All below as flat as melted iron, on three levels: first, Greenbank Hard; then a step down to the river, and a step up to the towpath; then away to the edge of the plate. A flat earth. A few knobs of trees and houses popping up to make it flatter. (HM 49)

In column 1 of his chart, Cary, this one time, substitutes for lines from "Traveller" the phrases "Clouds blue and soot" and "Moon rising." In the poem itself the "flat Earth," Blake's image of linear or unlimited vision, "becomes a Ball"—a reduction to the "dull round" of closed vision—at one of the more negative points in the poem, in Stanza 16, which Cary does not use in the novel. Here, however, Gulley's vision is enlarged in his perception of the "flat earth," and he sees three barges "like stranded whales with their waists in the water" (HM 49). This is a most positive foreshadowing, for a whale—unobscured by water—will appear as a central image in Gulley's final "Creation" painting.

For the moment Gulley continues to observe his surroundings: "It made my mouth water. I could have eaten those personal chunks of barges and that sweet individual flank of mud. But I thought, only another sketch and there's a million every day. . . . You damned old sorcerer" (HM 49). The "old sorcerer" or art has caught Gulley. As he explains to his friends, " 'I had a real job once, a job of work. But art got me and look at me now' " (HM 50). Thus does Cary lead into Gulley's memories of his life in art, his passage through the cycles seen by the traveler, which constitute Chapter 13.

III

Cary's most intense and provocative use of "The Mental Traveller" illuminates Gulley's passage through the various schools of art which have molded his work. His mentors are carefully chosen revolutionaries in art and ideas; their political and social connotations reverberate through the novel. Gulley

> never meant to be an artist. You say, who does? But I even meant not to be an artist because I'd lived with one and I couldn't forget seeing my father, a little grey-bearded old man, crying one day in the garden. I don't know why he was crying. He had a letter in his hand; perhaps it was to tell him that the Academy had thrown out three more Jimson girls in three more Jimson gardens. I hated art when I was young, and I was very glad to get the chance of going into an office. . . . When I came to London in '99, I was a regular clerk. I had a bowler, a home, a nice little wife, a nice little baby, and a bank account. I sent money to my mother every week, and helped my sister. A nice happy respectable young man. I enjoyed life in those days.[10] (HM 51)

But one day, doodling at his desk, he is seduced, like Gauguin, by art, and his entire life changes. "I started as a Classic. About 1800 was my period. And I was having a hell of a time with my anatomy and the laws of perspective."

> Her fingers numbered every nerve,
> Just as a miser counts his gold.
>
> (Stanza 5; HM 51–52)

The year 1800 began Blake's difficult time in Felpham and begins, in the novel, a capsule history of modern art. Like Blake, Gulley is antipathetic to formalism. But he seems to have been reasonably successful: "I had a picture in the old Water Colour Society that year. Very Classical. Early Turner. Almost Sandby" (HM 52). "Early Turner" had none of the glowing irridescence, the magnificent use of light and color of the late watercolors, which seem to foreshadow Impressionism. Like Paul Sandby, "the man who in some ways must be regarded as the central figure in English water-colours of the eighteenth century," [11] Turner in those days worked in the classical-academic tradition of topographical drawing. Unlike Gulley, however, he was good enough at perspective to become a teacher of that subject at the Royal Academy; but he, too, had trouble with anatomy, a problem he resolved by omitting human figures from most of his works.[12] Gulley also lacked Turner's comfortable financial state in the early years:

> My wife was nearly starving, and we had pawned most of the furniture, but what did I care? Well, of course I worried a bit. But I felt like an old master. So I was, very old. I was at about the period when my poor old father was knocked out. I'd gone through a lot to get my experience, my technique, and I was going to paint like that all my life. It was the only way to paint. I knew all the rules. I could turn you off a picture, all correct, in an afternoon. Not that it was what

you call a work of imagination. It was just a piece of stuff. Like a nice sausage. Lovely forms. But I wasn't looking any more than a sausage machine. I was the old school, the old Classic, the old Church.

> An aged shadow soon he fades,
> Wandering round an earthly cot,
> Full filled all with gems and gold
> Which he by industry had got.
>
> (Stanza 8; HM 52)

Cary's chart for this section includes more of the poem than he quotes at this point in the novel, revealing how subtly he has assimilated and condensed his various interpretations of the early stanzas into this brief passage of the novel:

2. Spiritual vision, born in joy [Stanza 2]	Constable Turner	Started as Turner, when art caught me. Papa's influence.
3. Given to materiality, law, necessity, technical problems [Stanza 3]	Papa at art school	
4. Until he learns how to dominate problems [Stanzas 6, 7]		dominate problems
8. An aged shadow, he rests on his laurels or picture. The old law, the wise old drunk Classical [Stanza 8]	Papa, the old classic	And quite pleased with myself. old papa. I'd got as far as 1850.

In the novel Cary stresses the limitation of Gulley's perceptions with the line, "I wasn't looking any more than a sausage machine." This is not seeing, not true vision, which looks through, not with the eye. It is an automatic process, having little to do with the creation of art. Suddenly, however, everything changes for Gulley: "one day I happened to see a Manet. Because some chaps were laughing at it. And it gave me the shock of my life. Like a flash of lightning. It skinned my eyes for me, and when I came out I was a different man. And I saw the world again, the world of colour. By Gee and Jay, I said, I was dead, and I didn't know it.[13]

> Till from the fire on the hearth
> A little female babe did spring.
>
> (Stanza 11; HM 52)

Gulley equates Manet with new vision, for Manet's *peinture claire* methods, his use of bright colors, "often deliberately juxtaposed clear acid tones . . . with his blacks and dark grays," shocked the *Salon public* "accustomed to 'opaque shades and dead tones.' " [14] Indeed, on the rare occasions when his paintings were accepted by the Salon, critical and public reaction was derisive, as Gulley well remembers.[15]

There is some question whether Manet was ever a true Impressionist. He never showed his work in their group exhibitions, but certainly his elimination of underpainting, glazing, and halftones—his rebellion against academic painting—was very likely to have influenced the Impressionists. And Manet's own later work shows a certain Impressionist delicacy.[16] Gulley both blurs the question and points up the connections as his reminiscences move easily from his discovery of Manet to his experiments with Impressionism:

> I had a bad time of it that year. I couldn't paint at all. I botched my nice architectural water-colours with impressionist smudges. And I made such a mess of my impressionist landscapes that I couldn't bear to look at them myself. . . . My old stuff made me sick. In the living world that I'd suddenly discovered, it looked like a rotten corpse that somebody had forgotten to bury. But the new world wouldn't come to my hand. I couldn't catch it, that lovely vibrating light, that floating tissue of colour. Not local colour but aerial color, a sensation of the mind; that maiden vision.
>
> And she was all of solid fire
> And gems and gold, that none his hand
> Dares stretch to touch her baby form,
> Or wrap her in her swaddling band.
> But she comes to the man she loves,
> If young or old, or rich or poor;
> They soon drive out the aged host,
> A beggar at another's door.
>
> [Stanzas 12, 13]
>
> I got her after about four years. At last I got rid of every bit of the grand style, the old church. I came to the pure sensation without a thought in my head. Just a harp in the wind. (HM 52–53)

Cary's depiction of the characteristics of Impressionism is both accurate and evocative of Romantic aesthetics. but the cycle continues: while Gulley at first appears to be "the man she loves," he quickly becomes "the aged host." He tires of Impressionism, stops painting again, and takes to drinking and argumentation: "I used to go out and get drunk, to keep some kind of illumination going in my dome" (HM 53).

> He wanders weeping far away,
> Until some other take him in;
> Oft blind and age-bent, sore distrest,
> Until he can a maiden win.
>
> [Stanza 14]

> And then I began to make a few little pencil sketches, studies, and I took Blake's Job drawings out of somebody's bookshelf and peeped into them and shut them up again. Like a chap who's fallen down the cellar steps and knocked his skull in and opens a window too quick, on something too big. I did a little modelling and tried my hand at composition. I found myself wandering round the marbles at the Brit. Mus. and brooding over the torso of some battered old Venus without any head, arms or legs, and a kind of smallpox all over the rest of her. Trying to find out why her lumps seemed so much more important than any bar-lady with a gold fringe; or waterlily pool.

> And to allay his freezing age
> The poor man takes her in his arms;
> The cottage fades before his sight,
> The garden and its lovely charms.
>
> [Stanza 15]

> Good-bye impressionism, anarchism, nihilism, Darwinism, and the giddy goat, now staggering with rheumatism. Hail, the new Classic. . . . And I studied Blake and Persian carpets and Raphael's cartoons and took to painting walls.
>
> But I rubbed most of them out again. They looked like bad imitations of the old masters; or made-up, pompous stuff. They didn't belong to the world I lived in. A new world with a new formal character. (HM 54)

This maiden is elusive, as fleeting as Blake's garden. Gulley's sources at this point reflect a blend of naturalism and classicism, the Michaelangelesque quality shared by Raphael and Blake. They represent a striking repudiation of the Victorian gimcrackery which seems foolish to Gulley and which Cary himself loathed.[17] But developments in art were beginning to move beyond Gulley, and he grew more and more unhappy with his work. "And of course no one would buy anything. They didn't know what I was driving at. I probably didn't know myself. I was like a chap under witchcraft. I didn't know if I was after a real girl or a succubus in the shape of a fairy" (HM 54–55).

Like many other artists at the beginning of this century, Gulley was having difficulty finding the appropriate form to express his vision. It was easy enough to reject Impressionism, more difficult, however, to find a satisfactory substitute. Imitating old masters is a valuable learning tool, but it is no more than that, and Gulley must find his own maiden, preferably "a real girl," rather than the parasitic unsubstantiality of "a succubus in the shape of a fairy." And so Gulley compares his own painful pursuit of the maiden with that of Cézanne.

On the single page which follows, Cary achieves an impressive density of quotation, allusion, and commentary on one of the most intriguing sections of "The Mental Traveller," the old man's pursuit of the maiden in a desert which becomes strangely verdant—"planted o'er / With labyrinths of wayward love"—and habitable—"many a city there is built, / And many a pleasant shepherd's home." Although most critics regard this vegetation and development as salutary, a movement away from the desert of Ulro, Cary perceives that it is false growth, based on "the various arts of love and hate." [18] Gulley first quotes Stanzas 18 and 20, and adds his own commentary:

> The honey of her infant lips,
> The bread and wine of her sweet smile,
> The wild game of her roving eye,
> Does him to infancy beguile;
> Like the wild stag she flees away,
> Her fear plants many a thicket wild;
> While he pursues her night and day,
> By various arts of love beguiled.
>
> [Stanzas 18, 20]

> "The job is to get hold of the form you need," [Gulley declares]. "And nothing is so coy. Cézanne and the cubists, when they chucked up old doddering impressionism, caught their maidens. But the cubists did it too easily. They knocked them down with hammers and tied up the fragments with wire. Most of 'em died and the rest look more like bird-cages than forms of intuition and delight. Cézanne was the real classic. The full band. Well, I suppose old Cézanne did more wandering in the desert even than me—he wandered all his life. The maiden flew away so fast that he hardly caught her once a year. And then she soon dodged off again." (HM 55)

The close connection between poem and novel at this point becomes clear through an examination of Cary's chart. He interprets Stanza 18: "And artist starts again in the desert . . . regeneration—a new girl but the same old solid idea" (col. 1); "Cézanne, Seurat" (col. 2); "Gulley caught by art. About 1900 . . . it got hold of Cézanne" (col. 3). Concerning Stanza 19, omitted from the text except for the reference to Cézanne wandering in the desert, Cary says, "And starts again in the desert . . . revolution, cubists etc. science" (col. 1). The term "Impressionism" is written and crossed out, replaced by "Classical again" (col. 2). The third column moves beyond art: "And went into the desert. Science revolution." These cryptic notes form the link between Blake's poem and Gulley's commentary. Cézanne, the father of modern art, was indeed a revolutionary, always searching for new means of expression, attacking traditional principles of perspective and using color to create volume. He also reaffirmed classical principles of construction—thus "Classical again." Impressionism was figuratively crossed out by both Cézanne and the Cubists, who worked primarily in reaction to its visual subjectivity and airiness of color. Seurat, placed alongside Cézanne on the chart, extended Impressionism to its scientific limits. Gulley himself experiments with Cubism, but ultimately finds it too limited for his personal vision.

Thus Cary follows—and expands upon—the traditional interpretation of the wandering in the desert as a search for vision. The old man's transformation to infancy is an indication of his creative potential, and the maiden—"a new girl but the same old solid idea"—represents the artist's ability to move on to new forms, to new methods; he "starts again in the desert." But when the maiden disappears, "Her fear plants many a thicket wild"—stunted growth, Cubist "bird-cages" rather than "forms of intuition and delight." Gulley's description of the Cubists knocking down their maidens with hammers and tying up the fragments with wire is a humorously accurate description of Picasso's early cubist female, reduced to carefully outlined geometric forms. But the maiden is also inspiration, vision, form itself, and Cary clearly feels that these are reduced in Cubism—partially as cause, partially as a result of societal pressures—specifically those of socialism. Indeed, his chart for Stanza 20 makes this explicit: "Material form flies from him and makes laws" (col. 1); "Cubists Surrealists Cézannists fly from him—The cubed square" (col. 2); "Begin with Darwin. Marx. And new rules appear. The coyness of idea produces rules" (col. 3). When imaginative vision eludes the artist, Cary believes, he turns to set patterns for art and for life itself. The cube closes the square as "the flat earth becomes a ball."

Cubism becomes the symbol of a reductivist social system, as Cary makes clear in the next section of the novel. Cary offers Stanzas 21 and 23 of "The Mental Traveller" interpolated with Gulley's commentary:

By various arts of love and hate,
Till the wide desert planted o'er
With labyrinths of wayward love,
Where roam the lion, the wolf and boar.

[Stanza 21]

I painted some cubists myself once and thought I'd got my maiden under padlock at last. No more chase, no more trouble. The formula of a new classical art. And of course a lot of other people thought so too. A lot of 'em are painting cubistry even now; and making a steady income and sleeping quiet in their beds and keeping their wives in fancy frocks and their children at school.

> The trees bring forth sweet ecstasy
> To all who in the desert roam;
> Till many a city there is built,
> And many a pleasant shepherd's home.
>
> [Stanza 23]

Cubiston. On the gravel. All services. Modern democracy. Organized comforts. The Socialist state. Bureaucratic liberalism. Scientific management. A new security. But I didn't live there long myself. I got indigestion. I got a nice girl in my eye, or perhaps she got after me. After 1930, even Hickson stopped buying me. And tonight it seems that I can't paint at all. I've lost sight of the maiden altogether. I wander weeping far away, until some other take me in. The police. It's quite time. I'm getting too old for this rackety life. (HM 55–56)

Gulley's equation of Cubism and socialism is quite clear: both, to him, are the enemies of individualism. Thus the terms "cubistry" and "cubiston" denote a formulaic approach to art and to life, respectively, for, as Gulley sees it, the creative artist is inevitably stifled in the socialist state. Cary's chart extends this point, stressing the closed circularity which results from the loss of imaginative vision. Of Stanza 20 he has said in his chart, "Material form flies from him and makes laws . . . Socialism." These laws, Blake's "thickets" planted by the maiden's flight, become widely planted "labyrinths" in Stanza 21, as Cary describes in his chart the socialist state which grows from such laws: "Under which cities grow up and a new liberal civilization, a new technique" (col. 1); "cities of art. old Cézanne" (col. 2); "Everybody paints Cézannes and is Gully [*sic*]. The new liberal socialism . . . an organized liberal state. The classic democracy" (col. 3).

Gulley's commentary on Stanza 21 points up such material benefits as "steady incomes." But the Blakean resistance to rule is most explicit in Cary's unique treatment of Stanza 23. The "sweet ecstasy" of "organized comforts" and "a new security" found in planned "cities of art" are undermined by the fact that, as Cary glosses the phrase "many a pleasant shepherd's home" in his six-column chart: "Laws *bind* art to build, to construct . . . Art builds the cities . . . Old mother . . . the law" (italics added). We have come full circle, it seems; the artist without imagination is offered material comforts, but he is bound by law to build—not Jerusalem but housing developments, perhaps (like those subsidized by several socialist states in the 1920s)—just as the babe is bound by the crone.

The transformation of the "wayward Babe" of Stanza 22, which Cary omits from the novel, into the "frowning Babe" of Stanza 24 links art with politics and sheds dazzling light on "The Mental Traveller" in *The Horse's*

Mouth. Cary annotates Stanza 22 in both of his charts. The six-column chart begins with the first two lines of the stanza, "Till he becomes a wayward babe / And she a weeping woman old," which Cary interprets as "pure visionary (modern art)" (col. 2); "He becomes a wayward babe and art drives him" (col. 3); "Plantie on the law" (col. 5); and "I gave way to her. But people can't go on like that. A weeping woman old" (col. 6). On the three-column chart, he has written "But he . . . learns from vision. Pure revolutionary spirit" and "But I don't agree with Cézanne. Nor the Surrealists."

It is Young Franklin, Gulley's political alter ego, who clarifies these lines in the novel. Franklin is convinced that Gulley is " 'finished anyhow. Done for himself, and why not? ' " (HM 56). But Ollier and Bert, Gulley's other friends, think that he should consult Mr. Plant, who had helped him after his previous telephone offense. Plant "loves to fight the law" (HM 57). When he had assured Gulley at the earlier time that they would get him off, Gulley responded, " 'No justice for me,' . . . 'What I need is special consideration on account of age and rheumatism and my services to the British nation in the future—about the year 2500. When they'll probably need a few good artists in their history or they won't be in history at all' " (HM 57). Through Plant's well-meaning intervention Gulley "got a month, instead of seven days, which was the usual equivalent. But it was a great victory for Plantie. It made him happy for weeks and gave him a big reputation round Greenbank. The real British hero. The man that whopped Old Woman the Law and frightened the magistrates" (HM 58).

Now, in "the Feathers," with some twenty minutes to spare before Plant's religious meeting, he praises Gulley's painting, "putting down his can like a law of Moses. 'Great subject, the Fall.' 'I'm giving up art.' I said, 'It's a bit late, but I may still learn to respect myself before I die' " (HM 60). Gulley continues in his self-abnegation: "What is art? Just self-indulgence. You give way to it. It's a vice. Prison is too good for artists— they ought to be rolled down Primrose Hill in a barrel full of broken bottles once a week and twice on public holidays, to teach them where they get off" (HM 61).

Gulley's spontaneous vision, which follows, of the earth as a Cézannist view of Eden, seems to belie his hostility to art and artists. But he continues, nonetheless, enlarging his theme in response to Plant's " 'I respect artists . . . they give their lives to it.' 'And other people's lives,' I said. 'Like Hitler.' 'Hitler,' said Frankie, not angry but sad; as if he couldn't bear any more' " (HM 61). Mr. Moseley, another patron,[19] declares that the problem with Hitler is that he " 'doesn't want anything. . . . He's got ideas. . . . When a chap gets ideas, you look out—' 'I believe you're right Mr. Moseley,' I said. 'He's got ideas that chap. And he wants to see them on the wall' " (HM 62). And Gulley thinks of "Artist Hitler":

> But when they find the frowning Babe,
> Terror strikes through the region wide;
> They cry "The Babe! the Babe is born! "
> And flee away on every side.
> And none can touch that frowning form,
> Except it be a woman old;
> She nails him down upon the rock,
> And all is done as I have told.
>
> [Stanzas 24, 26]

> "Since you've said it," said Franklin, "what is it all for—what's the good of art? You can have it. It's just another racket, it's a put-up job from start to closing time." "That's it, Frankie," I said, "a put-up job." "And they know it too," said Frankie, turning quite white and breaking into a sweat with indignation against the enemy. "The buggers know it—just like the bloody parsons know it. And the bloody government. Putting it over. Taking advantage." "That's it," I said, "they're all at it, like ticks on a mad dog. When he's too busy charming the moonshine to scratch himself in detail." (HM 62)

This is all too much for Plantie, who goes off to his meeting. " 'Meetings,' said Franklin. 'What's the idea? That's all I ask. What's the real idea? What are they getting at?' 'They aren't getting it, they're giving it,' I said, 'A chap has to get rid of his ideas somewhere, or they'll turn sour and give him a pain' " (HM 62–63).

When they are institutionalized, as Blake knew, religion, politics, and even art can simply be means of "taking advantage." But if individual ideas are repressed, the "wayward Babe," or vision which refuses to follow convention (even if that convention is avant-garde, like that of Cézanne and the Surrealists), becomes the "Frowning Babe" whom none dares touch—except the "Woman old" who will, of course, bind him down again.

At some future time, perhaps "about the year 2500" as Gulley suggests, the world will not turn in terror from the revolutionary—in the arts or sciences, biological or social. The Darwins and Marxes, the Blakes, Turners, Manets, and Cézannes will be accepted by society on their own terms, neither turned into "another racket" nor forced to hide their originality in obscurity. In his six-column chart Cary has said of the line "until he can a maiden win": "Drives out the old nature. And the old technique. He *paints Sara and gets back to infancy*." This is a reminder that the babe itself is potential—"wayward," "frowning," or terrifying, respectively, as the perceptions transform it. The "Eye altering alters all," Blake says in Stanza 16 of "The Mental Traveller." Unfortunately, the rebel against convention, the "modern artist" in any generation, is scorned by and scorns society. Hitler, in early life a thwarted artist, is seen by Gulley as the inevitable product of a society which has improper respect for its true artists. He is the "Frowning Babe" in a world that has lost its values. And Gulley, at this stage of the novel, has regressed to an earlier point in the cycle, the state of the old man about to begin his wandering in the desert. He has yet to find the maiden responsible for his true "Creation."

But the Blakean cycle continues in both its negative and positive aspects. The words Gulley uses to describe his friend Bert surely apply to himself: "All alive at seventy-five. But he's a bachelor. Driven in on himself. Banked down and still burning, the fire in the hearth" (HM 64). This is the fire from which the female babe is born. Gulley will paint a wall that he will not again rub out. And his "Creation" will come—in a new mode, his own form of Expressionism.

IV

"The Mental Traveller" is not an easy poem; its explicators have sometimes faltered in their attempts to elucidate it fully. Cary, too, appears puzzled at times and may at first glance seem simplistic in aspects of his interpretation. But he provides significant insights into this difficult work, and his enactment of the poem within his rich novel is a major creative achievement. Cary does not merely explicate, nor does he simply translate the poem's symbolic figures and events into modern equivalents. He integrates Blake's poem and his vision into the life, thought, and memory of his modern protagonist in ways that explain both his own and Blake's world views. These worlds center on the artist and his creation, but include as well the sociopolitical factors which restrain or stimulate him. The density of novelistic texture, the ultimate complexity of Cary's grasp of Blake is fully revealed by a reading of Blake's poem within Cary's novel, glossed by his intricate planning charts.

Cary's voluminous notes on Blake's other writings and his heavily annotated edition of Blake[20] attest to his lifelong interest in and thorough knowledge of Blake's poetry and thought. Cary's engagement with "The Mental Traveller" is stunning. When Cary appears to simplify or change the poem in his novel, he does so in order to convey the reactions and the point of view of his protagonist, an anarchic, pragmatic artist impatient with philosophical treatises or abstruse poems. Gulley Jimson's commentary within Joyce Cary's dramatization of "Traveller" reveals anew the timelessness of Blake's poem in a vital, nonscholarly idiom. Gulley's simplicity as narrator permits him to reduce Blake's line to mundane equivalents. Simultaneously, however, Cary builds up these equivalents, layer upon layer, creating a profundity of meaning unapparent to Gulley or to the unaware reader. When Cary translates the "Virgin bright" into Sara Monday; when the "aged host" becomes both Gulley and his father in their periods of imaginative sterility; when Turner, Manet, and Cézanne join Blake and Gulley as artists who reject conventional attitudes and modes and are in turn rejected by the academies of their days, then "The Mental Traveller" achieves its greatest depth, more than scholarly explication can offer.

"The Mental Traveller" has been interpreted in many ways, but the basic reading involves the pursuit of artistic vision. Joyce Cary dramatizes this pursuit, extending it into the past even as he modernizes and localizes it. In the life of Gulley Jimson he creates a portrait of the archetypal artist and his world as he traces Blake's cycles in *The Horse's Mouth*, extending and enriching our perception of "The Mental Traveller" as he thrusts it into the twentieth century.

Notes

1. See my article, "The Miltonic Progression of Gulley Jimson," *Mosaic* 11(1) (Fall 1977): 77–91.

2. Helpful interpretations of Blake's poem are provided by Hazard Adams, *William Blake: A Reading of the Shorter Poems* (Seattle: Univ. of Washington Press, 1963), pp. 77–100; Harold Bloom, *Blake's Apocalypse: A Study in Poetic Argument* (New York: Doubleday, 1963), pp. 316–325; Gerald Enscoe, "The Content of Vision: Blake's 'Mental Traveller,'" *Papers on Language and Literature* 4(4) (Fall 1968): 400–413; Martin Nurmi, "Joy, Love, and Innocence in Blake's 'The Mental Traveller,'" *Studies in Romanticism* 1 (1962): 97–104; Kathleen Raine, "Tharmas and the Mental Traveller," *Blake and Tradition*, vol. 1 (Princeton: Princeton Univ. Press, 1968), pp. 302–325; John Sutherland, "Blake's 'Mental Traveller,'" *Journal of English Literary History* 22 (1955): 136–147.

3. This statement appears at the top of one of three pages of planning charts for "The Mental Traveller" in *The Horse's Mouth* found in the James M. Osborn Collection of Joyce Cary Manuscripts in the Bodleian Library, Oxford University, Oxford, England. I am grateful to Mrs. Winifred Davin, Joyce Cary's literary executor, for permission to use the collection, and for her generous help and guidance.

4. They were taped together in 1971, when I first examined and photocopied the charts. By 1975, however, one of the sheets had disappeared.

5. Not every space on the charts contains an entry. Moreover, Cary's handwriting is so difficult to decipher that I have occasionally had problems in recognizing words; there may therefore be omissions or errors in transcription.

6. All references to *The Horse's Mouth* are to the revised edition (New York: Grosset & Dunlap, 1957); hereafter cited as HM. Quotations from "The Mental Traveller" appear as they are in the novel; Cary has occasionally changed or added to Blake's lines.

7. Chapter 11 also contains only two stanzas from the poem; these two chapters thus form a frame for the central chapters containing the bulk of the poem.

8. See, for example, the contrasting interpretations of Yeats, Bloom, and Adams: "The wealth of his soul consists of the accumulation of his own smiles and tears. . . . He is male, and mental, and these things make the joy of others, when he 'teaches in song'—as the overworked phrase has it—what he 'learned in suffering' " (Ellis and Yeats, *Works of Blake*, II, pp. 35–36); "His wealth is the proper equivalent of his aging into spectral form, for it consists of the morbid secretions of human suffering, particularly sexual repression based on courtly love conventions. He feeds on this and so clearly he is now a Urizenic figure. He extends this cannibal fare as charity, in an exemplification of the morality taught in 'The Human Abstract' " (*Blake's Apocalypse*, p. 293); "The gems and gold are the materialistic results of his 'husbandry'; they are, however, an abstraction from true creation, images of hard matter with monetary value. . . . As we read on, we realize that the 'aged shadow' has made his fortune by converting nature, which is the misery of others, into material gain for himself. The true gems of the world are gems of the mental states, particularly those of the eye and heart. But the shadow has converted these gems into their fallen analogies. . . ." (*A Reading of the Shorter Poems*, p. 92).

9. In the blending of these diverse female roles Cary anticipated Hazard Adams, who in 1963 wrote: "The babe is related by contrast to the aged female of the earlier stanzas. She is also related to the male babe who begins the poem, in that she is a harbinger of revolt. She is consistent with Blake's constant double representation of the fallen world. As against the aged and unprolific woman she is the prolific muse, the true Jerusalem. As against the male babe and her own delusory form, who as we see are circular conceptions, she is an image of positive achievement. She is not a representation of female selfhood, does not entice the male, but gives herself, thus finding her true place within him as emanation. . . ." (*A Reading of the Shorter Poems*, p. 94).

10. Cary's six-column chart prepares us for the youthful Gulley's antipathy to art and his concern with money. In column 6, paralleled with Stanza 11, he says, "But I hate art. Papa couldn't find art. . . . brooding over his old art." In column 3, equated with Stanza 3, is the line, "As a young man, devoted to Mammon."

11. Laurence Binyon, *English Water-Colours* (New York: Schocken Books, 1969), p. 21.

12. Jean Selz, *Turner* (New York: Crown, 1975), p. 18. Cary was an art student himself, informally in Paris in 1906, and at the Edinburgh College of Art (then the Board of Manufacturers School of Art) beginning in 1907. He, in contrast to Gulley, "master[ed] the basics and learn[ed] them so well that more than forty years afterwards he claimed he could still draw a cross section of the human body at any point his listener cared to suggest." Malcolm Foster, *Joyce Cary: A Biography* (Boston: Houghton Mifflin, 1958), p. 42.

13. Gulley's lines parallel Blake's in a letter to Hayley: "Suddenly, on the day after visiting the Truchsessian Gallery of pictures, I was again enlightened with the light I enjoyed in my youth, and which has for exactly twenty years been closed from me as by a door and by window-shutters" (E 703).

14. Phoebe Pool, "Introduction," *The Complete Paintings of Manet* (New York: Harry N. Abrams, 1967), p. 5, citing Théodore Duret.

15. There is no mention of Manet in Cary's chart. Instead he equates the "female babe" with "(a new vision) / the potential—idea . . . Darwin; Impressionists / Do What you like." The last phrase is evocative of "What You Will!," the title of a picture which Turner exhibited at the Royal Academy in 1822.

16. Pool, passim.

17. According to Malcolm Foster, the students at Edinburgh "discussed the new art and argued fauvism versus impressionism and agreed to despise the set pieces of Victorian art. . . ." (p. 41).

18. See in particular Bloom, p. 296; Enscoe, p. 412; Nurmi, p. 115; Paley, pp. 102–103; Sutherland, p. 146.

19. Possibly meant to recall Sir Oswald Mosley, head of the British Union of Fascists until the British government took him into custody in 1940.

20. The annotated text in the Bodleian collection is the Everyman edition, ed. Max Plowman (1927, reprint ed. 1942).

Susan Levin

A Fourfold Vision: William Blake and Doris Lessing

William Blake's myth of unitive consciousness illuminates the lives of Doris Lessing's protagonists. The joining of the prophetic Blake and Milton, the rebuilding of Jerusalem, the final resurrection of the Zoas in Eden describe a movement through the anguish of individualism to the epiphany of wholeness, to the awareness that things are not, after all, eternally separate from one another. Lessing's concerns are those of Blake as certain of her characters are pitched through the same divisions and reintegrations. Blake's antagonists, Locke and Newton, agape at a universe of objects, set theories for the world of hermetic individualism. "O Divine Spirit sustain me on thy wings!" Blake prays in *Jerusalem*, "That I may awaken Albion from his long & cold repose. / For Bacon & Newton sheathd in dismal steel, their terrors hang / Like iron scourges over Albion. . . ." (J I: 15, 9–12). Anna Wulf in *The Golden Notebook*, Charles Watkins in *Briefing for a Descent into Hell*, Martha Quest in *The Four-Gated City*, Kate Brown in *The Summer before the Dark*, and the nameless narrator of *Memoirs of a Survivor* each approximates in some way that awakened Albion, reenacting and then transcending the fundamental epistemological myth, which since Bacon and up through modern psychology of the self has expressed the controlling ethos of individualism. Most obviously in the Blakean phrases placed throughout and in the Blakean structures of these five books, most importantly in a vision of integrated personality, Lessing's texts intersect with those of Blake.

Certain novels are clearly structured after Blake. Patterned after *Jerusalem*, the work containing Blake's fullest description of his four-gated city, Lessing's *The Four-Gated City* is Blakean in design as well as in title. Both works are divided into four parts; maintaining Blake's emphasis on four, Lessing divides each of her four parts into four chapters. In an appendix, however, she modifies Blake's ending, in which Albion and Jerusalem embrace. Like Blake, Lessing creates a prophetic book, but hers foretells how the human race will destroy itself. In her *Memoirs of a Survivor*, the prophetic form prevails completely. These memoirs give another picture of the final breaking up of civilization. People live behind drawn blinds terrified of speaking to one another; individuals band together in packs to roam the earth for a while and then turn on one another to kill.[1]

The extreme cutting off of individuals from one another detailed in *Memoirs of a Survivor* makes explicit the divisions among people characterizing our century. Lessing uses the very form of her novels to comment on this fragmentation. In *The Golden Notebook*, the narrative "Free Women" is interrupted by the black, red, yellow, and blue notebooks. The novel, then, does not have a straight narrative line, but consists of fragments of thoughts and narratives, which interrupt one another. And, in pointing to "The Contrary Structure of . . . *The Golden Notebook*," Annis Pratt describes the ways in which Anna Wulf progresses through the Blakean contraries of her existence: "Just as *Jerusalem* describes the conflict between contrary attitudes towards the existence of contrary drives in human individuals, *The Golden Notebook* pivots upon Anna's coming to terms with dichotomies by accepting them openly rather than negating them or buttoning them up without closed conceptual systems." [2]

To build Jerusalem is to be freed of closed physical and mental structures. In Blake and Lessing, the cities men build both bring about and eradicate the closed systems of potential division. Lessing's characters populate Blake's cities of horror and of harmony. Stranded on a ship when his companions are absorbed into a huge crystal, Watkins, in *Briefing for a Descent into Hell*, is washed up on an apparently deserted shore, where two leopardlike creatures lead him on a torturous climb. He cannot depend on reason to show him a path, for he is in a state of "Innocence" and must find his way by using instinct. He finds himself in a city that seemed "itself a person, or had a soul, or being." [3] Watkins must preserve this city, must cleanse it from a bloody, cannibalistic feast, a process which also defines Los's building of the Holy City. The city Watkins encounters is not the mechanized, inhuman metropolis of "mind-forged manacles" that Blake deplores in "London," but rather an environment of harmony analogous to the New Jerusalem.

Blake's conception of Golgonooza also figures in *The Four-Gated City*. In one sense, London is "the city." Presented first as a city destroyed by World War II, London is, like Blake's Jerusalem, "scatterd abroad like a cloud of smoke thro' non-entity" (J I: 5, 13). Blake writes of the building of Golgonooza, and Martha sees London rebuilt, but the physical city must be replaced by the four-gated city of Imagination. Blake's task is "To open the Eternal Worlds, to open the immortal Eyes / Of Man inwards into the

Worlds of Thought" (J I: 5, 18–19). Like the poem *Jerusalem*, Lessing's novel is at once narrative, history, political tract, and prophetic book. Rebuilt London will be polluted and uninhabitable, the center of the contaminated zone, but the four-gated city may stand eternally.

Such an eternal city of "harmony, order and joy" is the subject of a novel within Lessing's novel. Mark Coldridge's visionary work describes a city in the desert. And around Golgonooza lies the "land of death eternal" (J I: 13, 30). The city is overrun by armies jealous of its happiness and becomes part of just another empire, but Mark's description is the basis of an imaginative creation which affects the rest of his life. Those around him try to set up "Utopias," cities in the desert, and since he has described such a place, demand that he participate in their schemes. In a grotesque parody of the ideal he imaginatively creates, Mark ends his life running plague-infested camps for the homeless masses; still he writes, "I cannot help dreaming of that perfect city. . . ." [4]

Martha Quest discovers that the city can be the body of every man. "These are the four Faces towards the Four Worlds of Humanity / In every Man. Ezekial saw them by Chebars flood. / And the Eyes are the South, and the Nostrils are the East. / And the Tongue is the West, and the Ear is the North" (J I: 12, 57–60). Martha's body becomes her instrument, her "receiving device": ". . . if she did not eat, slept very little, kept alert, she sharpened and fined down" (F 548, 534). Her search takes her into self-division, into madness until she finds, "Here, where else, you fool, you poor fool, where else has it been, ever. . . ." (F 591). The psychiatrist who tries to normalize Martha succeeds only in finding labels for her, prescribing the compartmentalizing Lessing abhors. Lynda Coldridge, "a first-class 'listener,' a first-class 'seer' " (F 365), is literally compartmentalized in a psychiatric hospital, a fate Martha avoids by using Lynda's experience and by finding what she can do for herself, without the doctors. Securing complete solitude, she faces herself and enters the grip of the "self-hater" or, in Blake's terms, the spectre, in *Jerusalem* the spectre of Urthona who derides imagination. The doctors, Martha realizes, keep those considered insane in the grip of the self-hater, in the grip of what is most despicable in oneself.

As the descent into madness shows Martha the depths of her psyche, so in *Briefing*, Watkins's descent into the hell of self requires that he face his own worst being. To reach apocalypse and Eden, one must work through Generation. Watkins participates in a cannibalistic orgy with three women and then faces the rat-dogs. The creatures seem at first animal horrors, "alien . . . in every way." "I hated everything about it. . . . Yet I was thinking that someone standing a hundred yards away might say, at a casual glance, that it and I were of similar species" (B 72). As he moves among them and observes them, he realizes that the rat-dogs are a part of him; he is on his way to the final awareness of Blake's *Jerusalem*: "All Human Forms identified even Tree Metal Earth & Stone" (J IV: 99, 1). Watkins's acceptance of the rat-dogs is not only a demonstration of the humanizing power of unfallen consciousness but is also a variation of the quotation from *The Marriage of Heaven and Hell* with which Lessing ends *Briefing*:

> *How do you know but every Bird that cuts the airy way,*
> *Is an immense world of delight, closed by your senses five?*

If a bird may be a world of delight, so may rat-dogs. Acceptance of these creatures leads to a literal working out of Blake's statement. As the patient sits brooding on the beach, a great white bird appears who takes him on a cleansing flight over the ocean, drawing him into an "immense world of delight." He becomes part of the bird and its universe.

He knows the rat-dogs; he cleanses the city; he lives the ritual of the women. Having thus been integrated with various forms of life on the island, and having entered the four elements, the patient can be absorbed into the crystal where what he sees parallels Blake's description of the Four Zoas in Eden: "To & fro in Eternity as One Man reflecting each in each & clearly seen / And seeing: according to fitness & order" (J IV: 98, 39–40). "In that dimension," Watkins relates, "minds lay side by side, fishes in a school, cells in honeycomb, flames in fire, and together we made a whole in such a way that it was not possible to say, Here Charles begins, here John or Miles or Felicity or Constance ends" (B 96). This is the unity described at the beginning of *The Four Zoas*:

> Four Mighty Ones are in every Man.
> a Perfect Unity
> Cannot Exist but. from the Universal
> Brotherhood of Eden
> The Universal Man.
>
> (FZ I: 3, 4–6)

Martha Quest can also participate in this unity, if she works especially hard: "well, of course, it is not a question of 'Lynda's mind' or 'Martha's mind'; it is the human mind or part of it, and Lynda, Martha can choose to plug in or not" (F 498).

From the time of *The Golden Notebook*, Lessing tells us, the horror of closed, fragmented selfhood finds expression in her work: ". . . the essence of the book, the organization of it, everything in it says implicitly and explicitly that we must not divide things off, must not compartmentalise." [5] The horrors and consequences of fragmentation and division are everywhere in Blake's writing. "The Spectre . . . in every man insane & most / Deformd," the death wound men receive as their emanations flee, the nailing of the lamb upon the tree of mystery all spring from division, from falling away from wholeness (FZ I: 5, 38–39). In Eden, the Zoas are "Unity"; in *Briefing*, Charles Watkins poses the problem of the four Zoas this way: ". . . but what awful blow or knock? What sent us off centre, and away from the sweet sanity of We?" (B 109).

In the first part of *Briefing*, futile conversations with psychiatrists alternate with Charles Watkins's seemingly insane narrative of a sea voyage to a strange land. Known only as "the Patient," Watkins faces the "idiot questioner" and manages "To cast off the rotten rags of Memory by Inspiration / To cast off Bacon, Locke, & Newton from Albions covering / To take off his filthy garments, & clothe him with Imagination" (M II: 41, 4–6). The voyage that Watkins describes leads him to the statement of *The Four Zoas*: man has fallen through division and can be resurrected through reintegration.

But the unity, the universal brotherhood of Eden, splinters into emanations and spectres, into warring male and female entities. The results are the separations that Lessing's patient sees characterizing "mad humanity":

> . . . these mad microbes say I,I,I,I,I, for saying I,I,I,I, is their madness, this is where they have been struck lunatic, made moon-mad, round the bend, crazy, . . . Some sort of a divorce there has been somewhere along the path of this race of man between the "I" and the "We," some sort of a terrible falling-away, and I (who am not I, but part of a whole composed of other human beings as they are of me) hovering here as if between the wings of a great white bird, feel as if I am spinning back (though it may be forwards, who knows?) yes, spinning back into a vortex of terror, like a birth in reverse, and it is towards a catastrophe, yes, that was when the microbes, the little broth that is humanity, was knocked senseless, hit for six, knocked out of their true understanding, so that ever since most have said, I,I,I,I,I,I,I, and cannot, save for a few, say, We. (B 109)

The Satanic I, I, I, selfhood of *Briefing* echoes *The Golden Notebook*. When Anna Wulf speaks with Saul Green, she feels his repeating "I's" are shot, "like bullets." "I,I,I,I,I he shouted, but everything disconnected, a vague, spattering boastfulness. . . . 'I am I, Saul Green, I am what I am what I am. I . . .' The shouting, automatic I, I, I speech began. . . ." [6] Anna and Saul cut themselves off from the world and descend into their own private madnesses. Throughout the novel, Anna sees herself as a series of I's, a divided personality represented by different notebooks. Her first words in the novel speak of this splintering: " 'The point is,' said Anna, as her friend came back from the telephone on the landing, 'the point is, that as far as I can see, everything's cracking up' " (GN 3).

Anna's inability to draw these various I's together is in part responsible for her writer's block. The novel "has been claimed by the disintegration and the collapse" (GN 110). Writing, it seems, furthers the destruction through naming, defining, oversimplification. In her naming game, however, she works out this problem in Blakean terms. "He who wishes to see a Vision; a perfect Whole / Must see it in its Minute Particulars," Blake tells us in *Jerusalem* (J IV: 91, 20–21). Anna tells us of the game, "Sometimes I could reach what I wanted, a simultaneous knowledge of vastness and of smallness" (GN 548). It is Blake's simultaneous macro-microcosm, "a World in a Grain of Sand," the holding of "Eternity in an hour" (E 481). To begin the game, Anna must return to a kind of innocence, "a state of mind I'd forgotten, something from my childhood." She then creates the room she sits in, naming each object, progressing out of one room to as much of the universe as she can: ". . . the point of 'the game' was to create this vastness while holding the bedroom, the house, the street in their littleness in my mind at the same time" (GN 548). Blake too describes the act of creating by naming, when he tells of the ancient poets in *The Marriage of Heaven and Hell*, those who "animated all sensible objects with Gods or Geniuses, calling them by the names and adorning them with the properties of woods, rivers, mountains, lakes, cities, nations, and whatever their enlarged & numerous senses could perceive" (MHH 11). Anna's naming game produces exhilaration but also exhaustion. And the person who sits alone playing the game is usually regarded by others as quite insane.

In Lessing's novels, the unity achieved through the naming game or through other kinds of madness is, as in *The Book of Urizen*, violated by a series of schisms, resulting in entities that are totally self-involved, unable to see anything but "I". Blake describes creation itself as a schism in which God, on an enormous ego trip, a "self-contemplating shadow," rends and divides. "Times on times he divided, & measur'd" (U 3: 8). This division informing Urizen's creation must be healed. The clinically insane people in *The Four-Gated City* or the patient in *Briefing* find that the healing process involves overcoming "your reason."

> The world was spinning like the most delicately tinted of bubbles, all light. It was the mind of humanity that I saw, but this was not at all to be separated from the animal mind which married and fused with it everywhere. Nor was it a question of higher or lower, for just as my having drunk blood and eaten flesh with the poor women had been a door, a key, and an opening, because all sympathetic knowledge must be that, in this spin of fusion like a web whose every strand is linked and vibrates with every other, the swoop of an eagle on a mouse, the eagle's cold exultation and the mouse's terror make a match in nature, and this harmony runs in a strengthened pulse in the inner chord of which it is a part. (B 97)

The doctors, men of science, deny this fusion of animal and human mind, this web of linked strands, and instead force their patients into an "I" existence, a categorized, individual identity. Watkins must be the college professor; Lynda must be Mark's wife and Francis's mother. When unable to fulfill these roles, when at sea on a raft or when groping around the walls of a flat to communicate with voices no one else can hear, a person must be put away. It is eventually discovered, we are told in *The Four-Gated City*, that "a significant proportion of the population had various kinds of extrasensory powers—not as a theoretical possibility but as a fact." In the 1960s, however, it is best to follow Lynda's advice: "I keep quiet about what I know" (F 622, 123). The person who sees connections, who refuses to accept one identity, is mad and must be normalized to accept the anti-Blakean dictum: we exist as discrete identities in a universe of discrete identities. Watkins as the patient, Anna in the naming game, Martha Quest alone in Paul's house become for a time those people who can articulate imaginative unity, the Los of Night the Fourth, the artist and prophet who builds from the ruins of Urizen. But as Los begins the Orc cycle, so Watkins goes back to his "normal" life, his identity as classics professor.

The stammer Watkins develops comes from his first attempts to recite the multiplicity within unity of the universe. His "kindred spirit," Frederick Larson, also stammers and notices that "as he talked, another stream of words paralleled the stream of words that he was actually using, and this parallel stream expressed opinions not precisely opposite to those he was using" (B 176). The patient is plagued by the necessity of using words in linear sequence to communicate. The stammer and the parallel stream both show that refusal to accept one-level reality, that seeing not of either/or relationships but of "and" relationships, or the seeing of simultaneous multiple levels of reality. Watkins can verbalize his fourfold vision, but only when he is not "normal," only when he is what the doctors consider insane. Lynda is given just enough pills to keep her from insisting on more than single-level reality, to keep her from insisting that she hears voices, "the parallel stream."

Sleep is one escape from the truths she sees. "I tell them, all right, if you won't let me have what I know, why can't I sleep? " (F 123). Often, however, refusal to accept "single vision" is paralleled by a literal attempt to escape Newton's sleep. When Lynda and Martha "work," when they are able to "plug into the universal mind" and to escape their habitual identities, they cannot allow themselves to sleep because sleeping thwarts energetic drives. In the hospital, the mad patient is given a variety of drugs to stop his steady talking, to harness the energy that allows verbalization of fourfold vision and to push him into what is considered restorative sleep.

Watkins differentiates between two doctors, "that man who pushes me under" and "the other, the fighting man," the physician who is wary about the administering of strong drugs and electric shock treatment. From birth we are praised for lack of energy, for sleeping: "He is a *good* baby, he sleeps all the time" (B 135). In normal terms, Blake tells us in the *Marriage*, "Evil is the active springing from energy" (MHH 3). We are conditioned away from energy, Rosemary Baines writes to Watkins. "The time of being awake, of being receptive, of *being energetic*—had consumed itself. We don't have much energy. Your words—or rather, what you had put into the words—had fed us, woken us, made us recognize parts of ourselves normally well hidden and covered over—and that was that" (B 165). Watkins, lecturing on education, wakes certain people momentarily, but we cannot fight the deadening passivity with which children are infused, and which Blake calls "good" or "the Passive that obeys reason."

With energy, awareness, and vision come the types of madness Lessing describes. In *The Divided Self*, R. D. Laing writes of the way our civilization suppresses "any form of transcendence. Among one-dimensional men, it is not surprising that someone with an insistent experience of other dimensions, that he cannot entirely deny or forget, will run the risk either of being destroyed by the others, or of betraying what he knows." Lessing's protagonists face the opposition Laing describes; so, writes Laing, did William Blake himself, a man who developed his own "piercing vision," perhaps as a result of "not sharing the common-sense (i.e. the community sense) way of experiencing oneself in the world." [7] Charles Watkins, Anna Wulf, Lynda Coldridge, Martha Quest, and Kate Brown find a new way of experiencing themselves in the world, but if they try to live that way, they can only be called insane. Doctors reduce their visions to symptoms which can be cured. Dorothy explains how patients in mental institutions joke about the pleasure the doctors get from being able to say, "You're nothing but—whatever it is. They've taken weeks and weeks to get to that point, you know, and it's, You're nothing but Electra. . . . It's nothing-but you want to sleep with your father. Nothing-but your brother" (F 224).

Explaining unitive vision as neurosis is one way the society of isolate individualism has of controlling that vision. In *The Four-Gated City*, for example, Lessing argues that psychiatry has been mistaken in its concept of schizophrenia. Lynda finally begins working with a doctor who understands the reality of what had been termed hallucination, "whose medical knowledge included what had been called 'mystical' or 'esoteric' " (F 621). People can see and hear each other telepathically. Martha from her isolated island can think her way into contact with Mark or with a Canadian trapper. Organized sanity is seen to be only fragmentation, imprisonment in selfhood.

While calling upon the presence of Blake to expand her novelistic visions, Lessing also consciously repeats the famous myth of selfhood singly forced from an alien environment—the story of Robinson Crusoe. Her protagonists first occupy this myth and then explode it from within as they drive through Defoe's archetypal modern man in order to approach the unified being of Blakean man. Charles Watkins has been on the ocean, on an island; Kate Brown travels to Turkey and to Spain; Martha Quest, in keeping with her name, discovers "this business of charting the new territory" (F 498). Through use of Blakean themes, however, Lessing turns Robinson Crusoe inside out, radically revising that voyage to the hell of self. The technique is perhaps most obvious in *Briefing*. The patient describes himself as swirling in the North Equatorial current. To get off the ship, he reports, "I began making a raft, using timber from the carpenter's store" (B 20). His syntax and detailed listings imitate Crusoe's as he tells of their similar adventures. Both build rafts; both are washed up on an apparently deserted shore. Robinson, however, fights the sea, whereas Watkins, emerging from divisive consciousness, manages to "breathe water." On land, Robinson trembles when he hears a lion roar, but Watkins is befriended by the leopards. Whereas Robinson's island adventures show him to be a perceiving subject using objects, the patient's experiences in the land of his shipwreck show him freeing himself from subject-object-animal-human-vegetable division to become like the fully integrated Albion.

Lessing shows us how we have defined Watkins's Blakean experience as the way of madness and have cut ourselves off from the world around us as well as from other people: ". . . the main feature of these human beings as at present constituted being their inability to feel, or understand themselves, in any other way except through their own drives or functions" (B 128). In this theory of self and civilization, Lessing finds her most important theoretical connection with Blake. The early eighteenth-century novel provides one theory of man and his environment. Blake, at the end of the century, provides the contrary, the view that our culture has largely overruled but which Lessing suggests may be the one that we must envision. No more than Blake does she promote any infantile nostalgia for totemic participation of mind in universe. Conceptually influenced by Blake, she celebrates the mind's power to lift the veil of Robinson Crusoe's object world. Her novels make contemporary readers conceive of that organized imagining of the human universe allowed by fourfold vision when "The Expanding Eyes of Man behold the depths of wondrous worlds" (FZ IX: 138, 25). With Blake, Lessing prophesies the terrifying realities that issue from the thwarting of ascent into the awareness of Martha Quest and Watkins-the-sailor in order to force descent to the organized sanity of Watkins-the-professor or Kate Brown–housewife, the sanity of warring negations, the civilized sanity that prohibits fourfold vision.

Notes

1. In her most recent work, a series of novels entitled *Canopus in Argos: Archives*, Lessing continues in the prophetic mode, creating works of science fiction which, in the words of Robert Scholes in *Structuralism in Literature*, "inform mankind of the consequences of actions not yet taken" (New Haven: Yale Univ. Press, 1974), p. 200. As she creates her own biblical account of the earth, she matches Blake's "sacred" texts. In his article "Doris Lessing and Romanticism," in *College English* 38(6) (1977): 531–532, Michael Magie describes Lessing's fascination with the Romantic imagination, especially with Wordsworth. He questions the models she offers, however. "Since she lacks the prophetic passion and commitment, she can only sidle into this role, hoping it might be hers" (p. 549). I find a more accurate description of Lessing's prophetic work in Scholes: her imagination does "not merely inform"; it makes "us feel the consequences of those actions, feel them in our hearts and our viscera" (p. 200).

2. Annis Pratt, "The Contrary Structure of Doris Lessing's *The Golden Notebook*," *World Literature Written in English* 12 (1972): 151. Although she does not mention Blake, Roberta Rubenstein arrives at conclusions similar to both Pratt's and my own in her fine book, *The Novelistic Vision of Doris Lessing* (Urbana: Univ. of Illinois Press, 1979). Rubenstein writes of how Lessing's "concern with the potentialities and forms of consciousness in its progress toward wholeness continues to occupy the central place in her fiction" (p. 200). Mary Ann Singleton notes Blake's influence on Lessing in *The City and the Veld* (Lewisburg, Pa.: Bucknell Univ. Press, 1977). Singleton posits three motifs in the novels: two cities and the veld. Against the strife-torn city of modern consciousness is set the ideal city, representative of unitive consciousness and in the tradition of Blake's Jerusalem.

3. Doris Lessing, *Briefing for a Descent into Hell* (New York: Bantam Books, 1972), p. 52; hereafter cited as B.

4. Doris Lessing, *The Four-Gated City* (New York: Bantam Books, 1970), p. 649; hereafter cited as F.

5. Doris Lessing, *A Small Personal Voice* (New York: Alfred A. Knopf, 1974), pp. 27–28.

6. Doris Lessing, *The Golden Notebook* (New York: Ballantine Books, 1962), pp. 580–586; hereafter cited as GN.

7. R. D. Laing, *The Divided Self* (Baltimore: Penguin Books, 1965), pp. 11, 189. Marion Vlastos gives a more complete discussion of the relationship between Lessing and Laing in "Doris Lessing and R. D. Laing: Psychopolitics and Prophecy," *PMLA* 91(2) (1976): 245–258.

PART III

Minna Doskow

The Humanized Universe of Blake and Marx

Both William Blake and Karl Marx address themselves to the central philosophical problem of their times, the relation of human subjectivity to the external world. Beginning with the new science of Bacon and his followers, and continuing through the philosophers of the Enlightenment, a breach between subject and object developed, between a self-defining subject who knows, wills, and reasons and a given, objectified nature, including human nature, with which the subject must deal. Nature was seen as "mechanistic, atomistic, homogenizing" and based on contingency as was man, who as part of nature partook of its character.[1] Reacting to this dualistic view, Blake and other European Romantics of the 1790s sought a way to heal the breach between subject and object and reintegrate man with his world. Building on the Romantic attempt, and Hegel's critical adaptation of it, Marx, too, a generation after Blake, attempted to heal the rift brought about by the Enlightenment.

Both Blake and Marx propose a humanistic alternative to the mechanistic world view which placed man as a single perceiving subject within a world of dead and mechanically operating objects, cut off from his world and his fellow man in this way, and seen as an object himself by his fellow man so that his relationships to his world and other men become objectified and reduced to mechanistic operations. They propose a human definition of man and his world, for both believe that the world has no meaning isolated from man, and it is only man's work upon the world which gives it shape, substance, and meaning. In doing so, both attempt to bridge the gap between subject and object posited by their Enlightenment predecessors by proposing an extension of the subject outward through consciousness and activity thereby creating a humanized universe as well as a fully developed self. For both, the world becomes subject as is evident in Blake's metaphor of unfallen man "who containd in his mighty limbs all things in Heaven &

Earth" (J I: 27 [prose]) and in Marx's naming nature man's "*inorganic body.*" [2] On the other hand, man becomes simultaneously objectified in all the objects of his world to which he gives shape and definition through the exercise of his mental and physical powers. Blake thus sees man simultaneously at the center and circumference of his world, and Marx sees him achieving subjective self-realization through his conscious objectification in productive activity. In either case, the resulting unity between subject and object brought about through the conscious activity of man in fully human development displaces the atomistic, dualistic model left by the Enlightenment.

For Blake, the subject actively expands to include the universe. Indeed, since Blake defines the universe itself as part of a human being, nothing can exist without man, and only through a human projection outward does the very universe come into being. Man's powers of imagination and reason (Los and Urizen) are repeatedly shown as responsible for the creation of the world. Without these powers, nothing would be, only chaos and the indefinite. Man creates the world by knowing, perceiving, and working upon it. He thereby gives it a human definition and makes the objects of the world subjects through his activities. Only man's actual work upon nature enables it to be fertile, flourish, and support life, for "Where man is not nature is barren" (MHH 10: 68). Blake's ideal world, then, is the garden or the city, nature influenced by civilization, and not the forest primeval, raw natural matter. Futhermore, ideal existence in that world is active labor and never simply idle bliss, which is the condition of Beulah's rest from imaginative labors rather than Eden's eternal state itself. Similarly, Eden, even when it appears in its historical guise as Blake's vision of revolutionary change in the earlier prophetic books, appears in terms of human imaginative action shaping the world.

As he acts on the world, man also creates his own human identity. He actively defines the world and himself intellectually, sensually, and physically through his mental pursuits and intellectual acts, through his senses and affections, and through his physical labor and crafts. Artistic activity is, of course, important, and Blake consistently calls on painters, sculptors, architects, poets, and musicians to shape the world in imaginative form through their activities. However, it is often tempting to stop there and in light of Blake's consistent condemnation of experiment, doubt, demonstration, of bare empirical science and philosophy, to ignore the vital part which he assigns to reason and science as dimensions of human intellect in shaping the world. Bacon, Newton, and Locke, however, join Shakespeare, Milton, and Chaucer in drawing Albion's visionary chariot in that Edenic realm pictured at the end of *Jerusalem*, for all "Mental pursuits" (J IV: 77), when they are truly human and not distorted, contribute to the imaginative shaping of the world. All the "labours of Art & Science" (J IV: 77) build the New Jerusalem, for all are in some way products of human intellect and activity. Indeed, the energetic exercise of human imagination in whatever form it appears develops human capacity and ability and through subjective action helps to achieve and define Blake's ideal renovated universe as mere passive contemplation, abstraction, or inactivity cannot. Without this imaginative activity the world is not, but only appears to be; it consists of dead objects rather than living forms. In this way, Blake's epistemology is a complete reversal of Locke's. For Locke, the human mind is empty, to be filled up by the perception of empirical stimuli which impinge upon consciousness, shape it, and may only be combined or judged, not altered by it. For Blake, the opposite is true. Man's consciousness is the active shaping agent which determines the human form of all phenomena in the universe. From the world of dead objects, Blake brings us to the humanized world subjectively determined.

Man's senses shape his world just as much as his intellect does. An infinitely variable and human way of seeing, hearing, smelling, tasting, and touching (and this last includes loving) determines the world, changes it from death to life, from discrete, mechanical, dead objects (the Enlightenment view) to unified, subjectively determined, and therefore, living reality. Blake's theories oppose the empirical and sensationalist theories of Locke, changing the perceptive function of man from passive reception to active determination of stimuli. When Orc comes to renew the world at the end of *America*, for example, he begins by abolishing Lockean sensuality as a prelude to renewal. Man's "five gates," the Lockean senses which provide mere entrances for outside stimuli, and "consum'd, & their bolts and hinges melted" (E 56) by Orc's revolutionary flames which proceed to abolish tyrannical governments also. The active function of man's ever-variable and potentially infinite powers of perception is necessary to shape a renewed world. In the same way, the hellish world which the Angel shows Blake in *The Marriage of Heaven and Hell* alters to an Edenic vision as Blake regards it, for it adjusts to the eye of the new beholder. Similarly, whether one sees the sun as a shining guinea in the sky or a band of angels depends on the eye of the beholder. In either case, the eye shapes the object, but whether it shapes it imaginatively or not depends on the state of the human eye.

In addition, man's senses in their Blakean rather than Lockean exercise determine man's human identity much as they do his humanized universe. For as Blake never tires of telling his readers, man becomes what he beholds; and if he beholds the discrete world of dead material objects which Locke describes, he, too, becomes objectified and deadened, as Reuben, fallen Albion, the historical tyrants and Urizenic characters generally do throughout Blake's prophetic works. If, on the other hand, he cleanses the doors of his perception, he regains life and becomes a living subject in a humanized or subjective universe as renovated Albion finally does at the end of *Jerusalem*.

Finally, man shapes his universe and himself through his labor. Imaginative activity is not simply intellectual, scientific, artistic, and perceptive, but also physical as Blake's images of the cultivated Edenic garden and civilized immortal city imply. Blake's earliest revolutionary hero, Orleans, envisions a postrevolutionary Edenic world based on human labor. He sees the priest joining the peasant "and putting his hand to the plow" (E 292) in a social and, therefore, truly human form of labor. The tools of human activity remain in his visionary world, but free rather than enslave man as in the prerevolutionary (or contemporary European) society. " ' "And the saw, and the hammer, the chisel, the pencil, the pen, and the instruments / Of heavenly song sound in the wilds once forbidden, to teach the laborious plowman" ' " (E 293). Once the restrictions of the old regime's oppressive tyrannical power are lifted, these human tools can once again, in Blake's view, civilize the world for man to live in. Not only are the tools of art (chisel, pencil, pen, and instruments of song) civilizing, but the tools of the farmer and worker (plow, hammer, saw) are equally so in the visionary world of Orleans's prophetic postrevolutionary dream. Nor does Blake ever abandon this view of human labor creating the imaginatively fulfilling universe. Even Los, the ultimate spirit of imagination, the eternal prophet, is viewed as a laborer, a blacksmith, who accomplishes his task of universal renovation within the metaphor of human labor. Whether we see him giving form to the earth with the tools of his trade, riveting, soldering, or forging, opposing the forces of reaction and dehumanization in the world in Urizen or the "Spectre," or creating the arts of the world in his furnaces by building Golgonooza, he is consistently pictured with his hammer, anvil, and bellows, working with the Promethean gift of fire through an approximation of human labor to remake the world in an eternal imaginative human image. His sons, too, labor at the furnaces to accomplish their civilizing and renovating task, joining him in blacksmith's labors, while his daughters accomplish their life-giving task through spinning and weaving as does Enitharmon herself. Golgonooza, the imaginative city of art, is itself laboriously built of bricks, stones, mortar, and cement by those golden builders, the children of Los, and "is namd Art & Manufacture by mortal men" (M I: 24, 50), for both are equally distinctive human products. Nor does Blake ignore agricultural labor. The shepherd, for example, constantly reemerges in both picture and poetry working to preserve innocence in the world, and the workers at the harvest and vintage preceding apocalypse perform the various agricultural tasks of plowing, harrowing, sowing, reaping, threshing, and grape crushing, to advance the time of renovation in the world.

Even in the corrupted or fallen world, human labor provides whatever ameliorating circumstances manage to exist. Science, mathematics, architecture, law, and commerce are among the activities which keep the universe from falling into complete chaos. If it were not for this modicum of human activity, of the products of human reason and labor in the world, chaos and death would prevail, solids would dissolve, Albion would become Satan, all would be indefinite night, there would be no physical basis for imagination to build upon, and creation would be impossible. So, even in a universe which distorts the ideal, human labor serves as an extenuating activity.

Although the distinction among man's intellect, senses, and labor is convenient for the purpose of discussion and analysis, it is not one which Blake advocates. For him, the energetic exercise of the human imagination in all its capacities (intellectual, sensual, and physical) is one, no matter in what form imagination temporarily appears, and it inevitably brings with it all the other forms in the unified man. He does not consider it important nor often even possible to distinguish between the products of mind and body. Imagination consists of the free exercise of both, and only this exercise makes man truly human, constitutes his "Human Form Divine." Therefore, Blake advocates the active or prolific in all its forms, for all human energies are needed to renovate man and humanize his world.

This same unbounded human development which renews man and the world establishes a bond between man and his fellows. Just as the universe becomes living form for Blake when man shapes it by extending his subjectivity in it, so too does one's fellow man. No longer seeing the world as dead objects, but as an extension of himself, man sees his fellow men similarly as extensions of his subjectivity and substitutes brotherhood for antagonism or self-interest in his relationships with them. They cannot exist as objects to be manipulated, for the entire world is a single subjective unity proceeding from man's imaginative activity, and all mankind is one. As one, mankind proceeds in perfect equality, in brotherhood, affirming self and other simultaneously. This is the political and social postrevolutionary vision glimpsed in the prophetic books and brought to fruition at the end of *Jerusalem*.

For Marx, as for Blake, man's exercise of his human capacities shapes the world he lives in as well as his self. Man is both part of nature and simultaneously the whole of which nature is a part. The two are inexorably linked since "nature is man's *inorganic* body" (EPM 112). Again for Marx as for Blake, nature without man is nonentity; "nature fixed in isolation from man—is *nothing* for man" (EPM 191). In the world, however, nature supplies the means of man's physical survival and also provides the raw material for man's physical activities in industry and agriculture and for his imaginative activities in art and science. Inarticulate nature is thus given expression through man's labors.

This human labor, which Adam Smith, for one, characterizes as an essentially and innately burdensome activity, Marx, like Blake, views as liberating activity, a "*positive, creative activity*" through which man achieves "self-realization, objectification of the subject, hence real freedom." [3] That is, man realizes himself through his activity in the world by extending his subjectivity to shape the objects he deals with. Marx is not talking about physical labor only, for he opposes Adam Smith's idea by specifically citing the example of a composer whose hard work is yet liberating and creative. Marx is, however, describing only truly human labor, that labor which is freed from its oppressive historical circumstances.

Through this kind of activity, man brings himself into existence, defining who he is by the way in which he impresses his physical and mental powers upon the natural world and learns to know himself by seeing what he thinks and what he does. "Productive activity is, therefore, the *mediator* in the 'subject-object relationship' between man and nature. A mediator that enables man to lead a *human* mode of existence, ensuring that he does not fall back into nature, does not dissolve himself within the 'object.' " [4] In his productive activity man, therefore, defines himself as human by changing nature, bringing it into line with himself rather than being absorbed by it. Just as the slave in Hegel's "Lordship and Bondage" [5] develops himself by working while the master who does no work remains undifferentiated and undeveloped, so, too, does man, in Marx's view, develop himself as he acts. Furthermore, by acting on the world and creating distinctively human products, he can view himself in the objects around him, and thereby see the human shape of the world rather than raw nature, and this further develops his consciousness. Man "duplicates himself not only, as in consciousness, intellectually, but also actively, in reality, and therefore he contemplates himself in a world that he has created" (EPM 114). He here obliterates the distinction between subject and object by objectifying himself in his activities and simultaneously through the consciousness and perception of this objectification, subjectivizing the entire universe, giving it a human form. Through his intellectual and physical labor, man makes the subject object by creating or acting upon the objects of the world, and, at the same time, makes the object subject by turning the world of objects into a function of man and thereby supplying the world with a subjective essence. Consequently, the world becomes a confirmation of man's essential human powers, "all *objects* become for him the *objectification of himself*, become objects which confirm and realize his individuality, become *his* objects: that is, *man himself* becomes the object" (EPM 140). Thereby the inner is made outer, the subject made object, and vice versa. By shaping the world and recognizing himself in that shape, man annihilates the opposition between self and other, and instead of the antagonism between antithetical concepts that modern Western thought has accustomed itself to, Marx's thinking substitutes a mutuality or unity of contraries within diversity.

Indeed, Marx sees man working to shape the world in "each of his *human* relations to the world—seeing, hearing, smelling, tasting, feeling, thinking, observing, experiencing, wanting, acting, loving . . ." (EPM 138–139) and, conversely, thereby shaping himself as well as the world. The effect of man's activity on the formation of the human senses which Marx depicts is particularly noteworthy, for it does not fall within the purely economic vision usually associated with him. Nevertheless, he claims that through man's efforts "the eye has become a *human* eye, just as its *object* has become a social, *human* object—an object made by man for man" (EPM 139). The senses are humanized in relation to the humanized object. The eye can see a beautiful statue because human art has shaped both the statue and the eye that can recognize its beauty. Conversely, the most beautiful music can have no sense for the unmusical ear, for "the meaning of an object for me goes only so far as *my* senses go" (EPM 140–141), and my senses are formed by what they behold. "Only through the objectively unfolded richness of man's essential being is the richness of subjective *human* sensibility (a musical ear, an eye for beauty of form—in short, *senses* capable of human gratification, senses affirming themselves as essential powers of *man*) either cultivated or brought into being" (EPM 141). The actions for Marx are reflexive: free labor humanizes the world which in turn educates the human senses. We become what we behold. "*Human* sense—the human nature of the senses—comes to be by virtue of its object, by virtue of *humanized* nature. The forming of the five senses is a labor of the entire history of the world down to the present" (EPM 141), Marx proclaims. It is also the story which Blake tells in *Europe*.

The social dimension of the humanized universe marks the vital culmination of Marx's vision. Not only does man see himself in the humanized world formed by his labor, but he sees his fellow men duplicated for him as well, and they too see him as well as themselves. Through his activities in the world man establishes a bond with his fellow men and thereby becomes a truly social being. Whether he acts alone or with others, if he engages in human action he inevitably works as part of the ongoing human species and not in unique relationship to simply raw nature. Therefore, "his *natural* existence become[s] his *human* existence, and nature become[s] man for him. Thus *society* is the unity of being of man with nature—the true resurrection of nature—the naturalism of man and the humanism of nature both brought to fulfillment" (EPM 137). Just as the human becomes the fulfillment of the natural, so the social (civilization) becomes the fulfillment of the human in Marx's thinking, and all form a single unity.

Yet as both Blake and Marx recognize, the humanized universe and fully human individual which are potentially our destiny are not actually our being in the world. What then has happened to create this disparity? For Blake, the answer lies in man's loss of imagination, while for Marx it lies in the alienation of his labor under capitalism. Yet these answers are not as different as they may at first appear, for the causes, evidences, and consequences of each are almost identical. Both writers see a distortion of human subjectivity which extends outward to encompass the world and results in distorted practices and a distorted world which are further reflected by the subject.

For Blake, the subject-object distinction underlies and exemplifies the lapse of human imagination which destroys the unity of the world and is responsible for man's unfulfilled, limited, and oppressed condition in it. This arbitrary division by the subject within himself prevents the extension of the subject outward, limits man to only objective perceiving and thinking, cuts him off from everything else in the universe, and proclaims universal reification. Man himself is isolated in the prison of his subjectivity, in an opaque cavern of obdurate bone admitting sensation through minimal sensual entrances, "till he sees all things thro' narrow chinks of his cavern" (MHH 14). His perception is restricted to the reception of empirically verifiable sensory stimuli which his intellect may combine, judge, or generalize upon in rational abstraction, scientific thought, or formal logic. Because he refuses to exercise his imaginative powers, he loses them and is left less than human too, cut off from his potential self, from nature, from his fellow man, and from divinity in a limited, shriveled being. But nature too is limited by this process. As other opposed to self, the dehumanized universe is left in dead objectivity cut off from its subjective essence, which is man. Man emerges, then, as an isolated independent unit in a world of isolated independent units—the atomized, objectified universe of Bacon, Newton, and Locke. Rather than seeing himself duplicated in nature, or shaping it through his perception, imagination, or action, he sees nature as operating independently of him and his only action consists in responding to it as already given. This is essentially the Lockean view of man as reactor to, manipulator, and abstractor of given, empirically verifiable stimuli, which Blake repeatedly attacks throughout his work as Urizenic perversion of intellect and the atomic, mechanistic Newtonian world, which Blake equally attacks. But for Blake the view is brought about not because of the way things are in the world, the natural given, but because of man's arbitrary subjective limitation. In *Jerusalem*, for example, when Albion refuses to recognize his divine imagination, he reduces his intellect to empirical rationalism, "demonstration," and darkens his world to its postlapsarian state. This denial of imagination also produces Reuben, the merely natural man of limited or earthbound perception who lives in the atomistic universe, "the Wilds of Newton & Locke" (J II: 30, 40). His narrowed senses narrow his world, for "If the Perceptive Organs close: their Objects seem to close also" (J II: 30, 56).[6]

Seeing the primary cause of man's fallen condition as internal, within man's consciousness, Blake yet sees the inevitable external consequences of this internal failure; and sees, furthermore, that these external consequences rebound upon man and further limit his being. Thus, man first denies his imaginative potential by withdrawing from unity with the world as Albion does at the beginning of *Jerusalem.* In doing so, however, he creates a dehumanized natural world and civil society which, in turn, oppress him and further limit his potential. Nature is left as an inhuman force (as Vala, Enitharmon, the fallen female, or Urizenic creation) which man may know only as his restricted senses allow through weight, measure, and distance, and not as part of himself. Society becomes the means by which others may be treated as objects, for man is as cut off from his fellow man as he is from nature and for the same reasons. He can only see them as other, too, as cut off from him and as objects for his isolated subjectivity. His relationship to his fellow man is thus a relationship to an other, to an object outside the single perceiving subject. Brotherhood is then impossible, and man manipulates the objects which are his fellow men as he does the objects of his natural world. Both become stuff for him to work upon for his own self-interest. Cut off in his isolated individuality or selfhood, he exists in a state of antagonism with other men and with the world. Blake reveals this state in recurrent images of ongoing warfare, of armed conflict and civil or religious struggles. As Blake retells human history, he unrolls a chronicle of bloodshed from the wars of Babel and Shinar to those upon the Rhine and Danube, showing man in a perpetual state of warfare with his fellow man of which the contemporary revolutions in America and France and the ensuing Napoleonic wars may mark the possible culmination. Thus time after time in Blake's prophecies, we see human beings at war and archetypal characters struggling in physical conflict with one another. This universal antagonism is not limited to literal armed warfare; it also exists as antagonistic relations in religion, politics, and economics. Oothoon sacrificed by restrictive moral codes, or the sons of Albion sacrificed by religion, the political victims imprisoned in the seven towers of the Bastille, or blasted by the plagues of Albion's angel, the family oppressed by tyranny, poverty, and hunger, by exploitive labor, drudgery, and ignorance, images of famine, plague, poverty, death, imprisonment, tyranny, oppression grimly detailed in the poetry and illustrations are only a few of the ways Blake shows how man torments his fellow man as a result of his imaginative failure. In each area of man's activity the repression and oppression of one man by another, whether in religious restriction, tyrannical denial, or economic exploitation, all stem from the same underlying cause: human limitation caused by imaginative failure. This failure affects not only man's consciousness but all his being and all his relationships in the world. Everything outside the subject, including other human beings, becomes an object for him and may, therefore, be manipulated.

In such a system God, too, is cut off from man in objectivity and is worshipped as an independent, foreign entity. No longer existing within man's developed subjectivity in the human form divine, He emerges as a shadow from Albion's intellect, part of man cut off and worshipped as other, and thereby becomes as tyrannical and oppressive as the other objectified forces in the world (Vala, Urizen, Albion's angel).

Marx, on the other hand, sees the alienation of man's labor affecting his entire being in the world, his consciousness and imagination as well as his activities, products, nature, fellow human beings, and deity. However, he notes the dialectical relationship of consciousness and practice in activity, for, like Blake, he sees man as a unified whole and not as a duality. Furthermore, he places the center of alienation as Blake does that of imaginative loss within the human subject, who, if distorted, defines a distorted universe.

Just as that which makes man fully human for Marx is his activity, so that which limits man is equally the distorted nature of this activity under capitalism. Then man's activity, instead of expressing his humanity and impressing it upon the world, becomes cut off from his essential nature and turns into simply a means to keep him alive. It denies rather than affirms him in the world, and turns him into a "*mentally* and physically *dehumanized* being" (EPM 121). In alienated activity, man does not exercise his humanizing power over nature but sinks to his animal existence using activity to satisfy simply physical need. He becomes a commodity selling himself (his labor) for the means of physical subsistence. This alienated activity dehumanizes not only man but also nature, which is thereby cut off from man and is changed to dead objectivity. Man's product becomes an alien object, "a *power independent* of the producer" (EPM 108) over which he has no control, but which, since it is cut off from man, turns into a dead and dehumanized object as does the world it controls. Here "realization of labor appears as *loss of realization* for the workers; objectification as *loss of the object* and *bondage to it*; appropriation as *estrangement*, as *alienation*" (EPM 108).

Man's potential self-realization in labor turns into its opposite, into the loss of realization for man, because he is not integrally connected to the object he creates which stands as an independent object outside of and controlling him. His labor does not serve human fulfillment; it serves instead to increase the power of the object and puts man under the control of dead matter, of things. Since the products of his labor are furthermore appropriated by another, man becomes fully alienated in his labor, turned into a thing himself, controlled and treated as a means for another.

Alienated from his life activity, man is alienated from his essential self. Because he does not function in human activity in shaping the world, he is cut off from "his spiritual essence, his *human* being" (EPM 114), his own body as well as his inorganic body (nature). His human needs for self-realization are submerged in crude animal needs for physical survival while his human senses are reduced to insensibility because they lack human objects to form them: "None of his senses exist any longer" (EPM 149). Furthermore, through the increased mechanization of industry, his activity is limited to "abstract mechanical movement" (EPM 149), and man is still further reduced to an adjunct of the machine, himself mechanized. The worker is changed "into an insensible being lacking all needs, [and] his activity into pure abstraction from all activity" (EPM 149).

Losing his essential humanity in alienated activity, man becomes isolated in his animal existence and loses his universal being in the human species. "Since mankind's deepest need is to produce, to create, and alienation makes productive life only a means to satisfy needs, individual man is alienated from mankind: 'man makes his essence only a means of his existence' " (EPM 47). All is subordinated to his isolated individuality, and he forms no bond of common humanity with his fellows. He is cut off from his fellow men, for "one man is estranged from the other, as each of them is from man's essential nature" (EPM 114). "The life of mankind is alienated as a whole; man is not what he should be as a human being, but finds himself treated as a means, a tool. Hence, man is alienated from his fellow man, since he treats him also as a means, a tool" (EPM 47). Since human essence is removed from the world in the alienation of labor, what is left is universal reification; everything and everyone turns into a dehumanized object for the other.

Isolated in his own individuality, surrounded by a world of objects which may be manipulated, man's relationship with his fellow man becomes antagonistic. The worker, alienated from his activity, falls under the power of the capitalist who appropriates the worker's activity and controls it as well as his product. Antagonism, therefore, becomes the normal relationship between the worker and the capitalist. For, "if the worker's activity is a torment to him [and under capitalism it is], to another it must be *delight* and his life's joy" (EPM 115). But antagonism is not limited to the worker–capitalist relationship; it exists everywhere as the normal relationship between men in an alienated world where men exist as objects for each other and not as parts of universal humanity.

Since essential human productive activity is displaced in the reified universe of alienation, money takes up its vacated position of universal mediator between man and the world, and, in a parody of human activity, measures everything by its inhuman form. Exercising control over all human beings and activities, it becomes the "*pimp* between man's need and the object" (EPM 165). Man's need exists as a real need for him only insofar as he has the money to satisfy it, and those who lack money have their needs abolished. Similarly, all human senses are reduced to the possession of money, and any other sensual expression is a useless distraction from it. Senses like needs become fiscal. The same reduction shapes man's relationship with his fellow man. In order to increase possession, the one remaining need and sense, man must spare himself "all sharing of general interest, all sympathy, all trust" (EPM 151). Again, isolated man opposes himself to his fellow man.[7]

The victim of universal alienation, man under capitalism is "wholly lost to himself" (EPM 120), cut off from all parts of his existence: from himself as alienated activity bestializes his labor, his perception, and his mind, from nature which becomes an object opposed to him rather than part of his inorganic body, from mankind generally in selfish, isolated individuality, and from his fellow men specifically as he utilizes them as objects or is himself utilized.

Having lost his fully human self, he turns in his intellectual confusion to God, an alien being he himself creates through abstraction. Observing the shattered unity between himself and nature, man reasons upon it and abstracts God from it, reducing himself still further in servile dependence upon an abstract deity.

Despite the universal evidence of man's distorted condition in the universe, neither Blake nor Marx sees the condition as unalterable or permanent. For both the possibility of transcendence is omnipresent, and for both it consists of a reintegration of man to realize his fully human potential. The distorted condition is a necessary historical stage along the way to human fulfillment. For Blake, Albion's sleep is a necessary precondition for Albion's awakening, as Thel had to be born to be saved; for Marx, capitalism is a necessary stage to be transcended along the way to communism, but a stage in advance of feudalism at any rate. For Blake error not only has to exist, but it also has to be consolidated, come to a crisis, and be recognized before it can be removed; for Marx the contradiction between labor and capital also has to exist and be recognized in self-consciousness, be sharpened and reach a crisis in order to hasten the resolution of contradiction in transcendence.

Although both Blake and Marx see political change as absolutely necessary, neither envisions the reintegration of man accomplished through purely political means. After *The French Revolution*, in which he postulates renewal effected by political change, Blake recognizes that renovation requires a complete change in man's consciousness, activities, and institutions. He explores these in later works and depicts changes in morality, religion, science, art, industry, perception, intellect, in human imagination and all its manifestations, not just its political ones. In *America*, for example, Blake sees revolutionary promise betrayed when only political change occurs, and at the end of the poem Orc soars off to France promising renewed sensuality and clerical disappearance as well as renovated politics as the sign of the coming of more complete revolution there. And in *Europe*, renewed sensuality and intellect assume the primary roles in revolutionary apocalyptic action. Milton repudiates his puritanical morality and artistic duplicity to renew himself and revive poetic inspiration. Finally, for Albion in *The Four Zoas* and *Jerusalem*, political change becomes simply one external change among many resulting from the abolition of his selfhood and his subsequent fully human reintegration in a humanized universe.

In his later works, Blake calls for a change in the nature of man, not just a change in the political status of man, such as resulted from the American and French revolutions. He sees, as his own poetical task,

> To open the Eternal Worlds, to open the immortal Eyes
> Of Man inwards into the Worlds of Thought: into Eternity
> Ever expanding in the Bosom of God. the Human Imagination
> (J I: 5, 18–20)

The inner imaginative development of man is here equated with God and renews both senses (eyes) and intellect (thought). As both Milton and Albion proceed along their journeys (in *Milton* and *Jerusalem*, respectively), they each accomplish this task of inner development; Milton by repudiating his old dualism and puritanical allegiance and embracing his emanation, thereby imaginatively renewing his own consciousness as well as Blake's, and Albion similarly by giving himself for another and also achieving reintegration thereby. However, this internal renewal and abolition of selfhood is not simply personal. It cannot be since it reintegrates man with the world. Milton becomes an inspiration to Blake and a savior to mankind, and Albion in renovating himself demonstrates the renewal of everyman. But this internal development is not simply a turning away from the world. Blake hardly encourages religious quietism, stoicism, or any system that requires a withdrawal from the outside world and cultivates isolated subjectivity. Rather his vision is energetic; imaginative vision includes imaginative action, and the self and the world are simultaneously renewed, for the two are really one after all. In *The Four Zoas*, for example, as "flames of mental fire" (FZ IX: 118, 18), of "intellect / And Reason" (FZ IX: 119, 19–20) surround the earth, "The thrones of Kings are shaken" and "The poor smite their opressors" (FZ IX: 117, 18, 19). Similarly, when Albion finally awakens at the end of *Jerusalem*, not only does he converse with "Visionary forms . . . creating exemplars of Memory and of Intellect" (J IV: 98, 28, 30), but he also abolishes war, sin, oppressive kingship, taxation, and poverty.[8] Indeed, the entire world turns human in his extended subjectivity, which takes in the human forms of "Tree Metal Earth & Stone" (J IV: 99, 1). No inhuman forms can possibly remain after his sacrifice of isolated self, that is, of the selfhood. This frees the true self, imagination, for action, and as imagination acts freely it inevitably remakes the world. Blake, in turning to the full renovation of man, never abandons the idea of political change; he merely sees it in its proper perspective as a part related to the whole.

For Marx, too, political change, although necessary, is insufficient in bringing about the renewed condition of man. While the first stage of communism is "still political in nature" (EPM 135), later stages transcend the political in forming the "reintegration or return of man to himself, the transcendence of human self-estrangement" (EPM 135). Mere political change is by definition incomplete. "Politics in this sense must be conceived as an activity whose ultimate end is *its own annulment* by means of fulfilling its determinate function as a necessary stage in the complex process of positive transcendence."[9] Taken by itself, political change postulates " 'Society' again as an abstraction *vis-à-vis* the individual" (EPM 137), but real transcendence sees no abstractions, only each man as individual and simultaneously social, and sees the end of all estrangement, not just in politics but in "religion, family, state, law, morality, science, art" (EPM 136). This final stage is Marxian communism, which is not simply the negation of private property but is a positive act of human development itself, the transcendence or raising to a higher positive state what began as the negation of an alien state. For Marx, "the transcendence of private property is therefore the complete *emancipation* of all human senses and qualities, . . . precisely because these senses and attributes have become, subjectively and objectively, *human*" (EPM 139). They finally serve to mediate between man and nature, to see man as the "being of nature" and nature as "the being of man" (EPM 145), to humanize the world and simultaneously to reflect objectivity as subjectivity and vice versa. Thus Marx's vision of reintegration is as complete as Blake's and also includes all human consciousness, activities, and institutions. The positive transcendence of private property that Marx envisions is simultaneously the transcendence of the entire process of man's self-estrangement, "the complete return of man to himself" (EPM 135), and "the real *appropriation of the human essence* by and for man" (EPM 135) instead of by and for capital. In this process all man's powers are returned to him from their alienated forms and are used to shape the humanized world. His action becomes human action, his needs human needs, and his consciousness human consciousness. He is returned to himself in all the processes of his being and his knowing, in a unity of idealism and materialism in true humanism, which Marx defines as communism.

While Marx, like Blake, sees man's inner development as inextricably connected with the outer conditions of his being, he reverses Blake's order. "Thus," he states, "the objectification of the human essence, both in its theoretical and practical aspects, is required to make man's *sense human*, as well as to create the *human sense* corresponding to the entire wealth of human and natural substance" (EPM 141). Only through the reflection of man's subjectivity in its objective appearance in the world can the development of fully humanized senses and self-consciousness occur. The relationship is fully dialectical for Marx as for Blake, but the qualitative change, if indeed there is one, seems to take place in productivity for Marx and in thought for Blake.

In both Blake's vision of inner imaginative renovation which has necessary consequences in the world, and Marx's analysis of the positive transcendence of private property which has necessary consequences for the inner man, a monistic vision triumphs over a dualistic one. In both writers the breach between subject and object is healed by a subjectivity which extends itself outward, humanizes the object that it beholds, and is further shaped by it in a dialectical but not a dualistic relationship. For Blake the basic unity of the world is variously expressed in the image of the universal man who contains the universe in his limbs, in the humanized identity of the phenomenal world, the inner definition of space and time, the vision of all as one when eternal man and his world merge in primal unity, or of the one as many when single natural objects such as a grain of sand or a flower expand to contain a universe. The subject is objectivized as the object is subjectivized, and the dialectical process once initiated continues as:

> . . . all
> Human Forms identified, livin, going forth & returning wearied
> Into Planetary lives of Years Months Days & Hours reposing
> And then Awaking into his [Albion's] Bosom in the Life of Immortality.
> (J IV: 99, 1–4)

For Marx the world becomes whole when the subject in the process of self-realization objectifies himself in the world and then returns the objectified human essence to subjectivity by the universal appropriation of that world through all his mental and physical powers. Again a dialectical relationship obtains as man shapes his world which in turn shapes him, and there is a coming and going from man to the world and back again. Unity and diversity also merge. "A *particular* individual is just as much the *totality*—the ideal totality—the subjective existence of thought and experienced society for itself; just as he exists also in the real world as the awareness and the real mind of social existence, and as a totality of human manifestation of life" (EPM 138). Finally, for both Blake and Marx, man by developing his fully human potential simultaneously gives the world its human shape. Subsequently, by seeing himself in the world, he recognizes it as human and establishes an identity with it. Thus both heal the breach between subject and object and establish a unity between man and his world based on an extension of subjectivity outward to embrace the no longer simply external world.

Notes

1. Charles Taylor, *Hegel* (Cambridge: Cambridge Univ. Press, 1975), p. 10.
2. Karl Marx, *The Economic and Philosophic Manuscripts of 1844*, ed. Dirk J. Struik, trans. Martin Milligan (New York: International Publishers, 1964), p. 112; hereafter cited as EPM.
3. Karl Marx, *Grundrisse: Foundations of the Critique of Political Economy*, trans. Martin Nicolaus (New York: Vintage Books, 1973), pp. 614, 611.
4. Istvan Meszaros, *Marx's Theory of Alienation* (New York: Harper & Row, 1972), pp. 80–81.
5. G. W. F. Hegel, "Independence and Dependence of Self-Consciousness: Lordship and Bondage," *The Phenomenology of Mind*, trans. J. B. Baillie (New York: Harper & Row, 1967), pp. 228–240.
6. The same process occurs in *Europe* (especially plate 10), where the limitation of man's once infinite senses and intellect produces the finite world of fallen reason and religion, in *The Book of Urizen* (plates 10–13), and in the limitation of Luvah and Albion as well as Reuben throughout *Jerusalem*.
7. Blake, too, sees money as universally corrupting and man's desire for it usurping the place of all his other human feelings and interests. The miser knows neither nature nor human sympathy because of it (E 49). The counselor uses it to destroy human senses and distort human life (E 67–68); and wherever it exists "Art cannot be carried on, but War only. . . ." (E 272).
8. As Eleanor Wilner points out, Blake was not only an imaginative visionary, but also "offered the first full-scale critique of the industrial age," for he "became aware of the contradictions in a system long before those contradictions, through their historical consequences, were to become apparent to the run of men." *Gathering the Winds: Visionary Imagination and Radical Transformation of Self and Society* (Baltimore: Johns Hopkins Univ. Press, 1975), pp. 47–48.
9. Meszaros, p. 160.

Eileen Sanzo

Blake, Teilhard, and the Idea of the Future of Man

No eighteenth-century ideal is more important than Blake's Jerusalem, his belief in a glorious future of mankind on earth, inspired by the Christian dissenting millennial tradition going back to Judaic and early Christian origins, expressed in Revelation by "John in Patmos" (M II: 40, 22).[1] In this century Pierre Teilhard de Chardin, who, like Blake, emerges from a background in the Christian tradition with its essentially optimistic interpretation of reality, shares and reinforces his futurism.[2] The Jesuit geologist, paleontologist, and philosopher, one of the discoverers of Peking man, provides, in fact, a scientific basis for the millenarian view of the "ultimate earth" [3] through his study of evolution and projection of it into the future. Blake's myth and symbolism and Teilhard's scientific writing are variations on a common, if sophisticated, millennial theme, which appears in Christian thought. Millenarianism in the eighteenth century was a Protestant, not a Catholic, tradition. As a Catholic, Teilhard extended the more universal Christian beliefs in the providential goodness of God and in the afterlife and thus, success of the world, to an optimistic view of history in terms of the earth, the future evolution of *this* world.

The works of both men, little known in their own lifetimes, are widely studied today. Teilhard reinforces in the contemporary mind Blake's central idea concerning a future based on the social ideals of Christianity, "Brotherhood & Universal love" (FZ IX: 133, 13). His optimism, belief in, and devotion to the future match Blake's and, while there is no reason to think he read Blake, their ideas now meet in the contemporary milieu. Because they are widely cited, they are to be distinguished from other Christian millenarian writers, such as the seventeenth-century Winstanley,[4] for example, whose audience today is more narrow, composed of a limited number of academic scholars.

Blake and Teilhard are read in a century when many, stunned by such things as world wars and the violence of the technological age, have succumbed to a pessimistic view of the world. After the optimism of the eighteenth and nineteenth centuries concerning man and his future, based on the concept of progress and that of the perfectibility of man and the advances of science as understood by positivists, the attitude of many in the twentieth century could be summed up by the title of the book published by Otto Spengler in 1918, *The Decline of the West*, and they would agree with Spengler that human history is cyclical rather than progressive. For others, the origin and development of the world are a result of chance, accident, not transcendent and immanent purpose. Even those within the Christian tradition do not share the futurism of Blake and Teilhard, for they by no means represent orthodox Christianity's concept of the future of the earth as it appears in either the eighteenth or the twentieth century.

The church disclaimed millenarianism, with its belief in a joyously transformed society in the future of this world, as early as the fourth century. In the next century, according to Norman Cohn in *The Pursuit of the Millennium*, Augustine's *The City of God* did not proclaim a Blakean Jerusalem, but rather taught that revelation "was to be understood as a spiritual allegory; as for the millennium, that had begun with the birth of Christianity and was fully realized in the Church." Cohn adds, "This at once became orthodox doctrine." [5] It is true that apocalypticism continued down through the centuries, as Bernard McGinn and others have shown, but McGinn makes a distinction between the narrower category of millenarianism (concerned with a terrestrial future) and the broader one of apocalypticism (concerned with the end of history, but not necessarily on earth).[6] The established view of the future on earth has been darker than that of Blake and Teilhard. From this point of view, the earth exists for the individual salvation of men and their reward in an afterlife. For many Christian believers today, the world does not have an evolutionary direction and purpose. Rather it presents a drama in which men as actors make certain choices which have significance for their personal salvation.

It is interesting that, in writing of the millenarianism of the fourteenth century, in which such fervor was strong though heterodox, Morton Bloomfield calls such people as Jan Hus, John Wyclif, and William Langland "prophets," to be distinguished from the great "mystics" of the century, who stressed individual salvation and individual union with the divine.[7] In the modern period, the distinction may still be made. Blake, in his writing, called himself a prophet, not a mystic, although some tried later to explain his work away as a "mysticism" which could not be comprehended. Blake and Teilhard, in their futurism concerning the earth, prophetically involve the totality of humankind, both socially and spiritually, while the more mystical today may emphasize an individual perfection and personal attainment to the divine. Blake and Teilhard, however, are prophets, not mystics, in the Christian millenarian, heterodox tradition.

In the modern period, Christianity, after denying evolution at first, never caught up with evolutionary theory, with Teilhard as a notable exception. Conventional belief was the same as it was in the Middle Ages—man fell; he has been redeemed; the world is static. There is no teaching concerning mankind's earthly future. Teilhard's writing on evolution and the direction it is taking was considered so unorthodox by some authorities in the Catholic Church that they would not allow him to publish his works, and only since his death in 1955 have they had widespread circulation.

If the Church early condemned millenarianism, the tradition, nevertheless, remained alive in Christianity, flourishing among dissenting sects and gathering force especially during many revolutionary periods in Western history. Marjorie Reeves, writing principally about the millenarianism of the twelfth-century Joachim of Fiore, traces what she calls the Joachist view of history and the coming Kingdom of God on earth in the religious orders, in the Renaissance Italy of Ficino and Savonarola, in Catholic missionary zeal, in Protestant reformers, and in eighteenth-century political prophecy.[8] The crude concept of Christ's presence on the earth for a thousand years was usually dropped, giving way instead to a belief in a prolonged period of peace, equality, and love among members of a transformed society on a fruitful and harmonious earth. In the post-Renaissance period millenarianism often took a secular form, as Carl Becker in *The Heavenly City of the Eighteenth-Century Philosophers* and J. B. Bury in *The Idea of Progress* point out. Ernest Tuveson, also, shows the religious, millennial background to the idea of progress in the modern West.[9] A secular millenarian whose work has had profound impact is Karl Marx.[10]

While sharing Marx's thirst for egalitarianism and social justice in a new society, the Blake of the epics, who opposed the "imaginative" or "eternal" to the "vegetative," would be antipathetic to Marx's materialistic view of reality. He believed in God and that man is divine because he participates in the life of God through the faculty of the imagination.[11] He believed in the afterlife ("Awaking into his Bosom in the Life of Immortality," J IV: 99, 4) and in the idea of the "Divine Humanity in Jesus" (VLJ, E 543), who appears as leader of the human family and reveals the divine:

> As one Man all the Universal Family; and that One Man
> We call Jesus the Christ: and he in us, and we in him,
>
> . . . .
>
> He is the Good shepherd, he is the Lord and master:
> He is the Shepherd of Albion, he is all in all. . . .
>
> (J II: 34, 19–20, 23–24)

His use of the myth of John to express these beliefs makes him a spokesman of dissenting Christian millenarianism.[12] His dedication to the future sprang from a deep personal humanitarianism and social conscience, which he identified with the social ideals of Christianity. Christian social ideals also inspire the futurism of Teilhard, which is based as well on far-reaching scientific study, while his social protest is less explicit than Blake's with its "minute particulars" (J II: 38, 23). Blake believed in Jerusalem as the earthly blessed future that will necessarily come into being with human effort, and which is imminent in the crisis of the modern period. His conviction was influenced in part by the American and French revolutions and the advances in knowledge of the period. Also, his belief was firmly situated in the imagination. Teilhard disclaimed a millennial connection for his futurism, but he denied a crude concept of the millennial, not its essence. His optimistic conviction concerning the future is part of his larger Christian confidence, his belief that Christ identifies himself with the evolutionary process. Both Teilhard and Blake are Christian millenarians in that they envision future mankind living as a family, with Christ as spiritual presence and unifying force. This is the Christian view of the afterlife, but they see it as a reality on earth.

The anthropological root of apocalypticism, according to Bernard McGinn, is an ability to validate present events in history by relating them to a transcendental End and purpose of history.[13] Blake, in the millennial tradition, relates the cataclysmic events of the French Revolutionary period to Old Testament prophecy and Revelation. More sophisticated because of his genius than the other millenarians of his day, he saw events mythologically and symbolically and, in many ways, related them to contemporary thought connected with the idea of progress, though formally he presented the millennial Jerusalem as a "return" to prelapsarian perfection rather than as an advance.

McGinn sees apocalyptic beliefs as "incapable of rational demonstration," but throughout his work, Blake expresses militant rejection of the modern West's test of truth by "Demonstration" and opposes it to perception of divine truth through "Imagination," intuition, and inspiration; while Teilhard, as a paleontologist and geologist, claimed a scientific basis for his interpretation of sacred history—not only cultural history, but now cosmic-evolutionary history. He proposed, in the modern period, a transcendental, millenarian validation of the sweeping time periods of the universe and the earth. Both accounts of history—cultural and cosmic-evolutionary—draw upon the Christian tradition.

Blake's Jerusalem is a vision of human unity, to include "All the Nations Peoples & Tongues throughout all the Earth" (J III: 72, 44). The idea of unity is the essential component of the thought of Teilhard, who draws, like

Blake, upon the idea of human unity in the New Testament, and John in particular. Unity is a vision of mankind awakened, as Blake put it; a mankind matured and grown up, as Teilhard saw it. Both Blake and Teilhard have a sense of the modern world as one of dramatic change and transition. A century and a half apart, they nevertheless use similar images. Blake, who had a limited exposure to Erasmus Darwin's concepts of evolution, rejected them because he believed in man's fall from a state of perfection. He had no knowledge of the evolutionary time sequence and conceived of the past, present, and future in the light of biblical revelation, interpreted esoterically. The world was only six thousand years old and the future would be the promised millennium that many Christians dared to hope for down through the centuries. Seemingly, the two thinkers would be separated by the vastness of the new scientific knowledge of the nineteenth and twentieth centuries. Tuveson points out that, in the nineteenth century, "the old teleological idea was transmuted into evolutionism," [14] but it was a secularized idea, a seemingly antireligious idea. Nevertheless, the two thinkers are together in their devoted and enthusiastic dedication to the future of man. They have the same intuition informed by their similar Christian beliefs. As Tuveson shows, "the germ of a concept of progress is implicit in the nature of the Christian religion," with the idea of development in history—of fall, degeneration, and salvation.[15] For orthodox Christianity, however, the idea of progress has generally been individual and spiritual, not in terms of the future of all on earth.

In a pessimistic age, Teilhard shares the confidence of Blake, who wrote his epics at a time when the French Revolution had seemingly failed and the counterrevolutionary measures of the British establishment further oppressed the poor. The poet believed all the more strongly in the future, symbolizing contemporary events as the night before the promised millennial dawn. If, after all, man lost faith and the age was materialistic, "Is it not that Signal of the Morning which was told us in the Beginning?" (J IV: 93, 26). It is indeed the future which is at the heart of the thought of both men. Each worked in his own way to "Labour in Knowledge" in order to "Build up Jerusalem" (J III: 77 [prose]).

The utopian idea, based on the nineteenth-century concept of universal progress, has taken many forms in the twentieth century, among them totalitarian dictatorships. Utopian dictatorships have created the anti-utopian visions of Orwell and Huxley, and in the contemporary period, nightmare fictions such as Vonnegut's *Player Piano*. These dictatorships are totally different from Blake's millennium; for him, "Jerusalem is called Liberty" (J III: 54, 5). He contrasts the "wheel without wheel, with cogs tyrannic / Moving by compulsion each other" with those of the New Jerusalem, "those in Eden: which / Wheel within Wheel in freedom revolve in harmony & peace" (J I: 15, 18–20). Blake and Teilhard, following John, for whom "God is love," both see the future as a world community based not on force but love. Unity for Teilhard is just that, union, not identification, for beings are further differentiated in unity.[16] Both Blake and Teilhard reject the individualistic tendencies of the eighteenth and nineteenth centuries and see the future in terms of collective man, but not in terms of totalitarian force. Teilhard calls Communism a distortion of something magnificent. Blake sees the millennium as a release of man from imprisoning restriction and oppressive inhibition. Man will be free to expand his creative energies in love. The eighteenth-century revolutionary discussion of the fraternal one and the many is given ultimate expression in Blake's image of the millennial unity of the many through love, with no loss of individuality. Such unity is plastic, expanding to oneness or contracting to multiplicity through shared consciousness made possible by love. The metaphor is of the family, which exists

> As one Man for contracting their Exalted Senses
> They behold Multitude or Expanding they behold as one
> As One Man all the Universal family & that one Man
> They call Jesus the Christ & they in him & he in them
> Live in Perfect harmony
>
> (FZ 1: 21, 2–6)

The family members referred to are "those in Great Eternity," who "met in the Council of God" (FZ I: 21, 1), but at the end of *Jerusalem* this state of "Expansion or Contraction" (J IV: 98, 36) is explicitly millennial and is, in *The Four Zoas*, meant for the entire human family. Blake's great "vision" is not private, as some have thought, nor is it one of only individual, subjective transcendence. His primary ideal is loving communal consciousness and he believes it will come about in the future.

Like Blake, Teilhard bases unity on the principles of brotherhood, rather than repression of the individual. Only love can unite people through what is deepest in them. Why should not the example of the couple or the team repeat itself on a worldwide scale in the future? Such synthesis of "unity with multitude" is even biologically necessary, as we see with lower forms of life. "Universal love" is the "only complete and final way in which we are able to love" (PM 267). Teilhard makes clear that what he has in mind is not a totalitarian collectivization but a very different socialization, one in keeping with mankind's differentiation as individuals:

> By virtue of the emergence of Thought a special and novel environment has been evolved among human individuals within which they acquire the faculty of associating together, and reacting upon one another, no longer primarily for

> the preservation and continuance of the species but for the creation of a common consciousness. In such an environment the differentiation born of union may act upon that which is most unique and incommunicable in the individual, namely his personality. Thus socialization, whose hour seems to have sounded for Mankind, does not by any means signify the ending of the Era of the Individual upon earth, but far more its beginning. All that matters at this crucial moment is that the massing together of individualities should not take the form of a functional and enforced mechanism of human energies (the totalitarian principle) but of a "conspiracy" informed with love.[17]

Is such a world of unity and freedom possible? From their common ground in Christian hope, Blake envisions it and Teilhard provides a scientific basis for Blake's vision. Evolution is on man's side. This is not to say that a millennial future is inevitable, for evolution is now in its partially "creative" phase as thinking, reflecting man comes to control more and more of the earth's destiny himself. Teilhard asserts that the biological evolution of the individual man has stabilized for the past few millennia; future evolutionary growth will not be of man but of mankind. Growth will take the direction of man influencing man as the planet, now fully discovered geographically, converges upon itself in unity. In his essay "The Atomism of Spirit," he holds that the surface of the earth is being compressed by the increase in population, much more by the growth of interconnections of all kinds and their acceleration than by numerical growth.[18] In *The Phenomenon of Man*, the ongoing physical expansion of the universe is related to a complementary compression of the earth; compression leads to the increasing complexity of the human group, and with this complexity comes increasing consciousness. It is Teilhard's central axiom that the greater the physical complexity of matter, the greater the consciousness, which is an extension of matter, the interior of matter. The growing complexity of mankind means an increase of the consciousness of mankind, and this consciousness is love as well as thought. Love then is the interior consciousness, accompanying the increasing complexity of union. Unity is not based on force, but on the instinctual and thoughtful affinities of man, which, once they have gained momentum, will be irresistible. As it is in John, love is the principle of the future for both Blake and Teilhard, who says that

> love has always been carefully eliminated from realist and positivist concepts of the world; but sooner or later we shall have to acknowledge that it is the fundamental impulse of Life, or, if you prefer, the one natural medium in which the rising course of evolution can proceed. . . . It is through love and within love that we must look for the deepening of our deepest self, in the life-giving coming together of mankind. Love is the free and imaginative

> outpouring of the spirit over all unexplored paths. It links those who love in bonds that unite but do not confound, causing them to discover in their mutual contact an exultation capable, incomparably more than any arrogance of solitude, of arousing in the heart of their being all that they possess of uniqueness and creative power. (FM 54, 55).

Teilhard sees the present as a critical evolutionary threshold into the future. Technology has united the world; spiritual unity must follow physical unity. As always in evolution, the spiritual proceeds from the physical. Union is the force of future evolution and Teilhard, like Blake, is trying to rouse humankind, to direct its energies in this time of creative evolution, to interpret the drift of the world's motion, so as to give understanding and reduce frustration. The great developmental force of the world that is evolution is sympathetic to man's growth, but man must also, to the degree to which he is free, choose to grow. Morton Bloomfield shows that, in most instances, the millenarianism of the Middle Ages considered man to have a primarily passive role in the bringing about of the Kingdom of God.[19] Blake and Teilhard, however, present modern mankind as needing to be an essentially active agent in contributing to the arrival of the millennial future. In the present period of world hostilities and creative evolution, humankind is encouraged by Teilhard and Blake, who wrote prophetically, to transcend division. Blake too sees the modern world as crucial. Teilhard would be sympathetic to Los as he announces the modern age:

> Fellow Labourers! The Great Vintage & Harvest is now upon Earth
> The whole extent of the Globe is explored: Every scatterd Atom
> Of Human Intellect now is flocking to the sound of the Trumpet
> All the Wisdom which was hidden in caves & dens, from ancient
> Time; is now sought out from Animal & Vegetable & Mineral
> The Awakener is come. outstretchd over Europe! the vision of God is fulfilled
> The Ancient Man upon the Rock of Albion Awakes. . . .
>
> (M I: 25, 17–23)

"The whole extent of the Globe is explored," says Blake; for Teilhard, the curvature of the globe and the world physically united means the convergence of the human family upon the earth, evolutionary compression and centering, a coming together and a reflection of mankind upon itself. The human monad belongs to the past, for mankind's unity as a whole is the direction of cosmogenesis.[20] Our age is a great period of evolutionary transition, including the tensions that change involves. Central to the work of Blake also is the unity of the human family. His Jerusalem is the earth-city of a united, all-inclusive mankind. Teilhard, writing during World War II, emphasizes the physical pressure upon mankind to unite:

> It took hundreds of centuries for man simply to people the earth and cover it with a first network: and further thousands of years to build up, as chance circumstances allowed, solid nuclei of civilizations within this initially fluctuating envelope, radiating from independent and antagonistic centres. Today, these elements have multiplied and grown; they have packed themselves closer together and forced themselves against one another—to the point where an over-all unity, *of no matter what nature*, has become economically and psychologically inevitable. Mankind, in coming of age, has begun to be subject to the necessity and to feel the urgency of forming one single body coextensive with itself. There we have the underlying cause of our distress. (AE 14–15)

For Blake, "Every scatterd Atom / Of Human Intellect now is flocking to the sound of the Trumpet." Similarly, Teilhard in "The Atomism of Spirit" announces the moleculization or coming together of the human. Blake was particularly sensitive to the currents of the modern age, and if the earth was physically united in his day, how much more so in Teilhard's electronic, accelerated period. Both thinkers realized that what must follow physical unity is spiritual unity and both urged mankind to work for it, to embrace it. Blake's scattered atom of intellect and Teilhard's "grain of thought" (AE 38) fuse with all the rest in researching the "Wisdom which was hidden in caves & dens, from ancient / Time," wisdom "sought out from Animal & Vegetable & Mineral." In Blake's day there was a new, enthusiastic interest in ancient mythology, not just classical but that of all peoples, and coupled with an interest in ancient history and primitive peoples of the past and present. The past was becoming present to the modern age. There was a new interest in the human and in the earth, which the new science was exploring. For Teilhard, the momentum that science has gained since Blake's day is one of the marks of the present evolutionary period. Millions are now engaged in research of all kinds. Mankind is even thinking together, forming a molecular "thought made up of thoughts" (AE 38):

> Now the type of solidarity which impresses itself upon us so palpably in the order of mechanics, is nothing but the tangible reflection of an even more profound psychological "setting." Leibniz and his closed monads have no place in today's world. Henceforth man is less capable than ever before of *thinking alone*. We have only to consider the series of our modern concepts in science, philosophy and religion, and it will be obvious that the more general and fruitful any one of these notions is proving, the more it, too, is tending to assume the form of a collective entity: we can, it is true, individually cover one

> angle of it, we can make a portion of it our own and develop it, but it rests in fact on a vault of mutually buttressed thoughts. The idea of the electron or the quantum, or the cosmic ray—the idea of the cell or heredity—the idea of humanity or even the idea of God—no single individual can claim these as his preserve or dominate them. In such things, what is already thinking, just as what is already working, through man and above man, is again mankind. And it is inconceivable, in virtue of the very way in which the phenomenon works, that the movement initiated should not continue in the same direction, tomorrow as today, becoming more pronounced and increasing in speed. (A E 37–38)

For Teilhard, Blake's "Awakener" is not "outstretched over Europe" but rather over the earth and is, in fact, evolution. In Blake's day, Europe was the center of the world. Now, the total earth is centered in what Blake calls the "Universal Man" (FZ I: 3, 6). At times, Blake's Albion is the cosmic man with all the universe contained in his body. At other times, he represents specifically the British ruling establishment. Teilhard sees mankind centering and moving in the direction of a personal Omega, his idea of Christ inspired by John's revelation of "the Lord" as "Alpha and Omega." Spiritually, multiple, evolving humankind is drawn upward into unity, attracted by a personal Omega-point, converging in love, one with each other and with the cosmic Christ, as in Blake's vision of "One Man all the Universal Family." The Omega-point of the universe, for Teilhard, is God, the personal center toward which the world is traveling through evolution. He makes universal human love possible because of his personalization of the world and evolution. Omega is a "pole of psychic convergence towards which matter, as it arranges itself, gravitates. . . ."[21] Since he believes in the divinity of Christ, Teilhard identifies him with Omega, who is "the Prime Mover, Gatherer and Consolidator, ahead of us, of evolution."[22] Blake believes in the final union of the cosmos with God and, at the end of *Jerusalem*, plate 99, as nature becomes human and humanity divine, there is a design of the future portrayed as the victorious Jerusalem, a female form embraced by a male image of Jehovah.[23] The greater and greater centricity resulting from the pull of the personal Omega from the future means that the united mankind achieves greater consciousness, what Teilhard calls "the ultra human" (FM 289). He says of the cosmic man:

> Mankind is more and more taking the form of an organism that possesses a physiology and, in the current phrase, a common "metabolism." We may, if we please, say that these ties are superficial, and that we will loose them if we wish. Meanwhile, they are growing firmer every day, under the combined action of all the forces that surround us; and history shows that, as a whole, their network (woven under the influence of irreversible cosmic factors) has never ceased to draw tighter. (AE 36–37)

For Blake, the millennium is imminent: "the Vision of God is fulfilled." Teilhard sees the modern age rather as a "critical threshold" (AE 284), the dawning of a new consciousness; a new age of evolutionary transition as the earth converges and mankind reflects back upon itself, centering and becoming one. He bases his belief in the future not on the millennial promise but rather on science; nevertheless, he figuratively uses the name Jerusalem, the "New Earth." [24]

Blake believed that the block to Jerusalem was man's "Selfhood" (J II: 29 [33], 17), selfish exclusion by the rich and powerful of the poor of the world. He addresses himself to the world-man Albion, who represents here specifically nationalism and the English ruling class:

> Is this thy soft Family-Love
> Thy cruel Patriarchal pride
> Planting thy Family alone,
> Destroying all the World beside.
>
> (J I: 27, 77–80)

In a similar way, Teilhard asks modern man what course he is to choose in terms of the future: "Is it to be a jealously guarded fostering of our own individuality, achieved in increasing isolation; or in the association and giving of ourselves to the collective whole of mankind? " (FM 54). Blind and selfish individualism is an obstacle to the future development of mankind.

Both Blake and Teilhard see human evil as division. Teilhard, unlike Blake, does not believe in a fall, interpreting the concept rather as a "promising beginning" of mankind's growth. He does not share Blake's distrust of nature, nor does he have the strong sense of evil found in Blake, as in John and most of the Christian millennial tradition. He regards evil rather as wastage in the process of a world rising from multiplicity and plurality and converging as it approaches perfection. Still, for Teilhard as well as Blake, evil is essentially division. At the beginning of *The Four Zoas*, Blake refers to the blessed state of unity as it existed before the fall:

> Four Mighty Ones are in every Man: a Perfect Unity
> Cannot Exist. but from the Universal Brotherhood of Eden
> The Universal Man. To Whom be Glory Evermore
>
> (FZ I: 3, 4–6)

He engraves on the page a reference to John 17 : 21–23:

> That they all may be one; as thou Father, art in me, and I in thee, that they also may be one in us: that the world may believe that thou has sent me. And

> the glory which thou gavest me I have given them; that they may be one, even as we are one; and that the world may know that thou hast sent me, and hast loved them, as thou hast loved me.

Further down the page, Blake refers to Los's "fall into Division & his Resurrection to Unity" (FZ I: 4, 4).

In *Jerusalem* Jesus invites Albion to give up the selfhood and become united to him and to all mankind. Here Blake's Pauline vision of the Body of Jesus with its many members[25] is close to Teilhard's Christology:

> Awake! awake O sleeper of the land of shadows, wake! expand!
> I am in you and you in me, mutual in love divine:
> Fibres of love from man to man thro Albions pleasant land.
>
> . . . .
>
> I am not a God afar off, I am a brother and friend;
> Within your bosoms I reside, and you reside in me:
> Lo! we are One; forgiving all Evil; Not seeking recompense!
> Ye are my members O ye sleepers of Beulah, land of shades!
>
> (J I: 4, 6–8, 18–21)

But the British establishment is interested in empire, its own concept of the millennium, seizing and grasping the world's resources, denying freedom or dignity to the poor and refusing to share the world with them. Albion answers Jesus:

> [. . . *We are not One: we are Many, thou most simulative*]
> Phantom of the over heated brain! shadow of immortality!
> Seeking to keep my soul a victim to thy Love! which binds
> Man the enemy of man into deceitful friendships:
>
> . . . .
>
> My mountains are my own, and I will keep them to myself:
> The Malvern and the Cheviot, the Wolds Plinlimmon & Snowdon
> Are mine. here will I build my Laws of Moral Virtue!
> Humanity shall be no more: but war & princedom & victory!
>
> So spoke Albion in jealous fears. . . .
>
> (J I: 4, 23–26, 29–32)

It is in Jerusalem that man is restored to personal and universal integrity. All men belong to Jerusalem. Plate 72 of *Jerusalem* contains not a dry epic catalog, as some have mistakenly thought, but rather a joyous chant of peoples. Blake dislikes selfish, exclusive nationalism as much as Teilhard does. In Jerusalem "the Vision of God is fulfilled," and Blake's own vision is ecstatic:

O Come ye Nations Come ye People Come up to Jerusalem
Return Jerusalem & dwell together as of old! Return
Return! O Albion let Jerusalem overspread all Nations
As in the times of old! O Albion awake! Reuben wanders
The Nations wait for Jerusalem. they look up for the Bride

France Spain Italy Germany Poland Russia Sweden Turkey
Arabia Palestine Persia Hindostan China Tartary Siberia
Egypt Lybia Ethiopia Guinea Caffraria Negroland Morocco
Congo Zaara Canada Greenland Carolina Mexico
Peru Patagonia Amazonia Brazil. Thirty-two Nations
And under these Thirty-two Classes of Islands in the Ocean
All the Nations Peoples & Tongues throughout all the Earth
(J III: 72, 33–44)

The agent of love in the universe for both Blake and Teilhard is the divine. For Teilhard, Jesus in his Sonship is united with creation, is the cosmic Omega, the pull on creation upward to a personalized center, himself. The object of evolution is not a cold abstraction, but a person and, through him, the universe is personalized and glows with warmth. Teilhard stresses the perfecting quality of the incarnation, rather than the crucifixion, since he does not believe in the fall of man or nature. At the end of Blake's *Jerusalem*, in the millennium, Jesus is revealed under the guise of the heroic Los, and Albion as world-man is united with him in friendship. Jerusalem, Albion's emanation, is fulfilled as "Bride of the Lamb." Evil and suffering, the "Furnaces of affliction" (J IV: 96, 35), are transformed into "Fountains of Living Waters" (J IV: 96, 37). Blake does not solve the seeming inexplicability of evil and suffering, but as man approaches Jerusalem, they are transformed and he transcends them. In a large body of his work, Blake addresses himself to the human cause of suffering, man's inhumanity to man, and this is resolved in *Jerusalem*. At the end of *The Four Zoas*, in the millennium, the oppressed do not forgive the oppressor and there is a hell, but at the end of *Jerusalem*, all are together in "Mutual Forgiveness forevermore" (J IV: 92, 18). Natural evil is also conquered in the millennium. It may be that, in the future, the wise use of technology by a loving mankind may limit natural evil, but what of death? Both Blake, as we see at the end of *Jerusalem*, and Teilhard believe in an afterlife. For Teilhard, immortality is not won through expiation, through Jesus' crucifixion, which Blake protested as the "tree of Mystery" (FZ IX: 119, 4), writing elsewhere "Doth Jehovah Forgive a Debt only on condition that it shall / Be Payed? . . . That Debt is not Forgiven!" (J III: 61, 17–19). Atonement is foreign to the thought of both Blake and Teilhard. For Teilhard, it is the universal Christ, the union of God with the cosmos, which overcomes physical entropy in each man and in the universe and draws the world in its final phase to spiritualization of matter. Blake proposes this radical transformation or consummation of the world, a form of evolution, when he writes in the very last lines of *Jerusalem* of the numinous humanization of matter and the realization of man's divinity in immortality:

> All Human Forms identified even Tree Metal Earth & Stone. all
> Human Forms identified, living going forth & returning wearied
> Into the Planetary lives of Years Months Days & Hours reposing
> And then Awaking into his Bosom in the Life of Immortality.
>
> (J IV: 99, 1–4)

In this ultimate phase of the millennium, nature becomes human and human beings become divine as the entire earth is consumed and spiritualized.

This is not to say that matter is evil for Teilhard; his position is just the contrary. He does not split the "noosphere," his word for the thinking part of the earth as found in man, from the biosphere, as the world ascends and evolves toward perfection. He defines his neologism in speaking of the phenomenon of man: "He is more than a branch, more even than a kingdom; he is nothing less than a 'sphere'—the noosphere (or thinking sphere) super-imposed upon, and coextensive with (but in so many ways more close-knit and homogeneous) the biosphere." [26] He writes of the "zonal composition of our planet," adding to the zones already named by science, the noosphere, "the thinking layer" of the earth (PM 182). The noosphere, which marks a "new era in evolution" (PM 181), evolves from the biosphere, as the biosphere evolves out of the geosphere. Teilhard differs in his attitude toward nature from the Blake of the epics, who divides the "Eternal or Imaginative" from the "Vegetable Universe" (J III: 77), symbolized as a threatening "Polypus" (M I: 15, 8). Teilhard believes in the ascendancy of the spiritual over the physical, but also in the evolving "spiritualization" of matter; matter is the precious base. Although Blake sees a division in the world, he does not reject it, for Jerusalem is an earthly as well as heavenly city. It is built according to vision. The work of David Erdman, especially, shows clearly that Blake envisioned Jerusalem as a transformation of the earth and not only as the "apocalypse by imagination" [27] or divine self-conception that M. H. Abrams and Thomas Altizer describe, respectively, with respect to Blake's Jerusalem. Teilhard opposes the renunciation of the world by Eastern religions and by Christian asceticism, for, with his knowledge of the time sequences of the world, the evolution of the higher from the lower and of the thinking world of noosphere from the biosphere, he sees no split in reality. Thus he does not distrust nature, as the Blake of the epics does. Evil is not identified with matter, but rather regarded as waste products of the world as it evolves from the imperfection of multiplicity to perfection in unity.

Teilhard seems to solve one of the problems Blake worked with in *The Marriage of Heaven and Hell*, where he seeks to achieve unity out of the Platonic, and conventionally Christian, duality of body and soul. In his later writing Blake divided the "eternal" and the "vegetative," but in *The Marriage of Heaven and Hell* he asserts that "All Bibles or sacred codes. have been the causes of the following Errors. / 1. That Man has two real existing principles Viz: a Body & a Soul. . . . But the following Contraries to these are True / 1 Man has no Body distinct from his Soul for that calld Body is a / portion of Soul discernd by the five Senses, the chief inlets of Soul in this age" (MHH 4). Teilhard, a self-styled materialist, calls himself a monist as he affirms both the within and the without of matter; his axiom, as we have seen, is that the greater the degree of complexity of matter, the greater the centricity and thus the greater the consciousness. He sees "an inflexible trend inherent in corpusculized energy towards progressively higher states of *complexity-consciousness*" (AE 377). As for the unity of body and spirit: "the great opportunity in my life will have been that I was so situated existentially that the 'spirit' of the philosophers and theologians was seen by me as a direct extension of universal physico-chemism. . . ." (AE 378). Here Teilhard provides the scientific base for the unity Blake was seeking.

Although Blake in his epic period distrusts nature, he is, like Teilhard, religious but also dedicated to the future of the earth. They do not reject the world, but rather work for its fulfillment. Though Blake bitterly protested the denial of the spiritual by scientific materialists, he was himself interested in science and technological inventions, as we see from his use of technology for images and symbols throughout the epics.[28] At the end of *The Four Zoas*, he even says that "The dark Religions are departed & sweet Science reigns" (FZ IX: 139, 10). Teilhard was a scientist who dedicated *The Divine Milieu* "To those who love the world." Blake and Teilhard are concerned with the future of the earth and of man on earth, but they do not limit their millennial Jerusalem to purely material progress, like many of the materialistic utopian designs of the nineteenth and twentieth centuries. Jerusalem is psychic as well as material.

What Blake, as artist and visionary, experienced as the "Imagination," Teilhard, as scientist and philosopher, experienced, intuitively and through research and observation, as the "noosphere." Both had a strong sense of the numinous in man. The faculty of imagination, for Blake, is the divine in man. Because the poorest beggar on the London streets possessed this faculty, Blake lashed out with protest at such people's oppression.

Indeed, the imagination is the spiritual means of human unity, to accompany the physical unity made possible by scientific discovery and invention. Through imagination, we transcend the "Selfhood" and feel empathetically what others feel, know what others know, experience what others experience. Man participates in Jerusalem through imagination, even before it is completely achieved. In Jerusalem, the divinity of man is realized as the members of the human family live for one another. Teilhard's view of the future is also represented when Blake writes as poetic spokesman of millennial vision that, in nearing Jerusalem,

> . . . we know
> That Man subsists by Brotherhood & Universal Love
> We fall on one anothers necks more closely we embrace
> Not for ourselves but for the Eternal family we live
> Man liveth not by Self alone but in his brothers face
> Each shall behold the Eternal Father & love & joy abound
> (FZ IX: 133, 21–26)

Both Teilhard and Blake, notwithstanding a strong sense of evil, are optimists. Living in a new age of materialism was not, for them, a reason to despair over humanity's spiritual decline. It is true that technology has united the world as culture and religion have not. In evolution, the spiritual evolves out of the physical, and for Blake and Teilhard physical unity calls for the spiritual to come. Teilhard reveals an ultimately beneficent universe, where cosmogenesis, the continued development and purpose of the world, mirrors humanity's highest ideals and provides a milieu favorable to its own positive choices concerning the future. Since it is the responsibility of modern man in this crucial period so to choose, work, and build, the vision of Blake and that of Teilhard are of great significance as a guide into the future. They derive their themes ultimately from their common Christian background, each performing a variation on an ancient subject. In both of them this belief in the future emerges fresh and strong, and they are perhaps its most notable spokesmen in the modern period. While Blake declares to the world that he will not cease from personal, creative "Mental Fight . . . Till we have built Jerusalem" (M I: 1, 13, 15) and portrays Jerusalem that Albion may "awake" to this vision of ultimate reality, the millennium which is inevitable with human effort, Teilhard urges man to believe in Jerusalem as a creative choice in order that it may come about: "The whole future of the Earth, as of religion, seems to me to depend on the awakening of our faith in the future" (AE 38). Although others, within Christianity as well as outside it, seem to have little concept of the future of mankind, Blake and Teilhard hold it up as our greatest hope.

Notes

1. Thus Joseph Anthony Wittreich, Jr., sees Blake's "definitive" poem *Jerusalem* as a "consolidation of the visions contained in . . . Revelation prophecy." "Opening the Seals: Blake's Epic and the Milton Tradition," in *Blake's Sublime Allegory: Essays on "The Four Zoas," "Milton," and "Jerusalem,"* ed. Stuart Curran and Joseph Anthony Wittreich, Jr. (Madison: Univ. of Wisconsin Press, 1973), p. 37.

2. George Mills Harper in *The Neoplatonism of William Blake* (Chapel Hill: Univ. of North Carolina Press, 1961), p. 269, identifies what he calls "the pessimism inherent in Blake's apprehension of reality" and asserts that "life on this earth . . . was merely a waiting period during which the fallen soul could batter down the door of the prison-house with the spears of intellect, could complete the Circle of Destiny and return to eternal rest in the oneness of the Divine Humanity." However, the work of David V. Erdman, especially, has shown that Blake was committed to the building up of *this* world, what he considered its regeneration and renewal, Jerusalem. See especially *Blake, Prophet against Empire: A Poet's Interpretation of the History of His Own Times*, rev. ed. (Princeton: Princeton Univ. Press, 1969).

3. Pierre Teilhard de Chardin, *The Phenomenon of Man*, trans. Bernard Wall (New York: Harper & Row, 1959), p. 273; hereafter cited as PM.

4. For the classic study of Gerrard Winstanley, see T. Wilson Hayes, *Winstanley the Digger: A Literary Analysis of the Radical Ideas of the English Revolution* (Cambridge: Harvard Univ. Press, 1979).

5. *The Pursuit of the Millennium*, rev. ed. (New York: Oxford Univ. Press, 1970), p. 29.

6. *Visions of the End: Apocalyptic Traditions in the Middle Ages* (New York: Columbia Univ. Press, 1979), pp. 28–30.

7. *Piers Plowman as a Fourteenth-Century Apocalypse* (New Brunswick, N. J.: Rutgers Univ. Press, n.d.), p. 99.

8. See Marjorie Reeves and Beatrice Hirsch-Reeves, *The Figurae of Joachim of Fiore* (Oxford: Clarendon Press, 1972); Marjorie Reeves, *Joachim of Fiore and the Prophetic Future* (New York: Harper & Row, 1976).

9. See *Millennium and Utopia: A Study in the Background of the Idea of Progress* (1949; reprint ed., Gloucester, Mass.: Peter Smith, 1972).

10. Marx may be said to belong to the secular branch of the millenarian tradition even though he and also Comte, as Robert Nisbet points out, "were fond of supposing . . . that all that had preceded them was altruistic sentiment, utopian speculation." *Social Change and History: Aspects of the Western Theory of Development* (New York: Oxford Univ. Press, 1969), p. 121.

11. Concerning Blake's humanism and his belief in God, Leopold Damrosch points out that Blake writes " 'God is Jesus' not because God is confined to the *merely* human, but because he does not exist in the superhuman or inhuman fictions of conventional religion. If Blake had wanted to say only that the human imagination is our sole experience of the divine, it would not have cost him so many years of brooding and such tortuous formulations to say so. As Frye reminds us, 'though God is the perfection of man, man is not wholly God, otherwise there would be no point in bringing in the idea of God at all.' " Damrosch writes that although "it is customary to deny the existence of a transcendent realm and to assert that God or Jesus is wholly human . . . we cannot describe [Blake's] poetry fairly or do justice to its peculiar emphases if we suppose that God or Jesus is wholly human." *Symbol and Truth in Blake's Myth* (Princeton: Princeton Univ. Press, 1980), p. 246.

This point of view contrasts with that of Thomas J. J. Altizer, who writes that "Blake's deepest vision refuses to allow any difference of nature between Man and God." *The New Apocalypse: The Radical Christian Vision of William Blake* (East Lansing: Michigan State Univ. Press, 1967), p. 18.

12. On Blake's own view of himself as a Christian, Damrosch writes of his "serious spiritual crisis in the late 1790s and early 1800s, the outcome of which was a passionate if idiosyncratic return to Christianity" (p. 245).

Kathleen Raine cites Blake's letter of November 22, 1802 to Thomas Butts to point out that, at this time, he "declares himself a Christian without reservation." She writes, however, that when Blake writes of himself that "I still & shall to Eternity Embrace Christianity and Adore him who is the Express image of God," he is "speaking not of the historical Jesus but rather the universal divine humanity." *Blake and the New Age* (London: George Allen & Unwin, 1979), pp. 32–33.

13. *Visions of the End*, pp. 30–36.

14. *Millennium and Utopia*, p. 4.

15. Ibid., p. 6.

16. Although this idea runs throughout Teilhard's work, see especially "Sketch of a Personalistic Universe," *Human Energy*, trans. J. M. Cohen (London: William Collins Sons, 1969), pp. 53–92.

17. "The Grand Option," *The Future of Man*, trans. Norman Denny (New York: Harper & Row, 1964), p. 54; hereafter cited as FM.

18. "The Atomism of Spirit," *Activation of Energy*, trans. René Hague (New York: Harcourt Brace Jovanovich), p. 36; hereafter cited as AE.

19. *Piers Plowman*, p. 176. Marjorie Reeves, however, writes that Joachim of Fiore envisioned inspired humanity as actively bringing about the age of the Holy Spirit on earth. See *Joachim of Fiore and the Prophetic Future*, p. 29.

20. Donald Gray writes concerning Teilhard's vision: "As he sees it, the great cultural and religious traditions of the human community, after a prolonged history of mutual isolation and divergence from one another, are beginning to converge through increased mutual contact and concentration. Something novel is being born—the world community. We have entered, if only recently, upon the planetary phase of human evolution. Today God is creatively seeking to bring about a new stage of human consciousness through the advent of a converging humanity." "Creative Convergence," *Anima: An Experiential Journal* 7(2) (Spring 1981): 112.

21. "The Formation of the Noosphere II," *Man's Place in Nature: The Human Zoological Group*, trans. René Hague (New York: Harper & Row, 1966), p. 120.

22. Ibid., p. 121.

23. Kathleen Raine sees plate 99 of *Jerusalem* as an engraving of the soul being embraced by God ("Seminar on Blake's Job," Lindisfarne Association, New York, fall 1978). The female Jerusalem can be understood as a person's soul or "Emanation"—the "Jerusalem in every individual Man" (J II: 39, 39). But Jerusalem is more. It is the "Emanation" or soul of Albion, all mankind; plate 99 shows the world-soul being embraced by the divine.

24. *The Divine Milieu* (New York: Harper & Row, 1965), p. 154.

25. Morris Eaves, "Romantic Expressive Theory and Blake's Idea of Audience," *PMLA* 95(5) (October 1980): 798.

26. "The Formation of the Noosphere I," *Man's Place in Nature*, p. 80.

27. M. H. Abrams, *Natural Supernaturalism: Tradition and Revolution in Romantic Literature* (New York: W. W. Norton, 1971), pp. 339–342; Altizer, *The New Apocalypse*.

28. Kathleen Raine may be said to represent most Blakeans when she writes that "William Blake is the only English poet whose central theme is the confrontation of science and imagination"; "Science and Imagination in William Blake," *Tenemos: A Review Devoted to the Arts of the Imagination* 1 (1981): 37.

However, the appeal of science to Blake's imagination, even as it challenges it, is less widely recognized. See my "William Blake and the Technological Age," *Thought* 46 (December 1971): 577–591; and my "Blake and the Symbolism of the New Iron Age," in *The Evidence of the Imagination: Studies of Interactions between Life and Art in English Romantic Literature*, ed. Donald H. Reiman et al. (New York: New York Univ. Press, 1978), pp. 1–11.

William Dennis Horn

William Blake and the Problematic of the Self

Any present-day study of Romantic attitudes toward the self should begin with the work of Harold Bloom, who, in locating the self in rhetoric, appears to stand as the "last Romantic" against post-Modernism's rather dogmatic rejection of all notions of centrality or agency. This is to say that Bloom is setting himself against those who insist that all talk of an identical self in phenomena is merely a "textual recurrence of metaphysics." A proper consideration of Bloom's theory of poetic repression leads, on the one hand, to contemporary interpretations of Freudian repression, and, on the other hand, back through William Blake to Gnostic images of bondage in the material world. While Modernists argue about "supreme fictions" and imaginary centers, there is little in their ideas which separates them from the Romantics, little in their critique of thought which cannot also be found in Blake's subtle and complex view of the self. What is more, like Blake, the other major figures of English Romanticism question the elusive self. The problematic self exists as an essential theme running from Enlightenment to Romantic thought, and from Romantic poetry to modern critical theories. An investigation of this theme in Romanticism reveals that there is nothing in contemporary notions of the fictional self which distinguishes Modernism from its Romantic roots. Even in the "post-Modern" notion of *deconstruction* we discover not the antithesis of Romanticism, but a viable description of the structure of much Romantic poetry.

Followers of Harold Bloom's endeavors to formulate a dynamics of literary influence on the Freudian model of psychic repression may become alarmed at discovering themselves in the "dense, wild, and tangled wood" of Kabbalistic lore. Indeed, the introjection of explanations of the Lurianic Kabbalah and Valentinian Gnosticism into a discussion of such concepts as the "anxiety of influence" and the "repression of the precursor" might require a map to that path which leads from Freud back to Kabbalism. While Bloom cites Wallace Stevens as his most important precursor,

William Blake lurks in the background as that strong poet whose Gnostic myths describe a world of psychic repression,[1] and furthermore, the poem *Milton* becomes the key work on the subject of poetic influences. In the progress of that poem Blake finds his poetic identity (fulfills his prophetic purpose) by bringing the poet Milton back to earth to correct his literary work. Bloom's theory rather admirably accounts for Blake's suppression of his large debt to Gnostic and Kabbalistic sources, influences on Blake which, while not unnoticed by readers from Crabb Robinson to Bloom himself,[2] have not received the critical attention they warrant. The theory itself accounts for the critic's tardiness in acknowledging his debt to Blake's poem of literary relationships. Further verification will be given when another critic misreads Bloom as a follower of Blake.

Among Bloom's precursors we should number, along with Blake and Freud, John Keble, whose poetic theories M. H. Abrams describes as anticipating Freud's. Abrams observes in *The Mirror and the Lamp*:

> Keble's chief importance, historically considered, is in his thesis that there is a conflict of motives in poetic creation, and in his view that poetry is, therefore, not a direct, but a disguised form of self-expression. This concept, as Keble says, "is the very pivot on which our whole theory turns." The impulse to express one's emotions is "repressed," in Keble's term, "by an instinctive delicacy which recoils from exposing them openly, as feeling that they never can meet with full sympathy." There ensues a conflict in poets between the need for relief on the one side, and the "noble and natural" requirements of reticence and shame on the other; a conflict which threatens "their mental balance."[3]

According to Bloom's configuration of the dynamics of literary creation, a poem is the result of anxiety over retaining one's literary identity in the context of a dominating precursor whose influence must be overcome, or at least repressed. Bloom's theory of poetic inspiration differs from ordinary Freudian theory and from Keble's in isolating the repression of a literary predecessor as the single important impetus in the production of poetic works. He virtually ignores the role of emotions in the creative process, other than those caused by anxiety over a kind of literary ego-annihilation which the poet fears will be the consequence of being dominated by the ideas and techniques of a "strong" precursor. When compared with Freud's wide-ranging theory of the repression of desires or even with Keble's poetic theory of conflicting emotions, Bloom's scheme appears rather narrow. But before we censure the critic for that kind of decadence which can see in a poem only other literary works and nothing of life, we should take notice of an important advance his theory makes over the more conventional Freudian theory of art. All Bloom's recent work rests on his assumption of a fundamental ego-insecurity in the poet, who needs to maintain, or, in fact, to establish a poetic identity by defining himself in opposition to his most important precursor. The ego which demands substantiation is not so much the personality of the poet as it is the literary identity behind a poetic work. Still, the anxiety behind "the anxiety of influence" is specifically ego-anxiety and the repression of "poetry and repression" results from the ego's denial of all that it cannot claim as its own. Bloom puzzles over the problem:

> Why must the ego be defended from the representations of its *own* desires? Whatever the answer is in a psychoanalytic context (and Freud is evasive in this area), I am certain that in the context of poetry the answer has to do with the anxiety of influence. The representations that rise up from the id are not wholly the ego's own, and this menaces the poetic ego. For the Precursor poem has been absorbed as impulse rather than as event, and the internalized precursor thus rises, or seems to rise, against the ego from what appear to be the alienated representations of the id.[4]

This passage can be read as an interpretation of the psychological meaning of the return and exorcism of Milton in Blake's poem by that name. It also agrees with Freud's reversal of his theory that repression causes anxiety.[5] In this case the ego is specifically anxious about maintaining its identity. For Bloom such anxiety is fundamental; it causes a repression of the precursor.

At the basis of Bloom's entire scheme of literary influence lies an ego trying to be born by separating itself from a literary context supplied by the strong poetic precursor. Such identity is most simply achieved by defining oneself in opposition to one's ruling context. The Romantics found the type of such self-assertion in the figure of the rebellious Satan of *Paradise Lost*. Bloom too as an "unreconstructed Romantic" points to Satan as the strongest example of his theory:

> If I can recognize the Sublime in poetry, then I find it in Satan, in what he is, says, does; and more powerfully even in what he is not, does not say, and cannot do. Milton's Satan is his own worst enemy, but that is his strength, not his weakness, in a dualizing era when the self can become strong only by battling itself in others and others in itself. Satan is a great rhetorician, and nearly as strong a poet as Milton himself, but more important he is Milton's central way through to the Sublime. As such, Satan prophesies the post-Enlightenment crisis-poem, which has become our modern Sublime. (*Poetry and Repression*, p. 23)

What Satan cannot do is exist as an entirely self-sufficient being; he finds his identity only in his opposition to God. The rhetoric by which he conceals this fact constitutes, for Bloom, the entire substance of Satan's rather problematic existence. Sophistic rhetoric is the very ground of his being. Bloom questions, "Against whom does Satan lie most persuasively: himself, his precursor, time? " [6] The reader of *Paradise Lost* grows aware that Satan is fooling himself; his suppression is actually a repression in the Freudian sense. Thus, for Bloom, Satan's rhetoric provides a model for the poet's denial of the literary context (i.e., the poems of the precursor) from which his poetry originates.

In placing the process of repression in the realm of rhetoric and trope Bloom has stepped beyond the psychological criticism of both Freud and Keble. Following the lead of the recent "French Freudians," he disembodies the mechanisms of the unconscious from their specific location in the individual psyche. He dislocates the self into that abstract structure from which it is supposed to originate. That is, he locates the process of literary influence in a structure to which the personality of the poet is only tangentially related. Of more importance to his criticism is the poetical identity defined by the relationship of a new poem to its precursor poems. Thus there are no poets outside of the context of influence: "Influence as a composite trope for poetic tradition, indeed for poetry itself, does away not only with the idea that there are poems-in-themselves, but also with the more stubborn idea that there are poets-in-themselves. If there are no texts, then there are no authors—to be a poet is to be an inter-poet, as it were." [7] Unfortunately such a poetic theory exalts poetry to the status of privileged discourse, while denying it meaning outside merely literary relationships.

Bloom's dislocation of the psychic process from the individual human personality should be viewed in the context of modern interpretations of Freudian psychodynamics which do about the same thing. Among the French Freudians Jacques Lacan and his followers argue that the structure of the unconscious is the structure of language. Such a claim emphasizes the role of language in Freud's discussion of the unconscious. Behind Lacan's view is an attempt to overcome Freud's hypostatization of unconscious activity as suggesting an actual realm or entity. In his philosophical analysis of the Freudian unconscious Alasdair MacIntyre observes that Freud "wishes to justify not just the adverb or the adjective but also the substantive form: the unconscious." [8] Freud's use of the concept in this way constitutes a key weakness in his entire theory: "In so far as Freud uses the concept of the unconscious as an explanatory concept, he fails, if not to justify it, at least to make clear its justification. He gives us causal explanations, certainly; but these can and apparently must stand or fall on their own feet without reference to it. He has a legitimate concept of unconscious mental activity, certainly; but this he uses to describe behaviour, not to explain it" (MacIntyre, p. 72). The problems raised by Freud's tendency to postulate a substantive unconscious are paradigmatic of all attempts to identify a central self. Freud eliminates naïve notions of a substantial self only to reestablish agency in the unconscious. His removal of the cause of human activity from the substantial self to a more remote, hidden entity repeats the pattern of the Romantic attempt to displace agency with a central will or spirit. Just this denial of the self as a central cause prompts Blake to assert: "We who dwell on Earth can do nothing of ourselves, every thing is conducted by Spirits, no less than Digestion or Sleep" (J I: 3). Such displacement calls into question all concepts of independent self-subsistence.

When the French Freudians consider the structure of the Freudian unconscious, they attempt to avoid reifying it by pointing out the dependence of the unconscious on its linguistic expression. In his discussion of Lacan's notion of the linguistic structure of the unconscious, Paul Ricoeur indicates that it successfully solves the problem presented by the Freudian unconscious:

> Thus the linguistic interpretation shows that the unconscious, though separated by repression and the other mechanisms that give it the form of a system, is nevertheless correlative to ordinary language. The linguistic interpretation does not constitute an alternative to the economic explanation; it simply prevents the latter from being reified by showing that the mechanisms that come under the economics are accessible only in their relation to hermeneutics. To say that repression is "metaphor" is not to replace the economic hypothesis but rather to parallel it with a linguistic interpretation and thus relate it to the universe of meaning without reducing it to that universe.[9]

"Repression is metaphor" in the sense that metaphor hides the fact that it has created a relationship where none existed before. For Bloom, the principle of metaphorical relationship is rendered as the poetic self. In Ricoeur's view, the mechanisms of Freudian repression resemble the tropes of language, because, as Freud observed, the analyst has access to them only through the mediation of the patient's language. But here perhaps a caution is in order. By displacing the unconscious into a structure and identifying that as the structure of langauge, the French Freudians have replaced one reification with another, disguising the fact that language like unconscious acts is a form of human behavior rather than an independent entity in its own right. Mere displacement of agency from a decentralized self cannot eliminate the problems arising in the concept of a purposeful, initiatory faculty.

Because Bloom attempts to found our experience of identity on the basis of rhetoric, his system succumbs to the same criticism as do those of the French Freudians. Bloom has had to reify the notion of trope as a prop for his metaphysical system. His use of Wallace Stevens, or more specifically of "Notes toward a Supreme Fiction," as his most significant precursor leads directly into the problem of the dislocated self. In a review of Bloom's work Joseph N. Riddel argues convincingly that Bloom has removed the self from "presence" only to find it again in the tropes of rhetoric: "Bloom's uncovering of the 'scene of instruction' is a refusal of the beginning that has all the nihilistic implications of Derrida's or Nietzsche's; yet at the same time it inaugurates a new 'grounding' of man in language, a new grounding of the 'self' (strong), will, psyche as the irreducible names of the primordial 'forces' traced in all trope." [10] Bloom's move reifies the functions of rhetoric to account for the appearance of the self. But the self he accounts for is not one that we can have knowledge of; it is only a rhetorical stance (supreme fiction) of the kind exemplified by Milton's Satan. As Riddel suggests:

> The evidence of "trope" is not what it represents, a real force or subject or will, but what it misrepresents or deviates from, that is, another trope or text. A stance is the figure of chiasmus, of a difference or deviation, a crossing or beginning again considered as an inaugural or originating event. Thus Bloom preserves, in an act he calls transumption, the Romantic ground of the "self" or the "will." The "will" . . . is itself only a trope: "The trope *is* a figure of will, rather than a figure of knowledge." Trope is persuasion, the sign of deviation and displacement. (R 1002)

Bloom's theory dislocates self, psyche, and even Romantic will to the realm of rhetoric, but all this results merely in "a hollowed-out figural notion of the 'self' " (R 1602). Perhaps, as Riddel implies, Bloom should have followed Nietzsche's advice and abandoned all notions of self or psyche from the beginning.

Why should the concept of the self be eliminated? And why should Bloom, as a "Romantic" critic, find it necessary to exhume the remains of a problem that modern criticism is making every effort to bury? Answers to such questions emerge more easily after a consideration of the ways in which Romantics confronted questions about the self.

Current advocates of Modernism seem to take it for granted that the basic weakness of Romanticism was its failure to abandon the project of substantiating the self as the ground or "origin" of knowing. Behind the Romantic interest in the self lies Descartes's project of founding a philosophy on the absolute certainty of the *cogito*. Such a project met its most formidable barrier in Hume's assertion that he could discover no self separate from the succession of his impressions:

> For my part, when I enter most intimately into what I call *myself*, I always stumble on some particular perception or other, of heat or cold, light or shade,

> love or hatred, pain or pleasure. I never can catch *myself* at any time without a perception, and never can observe any thing but the perception. When my perceptions are remov'd for any time, as by sound sleep; so long am I insensible of myself, and may truly be said not to exist.[11]

Hume observes, however, that we mean something quite different from a particular impression when we refer to the self: "But self or person is not any one impression, but that to which our several impressions and ideas are suppos'd to have a reference" (T 251). In considering this problem Hume turns to an examination of the identity of the physical object. He discovers that when we view a succession of similar perceptions the imagination tends "to ascribe to it a perfect identity, and regard it as invariable and uninterrupted." This tendency to mistake merely related perceptions for an identical object is so great that:

> Our last resource is to yield to it, and boldly assert that these different related objects are in effect the same, however interrupted and variable. In order to justify to ourselves this absurdity, we often feign some new and unintelligible principle, that connects the objects together, and prevents their interruption or variation. Thus we feign the continu'd existence of the perceptions of our senses, to remove the interruption; and run into the notion of a *soul*, and *self*, and *substance*, to disguise the variation. (T 254)

Hume's comments are witty and perhaps a bit ironic, but they do cause us to question our fundamental assumptions about identity. Hume might be asked for whom but itself does the self "disguise the variation," mistaking mere resemblance for the substantial object? Like Bloom's concept of trope, this self-deception functions to repress the radical variation (or difference) behind all judgments of identity.

When Hume turns to personal identity he finds that "the identity, which we ascribe to the mind of man, is only a fictitious one, and of a like kind with that which we ascribe to vegetables and animal bodies. It cannot, therefore, have a different origin, but must proceed from a like operation of the imagination upon like objects" (T 259). Thus Hume seems to speak, however ironically, of two selves. The one is only the succession of our perceptions. The other he refers to as the fictional self "to which our several impressions and ideas are suppos'd to have a reference" (T 251). Kant raises Hume's fictitious self to a transcendental status when he points out that the "I think," the "transcendental unity of apperception" is *necessary*, if we are to have the thoughts we do in fact have. Kant admits outright that the self is a mental assumption insofar as no particular perception of it could be found in experience, but his rather awkward phrase, "the synthetic unity of apperception," arises from his claim that experience presents itself in a formal unity, not in independent sensations. For Kant, the principle of that unity is the "I think." Every thought is connected to me insofar as I consider it my thought: "the one condition which accompanies all thought is the 'I' in the universal proposition 'I think.' "[12] Again Kant indicates the necessity of synthetic unity when he says, "All *my* representations in any given intuition must be subject to that condition under which alone I can ascribe them to the identical self as *my* representations, and so can comprehend them as synthetically combined in one apperception through the general expression, 'I think' " (CPR 157). Not only do we not have spatiotemporal intuition (i.e., perception) of this "I," but we are cautioned that it is nothing more than a "simple, and in itself completely empty, representation" (CPR 331).

While Kant overcomes Humean skepticism by securely establishing the "I" not as a fiction but as a transcendentally necessary condition of all thinking, the self which remains is virtually empty. It exists as a formal notion only, and not as a simple substance: "That the 'I' of apperception, and therefore the 'I' in every act of thought, is *one*, and cannot be resolved into a plurality of subjects, and consequently signifies a logically simple subject, is something already contained in the very concept of thought, and is therefore an analytic proposition. But this does not mean that the thinking 'I' is a simple *substance*" (CPR 369). More specifically on the substantiality of the "I" Kant argues:

> If by the term "substance" be meant an object which can be given, and it is to yield knowledge, it must be made to rest on a permanent intuition, as being that through which alone the object of our concept can be given, and as being, therefore, the indispensable condition of the objective reality of the concept. Now in inner intuition there is nothing permanent, for the "I" is merely the consciousness of my thought. So long, therefore, as we do not go beyond mere thinking we are without the necessary condition for applying the concept of substance, that is, of a self-subsistent subject, to the self as a thinking being. (CPR 372)

The "I" then is not self-subsistent, but exists as a necessary condition in the structure of thought. Its reality is similar to that of the phenomenal object about which Kant cautions us lest we "hypostatise outer appearances and come to regard them not as representations but *as things existing by themselves outside us, with the same quality as that with which they exist in us. . . .*" (CPR 356) (author's italics). In this way both "I" and external object exist not as independent subsistences, but only as they are interdependent in the structure of human understanding.

Kant establishes the "I" firmly enough, but he denies it all attributes as an independent entity. It is this concept of the "I" which Hegel in his critique of Kant finds particularly repugnant: "I = I; I must 'accompany' all our conceptions. This is a barbarous exposition of the matter. As self-consciousness I am the completely void, general I, completely indeterminate and abstract. . . ." [13] Hegel's attitude is characteristic of much Romantic thought on the subject. In fact the attempt to replace the vacuity at the center with a substantial "presence" can be seen as the guiding project of much Romantic literature, but not, as we shall soon see, of all that can be termed Romanticism.

Kant's description of the structure of understanding demonstrates the interdependence of mind and object, of object and the structure of thought. In that structure Kant makes the "I think" the principle of unity. But such a philosophy removes from the self most of its attributes and dislocates it from an exalted position as the substantial origin of judgment and understanding. Kant's "transcendental I" *is* the unity of apperception; it does not stand outside of cognition and *cause* unity. In this sense it is not an origin. While the "I" is shown to be necessary it is no longer substantial. The Romantics were thus faced with a prospect of self stripped of importance. On the one hand, the necessitarians simply denied freedom of choice; on the other hand, the subjective idealists subordinated it to the workings of a larger, cosmic will. Finally, in an ultimate undermining of the concept of the self, William Blake argues that it is not merely a fiction, but an error in thought. In fact, Blake considers self-consciousness to be the original error or sin which is signified by the Judeo-Christian account of the fall of man.[14] The mere postulating of a self as an independent entity results in a mistaken view of the world, a view in which self-subsistent egos are alienated from self-subsistent external objects. Thus it is not the concept of the "I" as a principle of unity which Blake names the original sin; rather it is the mistake of seeing the self as an independent entity. Therefore Blake, modeling his cosmology on a traditional scheme of fall and redemption, describes states of "innocence" (unself-consciousness), "experience" (self-consciousness), and higher "innocence" (an appreciation of the interdependence of all things)—in consideration of this last state we remember that Blake's most frequently used word is "all." [15] So severe is Blake's condemnation of the act of self-consciousness that he considers all consequences of that act to be equally fallen. The primary consequence of the self's assertion of independence is the concomitant hypostatization of the physical world as existing apart from the mind's activities. Blake then, without having read Kant, seems to have arrived at a similar conclusion, that the "I" and the objects of appearance are interdependent in perception.

Blake considers "creation" to be a continuous event in which the individual psyche divides off subjectivity in cognition, that is, the self, from the objects that self beholds. Like Kant, he names the faculty responsible for yielding our ordered perceptions in space and time the imagination. For Blake, too, Los and Enitharmon as manifestations of Urthona, imagination, work together to create the formal order of experience so that "Los is by mortals nam'd Time Enitharmon is nam'd Space" (M I: 24, 68). Blake's prophetic works repeat again and again the history of fallen cognition. His first and perhaps most concise account of that fall is given in *The Book of Urizen* which begins, as it must, when Urizen draws apart from the other immortals (of cognition) and asserts his independent existence, unaware that he is being viewed from above. Urizen, "a self-contemplating shadow" (U 3: 21), is modeled on Milton's Satan, the rhetorician who must deceive himself, but his name (your reason) also parodies Milton's concept of reason. In his satanic role he represents the emergence of a self-consciousness which divides and alienates. In the lines quoted below a creation motif is confounded with a parody of Satan's journey through chaos (PL II: 925–1033). But notice, throughout, the bravado with which Urizen asserts his self-importance:

> 5. First I fought with the fire; consum'd
> Inwards, into a deep world within:
> A void immense, wild dark & deep,
> Where nothing was; Natures wide womb[.]
> And self balanc'd stretch'd o'er the void
> I alone, even I! the winds merciless
> Bound. . . .
>
> (U 4: 14–20)

Read as an account of the advent of self-consciousness, such lines refer both to the development of the individual psyche and to reason's evolving recognition of its own nature. Thus Urizen writes his books:

> 6. Here alone I in books formd of metals
> Have written the secrets of wisdom
>
> . . . .
>
> 7. Lo! I unfold my darkness: and on
> This rock, place with strong hand the Book
> Of eternal brass, written in my solitude.
>
> (U 4: 24–25, 31–33)

In these last lines a parody of Moses receiving the tablets appears. Like Hegel, Blake considered the Ten Commandments to be a significant step in man's (reason's) recognition of his own nature. But for Blake reason, by attempting to codify its own being, misrepresents itself and binds men to laws they cannot keep.

Blake's extremely negative attitude toward the results of fallen cognition—its products are selfhood and the world of external objects—reveals his basically Gnostic attitude. While Blake critics frequently mention Blake's Gnostic leanings, Stuart Curran has been virtually alone in insisting, and insisting quite correctly, that Blake's outlook is fundamentally Gnostic.[16] For a basis on which to examine Blake's poetry I quote Philip Merlan's excellent summary of Gnosticism from his article on Plotinus in the *Encyclopedia of Philosophy*:

> The fundamental mood underlying Gnosticism is alienation from a hostile world, and Gnosticism undertakes to explain this mood and to open the road to escape from the world. The explanation is in the form of a history of the origin of the visible cosmos; according to Gnosticism, this cosmos is the result of the activity of an evil god sometimes identified with the Creator-God of the Old Testament or with Plato's divine artisan. This evil god is only the last in a succession of beings. The manner in which this succession takes place consists in a number of voluntary acts by which divinities of an ever lower order originate. The relation between these deities is often personal, based on such traits as curiosity, oblivion, daring, ambition. Man, as he exists in this evil world, contains in himself a spark of what was his original, divine substance, now imprisoned in his body owing to the scheming of the evil god. At a certain moment a messenger-savior in some way breaks the power of the evil god and makes it possible for those who hear the whole story (acquire gnosis) to regain their original standing and free themselves from the tyranny of the evil god.[17]

Blake finds his evil god in Urizen, who combines aspects of Milton's Satan and reason, the Creator-God of Genesis, and the "god of this world" so disparaged in the New Testament. Blake uses the phrase "god of this world" variously in "Notes on the Illustrations to Dante" (E 667), "The Everlasting Gospel" (E 515), and "Annotations to Watson" (E 608). His negative attitude toward this world and its god expresses that acosmism which is the distinguishing characteristic of Gnostic thought. Blake asserts that "Man Brings All that he has or Can have Into the World with him. Man is Born Like a Garden ready Planted & Sown This World is too poor to produce one Seed" (E 645–646). For Blake the human spark has no place in this world of evil.

Blake describes the presence of man in an alien world through traditional Gnostic images of bondage, which signify the way in which the mind is responsible for its own enslavement. Thus the "mind forg'd manacles" of the poem "London" (E 26–27) represent rigid laws in the form of "charters" and "bans" which bind men to their misery. More particularly Gnostic is Blake's notion that the material world is a kind of mental enslavement which constricts men to a single mode (Blake's "ratio of the five senses") of constructing from sensation a single material world. A fall into enslavement, into this single construction, results when the mind forgets it has supplied the perceptual world with the form in which it appears, or, to reinvoke Kant, it occurs when we "hypostatise outer appearances and come to regard them not as representations but *as things existing by themselves outside us, with the same quality as that with which they exist in us. . . .*" (CPR 356). Blake speaks of this kind of mental creation and fall (the theme of all the later "prophecies") as early as *The Marriage of Heaven and Hell* (circa 1790–1793). There he says: "The Giants who formed this world into its sensual existence, and now seem to live in it in chains, are in truth, the causes of its life & the sources of all activity, but the chains are, the cunning of weak and tame minds. which have power to resist energy . . ." (MHH 16). In "To Tirzah," the mother of matter binds sensations to their material organs:

> Thou Mother of my Mortal part
> With cruelty didst mould my Heart,
> And with false self-deceiving tears,
> Didst bind my Nostrils Eyes & Ears.
>
> Didst close my Tongue in senseless clay
> And me to Mortal Life betray:
> The Death of Jesus set me free,
> Then what have I to do with thee?
>
> (E 30)

This view of Jesus as the savior who frees the spirit from material bondage places Blake in a tradition of Christian Gnosticism which interprets Christ as the embodiment of that divine spark outside the cosmos who comes to redeem the divine within man. Throughout Blake's cosmic dramas the saving function is performed by Los, the personification of the imagination, who in turn is identified with Jesus.

While Gnostic ideas pervade Blake's poetry, his single most Gnostic work is clearly *The Book of Urizen*. Like many Gnostic works, it parodies the biblical Genesis by a peculiarly perverse inversion which insists that the God of Genesis represents an evil creator of an evil world. Originally Blake entitled the work *The First Book of Urizen* in a parody which suggests the title "The First Book of Moses" (Genesis), at once linking Moses the lawgiver (and thus the enslaver) with the God of creation described by the author of the book. Even as early as this poem Blake asserts his belief that a man forms his god in the image of himself. Blake's parody extends to the separation motif especially prevalent in the first chapter of Genesis.[18] There the creation is accomplished when God divides "the light from the darkness," and "the waters from the waters," and "the waters which were under the firmament from the waters which were above the firmament." In Blake's account creation begins when Urizen divides from the other immortals and supposes that he is self-sufficient. The mental nature of this account (Urizen's separation is merely an error) constitutes an interpretation of the first chapter of Genesis as an expression, if an obscure one, of the "mental creation" of the world, that is, of the division and distinction inherent in all cognition. Urizen/reason's separation from the immortals (and from Los, the imagination) signifies the more sinister results of the fall. Pleased with the objectivity yielded by perception according to its strictures, reason falls ignorant of the imagination's role in producing that world. By the same measure the imaginative spontaneity within is no longer considered a part of the codified logic which is reason's picture of itself.

The Book of Urizen may be read as an account of the development of the individual consciousness in its efforts to solidify sensations into the objects of the physical world, but it works as well—perhaps better—as a more abstracted account of the efforts of man's reason to objectify itself. The poem's receptivity to such interpretation has led E. D. Hirsch to characterize it as "a chapter in Blake's *Phenomenology of Mind*, written twelve years before the publication of Hegel's work."[19] But some fundamental differences stand between the positions of Blake and Hegel. Blake assumes that this world is evil, as its God is evil. He believes that reason, the god of this world, is inherently fallen; his codification of his own processes will never evolve into anything positive. At best, reason's picture of itself results in a kind of "consolidation of error," which, if man is lucky, will cause a complete abandonment of reason's project of attaining knowledge by abstraction. In short, Blake's stance is Gnostic. Unlike Hegel's dialectic, Blake's ends the moment one realizes the intrinsic impossibility of absolute knowledge. Blake, in recognizing a limitation to reason from the outset, is closer to Kant than to Hegel. Again, unlike Hegel, Blake sees reason as becoming more aware of itself *only* by realizing its intrinsic limitation: its objectification of spontaneity always distorts; hence its representation of itself is always a misrepresentation.

Another result of Blake's antagonism toward materiality arises from his belief that human desires are not to be satisfied in this fallen world. Just as in the Gnostic myths the divine spark that is humanity longs for its origin outside the world, so for Blake, what is truly human has nothing to do with the natural (phenomenal) world. In "Ah Sunflower," the sunflower serves as an emblem of the human ideal which longs for its source above. Not in this world, but in the world of its own desires can the sunflower achieve what it wants—in a world

> Where the Youth pined away with desire,
> And the pale Virgin shrouded in snow:
> Arise from their graves and aspire,
> Where my Sun-flower wishes to go.
>
> (E 25)

Here the images of frustrated desire are presented as that kind of divine spark (Blake identifies it with *the human*) which cannot be found in the material world. Blake's much-discussed apocalypse is ultimately Gnostic then, in that it occurs within an individual more than within an impersonal cosmic consciousness. Blake asserts that "whenever any Individual Rejects Error & Embraces Truth a Last Judgment passes upon that Individual" (E 551). Compare these words to Hans Jonas's description of the "pneumatic equation" of Valentinian Gnosticism: "The human-individual event of pneumatic *knowledge* is the inverse equivalent of the pre-cosmic universal event of divine *ignorance*, and in its redeeming effect of the same ontological order. The actualization of knowledge in the person is at the same time an act in the general ground of being." [20] Just as Gnosticism proposes to inform us "who we are, from whence we came, and whither we are going," so Blake's apocalypse informs us of the error of our misrecognition of our true selves. We rediscover our identity in those desires not to be satisfied by the world.

Los's efforts to give a body to Urizen constitute an interesting subplot, which is integral to the meaning of *The Book or Urizen* and essential to our investigation of Blake's view of the self. Los's efforts enact the mind's attempt to organize its activities in a form recognizable to itself. Urizen/reason, who takes credit for creating the material world, must be given a material body himself so that he will not remain unorganized. In a parody of God's creation of Adam from clay Los organizes the functions of Urizen under a uniform structure, the "Body of Urizen," which may be conceived of as a law code (the Ten Commandments), or as a body of mental rules (perhaps in the form of Aristotelian logic), or even as laws for the physical world (Newton's laws). This last group of laws is in Blake's view only the hypostatized projection, after all, of Urizen's self. Urizen reduces his nature to a fixed rule, and then writes in his "Book of Brass" the

> 8. Laws of peace, of love, of unity:
> Of pity, compassion, forgiveness.
> Let each chuse one habitation:

His ancient infinite mansion:
One command, one joy, one desire,
One curse, one weight, one measure
One King, one God, one Law.

(U 4: 34–40)

These lines have a sinister undertone because, in Blake's view, even human ideals of peace and love become restrictive when reduced to commands.

If *The Book of Urizen* is considered as an allegory of the mind, then Los's efforts to give a human form to the abstract selfhood, Urizen/Satan, can be interpreted as an account of the individual's identification of himself with his physical body. Los's activities are described in specifically anatomical terms. According to Carmen S. Kreiter's analysis of such imagery, Blake makes use of vivisectionist John Hunter's contemporary speculations on anatomy—it is Hunter whom Blake parodies as Jack Tearguts in "An Island in the Moon." [21] Kreiter singles out the following lines:

Many forms of fish, bird & beast
Brought forth an Infant form
Where was a worm before.

(U 19: 34–36)

This passage, according to Kreiter, expresses the biogenetic law: *ontogeny recapitulates phylogeny*. Whether or not such a complex biological theory had been anticipated by Hunter in his study of fetuses, Blake certainly makes use of images of embryonic development, but probably as a metaphor for psychic change. His insistent antimaterial theme, however, suggests that his use of physiological metaphors is parodic. The body of Urizen is his *idea* of independent material form. The ontogeny of his mental development recapitulates the phylogeny of reason's evolving objectification of its own nature. In the realm of the individual consciousness, however, the formation of Urizen's body represents both temporal development (the child comes to identify his body as himself) and the atemporal structure of thought (to the extent that the body plays a role in the individual adult's concept of himself). To better understand what role Urizen's body, as man's material body, signifies in terms of the individual's consciousness of self and of the perceived world, it is necessary to consider for a moment more modern speculations on the role of the body in self-identity.

In the twentieth century Freud has been the most influential of those thinkers who assign to the body an essential role in the development of consciousness. In this theory of the developing infantile consciousness, our present notion of self is preceded by a stage in which we are unaware of our own bodies: "The adult's ego-feeling cannot have been the same from the beginning. It must have gone through a process of development, which cannot, of course, be demonstrated but which admits of being constructed with a fair degree of probability. An infant at the breast does not as yet distinguish his ego from the external world as the source of the sensations flowing in upon him. He gradually learns to do so, in response to various promptings." Freud further speculates on the individual's differentiation of self from all feelings of unpleasure. He notes that "a tendency arises to separate from the ego everything that can become a source of such unpleasure, to throw it outside and to create a pure pleasure-ego which is confronted by a strange and threatening 'outside'."[22] We find in such speculations, I suggest, a developmental account of that Gnostic spark, Blake's "desire," which is alien to the world of the reality principle.

In other speculations on the nature of the self Freud remarks that "the ego is first and foremost a bodily ego; it is not merely a surface entity, but is itself the projection of a surface." [23] An important footnote to this line explains that "the ego is ultimately derived from bodily sensations, chiefly from those springing from the surface of the body. It may thus be regarded as a mental projection of the surface of the body, besides, as we have seen above, representing the superficies of the mental apparatus." [24] Among the more direct descendants of Freud, Jacques Lacan was distinguished in his earlier theorizing by his emphasis on the role of body identity in psychoanalytic theory. For Lacan the development of the body-ego has deeper psychological and philosophical implications that it has for Freud. Lacan suggests that the human infant organizes the chaos of his various sensations by identifying himself as an object form, his body. Arguing from analogies of animal physiological development, Lacan supposes that the human form or gestalt (as the infant's mother, or the infant's own form seen in a mirror) is a necessary component in his psychic development. At a point Lacan calls the *stade du miroir* (mirror-phase), the infant identifies himself as an object. This identification allows him to separate from himself (his body-self) the other objects of his experience; he sees himself as a spatiotemporal form in relation to his spatiotemporal body. It is just this kind of identification which gives a person the notion that his diverse sensations constitute a whole. The merely empirical self (to use Kant's words) is changed into our concept of a unified single self by means of this process. As Lacan puts it: "We have only to understand the mirror-phase *as an identification*, in the full sense which analysis gives to the term: namely, the transformation which takes place in the subject when he assumes an image—whose predestination to this phase-effect is sufficiently indicated by the use, in analytical theory, of the old term imago." [25] In Lacan then the self becomes an idealized mental image, *imago*, of singularity or unity. To the extent that the self is an idealization of singularity modeled on our notion of the permanence of the identical object, that self is a misrepresentation. Personal identity constitutes a kind of *misrecognition*, to use Lacan's term.

It is just this fundamental misrecognition intrinsic to all identifications of the self which Blake dramatizes in his cosmic dramas. Furthermore, the accounts of both Blake and Lacan have atemporal as well as temporal significance. Like Blake's *Book of Urizen*, Lacan's *stade du miroir* offers a synchronic description of the structure of adult cognition as well as a diachronic account of infant mental development. Of even greater significance for our present study is the notion that every act of identification entails a misrecognition, or error, in the form of the attribution of qualities such as singularity, substantiality, and permanence as a means of organizing the flux of sensory experience. Where Lacan speaks of misrecognition to indicate a structural quality of what is nonetheless an identity, Blake uses the word "error." The latter's questioning of identity results, not in the transcendental certainty of a Kant, but in a negative judgment (a skepticism) about all objects of cognition, about all of creation: "Error is Created Truth is Eternal Error or Creation will be Burned Up & then & not till then Truth or Eternity will appear It is Burnt up the Moment Men cease to Behold it I assert for My self that I do not behold the Outward Creation & that to me it is hindrance & not Action it is as the Dirt upon my feet No part of Me" (VLJ 95). Notice that here as in Freud "a tendency arises to separate from the ego everything that can become a source of . . . unpleasure." For Blake the source of unpleasure is the material world. This external world becomes hostile because man errs in supposing it has laws and intentions independent of the way in which the human mind perceives it. This independent intentionality of "female will" prevents man from identifying with his sensory experience. Mistaken man lives as a shadowy self in a world of objects stripped of "accidental" sensory qualities: "deduct from a rose its redness, from a lilly its whiteness from a diamond its hardness from a spunge its softness from an oak its heighth from a daisy its / lowness & rectify every thing in Nature as the Philosophers do. & then we shall return to Chaos" (E 584–585). In this way Locke's support for the notion that the center, self, or "real" object subsists in the primary qualities becomes for Blake a type of mistaken cognition.

Lacan fails to emphasize sufficiently the repression (Hume's "disguise") of the problematic nature of the identification process. Harold Bloom, however, recognizes the role of repression in the mental activity of creating identity. Bloom restricts his theorizing to the realm of literary identity, and in so doing "has performed," in the words of Joseph Riddel, "a critic's *stade du miroir*" (R 990). The repression of the mind's role in creating identity is not a function of personal identity only, but is a primitive condition of all identity formation. Such repression is fundamental to the existence of the object world as we know it. In the case of personal identity we pay for the maintenance of our own ego "fiction" and anxiety over the possible loss of our sense of the world as objective.

In interpreting the self and the world of separate objects as an error, a failure to appreciate the nature of the self, Blake thus looms as an even stronger precursor of Bloom. For Blake, reality is achieved in a personal apocalypse (uncovering) which reveals the form of identity, both of self and of objects in the world, to be an imaginative construct. The misrecognition intrinsic to identity makes all knowledge problematic. Even mind's representation of itself as an organized structure is a misrepresentation. In Blake such misrepresentations of mind are personified as Urizen. This is the meaning of Urizen's separation from the "Eternals" and his subsequent reification in terms of both a physical body and the metaphorical body of thought. Blake finds a type of the fall in Urizen's codification of himself in the decalogue, or again in Newton's laws, which interpret in the "external world" of space and time the order arising from the mind's organization of sensation. By means of such laws men are able to repress the terrible strife of their warring emotions and find solace in the contained vision of a regulated exterior universe. *The Song of Los* offers a concise "history" of that repression:

> The human race began to wither, for the healthy built
> Secluded places, fearing the joys of Love
> And the disease'd only propagated:
>
> . . . .
>
> Till like a dream Eternity was obliterated & erased.
>
> Since that dread day when Har and Heva fled.
> Because their brethren & sisters liv'd in War & Lust;
> And as they fled they shrunk
> Into two narrow doleful forms:
> Creeping in reptile flesh upon
> The bosom of the ground:
> And all the vast of Nature shrunk
> Before their shrunken eyes.
>
> (E 66)

As man shrinks to an abstract self so do the objects he beholds; he lives in a world which filters out concrete sensory experience in favor of abstract objects which he can reduce to laws:

> Thus the terrible race of Los & Enitharmon gave
> Laws & Religions to the sons of Har binding them more

And more to Earth: closing and restraining:
Till a Philosophy of Five Senses was complete
Urizen wept & gave it into the hands of Newton & Locke

(E 66)

Urizen's tears are hypocritical, while Newton and Locke merely offer a consolidated expression of what man has become. Newton's supposition that he has discovered laws of a world external to human cognition earns him a place at the bottom (Ulro) of Blake's mind-created cosmos, but he and Locke, along with Bacon, Milton, Shakespeare, and Chaucer join to herald Albion's apocalypse.

If Blake had known Kant, that philosopher's "Copernican Revolution" would have earned him a place somewhere on the level of Blake's world of "Generation." Blake would have seen the categories of understanding in the same way that Hegel actually did, as a major step in reason's self-recognition. But unlike Hegel, Blake would have considered this merely a further "consolidation of error," because of the problematic misrecognition which such reification demands. For Blake the fallen nature of cognition leads away from ultimate self-realization. Apocalypse can be achieved only by revealing that fallen character of thought and by exposing the falsity of both the self and the independently existing world of nature. Such a revelation, an exposure of our misrecognition of the self, can be achieved not through the abstract discourse of philosophy, but through the particular processes of artistic endeavor.

At one point in *The Book of Urizen* Blake comments on his own method of etching his stories on copper plate. The sulfurous fumes of Urizen's infernal realm become conflated with the smell of Blake's acid etching:

2. And Urizen (so his eternal name)
His prolific delight obscurd more & more
In dark secresy hiding in surgeing
Sulphureous fluid his phantasies.

(U 10: 11–14)

Blake's self-conscious parody of the very poem he is in the act of publishing underscores his inability to escape from the fallen form of identification by reification. Just as Los's act of creating a body for (hypostatizing) Urizen produces the originating fall, so Blake too, by giving the name *Urizen* to those aspects of experience we call reason, and by calling *Los* those aspects identified with the imagination, has committed the original sin of misrecognition. In his self-parody Blake attempts to reveal the problematic elusiveness of all thought which abstracts identical entities from sensation. The process is unavoidable because it lies within all cognitive experience.

Blake's creation of a character such as Los accentuates the enigma of thought. Los, or the imagination, like Kant's productive imagination or Coleridge's primary imagination, the "esemplastic" (form into one) power, provides us with spontaneous identification of objects. He "creates" the spatiotemporal world. He is also responsible for identifying, and thus objectifying, mental entities. When Blake's imagination creates Los, Los is reifying and misrepresenting his own nature. In the poetry his very existence as a personified abstraction marks him as a symbol of the fall, the "loss" of Eden. How else can mind know itself, but by becoming the object of its own thought? [26] This problematic of faculty psychology is expressed elsewhere in Romantic thought in Coleridge's claim that the son is himself the father of his own father. That is, the thought itself gives rise to the notion that it has a central origin. Los's conceiving of himself is a Urizenic act.

To recapitulate then briefly: In *The Book of Urizen* Blake's Gnostic reading of Genesis attempts to reveal the psychological "truth" behind the division motif in the biblical account of creation. Like his contemporary, Coleridge, Blake sees the act of perception in terms of mental organization of sensation. Such organization implies a separation of object from object and self from other. The creation of Urizen and the creation of the material world occur simultaneously because they are parts of an identical event. Fallen cognition perceives objects only in a spatiotemporal relation to a perceiving subject, and the subject finds its identity in relation to the objects it beholds. The idea of an independent self and independent "objects" in nature constitutes a kind of fallen cognition represented by Urizen/Satan's rhetorical self-affirmation and by his "discovery" of an independently existing world of external objects. "Knowledge," for Blake, results when one realizes, as a kind of mental apocalypse, or gnosis, that self and objects are *interdependent*, that our notion of either involves conceptual entailment—that is, that the concept of the one is a necessary part of the concept of the other. The forms in which experience presents itself are considered to be "mental"; the extension and duration of the natural object, in Blake's view, result from the way in which the mind organizes sensation. The hypostatization of such regularities as a structure or rule Blake calls Urizen, who is himself a reification of the mind's tendency to observe a causal self behind its perceptions. Blake assigns the name Los to the agency from which mental order spontaneously originates. Blake is not alone in emphasizing the importance of this faculty; the reification of the spontaneity of thought as the *imagination* (conceived of as agency, process, or structure) is the central statement of Romantic metaphysics.

In his efforts to define Romanticism in terms of the problems to which the poets addressed themselves, Morse Peckham cites the Romantic concern with the nature of the self as especially significant.[27] Peckham argues after Earl R. Wasserman that the Romantics were concerned with finding "a significant relationship between the subjective and objective worlds,"[28] and indicates that Wasserman himself employs the self as a focus for his comparison of various Romantic metaphysics. Peckham asserts that "throughout the century, and even at the present time, one form in which the problem was tackled was the hypostatization of the 'self.' The Romantics saw metaphysical construction as intimately related to the problem of the value of human experience, which, constituted by the self, as the result of the Enlightenment collapse, could be seen as the source of all value."[29] Peckham is correct in placing the self as a central problem of Romanticism, and in seeing that the poetic response to that problem was extremely subtle and diffuse. In the case of Blake we find a criticism, as problematic, of all notions of self, occurring in works which have as their main action the creation and psychomachia of mental agents. The drawback to such a definition of Romanticism lies in its absorption of the more essential attributes of what we call Modernism, for we find in Blake, as in Nietzsche, an important critique of the notion of agency. The obvious advantage to an approach to Romanticism along the lines suggested by Peckham is its inclusion of Blake and Byron among the Romantic poets. While each of the Romantics considers self from a different direction, they are in fact all facing the same general problem.

Peckham also correctly asserts that the twentieth century can be considered Romantic to the extent that it still addresses the problem of the self. Those who oppose Modernism to Romanticism err in supposing that all Romanticism takes refuge in a hypostatized notion of the self. The first modern poems are Blake's *Jerusalem* and "Vala," because of their fragmented narration with its lack of a single controlling voice or central consciousness. Even the claim of Derrida and his followers, that all centers such as self or mind are already interpretations of experience, is anticipated in the Romantic expression of the paradox that in the fallen form of cognition mind can only be presented as something other than itself. The Romantics inherited from the eighteenth century a concept of the self that had already been called into question. Their endeavors to rethink the nature of the self led them to deconstruct the epistemological ground of their thought.

The contemporary term "deconstruction" may be used properly to describe the epistemological questioning of much Romantic poetry. Harold Bloom quotes from Jacques Derrida a splendid definition of the latter's technique of "deconstruction": "To deconstruct philosophy would thus mean to think the structured genealogy of the philosophical concepts in the closest and most intimate way and yet to determine, at the same time, from a certain 'outside' unwarrantable, unnameable by philosophy itself, what this history might have dissimulated or forbidden. . . ." [30] Such a description especially fits the structure of the early chapters of the *Biographia Literaria*, a work which traces a "genealogy" of philosophy as it develops in the mind of the individual, Coleridge. In the same way Wordsworth's *Prelude* declares a history of the poet's mental progression from associationist psychology to an assumption of a transcendental ground—a movement which at the same time deconstructs the concept of the Imagination as it develops in the work. What Wordsworth and Coleridge do by tracing the history of their own philosophic positions, Blake achieves through a rhetorical technique which parodies, and thereby calls into question, the very method of presentation upon which his work, indeed all of his thought, depends.

In an essay entitled "The Rhetoric of Temporality" Paul De Man claims that critics such as M. H. Abrams and Earl Wasserman have erred in following too readily W. K. Wimsatt's suggestion that a movement from allegoric to symbolic language characterizes the Romantic period.[31] De Man argues to the contrary that the best of Romantic poetry exhibits the distancing between sign and what is signified that is peculiar to allegory. Allegory as a rhetoric of temporality, a rhetoric which insists on the temporal (problematic) nature of the self, reemerges to express those moments of revelation in which a man gives up his erroneous idea of himself as exhibiting the permanence of the natural object. De Man cites from Wordsworth episodes such as the crossing of the Alps, or the ascent of Mount Snowdon, which describe a personal apocalypse accompanying "the loss of self in death or in error" (RT 190). In such passages the speaker of the poem is able to look back through an experience which has revealed how his former self was mistaken in attempting to identify himself with the natural world. Such experience takes the form of a secular apocalypse in which an "unveiling takes place in a subject that has sought refuge against the impact of time in a natural world to which in truth, it bears no resemblance" (RT 190). As we have seen, such a temporal subject or self which "bears no resemblance" to the natural world is precisely that one whose alienation serves as the focus of Gnostic lament. Thus De Man's illustrations from Wordsworth could have been drawn even more readily from the poetry of Blake, whose parodic mode undercuts the metaphysics of selfhood.

De Man further argues against the mainstream of criticism that the dominant concern of Romanticism is *not* the dualism of subject and object, but rather that the central Romantic conflict is between self-revelation and the need to suppress our true nature:

> We are led, in conclusion, to a historical scheme that differs entirely from the customary picture. The dialectical relationship between subject and object is no longer the central statement of romantic thought, but this dialectic is now located entirely in the temporal relationships that exist within a system of allegorical signs. It becomes a conflict between a conception of the self seen in its authentically temporal predicament and a defensive strategy that tries to hide from this negative self-knowledge. On the level of language the asserted superiority of the symbol over allegory, so frequent during the nineteenth century, is one of the forms taken by this tenacious self-mystification. Wide areas of European literature of the nineteenth and twentieth centuries appear as regressive with regard to the truths that come to light in the last quarter of the eighteenth century. For the lucidity of the pre-romantic writers does not persist. (RT 191)

Here "negative self-knowledge" signifies the self's discovery of its impermanence and insubstantiality. De Man's identification of the rhetorical strategy which attempts to "hide from" (i.e., repress) this "negative self-knowledge" makes him yet another obvious precursor of Harold Bloom. And in his theory of rhetoric, as in Bloom's, the impetus behind such strenuous repression is ego anxiety, for the discovery of the nature of the self is of the most painful kind. De Man describes such self-realization in terms of a painful distancing, almost of bereavement and mourning. In such a theory Wordsworth's Lucy poem, "A Slumber Did My Spirit Seal," with its painful sense of loss and its present narration ("now") reflecting on a self in the past perfect ("I had no human fears"), becomes prototypical of the best in Romantic lyric. So too, it might be added, does Blake speak of the painful revelation of the temporal self; "In anguish of regeneration! in terrors of self annihilation" (J I: 7, 61).

For De Man, Romantic writers achieve the most when they are able to overcome repression of self-knowledge by adopting the distancing factor of the allegorical mode:

> Whereas the symbol postulates the possibility of an identity or identification, allegory designates primarily a distance in relation to its own origin, and, renouncing the nostalgia and the desire to coincide, it establishes its language in the void of this temporal difference. In so doing, it prevents the self from an illusory identification with the non-self, which is now fully, though painfully, recognized as a non-self. It is this painful knowledge that we perceive at the moments when early romantic literature finds its true voice. It is ironically revealing that this voice is so rarely recognized for what it really is and that the literary movement in which it appears has repeatedly been called a primitive naturalism or a mystified solipsism. (RT 191)

The assertion that early Romanticism finds its "true voice" in the moments of painful self-knowledge constitutes a value judgment which tells us much about contemporary criticism in an era whose most characteristic social phenomenon, psychoanalysis, finds therapeutic man's most bitter insights into himself. The post-Modern era exhibits a self-scrutinizing honesty which places it closer to the spirit of the late eighteenth century than to the interceding century whose literary repression was as severe as the previous period's insight had been clear and terrifying. The age returns from such repression to seek the knowledge offered in the best Romantic poetry, perhaps because historical realities impel man to abandon all illusions of permanence. If we see Romanticism not as an event of the late eighteenth century only, but as a movement which expresses the painful experience of abandoning our erroneous notion of a nontemporal self, then we must see William Blake as an early proponent of the most significant concept in contemporary critical thought. The resurgence of interest in his poetry during the middle of the twentieth century attests to its expression of the emotional dialectic of our time, a time in which the inexorable force of self-discovery repeatedly annihilates our fondest illusions about ourselves. Surely Blake's poetry of repression and self-discovery marks him as a declarer of the true voice of Romanticism. Only from the context of contemporary thought can we understand this poet who created for himself the literary identity of a prophet teaching a secular salvation through painful annihilation of the self. And only now can we begin to understand the historical figure who in 1826, near the end of his life, was able to sign himself in the autograph book of William Upcott: "WILLIAM BLAKE one who is very much delighted with being in good Company / Born 28 Nov, 1757 in London & has died several times since" (E 675).

Notes

1. For the question of Blake's Gnosticism, see Stuart Curran, "Blake and the Gnostic Hyle: A Double Negative," *Blake Studies* 4(2) (Spring 1972): 117–133. See also Piloo Nanavutty, "Blake and Gnostic Legends," *The Aligarh Journal of English Studies* 1 (1976): 168–190.

2. For Robinson's report of a particularly Gnostic conversation with Blake, see G. E. Bentley, Jr., *Blake Records* (London: Oxford Univ. Press, 1969), pp. 544–545. Virtually every major Blake critic mentions Blake's Gnosticism, but few pursue the subject.

3. *The Mirror and the Lamp: Romantic Theory and the Critical Tradition* (New York: W. W. Norton, 1958), p. 147.

4. *Poetry and Repression: Revisionism from Blake to Stevens* (New Haven: Yale Univ. Press, 1976), p. 144.

5. As Freud says, "Anxiety makes repression and not, as we used to think, the other way around." *The Complete Psychological Works of Sigmund Freud*, vol. 22, ed. James Strachey (London: Hogarth Press, 1964), p. 89. A repression of the basic nature of cognition would result from anxiety over a lack of ego self-subsistence. Such a lack, if acknowledged, would undermine the self's appearance of substan-

tiality. The notion of a definite self, it can be argued, is necessary to avoid an attitude of aporia toward phenomena. For Blake, Bloom's true precursor, the anxiety extends beyond mere poetic influence, because Blake is describing a process which extends beyond mere neurotic concerns over literary father figures.

6. "Poetic Crossing: Rhetoric and Psychology," *The Georgia Review* 30(3) (Fall 1976): 506.

7. *Kabbalah and Criticism* (New York: Seabury Press, 1975), p. 114.

8. *The Unconscious: A Conceptual Analysis* (London: Routledge & Kegan Paul, 1958), p. 71.

9. *Freud and Philosophy* (New Haven: Yale Univ. Press, 1970), p. 392.

10. See "Book Reviews" in *The Georgia Review* 30(4) (Winter 1976): 994; hereafter cited as R.

11. David Hume, *A Treatise of Human Nature* (London: Oxford Univ. Press, 1975), p. 252; hereafter cited as T.

12. Immanuel Kant, *Critique of Pure Reason*, ed. and trans. Norman Kemp Smith (New York: St. Martin's Press, 1965), p. 362; hereafter cited as CPR.

13. G. W. F. Hegel, *Lectures in the History of Philosophy*, vol. 3, trans. Elizabeth S. Haldane and Frances H. Simson (London: Routledge & Kegan Paul, 1892–1896), p. 437.

14. Thus Blake, like Jacob Boehme, identifies the self with all things satanic. In the poem *Milton*, Milton says, "I in my Selfhood am that Satan: I am that Evil One!" (M I: 14, 30).

15. *A Concordance to the Writings of William Blake*, ed. David V. Erdman (Ithaca: Cornell Univ. Press, 1967), 2 : 2181.

16. Curran observes that the Gnostics "see matter and all who serve it as intrinsically evil. Blake's view of Nature as a universe of death accords with Gnostic, not Neoplatonic doctrine." Curran, p. 119.

17. *Encyclopedia of Philosophy*, vol. 6 (New York: Macmillan, 1967), p. 356. For more extensive discussions of Gnosticism see Hans Jonas, *The Gnostic Religion* (New York: Columbia Univ. Press, 1959), and more recently Elaine Pagels, *The Gnostic Gospels* (New York: Random House, 1979).

18. For a more extensive account of this motif in Blake and in Genesis, see Leslie Tannenbaum, "Blake's Art of Crypsis: *The Book of Urizen* and Genesis," *Blake Studies* 5(1) (Fall 1972).

19. *Innocence and Experience: An Introduction to Blake* (New Haven: Yale Univ. Press, 1964), p. 73.

20. Hans Jonas, *The Gnostic Religion*, p. 176.

21. "Evolution and William Blake," *Studies in Romanticism* 4 (1964): 110–118.

22. *Civilization and Its Discontents* (New York: W. W. Norton, 1961), pp. 13–14.

23. See *The Ego and the Id . . . The Complete Psychological Works*, vol. 19, p. 26.

24. *The Ego and the Id*, p. 26n. The editor, James Strachey, indicates that "this footnote first appeared in the English translation of 1972, in which it was described as having been authorized by Freud. It does not appear in the German editions."

25. "The Mirror-Phase as Formative of the Function of the *I*," *The New Left Review* 51 (1968): 72.

26. The problem of whether mind can represent itself without distortion is central to Plotinus. In Ennead V, part iii, "On Gnostic Hypostases, and That Which Is beyond Them," Plotinus considers the problem in some detail. He says, for instance: "Does intellect, therefore, by one part of itself behold another part? In this case however, one part will be that which sees, but another, that which is seen.

And this is not for the same thing to see itself." *Select Works of Plotinus*, trans. Thomas Taylor (London: George Bell & Sons, 1895), p. 264.

27. "Romanticism: The Present State of Theory," *The Triumph of Romanticism* (Columbia: Univ. of South Carolina Press, 1970), pp. 58–83.

28. Earl R. Wasserman, "The English Romantics: The Grounds of Knowledge," *Studies in Romanticism* 4 (1964): 33.

29. Peckham, p. 73.

30. "Poetic Crossing," p. 505.

31. "The Rhetoric of Temporality," in *Interpretation: Theory and Practice*, ed. Charles S. Singleton (Baltimore: Johns Hopkins Univ. Press, 1969), pp. 173–209; hereafter cited as RT.

Notes on Contributors

HAZARD ADAMS is the author of *Blake and Yeats: The Contrary Vision* (1955), *William Blake: A Reading of the Shorter Poems* (1963), and various other books of criticism and fiction. He is currently Professor of English and Comparative Literature, University of Washington.

ROBERT J. BERTHOLF is currently Curator, The Poetry/Rare Books Collection, the University Libraries, the State University of New York at Buffalo. He is editor of a collection of essays *Robert Duncan: Scales of the Marvelous* (1980), published by New Directions, and author of *Robert Duncan: A Descriptive Bibliography*, to be published by Kent State University Press.

MINNA DOSKOW has taught at Goucher College, American University, and the University of Baltimore, where she is currently Dean of the College of Liberal Arts. Her book, *William Blake's "Jerusalem": Structure and Meaning in Poetry and Pictures* was scheduled for publication in 1982.

MYRA GLAZER has written on Blake's poetry and art, Joyce's treatment of perception, Lawrence's views of sex, and Shakespeare's presentation of mother-daughter relationships. She is the editor of *Burning Air and a Clear Mind: Contemporary Israeli Women Poets*, published by Ohio University Press, and the author of a forthcoming book on experiences of separation and the meaning of autonomy. A Senior Lecturer in Foreign Literatures at Ben Gurion University, she was a Visiting Scholar at UCLA in 1979–1980.

ROBERT GLECKNER is the author of *The Piper and the Bard: A Study of William Blake* (1959), *Byron and the Ruins of Paradise* (1967), *Selected Writings of William Blake* (1967), and *The Poetical Works of Lord Byron* (1975), and editor of *Romanticism: Points of View* (1962). He has recently completed a new study of Blake's *Poetical Sketches*. He is the author of two long studies on Blake and

Joyce, as well as over sixty other articles and reviews. Robert Gleckner is now Professor of English at Duke University.

William Dennis Horn received his bachelor's and master's in English from the University of California, Santa Barbara. In 1978 he received a doctorate in English from UCLA where he wrote a dissertation entitled "Blake's Gnosticism: The Material World as Allegory," under the direction of Professor Peter L. Thorslev, Jr. Professor Horn teaches at Clarkson College.

Susan Levin is currently an Assistant Professor of English at Stevens Institute of Technology. Her articles on Romantic poets have appeared in such journals as *South Carolina Review, Massachusetts Review*, and *CLA Journal*. She is writing a book about Dorothy Wordsworth.

Annette S. Levitt has taught at The Pennsylvania State University and Temple University, and has published articles and reviews on John Milton, William Blake, Joyce Cary, Garcia Lorca, and Roger Vitrac. She is currently writing a book on Blake and Joyce Cary.

Alicia Ostriker is the author of the critical study *Vision and Verse in William Blake* (1965), and the editor of the Penguin edition of *William Blake: The Complete Poems* (1977). As well as writing articles on contemporary poets, she is also a poet herself: *Songs* (1969) and *A Dream of Springtime* (1979) are collections of her work. Alicia Ostriker is currently Professor of English at Rutgers University.

Jay Parini has published a critical study, *Theodore Roethke: An American Romantic* (1979), a novel entitled *The Love Run* (1980), and a book of poems entitled *Anthracite Country* (1982). He reviews regularly for *The New Republic* and the *Times Literary Supplement*, and is a founding editor of *New England Review*.

Donald Pease's articles on American literature appeared in *PMLA* and other scholarly journals. An Associate Professor of English at Dartmouth College, he is writing a book on Whitman and the Romantic tradition in American literature.

Eileen Sanzo teaches at the Institute for Research in History. She has published articles in *The Evidence of the Imagination: Studies of Interactions between Life and Art in English Romantic Literature* (1978), *Thought, Blake: An Illustrated Quarterly*, and other scholarly journals.

LEROY SEARLE is an Associate Professor of English at the University of Washington. He is one of the founding directors of the Society for Critical Exchange, and his recent work includes essays on critical theory, criticism in photography, and a book in progress, *Speculative Poetics*, a study of the historical relation between criticism and philosophy.

Index

A note on the index. Since the chapters of this collection are themselves subject divisions, no attempt has been made to index themes, titles, and characters of the separate authors discussed. Only the pages where the major, and also minor, discussions of each author have been indexed. The principle Blakean themes, characters, and the titles of the poems of Blake have been indexed, along with other names and titles which are more than a casual reference.